The Revision Theory of Truth

The Revision Theory of Truth

Anil Gupta
Nuel Belnap

A Bradford Book
The MIT Press
Cambridge, Massachusetts
London, England

Set in Times Roman by Asco Trade Typesetting Ltd., Hong Kong.

Library of Congress Cataloging-in-Publication Data

Gupta, Anil, 1949–
  The revision theory of truth / Anil Gupta, Nuel Belnap.
    p.   cm.
  "A Bradford book."
  Includes bibliographical references and index.
ISBN 978-0-262-07144-4 (hc.: alk. Paper) -- 978-0-262-52695-1 (pb.)
The MIT Press is pleased to keep this title available in print by manufacturing single copies, on demand, via digital printing technology

  1. Truth. 2. Definition (Logic) 3. Liar paradox. I. Belnap, Nuel D., 1930–. II. Title.
BC171.G87   1993
121—dc20
                                    92-23160
                                       CIP

for Daniel and Gillian

Contents

	Preface	ix
	Acknowledgments	xi
1	**The Problem of Truth and Paradox**	1
2	**Fixed Points: Some Basic Facts**	33
2A	Preliminary Matters	33
2B	Definability and Indefinability of Truth	49
2C	Coherent Complete Partial Orders	63
2D	The Transfer Theorem	71
2E	The Extended Weak Kleene Scheme	80
3	**Fixed Points and the Signification of Truth**	85
3A	The Proper Interpretation of Fixed Points	85
3B	Expressive Incompleteness and Hierarchies	91
3C	The Signification Thesis	104
4	**The Revision Theory: An Informal Sketch**	113
5	**A General Theory of Definitions**	145
5A	The Semantical Systems S_n	147
5B	Completeness and Conservativeness	156
5C	Revision Sequences and Their Properties	166
5D	The Semantical Systems $S^\#$ and S^*	182
6	**Truth, Categoricalness, and Necessity**	199
6A	Truth I: The Main Lemma	199
6B	Truth II: Restricted Self-Reference	209
6C	Truth III: Rich Self-Reference	218
6D	The Concept "Categorical in L"	229
6E	The Logical Grammar of Necessity	235
7	**Truth and Other Circular Concepts**	253
	Bibliography	279
	Index	287

Preface

This book develops a way of viewing the concept of truth (and several other concepts) that we have come to believe, after much hesitation, to be fruitful and correct. The view can be stated quite simply, though its exact meaning can be made plain only during the course of the book: Truth is a circular concept. We shall argue that this viewpoint enables one to make sense of the perplexing behavior of truth (e.g., its behavior in the Liar paradox), and to explain much of its ordinary unproblematic behavior.

The *material* principles that are widely recognized as governing truth (the Tarski biconditionals) suggest strongly that truth is circular. (See section IV of chapter 4.) The difficulty in arguing for the thesis is created by widely accepted *formal* strictures which dictate that circular concepts do not exist and that circular definitions are illegitimate. Against these strictures we shall put forth and argue for the following claims:

- *General* theories of definitions are possible within which circular definitions—and, more generally, systems of mutually interdependent definitions—make logical and semantic sense.
- In the context of certain sorts of logical and philosophical inquiries, these formal strictures ought to be abandoned.

The theory of definitions, we believe, is the proper framework for the construction of a theory of truth. Indeed, the theory of truth is an immediate corollary of the theory of definitions.

We hope to show in this book that the viewpoint just sketched is attractive and plausible. We do not claim, however, to be setting down the theories of definitions and truth in their final form. Part of the reason for this is personal. Despite the many years we have spent on the subject, our study remains incomplete. But part of the reason is intrinsic to the subject. There are several conflicting desiderata one can impose on theories of definitions and truth, and it is not yet completely clear how these conflicts are best resolved.

How to Read the Book

This book may be read in two ways: either straight through or by first reading chapters 1, 4, and 7 and then reading the remaining chapters in order. Chapters 1, 4, and 7 explain the main philosophical ideas we wish to put forward in an accessible way. The remaining chapters are more technical. Chapters 2 and 3 present some basic facts about the fixed-point approach to the theory of truth and develop our argument against it. Chapters 5 and 6 contain a formal development of our approach. (Chapters 2, 3, 5, and 6 contain several open problems, which may be found via the index entry "open problems.")

A citation of the form Author 198+ or Author 199+ refers to an unpublished paper listed in the bibliography. For example, Thomason 198+ refers to Richmond Thomason's paper "Paradoxes of intentionality?" and indicates that we received it in the 1980s.

Prerequisites

Different parts of this book have different logical prerequisites. Chapters 1, 4, and 7 presuppose very little logical background and can be understood by anyone who has had a course in first-order logic. Chapters 2 and 3 presuppose some knowledge of set theory (in particular, of Zorn's lemma). These chapters do *not* presuppose any knowledge of arithmetization (except in a few skippable passages) or of the theory of ordinals. Chapters 5 and 6 presuppose a rudimentary acquaintance with the theory of ordinals, and three sections of chapter 6 (6C–6E) presuppose familiarity with arithmetization. All the technical chapters (2, 3, 5, and 6) assume that the reader has pencil and paper handy and is willing to work out the details of an example and to supply the missing proof of a straightforward theorem.

Acknowledgments

An enormous literature exists on the subject of this book, and we have benefited greatly from what we have read of it. Our most outstanding debt is to the work of Alfred Tarski and Saul Kripke. The ideas of these two authors have shaped the foundations of our subject, and have provided it with powerful conceptual and technical tools. We next wish to acknowledge Hans Herzberger, who investigated, completely independently, a theory of truth that is mathematically similar to one developed in this book. (See Herzberger 1982a, 1982b, 198+.) Charles Chihara, Robert L. Martin, Vann McGee, Albert Visser, and Peter Woodruff have also influenced our thinking significantly. We have had enjoyable and beneficial conversations and/or correspondence on the topics discussed in this book with all of the aforementioned authors except Tarski. Further, Gupta had the privilege of attending a seminar on truth by Kripke at Princeton University in the autumn of 1982.

We wish to thank Dorothy Grover, Vann McGee, and an anonymous referee for extensive written comments on the manuscript. Their comments have enabled us to correct several errors. We used parts of earlier drafts in seminars given at the University of Illinois, Indiana University, and the University of Pittsburgh. The feedback of our students has been valuable to us. We thank especially Paul Bartha, André Chapuis, Jerry Kapus, Tim O'Connor, Robert Rupert, Jeffrey Verman, Byeonguk Yi, Bosuk Yoon, and Ming Xu. We have presented our work on truth in lectures at several universities, and have discussed it on many occasions with friends and colleagues. The following are some of the people who were helpful to us through their good questions, interesting suggestions, etc.: Peter Aczel, Nicholas Asher, Jon Barwise, Wim Blok, John Burgess, Charles Chastain, David Copp, Steven Davis, Bill Demopoulos, Mike Dunn, Walter Edelberg, Dorothy Edgington, Mike Friedman, Bill Hart, Allen Hazen, Geoffrey Hellman, Chris Hill, Hans Kamp, John Macnamara, Penny Maddy, Tony Martin, Paul Teller, Richmond Thomason, Steve Yablo, Kent Wilson, and Mark Wilson. We have enjoyed working with Paul Bethge of The MIT Press and we wish to thank him for his careful editorial work. Thanks to David Beisecker and André Chapuis for help with the proofreading.

Substantial parts of two of our papers (Gupta and Belnap 1987; Gupta 1988–89) have been incorporated in this volume. Much of the first paper appears in section 3A, and much of the second in chapters 4 and 7. In addition, we have used a few paragraphs from Gupta 1982 and Gupta 1987. We wish to thank the *Journal of Philosophy*, the Aristotelian Society, and the Academic Press for permission to use this material here.

Gupta adds: I wish to acknowledge the research support provided to me by the University of Illinois at Chicago and by Indiana University. I also received support from the National Endowment for the Humanities. A Fellowship for University Teachers enabled me to devote the academic year 1988–89 to this book. Thanks to the members of the Padua group, especially Paolo Leonardi, for inviting me to discuss the theory of truth with them in the summer of 1985, and for the hospitality they extended to me and my family. I also wish to thank Dorothy Edgington for the good care she took of us during our stay in England in the summer of 1989. The friendly advice and suggestions of John Macnamara and Mark Wilson have been invaluable to me.

The Revision Theory of Truth

1 The Problem of Truth and Paradox

I

The concept of truth has a curious and perplexing double character. On the one hand, it appears to be so clear and simple that it seems as if a complete philosophical account of the concept can easily be given. On the other hand, the very intuition that creates the appearance of clarity and simplicity leads, on closer examination, to logical contradictions and seemingly insoluble problems.

The basic intuition that makes the concept of truth appear so clear and simple consists of two separable observations. The first can be found in the works of several philosophers and logicians—ancient, medieval, and modern. It is stated clearly enough by Aristotle in the *Categories*:

> ...there being a man reciprocates as to implication of existence with the true statement about it: if there is a man, the statement whereby we say that there is a man is true, and reciprocally—since if the statement whereby we say that there is a man is true, there is a man. ($14^{b}14-18$; Ackrill 1963, pp. 39–40)

The observation made in this passage clearly generalizes: a sentence of the form '"p" is true' implies the sentence p; and conversely, the sentence p implies '"p" is true'. John Buridan, in the second sophism of chapter 8 of his *Sophismata*, calls this coimplication Aristotle's Rule.[1] In more recent times, Gottlob Frege, Frank Ramsey, and others have made the related observation that the sentence 'that p is true' has the same meaning as p—that the addition of the truth predicate does not contribute any new content to the sentence p.[2]

The second observation that constitutes the basic intuition is not to be found, as far as we know, in the writings of the ancients or the medievals. It was first made in the twentieth century, and it can, with some justice, be attributed to Ramsey. Its clearest formulation, however, is to be found in Alfred Tarski's Convention T. Stated crudely, the observation is that the equivalences mentioned above are not only *analytic* of the concept of truth but also *exhaustive* of it. In Convention T this point is made more clearly and precisely: the equivalences are used to state a condition on the definition of truth—a condition whose satisfaction, it is suggested, is both necessary and sufficient for a definition of truth to count as adequate.

[1] See Hughes 1982, pp. 45 and 47.
[2] See Frege 1918/1956, p. 20, and Ramsey 1927, pp. 44–45.

Formulated a little loosely, Convention T requires of an adequate definition of truth (for a language L in L') that it imply

1. that the truths of L are sentences of L

and

2. all biconditionals of the form

> X is true (in L) if and only if p

> where X is replaced by the standard name of a sentence of L and p is replaced by the translation (in L') of the sentence.[3] (Biconditionals of this form will sometimes be called *T-biconditionals* and sometimes *Tarski biconditionals* for L in L'. The language L *for* which the definition is constructed is called the *object language*, and the language L' *in* which the definition is given is called the *metalanguage*.[4])

Clause 1 captures the idea that the objects of truth are sentences. This idea is acceptable only when L does not contain ambiguities, context-sensitive elements (such as indexicals and tenses), etc.[5] When such elements are present, Convention T requires major reformulation. A great deal of work has been done by philosophers working within Davidsonian semantics to formulate a version of Convention T that is adequate for natural languages.[6] Since we shall be concerned in this essay only with formalized

---

[3] The above formulation is not completely precise and exact. A precise formulation of Convention T can be given only for specific L', not for variable L'. A precise formulation requires that we state the sentences of L' that are to be implied by an adequate definition of truth, and this can be done only when the syntax and semantics of L' are known. In the above formulation we are forced to rely on an intuitive translation of English into L'. This is one respect in which the formulation given is loose.

[4] The notions of "object language" and "metalanguage" are also used outside the context of a definition. Here the object language is one *to* which the truth predicate refers, and the metalanguage is one that *contains* the truth predicate.

[5] One can call into question the idea that the objects of truth are sentences, and indeed the more general idea that truth is a predicate, on other grounds also. We shall discuss this later in the chapter. We shall argue that, at least for the issues that are of central concern in this essay, Tarski's assumption that truth is a predicate of sentences is a useful idealization.

[6] An observation concerning Davidsonian semantics: Even though some things like Tarski biconditionals play an important role in this semantics, and even though Donald Davidson has championed Tarski's work on truth, Davidson's goals are diametrically opposite to those of Tarski. Whereas Tarski took the notion of meaning (and translation) as unproblematic and attempted to define the notion of truth, Davidson does the very opposite. He takes the notion of truth as unproblematic (and undefined) and attempts to elucidate the notion of meaning in terms of it. There is an acknowledgment of this in Davidson's anthology on truth and interpretation. See Davidson 1984, p. xiv.

languages (and with simple fragments of English that are like formalized languages), we shall not pursue the question whether such a version of Convention T can be constructed.

Clause 2 is the distinctive and important part of the Convention. It requires of an adequate definition of truth (for English in English) that it imply, for example, the famous biconditional

(1)   'Snow is white' is true if and only if snow is white

(assuming that the standard names for sentences are formed by quotation). That the requirement is plausible can perhaps be brought out as follows: Any definition that implies the T-biconditional (1) is bound to define a concept that is coextensive with truth on at least one point—namely, the sentence 'snow is white'. Furthermore, this coextensiveness holds irrespective of the contingent facts that may obtain. Hence, with respect to the sentence 'snow is white', the defined concept is bound to agree with truth even in *intension*. Generalizing this observation, we conclude that if a definition implies a T-biconditional for *each* sentence then the defined concept will have the same intension as truth (assuming that the definition satisfies the first clause of Convention T).[7]

T-biconditionals like (1) are admittedly vacuous and trivial. However, one should not be deceived by this into thinking that Convention T is similarly vacuous and trivial. In fact, these properties of the biconditionals, far from weakening Convention T, add to its power. It is precisely because of these features that Tarski can write of the biconditionals that

Statements of this form can be regarded as partial definitions of the concept of truth. They explain in a precise way, and in conformity with common usage, the sense of all special expressions of the type: *the sentence x is true*. (Tarski 1936/1956, p. 404)

And he can say of the definition of truth that it

will fulfill what we intuitively expect from every definition; that is, it will explain the *meaning* of the term being defined in terms whose meaning appears to be completely clear and unequivocal. (Tarski 1944, section 9; emphasis added)

It is because the biconditionals are so vacuous that it is plausible to think that they are analytic of the concept of truth. And since the biconditionals fix the conditions under which the concept applies to any sentence of the

---

[7] See the discussion of the Intension and Implication Theses below.

language, it is plausible to think that they *fix* the meaning of 'true'. A definition satisfying Convention T is essentially a logical conjunction of these biconditionals. Hence, it is plausible to regard such a definition as giving the meaning of 'true'.[8]

It is a remarkable fact about the concept of truth that a plausible adequacy condition on its definition can be stated. For most concepts the formulation of such an adequacy condition is a difficult, if not impossible, task. In testing the adequacy of a definition (e.g., that of "free action" and "physical object") one is often forced to proceed in a piecemeal fashion, comparing the consequences of the definition against the ordinary uses of the concept in a case-by-case manner. One is forced to follow this procedure because the concepts have a diverse range of application and there is no viewpoint from which this diversity can easily be surveyed. Thus, for the definition of most concepts no *a priori* condition of adequacy can be laid down. For the concept of truth, however, Tarski surprisingly is able to put forward a clear, precise, and plausible condition of adequacy.

Convention T distinguishes Tarski's work on truth from all previous work. Logicians had discussed the T-biconditionals long before Tarski, and philosophers had constructed and debated definitions of truth for centuries before Tarski. But no one before Tarski saw a connection between the two projects.[9] No one put forward the idea that the T-biconditionals consti-

---

[8] There is abundant evidence in Tarski's works that he was concerned with giving the *meaning* of 'true'. For example, in section 1 of "The Semantic Conception of Truth" (1944), where Tarski is describing his project, he writes: "The desired definition does not aim to specify the meaning of a familiar word used to denote a novel notion; on the contrary, it aims to catch hold of the actual meaning of an old notion."

Curiously, numerous commentators have interpreted Tarski differently. Willard Van Orman Quine (1953b) sees Tarski as giving merely an extensionally correct definition of truth, and Hartry Field (1972) interprets Tarski as attempting a physicalistic reduction of the concept of truth. (Scott Soames [1984] also denies that Tarski's aim was to give the meaning of 'true'.) These interpretations not only fall afoul of Tarski's words; they also fail to explain the centrality of Convention T in Tarski's theory. If these interpretations were correct, it would be a mystery why Tarski should demand of a definition of truth that it imply the T-biconditionals, for the goals that Quine and Field attribute to Tarski can be attained even if the theory does not imply the biconditionals. It is obvious that a definition may be an extensionally correct definition of truth even though it does not imply the T-biconditionals. And, as we shall see, a theory that gives a physicalistic reduction of the notion of truth (assuming that such a theory is possible) need not imply the T-biconditionals. See the remarks on the Implication Thesis below.

We are not asserting that Convention T *is* the correct adequacy condition on a definition that aims to capture the meaning of truth. Our contention is that this is what Tarski is claiming and that his claim is plausible (even if it is not completely correct). The problem with the Quine and Field interpretations is that on them Convention T is highly implausible.

[9] Tarski's achievement did not occur in a philosophical vacuum, however. See Woleński and Simons 1989 for an account of the philosophical influences on Tarski's work.

tute the adequacy condition on a definition of truth.[10] No one even raised the *reflective* question: When would a definition of truth be adequate? Indeed, for most concepts this kind of question is not a good one. It does not help us to survey the diverse range of application of a concept. For the concept of truth, however, Tarski showed that the reflective question *is* a good question, and that it has a good answer. In fact, Tarski's answer is so good, so clear, and so precise that it turns the problem of constructing a definition of truth into a purely mathematical problem (at least for formalized languages). Convention T encapsulates Tarski's philosophical claim and provides the motivation for his mathematical results. It is the bridge that links the philosophical problem of understanding the concept of truth with the logico-mathematical problems that occupied Tarski. Tarski was aware of the importance of this linkage. In the "Historical Notes" added at the end of his "Wahrheitsbegriff" (1935/1956), Tarski lists a number of points on which his investigations were independent of those of others. The first point listed is "the general formulation of the problem of defining truth," and there follows a reference to the pages on which Convention T is formulated.

The biconditionals that make the concept of truth appear so simple and clear lead, unfortunately, to outright contradictions. This is the immediate lesson of the Liar paradox. Let us introduce into English the name 'The Liar' according to the following stipulation:

(The Liar)   The Liar is not true.

Now it is easily seen that the T-biconditionals for English imply a contradiction. For we have

(2)   The Liar = 'The Liar is not true',

and the T-biconditional for The Liar is

(3)   'The Liar is not true' is true if and only if The Liar is not true.

By substitutivity of identicals we deduce from (2) and (3) that

(4)   The Liar is true if and only if The Liar is not true,

which immediately yields a contradiction.

[10] Even though Frege remarks on the equivalence of 'that *P* is true' and *P*, he writes "it is probable that the content of the word 'true' is unique and indefinable" (1918/1956, p. 19). The gulf between the T-biconditionals and Convention T is wide indeed.

The version of the paradox just given is close to the one commonly attributed to Eubulides of Miletus (fourth century B.C.): "The statement I am now making is a lie." Another important version of the paradox is derived from a remark attributed to Epimenides (sixth century B.C.), a Cretan prophet. This remark is contained in the following famous lines from St. Paul's *Epistle to Titus*:

One of themselves, even a prophet of their own, said, The Cretans are always liars, evil beasts, slow bellies. This witness is true. (King James version)

The Epimenides remark "The Cretans are always liars" is paradoxical if we suppose that 'liar' applies to people who have never (even unintentionally) uttered a truth and that as a matter of fact all Cretan utterances, except perhaps the present one of Epimenides, are false.[11] One difference between the Eubulides version and the Epimenides version of the paradox is worth noting: The Eubulides version is *intrinsically* paradoxical in the sense that it is paradoxical no matter what the contingent facts may be. It is paradoxical in all possible worlds. But the Epimenides version is not intrinsically paradoxical. It is paradoxical if facts are one way (all other Cretan utterances are false, etc.), but not paradoxical otherwise.[12] We shall call sentences that exhibit this behavior *Contingent Liars*. Self-referential sentences such as The Liar above we shall call *Simple Liars*. All Simple Liars are intrinsically paradoxical, but there are intrinsically paradoxical sentences that are not of the form of the Simple Liar.

In summary: It is a fundamental intuition concerning truth that the T-biconditionals are analytic and that they *fix* the meaning of 'true'. The Liar paradox appears to show, however, that the fundamental intuition is incoherent. A central problem in the theory of truth is to resolve the paradox without damaging the fundamental intuition in any essential way.

[11] The discovery of the Liar paradox—as well as several other paradoxes of interest to logicians (e.g., the Sorites)—is generally credited to Eubulides. This attribution may well be correct even though Epimenides lived about two centuries before Eubulides. It could be that the paradoxical reading of the Epimenides remark is of later origin. Saint Paul himself shows no awareness of the potential paradoxicality of the remark. We have learned from Paul Vincent Spade (1973) that even the medieval literature on the Liar appears to have overlooked the potential paradoxicality of the Epimenides remark.
[12] This feature of the Epimenides-type paradoxes has been remarked on by several authors; see, e.g., Kneale 1972, p. 242. It is clearly brought out in Kripke 1975.

II

There are two types of approaches to the problem of truth and paradox that we do not wish to follow: One holds that the problem has a simple solution, the other that it is insoluble.

The philosophers who believe that a simple solution is possible typically think that the problem has arisen because of an error in the logical grammar of truth. These philosophers generally agree that truth is *not* a predicate of sentences. However, there is little agreement among them on what the correct logical grammar of truth is. One suggestion that has been accepted by many is that truth is a predicate of intentional entities such as *statements* or *propositions*. Yehoshua Bar-Hillel, who believed in a simple solution,[13] wrote in his 1966 essay "Do natural languages contain paradoxes?" that

[the] claim that natural languages contain semantic paradoxes ... can be met—or rather left without any basis—by making, among others, a clear distinction between sentences and statements, realizing that it is to statements that, primarily, truth-values have to be assigned and that the supposedly paradoxical situations can be shown to evaporate by realizing that in those situations no statements had been made at all, so that the question of truth and falsity does not arise to begin with. (p. 285)[14]

The way this maneuver in logical grammar is supposed to help solve the problem is this. Compare the Simple Liar with its propositional analogue: "This very proposition is not true" (or "The proposition expressed by this very sentence is not true"). We cannot say of the Simple Liar that it is true, nor can we say that it is false. Both claims lead immediately to absurdities. In contrast, it is plausible to assert of the propositional analogue that it contains a nondenoting singular term. For, it is suggested, the paradoxical sentence does not assert anything whatsoever and therefore does not express a proposition. We can thus rule on the truth value of the proposi-

[13] Buridan also appears to have subscribed to a simple solution. He took the objects of truth to be sentence tokens. See Hughes 1982.

[14] William Kneale (1971, 1972) also argues that the paradox is defused once propositions are recognized to be the primary objects of truth: "the paradox of the Liar holds no terrors for those who realise how the notion of truth is related to that of a proposition" (1971, p. 321). See Sobel 1992 for a recent defense of the same idea. The view that the paradoxical sentences do not *say* anything was proposed by the Stoic Chrysippus. It was also one of the first views to be elaborated in the early medieval literature on the Liar. See Bocheński 1961 and Spade 1987.

tional version in any one of the several ways that are familiar from the logic of nondenoting singular terms. If, following Bertrand Russell, we rule that it is false, we are not forced to conclude that it is true—for it is false because it does not express a proposition, not because it expresses a false proposition.

This approach succeeds, it appears, not only in resolving the paradox but also in preserving the fundamental intuition concerning truth. The propositional analogues of the T-biconditionals,

that p is true if and only if p,

seem to be always true (assuming 'that p' is a denoting term) and to fix the conditions under which 'true' is applicable to propositions. Hence, it appears that the biconditionals fix completely the meaning of truth. We have a simple theory of truth and a simple way out of the paradox.[15]

As was observed above, the presence in natural languages of indexicality, ambiguity, etc. makes the thesis that truth is a property of sentences highly implausible. In the final analysis of language and truth this thesis would have to be abandoned. And one plausible replacement for it is the idea that truth is a property of propositions.[16] However, the point to be observed here is that these factors that lead one to favor propositions as objects of truth do not lend any plausibility to the key idea that underlies the proposed resolution of the paradox—namely, that the paradoxical sentences do not express propositions. One can plausibly reject this idea even though one accepts the claim that the objects of truth are propositions.

The idea that paradoxical sentences do not express propositions has, in our opinion, some undesirable consequences. It complicates in numerous ways the semantics of language. Some examples:

1. *Belief sentences* A paradoxical sentence can be the complement of a belief attribution. A sentence such as

    (5) St. Paul believed that all Cretans are liars

---

[15] Many philosophers, including some who do not believe that the paradoxes can be resolved so simply, have been attracted to various elements in this account. Arthur Prior (1961), Charles Parsons (1974b), Saul Kripke (1975), and Richmond Thomason (198+)—to mention just a few—endorse the idea that paradoxical sentences do not express propositions/statements.

[16] But this is not the only plausible candidate. We may want to treat truth as a relation between sentences and various features of context.

can be true even though its complement is paradoxical. If we deny that paradoxical sentences express propositions, we will need to give a separate account of the logic and semantics of sentences like (5).

2. *Modality* Paradoxical sentences can be modalized: we can say truly 'it is possible that some Cretans weren't liars'. A special story would have to be told here also.

3. *Truth functions* Paradoxical sentences can appear in meaningful, even true, truth-functional compounds—e.g., 'if all Cretans are liars then indeed all Cretans are liars', 'either all Cretans are liars or some are not'.[17]

The idea that paradoxical sentences do not express propositions is attractive, it seems to us, only for sentences like (the analogue of) the Simple Liar. It is not attractive for the Contingent Liar. In our opinion it is better to say that the Simple Liar expresses a proposition because the Contingent Liar does than to deny that the Contingent Liar expresses a proposition because of the intuition that the Simple Liar does not. The Simple Liar is to the Contingent Liar as a tautology is to a contingent statement. Much as we say that a tautological sentence expresses a proposition because it is a limiting case of a contingent statement, we should say that a Simple Liar expresses a proposition because it is a limiting case of a Contingent Liar.[18]

A final argument against the proposed solution goes as follows: The proposal manages to evade one paradox only to fall into another. If in the propositional analogue of the Simple Liar we understand 'not' to have wide scope, we again land in difficulties. Consider this reformulation of the analogue:

(6)   It is not the case that there is a true proposition that this sentence—i.e., (6)—expresses.

Sentence (6) is paradoxical if we assume that it expresses a proposition. But there is a difficulty even if we assume that it does not. For now we must deny the existential claim that

---

[17] There are theories of truth that imply that these sentences are not true. However, to us this seems to be a false consequence of these theories.

[18] Until recently we did not have the tools to model paradoxical—and, more generally, circular—propositions in a natural way. The problem can be overcome in Peter Aczel's new set theory ZFC⁻ + AFA. See Barwise and Etchemendy 1987 and Aczel 1988.

There is a true proposition that (6) expresses.

Consequently, we must assert

(7)   It is not the case that there is a true proposition that (6) expresses.

But if we say that (6) does not express a proposition, it would appear that we should say equally that (7) does not express one either. This is strange: We are asserting (7) and yet denying that it expresses a proposition. This is no better than asserting of the sentential Simple Liar that it is not true and then refusing to conclude that it is true after all.

Our arguments so far do not *prove* that no simple solution to the problem will work. For one thing, the dialectic is not over even in connection with the particular idea under consideration.[19] For another, this is not the only "simple solution" to be found in the literature.[20] To make the point fully we would need to go through these solutions one by one and establish of each that it fails—something for which we have as little appetite as, we imagine, does our reader. Paul of Venice, a fourteenth-century logician, discusses fourteen proposals for solving the problem before offering one of his own.[21] A modern-day Paul of Venice would need to discuss as many as fourteen times fourteen solutions. We have no desire to fill this role. Instead we confine ourselves here to a few general observations that are based on our reading of the literature.

Studies of the paradoxes tend to fall into two categories. First, there are those that are best seen as responding to the *normative* problem posed by the paradoxes. The best of these studies yield interesting ways of blocking the paradox and of constructing paradox-free concepts of truth. Thanks to the logical work of the past ninety years or so, we now have several such ways. Russell's Ramified Type Theory, Tarski's Hierarchy of Truth Predicates, and the Fixed Points of Robert L. Martin, Peter Woodruff, Saul Kripke, and others are the most important examples of the methods that have been developed. These methods do not preserve all the features of our ordinary notion of truth and of our ordinary language. In fact, all known methods of constructing paradox-free truth concepts involve limiting the expressive power of the language; some methods restrict the range

---

[19] For discussions of some further stages of this dialectic, see Parsons 1974b and Thomason 198+.

[20] See Mates 1981 for a skeptical discussion of some that are not considered here. See Hazen 1987 for a critical discussion of Buridan's simple solution.

[21] The relevant passages can be found in Bocheński 1961.

of the quantifiers, others rule out certain types of negation, yet others ban self-reference from the language, and there are other possibilities. These methods are useful nonetheless, for there are contexts in which we need a clear, paradox-free notion of truth (property, set, etc.) but in which the loss of certain kinds of expressive power is quite acceptable (e.g., when we are trying to clarify the distinction between truth and proof in mathematics).

The studies of the second category attempt to solve the *descriptive* problem posed by the paradoxes—the problem of giving an account of truth and paradox that is adequate to a language in actual use. Numerous proposals for the solution of this problem are found in the literature, but none is successful. Sometimes it is suggested that the problem is to be solved through a maneuver in the logical grammar of truth, as in Bar-Hillel's proposal considered above. But it has been our experience that no maneuver in logical grammar succeeds *by itself* in solving or dissolving the paradox. Some secondary maneuvers are invariably necessary. The simpler of these (e.g., Bar-Hillel's idea that paradoxical sentences do not express propositions) do sometimes succeed in creating the impression that they solve a version of the paradox, but these maneuvers turn out to be impotent against other closely related versions. The interesting attempts to solve the descriptive problem generally end up relying on the results of studies of the first type: It is argued of a given normative proposal that it describes the workings of truth and paradox in ordinary language. (Charles Parsons and Tyler Burge, for example, have argued that a Tarskian hierarchy of truth predicates can be used to give an account of the ordinary notion of truth.) Such theories face two problems. First, they need to establish their descriptive adequacy. Second, they need to show *why* the expressive incompleteness that is inherent in their proposal must, despite appearances, be present in ordinary language. We shall discuss these problems in chapter 3. Here we wish to emphasize only that neither problem is easy to solve. The easy optimism of the simple approach seems to be entirely misplaced.

A final observation on these problems: They remain equally difficult no matter what account one gives of the logical grammar of truth. For any move available within one framework, there is usually an analogous move available in any other framework.[22] For any problem that arises in one

---

[22] Example: The fixed-point approach to the paradoxes can be adapted to fit different conceptions of the logical grammar of truth. Martin, Woodruff, and Kripke treated truth as a predicate of sentences in their development of the approach. Jon Barwise and John

framework, one can usually cook up an analogous problem for the other framework. The issues of logical grammar *are* of importance in connection with some problems, but we have yet to see a reason to believe that they are of importance in connection with the problems posed by the paradoxes.[23] For this reason, we shall accept in this work the most convenient account of the grammar of truth: We shall treat truth as a predicate of sentences.

III

Diametrically opposite to the idea that the paradoxes have a simple solution is the view that they are insoluble. According to this view, the proper thing to say about the Liar argument is that it is valid and that it proves the notion of truth to be inconsistent. An early expression of this idea can be found in Tarski's works. In the "Wahrheitsbegriff" (1935/1956), Tarski writes that the paradoxes "prove emphatically that the concept of truth (as well as other semantical concepts) when applied to colloquial language in conjunction with the normal laws of logic leads inevitably to confusions and contradictions" (p. 267). It is interesting that Tarski does not take the paradoxes to be a *reductio* of his Convention T. Despite the paradoxes, he continues to maintain a strong conceptual link between the biconditionals and the concept of truth. Instead, he reads the paradoxes as showing that our ordinary notion of truth "when applied to colloquial language" leads to contradictions. Charles Chihara (1979, 1984) has endorsed Tarski's view, which he calls the *Inconsistency View of Truth*.[24] Chihara writes that "there are generally accepted conventions which give the meaning of 'true' and which are expressed by [the T-biconditionals],"[25] and he views the paradoxes as showing that these conventions imply contradictions.

Etchemendy's Russellian account (1987) also follows the fixed-point approach, but it treats truth as a predicate of propositions. Dorothy Grover (1977) uses the approach in the context of a Prosentential Theory of Truth, which treats certain truth locutions as analogous to sentential variables. (See Grover, Camp, and Belnap 1975 for an exposition of this view.)

[23] We believe the same holds for the problem posed by the Hangman Paradox for the notions of knowledge, necessity, etc. See section 6E.

[24] Graham Priest too has argued for the Inconsistency View in a number of papers (1979, 1984, 1985–86, 1987). In one respect he goes further than Chihara and Tarski: He believes that the Liar argument provides a good reason for thinking that some contradictions are true.

[25] Chihara 1979, p. 611. Chihara's actual reference is not to the T-biconditionals but to the

The Inconsistency View is more attractive than it may appear at first sight. As Chihara points out, it gives a simple account of the meaning of 'true'. Unlike other theories of truth that end up appealing to what Chihara calls "sophisticated" logical notions, the Inconsistency View has no difficulty explaining how ordinary humans, even children, can so easily learn the meaning of 'true'. Furthermore, the theory does not imply that the notion of truth is incoherent or unusable, for the claim that the conventions and rules governing 'true' are inconsistent does not imply that they cannot guide our judgments in unproblematic cases. We can work with inconsistent conventions, and follow inconsistent rules, without falling into incoherence. For example, the laws and ordinances governing our nations and cities are inconsistent on numerous points, and yet this does not mean that the entire legal system is incoherent. (See Chihara 1979 for some different kinds of examples.) A final strength of the Inconsistency View is that it provides a way of dealing with a question that proves to be an embarrassment for many (perhaps most) theories of truth: Is the Simple Liar true, or untrue? If the theory says that it is untrue, and the theory is consistent, then it must deny that the Simple Liar is true even though the Simple Liar says of itself exactly what the theory says about it. On the other hand, if the theory says of the Simple Liar that it is true, the theory attributes truth to a sentence that contradicts what the theory asserts.[26] In either case we have a strong argument against the theory. We have here a mechanical procedure for refuting many theories of truth. It is a virtue of the Inconsistency View that it seems to provide a way of evading this refutation: We accept the contradictory conclusions drawn in the argument but argue that their source is in the fact that the principles governing truth are inconsistent. As Chihara (1979, p. 613) writes, "... the contradictory intuitions are not to be explained away at all, since ... these intuitions correctly reflect the meaning we have given to the word 'true'."

The main reason we do not find the Inconsistency View acceptable is that it does not have the resources to explain the meaning and use of

principle that "a sentence is true if, and only if, what is said to be the case by the sentence is in fact the case." However, he takes the T-biconditionals to give the content of this principle in a clearer form. See p. 605 of his paper.

[26] If the theory attempts to evade the question by saying that the Liar is meaningless (or truth-valueless, or sortally incorrect, ...), then, since no meaningless (or truth-valueless, or sortally incorrect, ...) sentence is true, the theory must say that the Liar is untrue—thus landing on the first horn mentioned above.

ordinary, everyday sentences containing the word 'true'.[27] If the T-biconditionals, read in the naive way, represent the conventions governing 'true', it is a mystery how on the basis of these conventions we arrive at our ordinary unproblematic assessment of the truth values of numerous sentences. The T-biconditionals imply not only of the paradoxical but of *all* sentences that they are both true and untrue. An indirect argument to this conclusion is easy; we need only combine the reasoning of the Liar argument with the classically valid principle that from a contradiction anything follows (*ex falso quodlibet*). However, this is not the only argument available. There are direct arguments to the same conclusion. For example, the T-biconditional of (8) implies in very weak systems of logic—including systems that deny *ex falso quodlibet*—that God exists.

(8)   If this sentence is true then God exists.

To make the argument a little clearer, let us remove the indexical 'this' from (8). Consider (9).

(9)   If sentence (9) is true then God exists.

The T-biconditional for this sentence is (or, more strictly, implies) sentence (10).

(10)   Sentence (9) is true if and only if (If (9) is true then God exists).

Suppose that

(11)   Sentence (9) is true.

In virtue of (10), the T-biconditional for (9), we have (12).

(12)   If sentence (9) is true then God exists.

Applying *modus ponens* to (11) and (12) yields (13).

(13)   God exists.

On the supposition that (9) is true, we have established that God exists. We can conclude, therefore, that

(14)   If sentence (9) is true then God exists.

This implies, in view of (10), that

[27] For another kind of criticism of the Inconsistency View, see Herzberger 1966, 1967.

(15)   Sentence (9) is true.

The desired conclusion that

(16)   God exists

follows from (14) and (15) by *modus ponens.*[28] Thus, a direct argument to any conclusion whatsoever can be constructed from the T-biconditionals.

It may be said (as Chihara [1984] does say in connection with *ex falso quodlibet*) that, even though there is a proof of God's existence from the T-biconditionals, it does not follow that it is *reasonable* to infer God's existence from the biconditionals. Chihara (1984, p. 226) writes that "in 'real life' situations, one doesn't simply accept blindly the logical consequences of whatever one may initially have reason to believe." The suggestion is that although the T-biconditionals represent the rules governing the word 'true', we need not accept all the logical consequences of these rules. We need accept only those consequences that are "reasonable." The problem with this suggestion is that by putting the entire burden of the theory on the notion of "reasonable inference"—a notion of which no theoretical or even intuitive account[29] is given—it obscures completely the contribution of the T-biconditionals to the meaning of 'true'. Without an account of "reasonable inference," any inconsistent—or consistent— set of sentences can be put forward as giving the rules and conventions governing 'true' and this set would not be any worse off as far as explaining our use of 'true' is concerned.

We do not think that we can expect an account of "reasonable inference" that would explain our ordinary uses of 'true' in terms of the T-biconditionals. The reason is that when the T-biconditionals are interpreted in the ordinary way they are inconsistent not only on a few isolated points; as Curry's paradox shows, they are *thoroughly* inconsistent: for any conclusion *A* whatsoever, there is a direct argument from the bicondi-

---

[28] The combinatory structure underlying this argument was first discovered by Haskell Curry and is known as *Curry's Paradox.* Medieval logicians were aware of closely related arguments and used them to construct fallacious proofs of God's existence. Note that Curry's argument is similar to the argument for Löb's Theorem. In fact, Löb's Theorem is to Curry's Paradox as Tarski's Theorem on the Indefinability of Truth is to the Liar Paradox.

[29] We are unclear as to why it would be unreasonable for a person *who accepts the biconditional for* (9) to infer God's existence from it. Furthermore, it is not clear why it would not be reasonable for such a person simply to revise his beliefs and abandon the problematic T-biconditionals, such as those for (9) and those for the Simple Liar. If this *were* reasonable, then there would be no sense in which the inconsistent T-biconditionals governed the use of 'true' *after* the revision took place.

tionals to the conclusion that A is true, and there is another to the contradictory conclusion that A is not true. It is difficult to see how such a
thoroughly inconsistent set of conventions could guide any behavior, let
alone the coherent and stable body of judgments we produce concerning
'true'.[30] Further, it seems that what is reasonable to infer from a given
body of inconsistent sentences depends not only upon the syntactic features
of the sentences but also upon the meanings of the constants occurring in
them, and sometimes also on pragmatic factors.[31] Thus, what is reasonable to infer from the T-biconditionals (on their ordinary interpretation)
would be different if we were to take 'true' to express the concept "identical
to itself."[32] If this is so, then we need an account of the concept of truth to
explain what is reasonable to infer from the inconsistent biconditionals,
not the other way around; the concept of truth is not to be explained in
terms of the T-biconditionals and "reasonable inference." There is another
consideration that suggests this conclusion. What is "reasonable" to accept on the basis of inconsistent conventions, we have noted, depends
sometimes on context. The more thoroughly inconsistent a set of conventions is, the less guidance it provides to behavior and the more context
dependent are its applications. Hence, if the Inconsistency View is correct,
we should expect our use of 'true' in a given context to depend on how we
choose, in that context, to interpret and apply the inconsistent conventions governing it. As a result, we should expect our use of 'true', even in
reference to context-independent sentences, to be highly dependent on
context. This expectation, however, is not borne out in our ordinary uses
of 'true'. The Inconsistency View loses much of its attractiveness, it seems
to us, when we seek from it an explanation of our ordinary, unproblematic
uses of 'true'.

These considerations point to an important methodological observation. It is remarkable that despite the enormous effort that has been devoted to solving or dissolving the Liar paradox, the paradox and the
mystery that surrounds it are still with us. It seems to us that a reason for

---

[30] Analogy: If our laws were thoroughly inconsistent (in the sense that for *every* course of
action there were explicit rules that directly implied that the action was illegal and others
that directly implied that it was not), then it would be difficult to understand our legal
practices in terms of these laws.

[31] On such factors as our degrees of belief in the sentences, the risks involved if our beliefs are
wrong, and our sources of information and our views about them.

[32] For example, it would then be reasonable to infer (presumably) that "'snow is white and
snow is not white' is true."

this failure may be that insufficient attention has been paid to the ordinary, unproblematic uses of the concept of truth. When confronted with some perplexing and extraordinary phenomenon, one is tempted to focus on it and to ignore the ordinary and familiar phenomena that are related to it. However, this may not be the best strategy for achieving an understanding of the puzzling phenomenon. An analogy may help to make the point clear. Imagine that before the development of astronomy the members of a tribe observe a solar eclipse. Naturally perplexed by this extraordinary occurrence, they seek an explanation of it. Their first tendency may well be to speculate on the causes of the event. We can imagine the kinds of hypotheses that would appear natural: the wrath of gods, the swallowing of the sun by an evil demon, and what not. But it is unlikely that such speculations will yield an understanding of the eclipse. The proper method for gaining understanding here is to undertake a patient and systematic study of the ordinary and familiar behavior of the sun, the moon, and the stars. Often we come to understand the extraordinary only when we see it in terms of the ordinary. The suggestion we are making is that in order to gain a proper understanding of the Liar paradox we should try to understand the principles that underlie the ordinary, unproblematic uses of the concept of truth. In order to gain a better understanding of the Liar, we need to give *less* attention to the paradoxes than we have given them.

What makes it easy to ignore the ordinary phenomena is that it is not always clear at first sight that there is anything to explain. A little reflection on ordinary discourse concerning truth reveals, however, that there are elements in it that deserve a systematic explanation. Consider an ordinary assertion. Imagine that on a certain occasion Ravi says that

(17)   Everything that Kamal said is true

and suppose that the relevant assertions of Kamal are that snow is white and that two plus two is four. We notice that we can determine the truth value of Ravi's statement once we know what things Kamal has asserted and whether snow is white and two plus two is four. We can make the example more complex by imagining that Kamal makes claims about the truth and falsity of Anita's remarks and Anita in turn makes claims about the veracity of yet another person. Still, in each case the truth or falsity of Ravi's original statement is completely fixed by certain facts about the world—facts such as that Kamal has made such-and-such assertions, that snow is white, and that Anita's third remark was such-and-

such. Let us call facts of this sort *nonsemantical facts*. We will not attempt
to give a precise explanation of this notion.[33] For present purposes, nonsemantical facts may be taken as those that do not contain the concept of
truth as a constituent. Thus, facts such as that snow is white and that
Anita's third remark was such-and-such count as nonsemantical. But facts
such as that the sentence 'Two plus two is four' is true and that Darwin's
theory is true do not count as nonsemantical. The feature of the concept
of truth we have just observed can be stated as follows: The truth and
falsity of the unproblematic sentences are completely determined by the
nonsemantical facts. One goal of a theory of truth ought to be to explain
in a systematic way *how* the truth values of unproblematic sentences depend on nonsemantical facts. This task is harder and more illuminating
than it may appear at first sight.

The nonsemantical facts, as the paradoxes show, do not necessarily fix
a definite truth value for each and every sentence of the language. In the
example given above, if we assume that Kamal's only assertion is

(18)   Ravi's statement (17) is not true

then we find that in trying to evaluate Ravi's statement (17) we are led to
evaluate Kamal's assertion (18), and this leads us back to (17). We notice
also that if we say that (17) is true then we are led to say that (18) is true,
and this leads us to contradict our earlier judgment and say that (17) is not
true. On the other hand, if we say that (17) is not true we are forced to
conclude that (18) is not true. And this leads us to revise our earlier claim
and say that (17) is true after all. And the process repeats. Thus we find
that, if the nonsemantical facts are as described in this example, we cannot
coherently assign any truth value to (17) or (18). These sentences exhibit
paradoxical behavior. Still, even here there is a fact that needs explaining:
Once we are given the nonsemantical facts, we can determine which sentences are problematic and paradoxical and which are not. The general
point is this: *If all the nonsemantical facts are given, then the status of
a sentence—that is, whether the sentence is problematic, and, if unproblematic, whether it is true—is completely determined.* In particular cases
we can calculate, and even intuit, the status of a sentence once the nonsemantical facts are given. But the general principles that govern our cal-

---

[33] Later we shall replace it by a more exact notion. The inexact notion just introduced is
useful in the interim.

culations and intuitions are not known to us. One task of a theory of truth is to explain in a systematic way how the statuses of various sentences depend upon the nonsemantical facts.[34]

Our main criticism of the Inconsistency View is that it does not perform the task just outlined. No account of "reasonable inference" is available that would systematically explain our intuitive judgments concerning truth, falsity, and paradoxicality. And, for the reasons given earlier, there is little hope that such an account can be constructed.

These considerations show that Chihara's argument on behalf of the Inconsistency View that it is simple is not only premature but unsound. The theory without an account of "reasonable inference" is simple. It is simple, however, not because it performs the desired task simply, but because it evades the task altogether. On the other hand, there is little reason to think that the theory will remain simple once an account of "reasonable inference" is adjoined to it (assuming that such an account is possible). Hence, the Inconsistency View has no better prospect of explaining children's acquisition of the concept of truth than other theories that rely on what Chihara calls "sophisticated" logical notions. Concerning the second point in favor of the Inconsistency View mentioned above: One can grant Chihara's claim that the view is not committed to saying that the notion of truth is incoherent and unusable. However, this claim is too weak to make the view plausible. What must be shown is not merely that the Inconsistency View is compatible with the ordinary uses of 'true', but that it can *explain* these uses. Finally, concerning the argument that the Inconsistency View escapes the dilemma that fells many theories of truth: It *is* plausible to see the paradoxes as arising from the rules governing 'true'— and this idea may even provide a basis for dealing with the dilemma. However, it is not so plausible to maintain that the rules governing 'true' are inconsistent. We shall see in chapter 4 how we can gain the former advantage without incurring the latter burden.

The arguments just given against the Inconsistency View do not, and are not meant to, call into question the fundamental intuition that the T-biconditionals fix the meaning of truth. What the arguments do show, we hope, is that there is a problem if we accept the fundamental intuition *and* interpret the T-biconditionals naively, for then it is completely unclear how the meaning that we attribute to 'true' contributes to its use. We

---

[34] For a more extended discussion of this demand, see Gupta 1987.

should seriously consider the possibility that the fundamental intuition is correct and the problem lies in the naive interpretation of the T-biconditionals. Our judgments concerning the status of both the unproblematic and the paradoxical sentences *do* seem to have their source in the equivalences expressed in the T-biconditionals. But the logic and the semantics of the T-biconditionals may not quite be what they appear to be. It is only through the construction of a theory of truth—a theory that offers a systematic explanation of our ordinary uses of 'true'—that we can arrive at the proper interpretation of the T-biconditionals. Only then can we hope to understand how these biconditionals contribute to our use of 'true'.

IV

The existence of the paradoxes, then, does not invalidate the fundamental intuition, formalized in Convention T, that the meaning of truth is fixed by the T-biconditionals. For reasons independent of the paradoxes, however, this intuition must be qualified and sharpened. We need to isolate the special sense of 'true' and the special sense of 'meaning' in which these expressions are to be interpreted in the fundamental intuition.

Tarski (1969, p. 63) noted that a definition that satisfies Convention T does not capture *all* the diverse uses of 'true':

The notion of truth occurs in many different contexts, and there are several distinct categories of objects to which the term "true" is applied. In a psychological discussion one might speak of true emotions as well as true beliefs; in a discourse from the domain of esthetics the inner truth of an object of art might be analyzed.... We concern ourselves exclusively with the meaning of the term "true" when this term is used to refer to sentences.[35]

Tarski does not delineate Convention T's domain of applicability any further. However, even in reference to sentences, we have several distinct notions of truth, and Convention T is the appropriate adequacy condition for one notion but not for the others.

We need to distinguish, in the first place, what may be called the *logical* notion of truth from the *nonlogical* notion. Consider the following two sentences, both of which can be truly asserted:

---

[35] Tarski goes on to say "Presumably this was the original use of the term "true" in human language." Fortunately the value and the validity of Tarski's work do not depend upon this claim's being right.

(19) The sentence 'snow is white or snow is not white' is necessarily true.

(20) If 'or' had meant what 'and' means then the sentence 'snow is white or snow is not white' would not have been true.

How can the sentence 'snow is white or snow is not white' be both necessarily true and possibly untrue? A simple and natural resolution of the puzzle is to say that two different notions of truth are being employed in these sentences. Using the metaphor of possible worlds, we can explain the differences between the two notions as follows: To determine whether a sentence falls, in a world w, under the first notion of truth—the notion that is employed in (19), and which we shall call the *logical* notion—we determine whether the sentence is true in w with *the meaning it has in the actual world*. On the other hand, to determine whether it falls under the second notion of truth in w—the notion that is employed in (20), and which we shall call the *nonlogical* notion—we determine whether it is true in w with *the meaning it has in the world* w. Truth depends both on meaning and on facts. In its first (logical) sense, the truth of a sentence in a world w depends on the meaning of the sentence in the *actual* world and on the facts in w. It is sensitive, therefore, to the variation of facts from world to world, but *not* to the variation of meaning. In its second (nonlogical) sense, truth has a simpler dependence on meaning and facts. It is sensitive both to the variation of meaning and to the variation of facts from world to world.[36]

Only for the logical concept of truth are the T-biconditionals necessarily true, and only for this concept is Convention T a plausible adequacy condition.[37] The concession that Convention T is not adequate for the nonlogical concept, it seems to us, does not detract from Convention T's importance. The concept of truth that is useful in Logic and Philosophy of Language is the first one. It is this concept that is needed in the definition of validity and in the thesis that meaning is given by truth conditions.[38]

---

[36] The distinction between the two notions of truth is significant only if some languages are contingent entities or, if they are all necessary, the semantic properties of some are not essential to them. Otherwise the semantic properties of languages would not exhibit any variation across worlds, and thus the distinction between the two notions would collapse.

[37] A concept whose definition satisfies Convention T is *extensionally* but not *intensionally* equivalent to the nonlogical notion of truth.

[38] Here we disagree with Etchemendy, who assumes that the notion of truth used in Semantics is, in our terminology, the nonlogical one. See Etchemendy 1988, p. 61.

And Convention T appears to formulate the correct material-adequacy condition for this concept.[39]

Another distinction that we need to recognize is that between the *weak* and the *strong* notions of truth (Yablo 1985). With the weak notion, the semantic status of '"*P*" is true' is exactly the same as that of *P*. If *P* is neither true nor false, then so is '"*P*" is true'. If *P* is both true and false, then so is '"*P*" is true'. If *P* has a certain degree of truth, then '"*P*" is true' has the same degree of truth. And so on. With the strong notion(s) of truth the equivalence between *P* and '"*P*" is true' is not perfect. For example, with this reading, '"*P*" is true' may be false even though *P* is not false but only neither true nor false.

For purposes of illustration, suppose someone makes an assertion that lacks truth value. Suppose it is the logician's favorite, (21).

(21)   The present King of France is bald.

Further, suppose that another person affirms this by saying

(22)   That is true.

It is natural to hold that (22), like (21), is without truth value, for (21) and (22) say the same thing. On this reading, 'true' in (22) expresses the weak notion. But in the sentence '(21) is neither true nor false', it is natural to interpret 'true' as expressing a strong notion.[40]

It is clear that the T-biconditionals are true, and that Convention T is plausible, only for the weak notion of truth. Combining this with our earlier observation, we conclude that Convention T is appropriate only for those uses of 'true' where it expresses the weak, logical notion. Henceforth, unless we state otherwise, it is this notion that we will be discussing.

One final distinction concerning truth should be noted: that between the absolute notion "*truth simpliciter*" and the relativized notion "*truth in a model.*" The two notions are related. Truth simpliciter is truth in the

[39] It may be that the phenomenon exemplified by sentences (19) and (20) above can be explained without positing an ambiguity in truth—say, by assigning to predicates a more complex meaning and by complicating the semantics of necessity and possibility. In this case the proper conclusion would be that Convention T takes into account only a limited range of the uses of 'true'. The fact remains, however, that the uses it does take into account constitute an important class.
[40] The strong reading is not forced, however. We can defend the weak reading if we interpret 'neither *P* nor *Q*' so that its truth does not require the falsity of the components *P* and *Q*. In general, the weak notion of truth carries more information than any of the strong notions and can do their work if the language is rich in logical resources.

unique model that represents the actual world. Truth in a model M can, in turn, be explained using absolute truth roughly in the following way: Truth in M is what would be true simpliciter had the situation represented by M obtained. Though the two notions are related, the projects of defining them are quite distinct. The definition of absolute truth requires (at least arguably) that the demands of Convention T be met. But Convention T is quite inappropriate for the definition of the relativized notion. The T-biconditionals make no sense if they are taken to be about "truth in a model." Their right-hand sides do not even mention the variable on which relativized truth so crucially depends.

No definition of either one of these notions can be obtained in a straightforward way from a definition of the other. The transformation of a definition of relativized truth into a definition of absolute truth requires one to define the model M that represents the actual world, and that is an entirely nontrivial task. Sometimes, depending upon the resources of the object language and the metalanguage, it can even happen that the relativized notion has an easy definition but the model M is indefinable. For example, suppose one has a first-order formalization of the language of physics. The relativized notion of truth for this language can be defined using only set-theoretic resources. But the model that represents the actual world cannot be so defined; obviously it requires the use of physical vocabulary. Often it is easier to give a direct definition of absolute truth than it is to convert a definition of relativized truth into one of absolute truth.

Nor does a definition of absolute truth provide us with the resources necessary for the construction of a definition of relativized truth. The key problem that one must solve in constructing this latter definition concerns the notion of "model." One needs to articulate this notion so that it is general enough to capture the broad notion of logical possibility and yet precise enough to be of use in characterizing validity. This task in turn requires, among other things, that one distinguish between the logical and the nonlogical signs of the language and that one give an account of the range of possible interpretations of the nonlogical signs. Even though some philosophers (especially those attracted by the Davidsonian conception of semantics) have seen in Convention T a demand that would lead to a systematic solution of these problems,[41] the fact is that a definition

---

[41] Tarski himself did not view Convention T in this way. But Davidson (1973, p. 71) has written: "Theories of absolute truth necessarily provide an analysis of structure relevant to truth and to inference. Such theories therefore yield a nontrivial answer to the question what

satisfying Convention T need provide no insight into the logical structure of the language, or into the distinction between the logical and nonlogical signs, or into the notion of logical possibility. This point can be made clear by means of an example first constructed by Tarski (1969, p. 65) for another purpose.

Suppose the object language L is finite. Say it has n sentences, A_1, A_2, ..., A_n (where n may be as large as one likes). Suppose the metalanguage contains the object language and has, besides the usual logical resources, quotational names for all the sentences of L. Now a definition of absolute truth for L can easily be constructed:

(23)   For all objects x: x is true (in L) if and only if either $x = $ 'A_1' and A_1 or $x = $ 'A_2' and A_2 or ... or $x = $ 'A_n' and A_n.[42]

This definition satisfies Convention T.[43] But it does not reveal the logical structure of L. It does not help us to mark the distinction between the logical and the nonlogical signs of L, nor does it help us to articulate the notion of logical possibility. The example should not be dismissed on the ground that L is finite. The first reason is that a theory of logical structure should be general. Since the finiteness of L does not preclude L's having interesting logical structure, the example ought to be covered by the theory. Second, even when the object language is infinite, truth definitions can be given which do not reveal logical structure and which do not yield a notion of logical possibility. (See Belnap and Grover 1973 for an example. Further, the theories of truth for modal languages constructed in Gupta 1978 satisfy Convention T but do not yield a notion of model.) It is true that under certain conditions a definition of truth is best constructed by means of a recursion on all and only the logical constants of the object language, but these conditions may well be impossible to specify. Furthermore, it is doubtful that illumination concerning such things as the distinction between the logical and the nonlogical is to be found in the specification of these conditions.

---

is to count as logical form of a sentence.... The logical constants may be identified as those iterative features of the language that require a recursive clause in the characterization of truth and satisfaction."

[42] Tarski notes that this definition cannot itself be in L, for it contains all the sentences of L as proper parts. Thus, this kind of definition does not allow one to define "true in L" in L.

[43] Assuming that various elementary syntactic facts about L (facts such as that 'A_1' is a sentence of L and that 'A_1' $\neq$ 'A_2') are available in the metalanguage.

The projects of defining the absolute and relativized notions of truth, though related, are distinct. They face their own distinctive problems and hold forth their own distinctive promises.

V

Thus, one qualification that must be put on the fundamental intuition (that the T-biconditionals fix the meaning of truth) is that it concerns only the absolute, weak, logical notion of truth. Another necessary qualification is that the relevant sense of 'meaning' here is that of *intension*.[44] Let us call this reading of the fundamental intuition the *Intension Thesis*.

Intension Thesis   The T-biconditionals fix the intension of truth.

Observe that this thesis is committed to a weaker linkage between the biconditionals and the concept of truth than that expressed in Convention T. Convention T is committed to the following claim:

Implication Thesis   A definition of truth should *imply* the biconditionals.

The differences between the two theses may appear insignificant, but actually they are of great philosophical importance. The Intension Thesis is more plausible than the Implication Thesis, and it is philosophically neutral in several ways in which the Implication Thesis is not.

One aspect of the neutrality is brought out by reflection on the relationship of the two theses to the Correspondence theory of truth. The Intension Thesis, it will be observed, is consistent with this theory: a Correspondence theorist can acknowledge the Intension thesis for the *logical* notion of truth and can even give a correspondence account of this notion.[45] However, a Correspondence theorist would not, and should not, accept the Implication Thesis. It is neither a necessary nor a sufficient condition on an adequate Correspondence theory that it imply the T-biconditionals. Tarski's work shows that a theory can imply the bicondi-

---

[44] We use *intension* to isolate that aspect of meaning that concerns alethic modalities such as possibility. Roughly, the intension of an expression is determined by its extension through all possible worlds.

[45] The account would have to use modal notions, such as 'actually'. One part of the account might say, for example, "The sentence 'a is F' is true (in L) if and only if there is an object x and a property P such that a actually refers to x and F actually denotes P (in L) and x has the property P."

tionals without spelling out the correspondence relationship between the words and the world. The converse holds also. A theory may give a satisfactory account of the correspondence relationship but not imply the biconditionals. This can be seen through an example.

Suppose we build a Correspondence theory of truth for English by giving a detailed account—even, say, in physicalistic terms, as Field (1972) desires—of the relationship that holds whenever a name of English denotes an object, a one-place predicate of English is true of an object, and so on. Let us abbreviate an account of this relationship to 'R'. Such a theory would imply that

For all names and predicates x and for all objects d: x denotes d or is true of d (in English) if and only if x R d

and would yield the biconditional

'Snow is white' is true if and only if there is an object d such that 'snow' R d and 'is white' R d.[46]

However, just as a biological theory of fatherhood (say, in genetic terms) does not by itself imply the particular instances of the father-child relationship, the theory of correspondence between the words and the world does not *by itself* imply the particular instances of the correspondence relationship—instances such as

'snow' denotes snow.

This instance follows from the theory once we add to it the specific information that

'snow' R snow.

However, in the absence of this information, the theory would not imply the T-biconditional for 'snow is white'.

More generally, theorists defending correspondence, coherence, or any other traditional philosophical account of truth can accept the T-biconditionals. They can accept also the further idea that the totality of T-biconditionals fixes the intension of truth. But they cannot accept the claim that an adequate account of truth should imply the T-biconditionals.

---

[46] We are treating 'snow' as a proper name and ignoring the complication that it is actually a mass term.

The T-biconditionals are philosophically neutral. This neutrality does not carry over, however, to Convention T.[47]

Another illustration of the philosophical neutrality of the Intension Thesis is provided by its relationship to *disquotationalism* and *deflationism*. The Implication Thesis, by making the T-biconditionals a consequence of the definition of truth, suggests that sentences such as 'snow is white' and ''snow is white' is true' are perfectly equivalent: The two say the same thing and play exactly the same role in our language. But if such pairs of sentences are perfectly equivalent, what is the utility of the truth predicate? A natural response is that the truth predicate is a device of *disquotation*. Quine (1970, p. 12) explains the usefulness of the device in the following way:

> We may affirm the single sentence by just uttering it, unaided by quotation or by the truth predicate; but if we want to affirm some infinite lot of sentences that we can demarcate only by talking about the sentences, then the truth predicate has its use. We need it to restore the effect of objective reference when for the sake of some generalization we have resorted to semantic ascent.

The picture of the role of truth that Quine sketches, and one that is suggested by the Implication Thesis, can be put as follows: In semantic ascent, often signaled by the use of quotation marks, one shifts from talk of reality to talk of language. Truth as a device of disquotation undoes the effect of quotation. It allows us to say things about the world while talking about sentences. This shifting of levels from reality to language and back to reality, as Quine points out, is useful. It enables us to express certain generalizations—such as 'every alternation of a sentence with its negation is true' (Quine's example)—that would otherwise be inexpressible in a first-order language.

It is in the additional expressive power which semantic ascent gives us that Quine and the other disquotationalists see the utility of the truth predicate. Truth, on the disquotational view, is assigned a purely logical role, a role on par with that of the logical connectives and quantifiers. This

---

[47] Tarski says in a number of his essays that he is concerned to capture the classical correspondence conception of truth. In Tarski 1969 he suggests that, although the correspondence conception is in accord with the ordinary notion, the coherence and pragmatic conceptions "have little connection with the actual usage of the term 'true'" (p. 64). Tarski's opinions on these matters were not entirely stable, and his discussions of them were always very brief. We shall not attempt to interpret and criticize his remarks. We shall note only that, in our opinion, although the T-biconditionals are neutral with respect to the various philosophical theories, Convention T is not. Convention T sets a demand that is not met (nor, in our view, is there any reason to think that it should be met) by the traditional philosophical theories.

raises another puzzle: If truth is solely a device of disquotation, how can it play the role that has traditionally been assigned to it? How can it be of any importance in such philosophical concerns as the theories of inference and meaning, and in the metaphysical dispute over realism? A number of philosophers, in response to this problem, have been willing to deny that the notion of truth can play any significant philosophical role. Some declare the traditional issues themselves to be bogus. Others try to redefine them so that they concern some notion other than that of truth, such as verification. In either case the resulting view is *deflationist* toward truth.[48]

We cannot discuss here the numerous issues raised by disquotationalism and deflationism. For now, we wish to emphasize only that the Intension Thesis does not lead to, and does not motivate, these views. The Intension Thesis implies only that such pairs of sentences as 'snow is white' and ''snow is white' is true' are intensionally equivalent. It is not committed to maintaining that they have the same role in our language. Expressions that have the same intension may, nonetheless, have radically different functions in our language. A stereotypical example is 'water' and 'H$_2$O'. Many philosophers accept the idea that these expressions have the same intension,[49] but no one holds that they have the same role. A philosopher can subscribe to the Intension Thesis and at the same time reject (or accept) disquotationalism and deflationism.

That the Implication Thesis goes beyond the Intension Thesis is also evidenced by the fact that the latter is immune from certain doubts that arise naturally in connection with the former. The Intension Thesis has the same plausibility whether we consider the homophonic examples (i.e., those examples in which the translation of the object language into the metalanguage is the identity function) or the heterophonic ones (those in which the translation is not the identity function). The claim that the T-biconditionals of English fix the intension of "true in English" is no more (or less) plausible than the claim that the T-biconditionals for German fix the intension of "true in German" (assuming that a T-biconditional for each German sentence is formulable in English). In contrast, however, the Implication Thesis is plausible only in the homophonic examples, not in the heterophonic ones. A biconditional such as

[48] See Devitt 1984, Horwich 1990, and Kapus 1992 for more information on deflationism.
[49] Mark Wilson has pointed out that as a matter of fact these expressions are not even coextensional. He would reject the example but not the philosophical point.

'Schnee ist weiss' is true in German if and only if snow is white

cannot be regarded as being true in virtue of the concept "true in German." A person may have a perfect grasp of the concept "true in German" and yet not know any of the biconditionals, and may not even be able to distinguish grammatical strings of German from ungrammatical ones. T-biconditionals such as the one above carry empirical information about German, and the possession of this information is not a precondition for the grasp of the concept "true in German". Hence, it is not plausible to require that a definition of 'true in German' imply the biconditionals.[50] A failure to distinguish clearly the Implication Thesis and the Intension Thesis may well have made the former appear more plausible than it is.[51]

VI

The problem of truth and paradox can now be stated as follows. We want a theory that will explain the *absolute, weak, logical* notion of truth. More specifically, we would like to construct, if possible, a theory of the *intension* of 'true' (in its absolute, weak, logical sense) that (a) would yield a systematic account of its use in our language, and (b) would validate the Intension Thesis. In its present formulation, however, the problem is much too rough and much too hard to be tackled directly. Let us begin by making it a little sharper and a little easier.

It is a feature of the concept of truth that it reflects virtually all the semantic complexities present in the object language. If there are terms in the language that are vague, then 'true' is vague also.[52] If there are truth-value gaps in the language, then the truth predicate is gappy also. If there

[50] One cannot evade this conclusion by taking the aim of the definition to be something weaker than the analysis of meaning—say, by taking the aim to be extensional or intensional equivalence with truth. Although a definition that implies the biconditionals would suffice for these aims, a definition that does *not* imply the biconditionals might well suffice also. So it is not a requirement on such definitions that they *imply* the biconditionals.

[51] Another source of the plausibility of the Implication Thesis may be the fact that it is reasonable to require of a theory of truth (and translation) that *it imply that the T-biconditionals are true* (for the moment, ignoring the paradoxes). The difference between this requirement and the Implication Thesis is that the latter gives a *de re* reading to the expression "T-biconditionals" in the italicized statement—a reading that is not permissible. The following parallel may help to bring out the distinction: We (the authors) know *a priori* that the T-biconditionals of Bulgarian formulated in English are true (ignoring the paradoxes); however, for no such biconditional X do we know, *a priori* or otherwise, that X.

[52] We remind the reader that we are concerned with 'true' in its *weak* sense.

is context dependency, then 'true' is similarly context dependent. And so on. In view of this feature, a complete solution of the problem posed above requires us to solve virtually every known semantic problem. Clearly, if we are to make any progress in giving a description of our concept of truth, we need to set some of these problems aside. For this purpose let us assume that the language (or language fragment) under study has, aside from the concept of truth, none of the other complicating factors: indexicals, vagueness, ambiguity, intensional constructions, truth-value gaps, etc. We assume that, apart from the concept of truth, the language L under study can be viewed as a classical first-order quantificational language. This assumption is satisfied only by very limited fragments of natural languages. We believe, however, that it removes little that is of immediate interest to us in our study of paradox and truth.

One benefit of this assumption is that it enables us to accept a simple account of the semantics of all atomic terms of L other than the truth predicate (say, T). We can assume that all terms other than T are well behaved: that names have denotations, predicates have classical extensions, and function symbols have well-defined graphs in all possible situations. We want to emphasize that we are not making any assumptions concerning the semantics of T. We leave open all possibilities: The interpretation of T may be two-valued, three-valued, n-valued, vague, or something else yet unknown. What the form of the semantics of T should be is one of the central questions that a theory of truth has to answer. It is useful to introduce some terminology to facilitate later discussion of this question. Let the (*extensional*) *signification* of an expression (or a concept) in a world w be an abstract something that carries all the information about the expression's extensional relations in w. The signification of a *classical* predicate can be represented by its extension or by a function that determines of each object whether the predicate is true or false of it. The sigification of a *three-valued* predicate determines, and is determined by, the extension and the antiextension[53] of the predicate. The signification of a *vague* predicate determines the degree to which the predicate is true of any given object. In short: Signification is a generalization of the notion of extension. Within a two-valued context the signification of a

---

[53] The antiextension of a predicate in a world w is the set of objects of which the predicate is false. Objects that lie outside both the extension and the antiextension are those of which the predicate is neither true nor false.

predicate can be identified with its extension, but in general signification is richer and carries more information.[54]

In classical modal logic the intension of a predicate is understood as a function that yields the extension of the predicate in each world. Generalizing this idea to suit the present context, we say that the intension of *T* is a function that yields at a world w the signification of *T* in w. We thus arrive at the following useful reformulation of the Intension Thesis:

Signification Thesis   The T-biconditionals fix the signification of truth in every world.

Note that this thesis is actually only a thesis *schema*, or an *equation*. It makes a definite assertion only when precise values are specified for the two crucial variables in it: the T-biconditionals and the signification of truth. The second problem formulated above—problem (b)—sets us the task of solving this equation, i.e., of discovering an account of the T-conditionals and the signification of truth so that the Signification Thesis will be rendered true. We take this to be a principal task of this book.

We must make the notion of possible situation a little clearer before we can give a satisfactory formulation of the problem of truth and paradox. This is made easier by our decision to work with a language *L* whose *T*-free fragment, *L'*, is completely classical. This implies that *L'* is extensional and, consequently, that the truth value of each of its sentences is completely determined by the extensional properties of its atomic terms (i.e., by the denotations of the names, extensions of the predicates, and the graphs of the function-symbols). Hence, as far as the *T*-free fragment *L'* is concerned, the possible situation can be identified with a classical model[55] (sometimes also called 'structure') of the language. Turning now to the language as a whole, what additional information do we need to fix the status of sentences that contain *T*? The answer is: None. As we saw above, the statuses of all the sentences of the language are completely determined

---

[54] It is with some hesitation that we reintroduce the medieval term 'signification' into semantics, though not with the meaning it had before. We want to be able to talk about what we are calling the signification of a term without any theoretical commitments concerning it. "Extension" does not always give all the information about a term's extensional relations, and in our view not all concepts have extensions. 'Interpretation', in its contemporary usage, is a flexible term, meaning different things in different contexts. Sometimes it means "extension," sometimes "intension," sometimes "meaning," and on occasion also "signification." Since its flexibility is useful, we have chosen to leave 'interpretation' alone and introduce some new terminology.

[55] Definitions of this and other notions are reviewed in section 2A.

by the nonsemantical facts. And models of the T-free fragment carry all the relevant nonsemantic information.[56] Conclusion: The notion of possible situation can, for our purposes, be identified with that of model of the T-free fragment of L.

The problem to be solved, then, is this: Given a first-order language L with a distinguished predicate T that means "true-in-L," and given a classical model M of the T-free fragment of L, construct a systematic account of the signification of T that

- yields a classification of the sentences of L into true/false/paradoxical/ etc.—a classification that conforms to our ordinary intuitions and uses of 'true'

and

- yields an interpretation of the T-biconditionals that is in accord with the Signification Thesis.

It is through attempting to solve this problem, we believe, that we can hope to discover principles that will illuminate the nature and the source of the paradoxes.

[56] A simple example: The status of the sentence "'Socrates is wise' is true" is completely determined by whether Socrates is wise or not, and this information is carried by the model of the T-free fragment. This model tells us the denotation of 'Socrates' and the extension of 'is wise'.

2 Fixed Points: Some Basic Facts

We shall argue in chapter 3 that the desiderata posited above for the theory of truth cannot be secured if the signification of truth is viewed in traditional ways—that is, if truth is treated as a two-valued, or three-valued, or four-valued predicate. The present chapter provides an introduction to the concepts and results that are needed for an understanding of the traditional approaches and for the arguments we shall develop against them. These concepts and results will be useful in later chapters also.[1]

2A Preliminary Matters

This section is devoted to a review of the key elements of the classical and of some nonclassical semantics. We shall be concerned primarily with extensional first-order languages. We suppose for concreteness that the logical constants of our languages are = (identity), $\sim$ (negation), & (conjunction), $\perp$ (falsity), and $\forall$ (universal quantifier), and that the usual definitions are given for $\vee$ (disjunction), $\rightarrow$ (material conditional), $\leftrightarrow$ (material equivalence), and $\exists$ (existential quantifier). Sometimes we shall consider languages with additional, and sometimes with fewer, logical resources. When this is so, we shall state the additions and subtractions explicitly. The nonlogical resources of our languages may consist of some or all of the following: names, n-place function symbols, n-place predicates. Unless we state otherwise, we shall assume that the nonlogical constants of the language are at most denumerable. We use L, L', L_1, ... to range over languages syntactically construed. (We may, if we wish, think of these as variables ranging over set-theoretic constructs that carry sufficient syntactic information about the language.) We suppose that notions such as *term of L*, *formula of L*, *a variable x being free in a formula A*, and *sentence of L* are defined in the usual way. In particular, *sentences* of a language are formulas in which no variable occurs free.[2]

We shall consider languages under the classical two-valued interpretations and also under three-valued and four-valued interpretations. These

[1] Chapters 4 and 7 are, however, entirely independent of this and the next chapter. Readers unwilling to work through technical material should skip to chapter 4.
[2] We use italicized symbols as metalinguistic variables ranging over the symbols and expressions of the object language. In particular, we use x, y, z, x', ... to range over the variables of the object language; a, b, c, ... as variables ranging over names; s, t, t', ... over terms; f, g, f', ... over function symbols; F, G, R, F', ... over predicates; A, B, C, A', .. over formulas; and X over expressions (= terms and formulas).

latter interpretations, which many theoreticians of truth have thought to be crucial to the problems with which we deal, are like the classical ones except that the predicates of the language may be neither true nor false (the three-valued case) or, in addition, both true and false (the four-valued case) of an object in the domain. Thus, whereas under the classical interpretation sentences have one of the two semantic values **t** (The True) and **f** (The False), under the three-valued interpretation they may have any one of the three values **t**, **f**, and **n** (The Neither-True-Nor-False); and under the four-valued interpretation they may have any one of the four values **t**, **f**, **n**, and **b** (The Both-True-And-False).

It is useful to note the "told" interpretation of these values. One may think of the assignment of the value **t** (**f**) to a sentence as representing that one has been *told* that the sentence is true (false). The assignment of **n** then means that one has been told neither that the sentence is true nor that it is false. Similarly, the assignment **b** means that one is unfortunate enough to have been told that the sentence is true and that it is false. (For an extended motivation and discussion of the "told" interpretation see Belnap 1976, 1977.)

The "told" interpretation is not the only one possible or the only one appropriate for the applications of the semantics. Nonetheless, it does show that acceptance of the semantics as useful or as governing one's own communicative context does not necessarily commit one to any ontological claims; for example, it does not commit one to the existence of incompleteness or inconsistency in the world (whatever that may mean), or even to anyone's having inconsistent beliefs. More important for our purposes, the "told" interpretation motivates the following ordering of the values: The value **n** indicates a state of least information, a state in which one has been told nothing. The values **t** and **f** indicate states of greater information than **n**; so we have $n \leq t$ and $n \leq f$. Neither **t** nor **f** indicates a state of greater information than the other, so neither $t \leq f$ nor $f \leq t$. The value **b** indicates a state of greatest information, a state in which one has been told much too much. Thus, we have $n \leq b$, $t \leq b$, and $f \leq b$.[3]

Let **A3** and **A4** be, respectively, the structures $\langle \{t, f, n\}, \leq \rangle$ and $\langle \{t, f, n, b\}, \leq \rangle$. They can be pictured thus:

---

[3] We use the same sign '$\leq$' for the ordering of truth values in both the three-valued and the four-valued logic. The resulting ambiguity should not be misleading. The context will always make it sufficiently clear which relation is under discussion.

A3 t   f

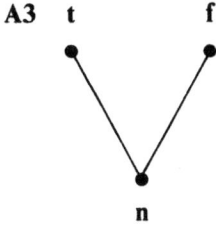

n

A4   b

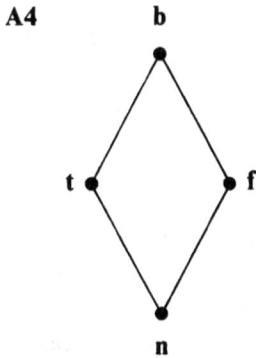

t   f

n

Observe that **A3** and **A4** are *partially ordered*; that is, in each structure the relation ≤ has the following properties:

Reflexivity For all objects u in the domain, u ≤ u.

Antisymmetry For all u and v in the domain, if u ≤ v and v ≤ u then u = v.

Transitivity For all u, v, and w in the domain, if u ≤ v and v ≤ w then u ≤ w.

We shall see that **A3** and **A4** are the structures underlying the three- and four-valued logics, respectively, considered below. Let us observe a few further useful properties of these structures. First, we recall some definitions from the theory of partial orders.

2A.1 Definition (Partial-order definitions) Let $\mathcal{X} = \langle X, \leq \rangle$ be a partial order, and let $Y \subseteq X$ and $x \in X$. Then:

  (i) x is an *upper bound* of Y iff, for all $y \in Y$, $y \leq x$.[4]

----

[4] Here and below, 'iff' abbreviates 'if and only if'.

(ii) x is a *lower bound* of Y iff, for all y ∈ Y, x ≤ y.

(iii) x is a *supremum* (alternatively, *least upper bound* or *l.u.b.*) of Y iff x is an upper bound of Y and for all upper bounds y of Y, x ≤ y. $\bigvee$Y is the supremum of Y provided that it exists.[5]

(iv) x is an *infimum* (alternatively, *greatest lower bound* or *g.l.b.*) of Y iff x is a lower bound of Y and for all lower bounds y of Y, y ≤ x. $\bigwedge$Y is the infimum of Y provided that it exists.

(v) $\mathcal{X}$ is a *lattice* iff every nonempty finite subset of X has a supremum and an infimum.

(vi) $\mathcal{X}$ is a *complete lattice* iff *every* subset of X has a supremum and an infimum (equivalently: every subset of X has a supremum (infimum)).

Examples   The set {**t, n**} has a supremum, **t**, and an infimum, **n**, in **A3**. But the set {**t, f**} has only an infimum, **n**. It does not have a supremum, or even any upper bounds, in **A3**. In **A4**, however, {**t, f**} has a supremum, namely **b**. In fact, every subset of {**t, f, n, b**} has a supremum and an infimum in **A4**. Thus, **A4** is a complete lattice. On the other hand, **A3** is not a lattice. **A3** does satisfy a weaker condition that is useful to isolate.

2A.2   Definition   (Consistency and ccpo)   Given $\mathcal{X}$, Y, and x as before, let us say, following Visser (1984, 1989), that

(i)   Y is *consistent* (in $\mathcal{X}$) iff each {u, v} ⊆ Y has an upper bound in $\mathcal{X}$

and

(ii) $\mathcal{X}$ is a *coherent complete partial order* (*ccpo*) iff every consistent subset of X has a supremum.

We saw that the set {**t, f**} does not have a supremum in **A3**, but it is also not consistent. It can be verified that every *consistent* subset of {**t, f, n**} does have a supremum in **A3**: **A3** is a ccpo. We shall see in section 2C that ccpo's have some nice mathematical properties—properties that are useful in investigating truth in three-valued languages.

We have motivated **A3** and **A4** through the "told" interpretation of the truth values. We want to emphasize, however, that the utility of these structures is independent of this interpretation. Whether we accept a

[5] If a supremum for Y exists, then it is unique; thus, if it exists, "$\bigvee$Y" is well defined. Similarly for infima in the next definition.

"told" interpretation or not, these structures remain useful in that they enable us to state important properties of the semantics in a concise way.

Central to a semantic explanation of the logic of a language is the elucidation of the notions of "possible situation" and "truth in a possible situation." The former notion is elucidated by isolating the semantic information about the atomic terms that is relevant to determining the truth and falsity of the sentences of the language, and the latter by showing *how* the truth and falsity of sentences depends upon this semantic information. For a first-order *extensional* language L the first of these tasks is straightforward. To determine the truth or falsity of the sentences of L in a possible situation w, the relevant semantic information is constituted by the denotations of the names, the graphs of the function symbols, and the significations of the predicates in w. This motivates the following definition:

2A.3 Definition (Standard models) A *standard two-valued [three-valued; four-valued] model* for a language L is an ordered pair $\langle D, I \rangle$ such that

(i) D is a nonempty set

and

(ii) I assigns to each name of L a member of D, to each n-place function symbol of L a member of $D^{(D^n)}$, and to each n-place predicate of L a member of $\{t, f\}^{D^n} [\{t, f, n\}^{D^n}; \{t, f, n, b\}^{D^n}]$.

If we think of possibility in linguistic terms as consistency with some antecedent assumptions, then standard models represent a notion of possibility that is constrained by the most minimal assumptions. We make no assumptions about how things are, or about the laws by which things are governed, or about the connections between the meanings of the various terms of the language. We assume only a few very general things about the language and the world. We assume such things as that all the names in the language have denotations and that the possible semantic values of the sentences are t, f, and n (the three-valued case). There are contexts in which these assumptions are not acceptable. In the present context, however, they are a small price to pay for the gain in precision and clarity that they bring to the notion of possible situation.

The *signification* (sometimes also called *interpretation*) of an n-place predicate F in a standard model $\mathcal{M}$ $(= \langle D, I \rangle)$ is the function $I(F)$; its *extension* is the set of n-tuples $\{\bar{d}: t \leq I(F)(\bar{d})\}$, and its *antiextension* is the set $\{\bar{d}: f \leq I(F)(\bar{d})\}$.[6] The *range of applicability* of F in $\mathcal{M}$ is the union of its extension and its antiextension in $\mathcal{M}$. Note that in all the models defined above extension and antiextension jointly carry the same information as signification; given one, we can recover the other. Hence, in these models one can represent the signification of a predicate with an ordered pair consisting of the predicate's extension and its antiextension. Sometimes, when it is convenient, we shall represent signification in this way. In the two-valued models the extension and the antiextension are disjoint sets and their union exhausts the domain. In these models even extension (alone, without antiextension) and signification carry the same information and can (and sometimes will) be identified. In the three-valued models the extension and the antiextension are disjoint but need not exhaust the domain. In the four-valued models they may fail to be both disjoint and exhaustive. In three- and four-valued models we cannot recover signification from extension alone; we need the antiextension as well.

The orderings **A3** and **A4** introduced above yield orderings on the possible interpretations of a predicate in a model $\langle D, I \rangle$. Let f and g be possible interpretations of an n-place predicate. That is, let

$f, g \in \{t, f, n, b\}^{D^n}$.

We define

$f \leq g$ iff $f(\bar{d}) \leq g(\bar{d})$ for all $\bar{d} \in D^n$.

Intuitively we can read $f \leq g$ as saying that the interpretation f carries less (though not necessarily strictly less) information than g. It can be verified that for the three-valued interpretations the resulting structure is a ccpo. And for the four-valued interpretations it is a complete lattice. (See Theorem 2C.4.) The structures induced on the possible interpretations of a one-place predicate are of special interest to us. Let

$D3 = \{t, f, n\}^D, D4 = \{t, f, n, b\}^D$

and

$\mathbf{D3} = \langle D3, \leq\uparrow D3 \rangle, \mathbf{D4} = \langle D4, \leq \rangle$.[7]

---

[6] We use $\mathcal{M}, \mathcal{M}', \mathcal{M}_1, \ldots$ to range over standard models and $\bar{d}$ to range over the n-tuples of D.
[7] $\leq\upharpoonright Z = \leq \cap (Z \times Z)$.

Finally, note that the ordering of the interpretations results in a parallel ordering of the models themselves. Given $\mathcal{M}$ $(= \langle D, I \rangle)$ and $\mathcal{M}'$ $(= \langle D', I' \rangle)$, define

$\mathcal{M} \le \mathcal{M}'$ iff (a) $D = D'$; (b) $I(X) = I'(X)$, for all names and function symbols X; (c) $I(F) \le I'(F)$ for all predicates F.

Intuitively: $\mathcal{M} \le \mathcal{M}'$ iff $\mathcal{M}$ and $\mathcal{M}'$ are alike except that $\mathcal{M}'$ may assign more informative interpretations to the predicates than $\mathcal{M}$.

We now turn to the task of defining the notion "truth in a model." Once we are given a model $\mathcal{M}$ $(= \langle D, I \rangle)$ for a language L, the only element we need to specify the semantic status of each sentence of L is the scheme that gives the semantic rules for the logical constants—rules that determine how the semantic status of a complex sentence depends on those of its parts. Even if we adopt (as we shall) the principle that compounds are to be evaluated by the classical rules whenever their components have classical values $\{t, f\}$, there is an unfortunate abundance of choice here; for example, the principle leaves it completely open what the value of a conjunction should be if one of the conjuncts is n. In this section we review two schemes for evaluating formulas in the three-valued semantics and one for the four-valued semantics. (A few more schemes will be introduced later.)

We wish to define for each scheme the following fundamental notion:

the semantic value of the expression X in the standard model $\mathcal{M}$ $(= \langle D, I \rangle)$ relative to the assignment s of values to the variables (abbreviated to $\mathrm{Val}_{\mathcal{M}, s}(X)$),

where an *assignment* of values to the variables is a function that assigns to each variable a member of D, and *expressions* encompass all and only the terms and formulas of the language. For the quantifier clause it is convenient to have available notation for the "shifted assignment" $s[d/x]$; that is, where s is an assignment of values, d is a member of D, and x is a variable, $s[d/x]$ is that assignment that agrees with s at all variables except perhaps x and gives x the value d. The general form of the definition of $\mathrm{Val}_{\mathcal{M}, s}(X)$ is the same for each scheme,[8] and is as follows.

---

[8] That is, the definition is the same except for the differences due to the different truth functions represented by $\sim$, &, and $\forall$ in the various schemes.

2A.4 Definition   (Semantic value: Val $_{\mathscr{M},s}(X)$)

  (i) If X is a name, then Val $_{\mathscr{M},s}(X) = \text{I}(X)$.

  (ii) If X is a variable, then Val $_{\mathscr{M},s}(X) = s(X)$.

  (iii) If X is the term $f(t_1,\ldots,t_n)$, then Val $_{\mathscr{M},s}(X) = \text{I}(f)(\text{Val}_{\mathscr{M},s}(t_1),\ldots,$ Val $_{\mathscr{M},s}(t_n))$.

  (iv) If X is the formula $\perp$, then Val $_{\mathscr{M},s}(X) = \mathbf{f}$.

  (v) If X is the formula $t_1 = t_2$ then Val $_{\mathscr{M},s}(X) = \mathbf{t}$ if Val $_{\mathscr{M},s}(t_1) =$ Val $_{\mathscr{M},s}(t_2)$; Val $_{\mathscr{M},s}(X) = \mathbf{f}$ otherwise.

  (vi) If X is the formula $F(t_1,\ldots,t_n)$, then Val $_{\mathscr{M},s}(X) = \text{I}(F)(\text{Val}_{\mathscr{M},s}(t_1),$ $\ldots,$ Val $_{\mathscr{M},s}(t_n))$.

  (vii) If X is the formula $\sim A$, then Val $_{\mathscr{M},s}(X) = \sim[\text{Val}_{\mathscr{M},s}(A)]$.

  (viii) If X is the formula $(A\&B)$, then Val $_{\mathscr{M},s}(X) = [\text{Val}_{\mathscr{M},s}(A) \ \&$ Val $_{\mathscr{M},s}(B)]$.

  (ix) If X is the formula $(\forall x)A$, then Val $_{\mathscr{M},s}(X) = \forall\{\text{Val}_{\mathscr{M},s[d/x]}(A): d \in D\}$.

To complete the definition we need only state the truth functions represented by $\sim$, $\&$, and $\forall$ in the various schemes. The classical scheme is familiar:

The Classical Scheme (τ)

Negation

$\sim: \{\mathbf{t},\mathbf{f}\} \to \{\mathbf{t},\mathbf{f}\}$

$\sim\mathbf{v} = \mathbf{t}$ iff $\mathbf{v} = \mathbf{f}$, for all $\mathbf{v} \in \{\mathbf{t},\mathbf{f}\}$.

Conjunction

$\&: \{\mathbf{t},\mathbf{f}\}^2 \to \{\mathbf{t},\mathbf{f}\}$

$\mathbf{v} \ \& \ \mathbf{v}' = \mathbf{t}$ iff $\mathbf{v} = \mathbf{v}' = \mathbf{t}$, for all $\mathbf{v}, \mathbf{v}' \in \{\mathbf{t},\mathbf{f}\}$.

Universal Quantifier

$\forall: \mathscr{P}\{\mathbf{t},\mathbf{f}\} - \{\varnothing\} \to \{\mathbf{t},\mathbf{f}\}$

$\forall Y = \mathbf{t}$ iff $Y = \{\mathbf{t}\}$, for each nonempty $Y \subseteq \{\mathbf{t},\mathbf{f}\}$.

The three-valued schemes we shall discuss are Kleene's *weak* and *strong* valuation schemes.[9] Both schemes are designed to have the following important properties. First, they are *truth-functional*: The value of a compound is a function of the values of its immediate components. Hence the semantic rules that these schemes associate with the logical constants are truth functions over $\{t, f, n\}$. Second, these schemes are *normal* in the sense that they accord with the principle mentioned above: The value of a compound is determined by the classical rules whenever the components have classical values. Finally, both schemes are *monotonic*: The truth functions associated with the logical constants have the property that as the arguments become more informative the values become more informative also. Formally: An n-ary truth function f is *monotonic* if and only if it preserves the relevant order (in the present instance, A3); that is, if $v_1 \leq v'_1$ and ... and $v_n \leq v'_n$, then

$$f(v_1, \ldots, v_n) \leq f(v'_1, \ldots, v'_n).$$

These three properties fix completely the semantics for $\sim$. Normality implies that $\sim t = f$ and $\sim f = t$; monotonicity now yields that $\sim n = n$. The semantics for &, it can be verified, is also settled except for the values of $(f \& n)$ and $(n \& f)$. Neither can be t, as that would violate monotonicity. So, assuming commutativity of &, the properties leave open only two tables: $(f \& n)$ $[= (n \& f)]$ can be either n or f. The first choice yields the Weak Kleene table and the second yields the Strong Kleene table.

We have the following rules for the logical constants. Note that $\forall$ is treated as a generalized conjunction.

The Weak Kleene Scheme (μ)

Negation   *Conjunction*

$\sim$	
t	f
f	t
n	n

&	t	f	n
t	t	f	n
f	f	f	n
n	n	n	n

---

[9] See Kleene 1938 and section 64 of Kleene 1952. Kleene's weak rules for $\sim$ and & are the same as those of D. A. Bochvar for what he calls "formal internal negation" and "formal internal logical sum" (see Bochvar 1937/1981 and Herzberger 1970b). Kleene's strong rules for $\sim$ and & were anticipated by Jan Łukasiewicz. In Bochvar's and Łukasiewicz's logic, however, there are connectives that violate the important property of monotonicity described below.

Universal Quantifier

$\forall: \mathscr{P}\{\mathbf{t}, \mathbf{f}, \mathbf{n}\} - \{\varnothing\} \to \{\mathbf{t}, \mathbf{f}, \mathbf{n}\}.$

For all nonempty $Y \subseteq \{\mathbf{t}, \mathbf{f}, \mathbf{n}\}$:

$\forall Y = \mathbf{t}$ iff $Y = \{\mathbf{t}\}$,

$\forall Y = \mathbf{n}$ iff $\mathbf{n} \in Y$.

The Strong Kleene Scheme (κ)

Negation   *Conjunction*

~	
t	f
f	t
n	n

&	t	f	n
t	t	f	n
f	f	f	f
n	n	f	n

Universal Quantifier

$\forall: \mathscr{P}\{\mathbf{t}, \mathbf{f}, \mathbf{n}\} - \{\varnothing\} \to \{\mathbf{t}, \mathbf{f}, \mathbf{n}\}.$

For all nonempty $Y \subseteq \{\mathbf{t}, \mathbf{f}, \mathbf{n}\}$:

$\forall Y = \mathbf{t}$ iff $Y = \{\mathbf{t}\}$,

$\forall Y = \mathbf{f}$ iff $\mathbf{f} \in Y$.

Note that the Weak Kleene scheme has the property that it evaluates a compound as **n** if any of the components has the value **n**. This treatment is natural if, following Bochvar (1937/1981), we read **n** as indicating "meaninglessness": a compound with a meaningless part is itself meaningless. The Strong Kleene scheme, on the other hand, is natural if we give **n** a "told" reading. This interpretation makes it natural to say that (**f** & **n**) is **f**, for if one has been told that the first conjunct is false and has not been told anything about the second conjunct then one has been told (by implication) that the conjunction is false. This interpretation also motivates the requirement that the connectives be monotonic.

   The Four-valued scheme we shall discuss also has all three of the properties mentioned earlier: truth-functionality, normality, and monotonicity (the relevant ordering now is **A4**). As before, these properties fix completely the semantics for $\sim$, but we have some choice in connection with

&. In the scheme we shall work with the choice is made along the Strong Kleene lines.[10]

The Four-Valued Scheme (v)

Negation

$\sim$	
t	f
f	t
n	n
b	b

Conjunction

&	t	f	n	b
t	t	f	n	b
f	f	f	f	f
n	n	f	n	f
b	b	f	f	b

Universal Quantifier

$\forall: \mathscr{P}\{\mathbf{t}, \mathbf{f}, \mathbf{n}, \mathbf{b}\} - \{\varnothing\} \to \{\mathbf{t}, \mathbf{f}, \mathbf{n}, \mathbf{b}\}.$

For all nonempty $Y \subseteq \{\mathbf{t}, \mathbf{f}, \mathbf{n}, \mathbf{b}\}$:

$\forall Y = \mathbf{t}$ iff $Y = \{\mathbf{t}\}$,

$\forall Y = \mathbf{f}$ iff $\mathbf{f} \in Y$ or $\{\mathbf{n}, \mathbf{b}\} \subseteq Y$,

$\forall Y = \mathbf{n}$ iff $Y = \{\mathbf{n}\}$ or $Y = \{\mathbf{t}, \mathbf{n}\}$.

The functions & and $\forall$ become a little clearer once it is observed that they represent the greatest-lower-bound operation in the following lattice:

L4

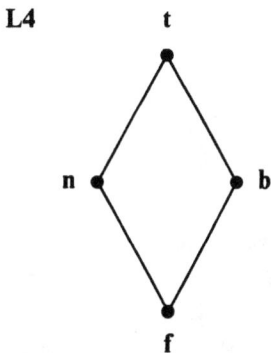

---

[10] This scheme was first worked out by T. J. Smiley, who used it to give a semantics for the "tautological entailments" of Anderson and Belnap (1975). For an extended motivation of the scheme, see Dunn 1976, Belnap 1976, and Belnap 1977.

Table 2.1
The four schemes.

Code	Scheme	Values	A key feature
τ	Classical	$\{f, t\}$	
μ	Weak Kleene	$\{f, n, t\}$	$f \& n = n \& f = n$
κ	Strong Kleene	$\{f, n, t\}$	$f \& n = n \& f = f$
υ	Four-valued	$\{f, n, b, t\}$	$n \& b = b \& n = f$

We have

$\mathbf{v} \& \mathbf{v}' =$ the infimum of $\{\mathbf{v}, \mathbf{v}'\}$ in **L4**

and

$\forall Y =$ the infimum of Y in **L4**, for all $Y \neq \varnothing$.

Under the usual definitions, $\vee$ and $\exists$ represent the operation of supremum in **L4**. Similarly, in the Strong Kleene scheme & and $\forall$ represent the operation of infimum, and $\vee$ and $\exists$ represent the operation of supremum, in the following lattice **L3**:

Table 2.1 summarizes the four principal schemes presented above.

By an *interpreted language* we understand a language L together with an interpretation for *all* its constants. We identify an interpreted language with an ordered triple $\langle L, \mathcal{M}, \rho \rangle$ where L codes the syntactic information about the language, $\mathcal{M}$ is a model that gives the interpretation of the nonlogical constants, and ρ is a scheme that interprets the logical constants.[11] (Note that ρ is required to have at least the values that $\mathcal{M}$ uses. If (for example) $\mathcal{M}$ interprets some predicates in the three-valued way, then ρ cannot be classical, for that would be meaningless. Observe that $\langle L, \mathcal{M}, \rho \rangle$ is meaningful if ρ allows *more* values than $\mathcal{M}$ happens to use.) We use $\mathcal{L}$, $\mathcal{L}'$, $\mathcal{L}_1$, ... to range over interpreted languages, and we take such notions as formula of $\mathcal{L}$ and domain of $\mathcal{L}$ as understood in the natural way. We do not give explicit definitions for them.

For the remainder of this section let $\mathcal{L}$ ($= \langle L, \mathcal{M}, \rho \rangle$; $\mathcal{M} = \langle D, I \rangle$) and $\mathcal{L}'$ ($= \langle L', \mathcal{M}', \rho' \rangle$; $\mathcal{M}' = \langle D', I' \rangle$) be interpreted languages. Let s be an assignment of values to the variables, A a formula, and X an expression of $\mathcal{L}$.

2A.5 Definition ($\mathcal{L}$-concepts, i.e., concepts for interpreted languages)

(i) $\mathcal{L} \leq \mathcal{L}'$ if and only if (a) $L = L'$, (b) $\rho = \rho'$, and (c) $\mathcal{M} \leq \mathcal{M}'$.

(ii) $\mathcal{L}$ is *classical, Weak Kleene, Strong Kleene*, and *four-valued* according as ρ is classical, Weak Kleene, Strong Kleene, and four-valued; that is, according as $\rho = \tau$, μ, κ, υ. If $\mathcal{L}$ is Weak or Strong Kleene then it is said to be a *three-valued* language.

(iii) *The set of truth values of* $\mathcal{L}$ is $\{\mathbf{t}, \mathbf{f}\}$ $[\{\mathbf{t}, \mathbf{f}, \mathbf{n}\}; \{\mathbf{t}, \mathbf{f}, \mathbf{n}, \mathbf{b}\}]$ if $\mathcal{L}$ is classical [three-valued; four-valued].

(iv) A function g is an *n-ary propositional function* for $\mathcal{L}$ iff the domain of g is D^n and the range of g is the set of truth values of $\mathcal{L}$.

(v) $\mathrm{Val}_{\mathcal{L}, s}(X) =$ the semantic value of X in the model $\mathcal{M}$ relative to the assignment s and scheme ρ.

Our first theorem records some relationships between the various schemes, emphasizing for instance some cases in which they give all formulas the same truth values even when the schemes themselves use different numbers of truth values.

---

[11] We are following common practice in calling these ordered triples "interpreted languages." However, the specification of these triples does not fix the *meanings* of the nonlogical constants, only their *significations*. One cannot determine the meaning of an expression from its signification, since expressions with identical signification may differ in meaning. Nor can one determine signification from meaning alone; one needs to know the relevant facts also. Hence, the constructs we are calling "interpreted languages" are not *interpreted* languages in the ordinary sense of the term. Nonetheless, these constructs are useful, since they carry the kind of information that is needed to fix the truth or the falsity of every sentence of the language.

2A.6   Theorem   (Schemes compared)   Let $L = L'$ and $\mathcal{M} = \mathcal{M}'$. Then

(i) $\text{Val}_{\mathcal{L},s}(X) = \text{Val}_{\mathcal{L}',s}(X)$, if $\rho = \tau$, regardless of what ρ' may be.

(ii) $\text{Val}_{\mathcal{L},s}(X) = \text{Val}_{\mathcal{L}',s}(X)$, if $\rho = \kappa$ and $\rho' = \upsilon$.

(iii) $\text{Val}_{\mathcal{L},s}(A) \leq \text{Val}_{\mathcal{L}',s}(A)$, if $\rho = \mu$ and $\rho' = \kappa$.

Proof   The theorem is established by a straightforward induction on the complexity of X (A). Note that in (i) $\rho = \tau$ yields that $\mathcal{M}'$ must be classical (even if ρ' is not), and similarly in (ii) $\rho = \kappa$ yields that $\mathcal{M}'$ is three-valued even though ρ' is four-valued.   ∎

A local, stronger version of this theorem holds also: We can weaken the condition $\mathcal{M} = \mathcal{M}'$ by requiring only that the languages[12] have the same domain and agree on the interpretations of the nonlogical constants occurring in X (A). Two further facts, the first a monotony property, the second a matter of local determination:

2A.7   Theorem   (A monotony)   If $\mathcal{L} \leq \mathcal{L}'$ then $\text{Val}_{\mathcal{L},s}(A) \leq \text{Val}_{\mathcal{L}',s}(A)$.

2A.8   Theorem   (A local determination property)   Let s and s' be assignments for $\mathcal{L}$ that agree on all the free variables in X. Then $\text{Val}_{\mathcal{L},s}(X) = \text{Val}_{\mathcal{L},s'}(X)$.

Theorem 2A.7 is a direct consequence of the monotonicity of the schemes. It will be of fundamental importance in the later applications of the languages. Theorem 2A.8 entitles us to the following definitions:

2A.9   Definition   (Concepts depending on $\text{Val}_{\mathcal{L},s}(X)$)

(i) Let X be an expression with exactly n free variables $x_{i_1}, \ldots, x_{i_n}$, and let $\bar{d}$ be an n-tuple of members of D. Then $\text{Val}_{\mathcal{L}}(X, \bar{d}) = \text{Val}_{\mathcal{L},s}(X)$, where s is an assignment that assigns to a variable x_{i_j} ($1 \leq j \leq n$) the jth object in $\bar{d}$.[13,14]

(ii) If X is a closed expression (for example, a sentence), then $\text{Val}_{\mathcal{L}}(X) = y$ iff there is an assignment s such that $\text{Val}_{\mathcal{L},s}(X) = y$.

(iii) A formula A *defines* g *in* $\mathcal{L}$ iff for some $n > 0$ (a) g is an n-ary propositional function for $\mathcal{L}$, (b) A has exactly n free variables, and (c) for all

---

[12] Here, and below, we sometimes drop the adjective 'interpreted' if the context allows it.
[13] It is assumed that the variables of $\mathcal{L}$ are ordered and that $x_{i_1}, \ldots, x_{i_n}$ respect that order.
[14] We shall identify a one-tuple $\langle d \rangle$ with d itself.

n-tuples $\bar{d}$ of D

$\text{Val}_{\mathscr{L}}(A, \bar{d}) = g(\bar{d})$.

If g is the propositional function defined by A in $\mathscr{L}$,[15] we say that g is the *signification*, that $\{\bar{d}: \mathbf{t} \leq g(\bar{d})\}$ is the *extension*, and that $\{\bar{d}: \mathbf{f} \leq g(\bar{d})\}$ is the *antiextension* of A in $\mathscr{L}$. As before, the union of the extension and the antiextension of A in $\mathscr{L}$ is said to constitute the *range of applicability* of A. In classical languages, a formula is also said to *define* its extension.

Here is a small fact concerning the semantics of substitution that relates some of the notions just defined. (A more general theorem holds also.)

2A.10 Theorem (Semantics of substitution) Let t be a closed term of $\mathscr{L}$, let $A(x)$ be a formula with exactly one free variable x, and let $A(t)$ be the result of replacing all the free occurrences of x in A by t. If $d = \text{Val}_{\mathscr{L}}(t)$ then

$\text{Val}_{\mathscr{L}}(A(x), d) = \text{Val}_{\mathscr{L}}(A(t))$;

in other words,

$\text{Val}_{\mathscr{L}}(A(t)) = \text{Val}_{\mathscr{L}}(A(x), \text{Val}_{\mathscr{L}}(t))$.

2A.11 Definition (True, false (of $\bar{d}$)) Let A be a formula with exactly n free variables, and let $\bar{d}$ be an n-tuple of members of D. We say the following:

 (i) *A is true of $\bar{d}$ in $\mathscr{L}$* iff $\mathbf{t} \leq \text{Val}_{\mathscr{L}}(A, \bar{d})$.

 (ii) *A is false of $\bar{d}$ in $\mathscr{L}$* iff $\mathbf{f} \leq \text{Val}_{\mathscr{L}}(A, \bar{d})$.

 (iii) *A is true (false) in $\mathscr{L}$* iff A is a sentence of $\mathscr{L}$ and $\mathbf{t}(\mathbf{f}) \leq \text{Val}_{\mathscr{L}}(A)$.[16]

The notions of truth and falsity defined above have the expected properties, and interact nicely with the logical connectives of the schemes τ, κ, and υ:

2A.12 Theorem (Properties of truth and falsity in τ, μ, and κ) Let $\mathscr{L} = \langle L, \mathscr{M}, \rho \rangle$, where $\mathscr{M} = \langle D, I \rangle$. Let A be a sentence of $\mathscr{L}$, and let B be a

---

[15] Clearly, A defines a unique propositional function.

[16] If the context fixes L and ρ, we shall also speak of "truth (falsity) in a model $\mathscr{M}$."

  Note that "$\text{Val}_{\mathscr{L}}(A) = \mathbf{t}$" and "$A$ is true in $\mathscr{L}$" are not equivalent in every scheme, υ being a counterexample. The former implies, and the latter does not, that A is not false in $\mathscr{L}$. Similarly for "$\text{Val}_{\mathscr{L}}(A) = \mathbf{f}$" and "$A$ is false in $\mathscr{L}$."

formula with exactly n free variables. Let $\bar{d}$ be an n-tuple of members of D. Then

(i) If $\rho = \tau$ then A (B) is either true or false (of $\bar{d}$) in $\mathscr{L}$ but not both.

(ii) If $\rho = \kappa$ or $\rho = \mu$ then A (B) is not both true and false (of $\bar{d}$) in $\mathscr{L}$.

2A.13 Theorem (Properties of connectives in τ, κ, and υ) Let $\mathscr{L}$ and $\mathscr{M}$ be as in the previous theorem and let ρ be one of τ, κ, υ. Then for all sentences A and B of $\mathscr{L}$

(i) $(A \ \& \ B)$ is true in $\mathscr{L}$ iff A and B are true in $\mathscr{L}$.

(ii) $(A \ \& \ B)$ is false in $\mathscr{L}$ iff either A or B is false in $\mathscr{L}$.

(iii) $\sim A$ is true in $\mathscr{L}$ iff A is false in $\mathscr{L}$.

(iv) $\sim A$ is false in $\mathscr{L}$ iff A is true in $\mathscr{L}$.

With the μ scheme (ii) fails, for if A is false but B is neither true nor false then the conjunction $(A \ \& \ B)$ is neither true nor false.

The notions "model" and "truth in a model" defined above are formal analogues of the intuitive notions "possible situation" and "truth in a possible situation." They can be used to give precise definitions of logical concepts. The following definition mimics the usual intuitive explanation of implication: A set of sentences Γ (we reserve Γ for such sets) implies A iff A is true in all possible situations in which all the members of Γ are true.

2A.14 Definition (Classical implication) Let A and the members of Γ be sentences of L. Then, Γ *classically implies* A ($\Gamma \models^{\tau} A$) iff, for all classical models $\mathscr{M}$ of L, A is true in $\langle L, \mathscr{M}, \tau \rangle$ ($= \mathscr{L}$) if all members of Γ are true in $\mathscr{L}$.

Classical implication is defined as truth preserving. In virtue of the two-valued character of classical semantics, this implication is also "non-falsity" preserving: If the premisses are nonfalse then so is the conclusion, or equivalently, if the conclusion is false then so also is one of the premisses. In the three- and four-valued contexts, however, this equivalence breaks down and consequently we can define and study several different notions of implication. We confine ourselves here to one that requires that implications preserve both truth and nonfalsity.

2A.15 Definition (Implication in four schemes) Let A and the members of Γ be sentences of L, and let ρ be any scheme. Then Γ *implies A in ρ* $(\Gamma \models^\rho A)$ iff for all interpreted languages $\mathscr{L} = \langle L, \mathscr{M}, \rho \rangle$

(i) A is true in $\mathscr{L}$ if all members of Γ are true in $\mathscr{L}$

and

(ii) some member of Γ is false in $\mathscr{L}$ if A is false in $\mathscr{L}$.

Equivalently,

the infimum of $\{\mathrm{Val}_{\mathscr{L}}(B): B \in \Gamma\}$ in **L4** $\leq \mathrm{Val}_{\mathscr{L}}(A)$.

In virtue of the first part of Theorem 2A.6, all implications that hold in μ, κ, and υ hold also in τ. And in virtue of the second part of this theorem, implications that hold in υ hold also in κ. The examples below show that no other schemes are related in this way.

2A.16 Example (Nonimplication examples) Let A, B, and C be sentences of L. Consider the following implication statements

(i) $A \ \& \ \sim A \models^\rho B$,

(ii) $A \ \& \ \sim A \models^\rho B \vee \sim B$,

(iii) $A \ \& \ B \models^\rho A$,

(iv) $A \ \& \ \sim A \models^\rho B \ \& \ (A \ \& \ \sim A)$.

All these implications hold if $\rho = \tau$. Implication (i) fails for all other schemes. Implication (ii) holds in μ and κ but not in υ. Implication (iii) holds in all schemes except μ. Implication (iv) holds in μ but fails for κ and υ.

Syntactic characterizations of the notions $\models^\rho$ can be found in the literature; see Wang 1961, Anderson and Belnap 1975, Scott 1975, and Kremer 1986.

2B Definability and Indefinability of Truth

Every theory of truth must take account of two important types of mathematical theorems. First, there are the Indefinability Theorems that establish of certain types of languages that they cannot contain a definition of their own truth. The most famous of these is Tarski's theorem on the indefinability of arithmetical truth within classical arithmetic. Second, there are the Definability Theorems that establish of certain other languages that they *can* contain a definition of their own truth. The most famous of these are the theorems of Kripke, Martin, and Woodruff on the definability of truth within certain three- and four-valued languages. Both the Definability and the Indefinability theorems concern interpreted languages of the sort discussed in section 2A. The notions of truth and falsity for such languages are perfectly clear (see Definition 2A.11). Also, for any formula of such a language $\mathscr{L}$, it is perfectly clear what its extension and its antiextension are (Definition 2A.9). Hence, for any formula of $\mathscr{L}$, the following question has a determinate answer: Does the extension of the formula consist of all and only the truths of $\mathscr{L}$, and the antiextension of all and only the falsehoods of $\mathscr{L}$? The Definability and Indefinability theorems arise from attempts to answer various instances of this question. Let us isolate an important notion that is implicit in the question.

Let $\mathscr{L}$ $(= \langle L, \mathscr{M}, \rho \rangle;$ $\mathscr{M} = \langle D, I \rangle)$ and $\mathscr{L}'$ $(= \langle L', \mathscr{M}', \rho' \rangle;$ $\mathscr{M}' = \langle D', I' \rangle)$ be interpreted languages. Let us say that a *coding* of the sentences (or the formulas) of $\mathscr{L}$ into $\mathscr{L}'$ is a 1-1 function whose domain is the set of sentences (formulas) of $\mathscr{L}$ and whose range is a subset of the domain D' of $\mathscr{L}'$. (If D' contains the sentences of $\mathscr{L}$ then the coding may be the identity function.)

2B.1 Definition (T-predicate) Let c be a coding of the sentences of $\mathscr{L}$ into $\mathscr{L}'$, and let A be a formula of $\mathscr{L}'$ with exactly one free variable.

(i) A is a *T-predicate for $\mathscr{L}$* (*relative to the coding* c) iff the extension of A consists of (the codes of) the true sentences of $\mathscr{L}$ and its antiextension consists of (the codes of) the false sentences of $\mathscr{L}$ and of things that are not (codes of) sentences of $\mathscr{L}$.[17] If G is a one-place predicate of $\mathscr{L}'$, we say G is a *T-predicate for $\mathscr{L}$* iff Gx is a T-predicate for $\mathscr{L}$.[18]

---

[17] The requirement that a T-predicate for $\mathscr{L}$ be false of objects that are not (codes of) sentences of $\mathscr{L}$ is convenient and natural, but inessential.

[18] By "predicate" we generally mean "predicate letter" or (for English) "predicate phrase." Our official definition of a T-predicate, however, makes a T-predicate a formula with a free variable, and so we add this last clause in order to be able to move easily between T-predicates in the sense of predicate letters and T-predicates in the sense of formulas with a free variable. (What the two conceptions of predicates have in common is this: If either is supplied with a term, the natural result is a sentence—obtained by affixing the term to the predicate letter or substituting the term for the variable in the open formula.)

(ii) *Truth for $\mathscr{L}$ is definable in $\mathscr{L}'$ (relative to the coding* c) iff $\mathscr{L}'$ has a T-predicate for $\mathscr{L}$ (relative to the coding c).[19]

The following characterization of a T-predicate is an immediate consequence of the definitions. (See, in particular, Definition 2A.9.) We shall use it without always citing it explicitly.

2B.2 Lemma (T-predicate characterized) Let $\mathscr{L}'$ be a language whose domain D' contains all the sentences of $\mathscr{L}$, and let A be a formula of $\mathscr{L}'$ with exactly one free variable. Assuming that A is not true but false of all the elements of D' that are not sentences of $\mathscr{L}$, the following are equivalent:

(i) A is a T-predicate for $\mathscr{L}$.

(ii) For all sentences B of $\mathscr{L}$ the following hold:
  1. A is true in $\mathscr{L}'$ of B iff B is true in $\mathscr{L}$,
  2. A is false in $\mathscr{L}'$ of B iff B is false in $\mathscr{L}$.

(iii) For all sentences B of $\mathscr{L}$,

$$\mathrm{Val}_{\mathscr{L}'}(A, B) = \mathrm{Val}_{\mathscr{L}}(B).$$

Let us now consider some simple indefinability theorems.

2B.3 Theorem (Sufficient condition for $A(x)$ failing to be a classical T-predicate) Suppose $\mathscr{L}$ is a classical language whose domain D contains all its sentences. If $A(x)$ is a formula with exactly one free variable and t is a closed term of $\mathscr{L}$ such that

$$\mathrm{Val}_{\mathscr{L}}(t) = \sim A(t)$$

(i.e., the term t in $\mathscr{L}$ denotes the sentence $\sim A(t)$ of $\mathscr{L}$), then $A(x)$ is not a T-predicate for $\mathscr{L}$. As a special case, if $\mathscr{L}$ has a one-place predicate G and a name b such that $I(b) = \sim Gb$, then G is not a T-predicate for $\mathscr{L}$.

Proof Suppose, for reductio, that $A(x)$ is a T-predicate for $\mathscr{L}$ itself, so that we have for all B

$$\mathrm{Val}_{\mathscr{L}}(A(x), B) = \mathrm{Val}_{\mathscr{L}}(B).$$

[lemma 2B.2(iii) on T-predicates]

---

[19] Except where it is necessary to emphasize the relativity to a coding c, we shall omit the parenthetical expression. Further, unless stated otherwise, c will be assumed to be the identity function.

Then calculate as follows.

$$\text{Val}_{\mathscr{L}}(A(x), \sim A(t)) = \text{Val}_{\mathscr{L}}(\sim A(t))$$

[putting $\sim A(t)$ for B]

$$\text{Val}_{\mathscr{L}}(A(x), \sim A(t)) = \sim \text{Val}_{\mathscr{L}}(A(t))$$

[definitions 2A.9 and 2A.4 (vii)]

$$\text{Val}_{\mathscr{L}}(A(x), \text{Val}_{\mathscr{L}}(t)) = \sim \text{Val}_{\mathscr{L}}(A(t))$$

[by hypothesis as to what t denotes in $\mathscr{L}$]

$$\text{Val}_{\mathscr{L}}(A(t)) = \sim \text{Val}_{\mathscr{L}}(A(t))$$

[theorem 2A.10 on the semantics of substitution]

But in the classical scheme no truth value is identical to its own negation, so that the supposition that $A(x)$ is a T-predicate for $\mathscr{L}$ itself has been reduced to absurdity when $\text{Val}_{\mathscr{L}}(t) = \sim A(t)$. The proof for the special case is exactly the same.

Because the idea of this proof has been so crucial to many discussions of the indefinability of truth, including ours to come, we put the same argument again in the language of "true" and "true of" familiar from discussions of the Liar. Suppose, for *reductio*, that $A(x)$ is a T-predicate for $\mathscr{L}$, so that it is true of just the true sentences of $\mathscr{L}$, and suppose that t denotes in $\mathscr{L}$ the sentence $\sim A(t)$. Now suppose $\sim A(t)$ is true (false). Then $A(x)$, because a T-predicate, is true (false) of it and hence true (false) of what t denotes. But this makes $A(t)$ itself true (false) by the standard semantics of substitution. Hence $\sim A(t)$ and $A(t)$ are either both true or both false, which is classically impossible. ■

In virtue of the above theorem, the existence of a self-referential sentence $\sim Gb$, a sentence that says of itself that it is not G, implies that G cannot be a T-predicate for the language $\mathscr{L}$. By ensuring the existence of a similar self-referential sentence for each formula of the language, we obtain classical languages in which truth is not definable.

2B.4   Theorem   (Indefinability Theorem I)   Let $\mathscr{L}$ be a classical language whose domain contains all its sentences. Let $A_0, A_1, \ldots, A_n, \ldots$ be an enumeration of all the formulas of $\mathscr{L}$ with exactly one free variable. Let $\mathscr{L}$ have denumerably many constants c_i $(0 \leq i)$ such that $I(c_i) = \sim A_i(c_i)$. Then, truth for $\mathscr{L}$ is not definable in $\mathscr{L}$.

Proof Since $\text{Val}_{\mathscr{L}}(c_i) = I(c_i)$ (Definitions 2A.9 and 2A.4), and since the nondefinability of truth means the nonexistence of a T-predicate, the theorem is an immediate corollary of Theorem 2B.3. ∎

Self-reference of the sort needed for the theorem can be achieved without using names. One device, that of the "substitution" operator, is familiar from Gödel.

2B.5 Theorem (Indefinability Theorem II) If a classical language $\mathscr{L}$ has (i) standard names for all its formulas and (ii) a two-place function symbol *sub* such that

$$I(sub)(d_1, d_2) = \begin{cases} d_3, \text{ if } d_1 \text{ and } d_2 \text{ are formulas of } \mathscr{L} \text{ and } d_3 \text{ is the result} \\ \text{of substituting the standard name of } d_2 \text{ for the free} \\ \text{occurrences of } x \text{ in } d_1 \\[6pt] \text{some arbitrarily chosen object if } d_1 \text{ or } d_2 \text{ is not a} \\ \text{formula of } \mathscr{L}, \end{cases}$$

then truth for $\mathscr{L}$ is not definable in $\mathscr{L}$.

Proof Suppose, for *reductio*, that truth for $\mathscr{L}$ is definable in $\mathscr{L}$. So $\mathscr{L}$ contains a T-predicate—say, $A(y)$—for itself. We may suppose without loss of generality that the variable x is free for y in $A(y)$. (If it is not, we can construct, by changing the bound variables in $A(y)$, a formula $A'(y)$ which remains a T-predicate for $\mathscr{L}$ but in which x is free for y. The ensuing argument can then be given for $A'(y)$.) Consider the formula

$\sim A(sub(x, x))$.

It has a standard name in $\mathscr{L}$, say $\ulcorner \sim A(sub(x, x)) \urcorner$. So (1) is a term of $\mathscr{L}$.

(1) $sub(\ulcorner \sim A(sub(x, x)) \urcorner, \ulcorner \sim A(sub(x, x)) \urcorner)$.

By the condition on the interpretation of *sub* we know that the denotation of (1) in $\mathscr{L}$ is

(2) $\sim A(sub(\ulcorner \sim A(sub(x, x)) \urcorner, \ulcorner \sim A(sub(x, x)) \urcorner))$.

That is,

(3) $\text{Val}_{\mathscr{L}}((1)) = \sim A((1))$.

Hence Theorem 2B.3 applies, yielding that $A(y)$ is not a T-predicate of $\mathscr{L}$. This contradicts our initial hypothesis. ∎

The crucial element in the above argument is the construction of the sentence (2) that says of itself that it is not A. The construction relies on the function symbol *sub* whose special interpretation ensures that the term (1) denotes the sentence (2), thus making (2) self-referential. There are other ways of achieving this effect. One that we would like to mention occurs in Raymond Smullyan's ingenious Chameleonic Languages. The distinctive feature of these languages is that they have a term '*this*' which has the intuitive meaning that its occurrences in a formula denote the formula itself. So, for example, the occurrence of '*this*' in

(4) $F(this)$

denotes (4). As a result, (4) says of itself that it is F. A curious feature about '*this*' is that, although it is context sensitive (in the sense that its denotation depends upon the context of its occurrence), the sentences in which it occurs are context independent (in the sense that all assertions of a sentence have the same truth value in all contexts). A second curiosity worth noting is that in Smullyan's Chameleonic Languages a sentence and its negation may both be true, and yet no contradiction is ever true. If, for example, (4) falls in the extension of F but its negation does not then (4) and its negation will both be true (the two are about different objects). But the conjunction of (4) and its negation is about one object (namely, itself) and says of that one object that it is both F and not F. Hence it cannot be true. For a similar reason, the set of true sentences of a Chameleonic Language is not closed under *modus ponens*.[20] Following Smullyan, call a formula *normal* if it contains no occurrences of '*this*'. It is easy to see that normal formulas cannot be T-predicates. (The proof of Theorem 2B.4 applies.) Smullyan shows further that non-normal formulas fail to define truth also.

The indefinability theorems considered so far are applicable only to classical languages that meet very specific requirements. Our next theorem is more general and more useful.

2B.6   Theorem   (Indefinability Theorem III)   Let $\mathscr{L}$ be a classical language, and let c be a coding of formulas of $\mathscr{L}$ into (the domain of) $\mathscr{L}$ itself.

---

[20] See Smullyan 1984 for further curiosities. Languages containing devices similar to '*this*' have also been constructed by van Fraassen (1970b) and by Barwise and Etchemendy (1987).

Further, let $\mathscr{L}$ contain the standard name $\ulcorner A \urcorner$ for the code of each formula A, and let $R \subseteq D^3$ be the relation such that

$\langle d_1, d_2, d_3 \rangle \in R$ iff d_1, d_2, and d_3 are codes of some formulas A', B', and C' (respectively) such that C' is the result of substituting the standard name of the code of B' (i.e., of d_2) for the free occurrences of the variable y in A'.

If R is definable in $\mathscr{L}$, then (i) for each formula $A(x_{i_1}, \ldots, x_{i_m})$ of $\mathscr{L}$ there is a formula $B(x_{i_2}, \ldots, x_{i_m})$ such that the universal closure of

$$B(x_{i_2}, \ldots, x_{i_m}) \leftrightarrow A(\ulcorner B \urcorner, x_{i_2}, \ldots, x_{i_m})$$

is true in $\mathscr{L}$ and (ii) truth for $\mathscr{L}$ is not definable in $\mathscr{L}$.

Sketch of Proof

(i) Let $C(u, v, w)$ define R in $\mathscr{L}$ and let $A(x_{i_1}, \ldots, x_{i_m})$ be an arbitrary formula. Let a be the standard name of the code of

$$(\exists w)(C(y, y, w) \ \& \ A(w, x_{i_2}, \ldots, x_{i_m})).$$

Take B to be the formula

$$(\exists w)(C(a, a, w) \ \& \ A(w, x_{i_2}, \ldots, x_{i_m})).$$

Then, the universal closure of

$$B(x_{i_2}, \ldots, x_{i_m}) \leftrightarrow A(\ulcorner B \urcorner, x_{i_2}, \ldots, x_{i_m})$$

is true in $\mathscr{L}$.

(ii) If $A(u)$ is a formula with exactly one free variable, then by (i) there is sentence B such that $B \leftrightarrow \sim A(\ulcorner B \urcorner)$ is true in $\mathscr{L}$. B "says" of itself that it is not A. It follows by an argument similar to those given above that A is not a T-predicate for $\mathscr{L}$. ∎

This theorem is more general than the earlier ones. It applies even when the domain of $\mathscr{L}$ does not contain formulas of $\mathscr{L}$, but only codes of formulas. These codes can be anything: numbers, space-time points, formulas, and even physical objects. Further, the theorem does not require $\mathscr{L}$ to have *specific* kinds of names and function symbols. (It may apply even if $\mathscr{L}$ has no function symbols at all.) Illustration: Consider the interpreted language of arithmetic $\mathbb{N} = \langle L_{\mathbb{N}}, \mathscr{M}_{\mathbb{N}}, \tau \rangle$, where $L_{\mathbb{N}}$ represents the usual syntax, and $\mathscr{M}_{\mathbb{N}}$ the standard model, of arithmetic. Let the coding be via some Gödel numbering and let the standard names of the codes be the numerals $0, 0', 0'', \ldots$. Now the relation R of substitution is definable in ℕ. (In fact, it has a "simple" definition—the relation is primitive recursive.) Our third indefinability theorem applies, yielding the following theorem.

2B.7 Theorem (Tarski's Indefinability Theorem; Indefinability Theorem IV) Truth for ℕ (relative to the Gödel coding) is not definable in ℕ.

The proof of each of the indefinability theorems considered above consists of two parts. First, it is shown that the language under consideration has the resources to form for each formula A (containing one free variable) a sentence B that "says" of itself (or its own code) that it is not A. Second, it is shown, using an argument parallel to that found in the Liar paradox, that A cannot be a T-predicate for the language. The mere existence of a sentence that says "I am not A" is sufficient to prove that A is not a truth predicate. This raises a small puzzle: Why does the Liar argument result in an indefinability theorem in one context but in a paradox in another? Why don't we take the argument to show that 'true' is not a truth predicate of English?

The answer is that there is a crucial difference between the two cases: In one case the semantics of the *entire* language is completely clear and fixed, but this is not so in the other. Once we stipulate that $\mathscr{L}$ is a classical language, the mere existence of the self-referential sentence for A ensures that A is not a T-predicate for $\mathscr{L}$, for there is now bound to be a difference in the extension of A and the extension of "true in $\mathscr{L}$." We have a theorem, not a paradox. The existence of the self-referential sentence "This very sentence is not true" in English, however, does not imply that 'true' is not a "truth predicate" of English. Even if we ignore all other sources of non-classicality in English, we are not entitled to assume that 'true' has a classical interpretation. Hence, when applied to English, the Liar argument does not yield a theorem (unless it be the unsurprising claim that English is not a classical language); it yields only a paradox. It forces us to rethink our ordinary preconceptions concerning the logic and semantics of 'true'.

Many authors have observed that if truth-value gaps are allowed in the language then the Liar argument does not yield a contradiction. All it shows is that if the Liar sentence is true then it is false, and if false then it is true. The possibility remains open that the Liar is neither true nor false.[21] The formal analogue of this observation is that the above proofs of the indefinability theorems are blocked if we shift to a three-valued language. Illustration: Suppose in the manner of Theorem 2B.3 that a language $\mathscr{L}$ has a name b that denotes $\sim Gb$. As the proof of the theorem shows, G cannot be a T-predicate if $\sim Gb$ is true in $\mathscr{L}$ (for then G is false of this sentence) or if $\sim Gb$ is false (for then G is true of this sentence). But if $\mathscr{L}$ is, say, a Strong Kleene language, the possibility exists that $\sim Gb$ is neither true nor false. And if it *is* neither true nor false, then (by the semantics of $\sim$), G is also neither true nor false of $\sim Gb$. Thus, it is not ruled out that G is a T-predicate for $\mathscr{L}$. In three-valued languages the existence of Liar-type self-reference for a predicate does not imply that the predicate is not a T-predicate for the language.

This point may be isolated by considering schemes τ, μ, κ, and υ. Theorem 2B.3 shows as the last step of its calculation that the classical scheme τ cannot tolerate a Liar sentence precisely because it is never true that the negation of a value is precisely that value itself. On the other hand, each of the three other schemes has at least one value whose negation is just that value itself, so for those schemes the calculation of Theorem 2B.3 would not go through to absurdity.

The possibility is therefore open that three-valued languages can contain self-reference and also their own T-predicates. Logicians and philosophers were aware of this possibility early in their investigations of the semantic and set-theoretic paradoxes; Bochvar (1937/1981) is one example. However, curiously, the existence of such languages was not proved until much later. Martin and Woodruff showed in 1975 that a Weak Kleene language rich in syntactic resources can contain its own T-predicate. Kripke proved, independently and at about the same time, a similar result for the Strong Kleene languages.[22] Analogous results had been obtained much earlier by logicians working on the set-theoretic paradoxes,[23]

---

[21] This possibility was considered by the medievals. It is the sixth of the fourteen opinions mentioned by Paul of Venice. Unfortunately, he dismisses it with the remark that "every proposition is true or false, and every insoluble is a proposition, therefore every insoluble is true or false." See Bocheński 1961, p. 242.

[22] Kindt (1978) and Aczel (1980) also appear to have obtained similar results independently.

[23] See, in particular, Gilmore 1974, where use is made of an inductive construction that did not appear in the truth literature until much later. (Paul Gilmore's work was available from 1967 on, though it was not published until 1974.) Gilmore attributes the inductive construction to Fredric B. Fitch (1948). Throughout his life Fitch urged the philosophical motive of universal applicability and therefore self-applicability (1946, 1964), and his entire "basic logic" program was informed by it. (One of us—NB—was educated in these attitudes and methods by Fitch during the mid 1950s.)

but their work had little influence on the philosophical literature devoted to the Liar paradox. This is especially curious because in the late 1960s and the early 1970s many philosophers held the working assumption that the Liar sentence is neither true nor false and presupposed the possibility of three-valued languages that contain T-predicates for themselves.[24]

A partial explanation of this curiosity may be that the formal problem was not perceived by the researchers in the area to be the central one. The problem that commanded the greatest attention was to find a justification for the claim that the Liar is neither true nor false, a justification that is independent of the paradoxes.[25] A number of ideas were put forward: Martin (1967, 1968, 1970b) proposed that the Liar lacks a truth value because it is sortally incorrect; van Fraassen (1968, 1970a) sought to explain it in terms of a failure of presupposition in the Liar statement; and there were other ideas also. These authors attempted to answer an important question, one that any three-valued theory has to address, but their works were unsystematic in character and did not offer a developed theory of truth. With the publication of Martin and Woodruff 1975 and Kripke 1975, not only was it established once and for all that three-valued languages could contain T-predicates for themselves, but tools became available that could be used to construct systematic theories of truth. Now one could determine more exactly what the consequences of a given philosophical conception were. Thanks to these papers, a systematic and plausible semantic account of the concept of truth appeared to be possible.

Let us see now how the definability results for nonclassical languages are established. We shall follow the algebraic approach of Visser (1984, 1989) and Fitting (1986). Kripke's inductive construction will be introduced later.

Some other relevant works are Myhill 1950, Skolem 1960, Skolem 1963, Brady 1971, and Nepeivoda 1973. Scott's (1972, 1973, 1975, 1980) work on the lambda-calculus and combinatory logic is closely related. See Feferman 1984 for further historical remarks and for a unified account of the set-theoretic and semantical paradoxes within a three-valued context.
[24] See Martin 1967, 1968, 1970b; van Fraassen 1968, 1970a; and Skyrms 1970a, 1970b. Martin (1970b) formulates the problem of establishing the existence of such languages and, in fact, introduces the important notion of "fixed point" (he calls it 'standard interpretation'). But the proof Martin gives of their existence is inadequate, and he later disowned it.
[25] Another problem that attracted attention was that of the Strengthened Liar. Brian Skyrms' work, in particular, is motivated by this problem.

Let L be a language with a one-place predicate G. Let M $(= \langle D, I \rangle)$ be a model (1) whose domain D contains all (the codes of) the sentences of L and (2) that assigns classical interpretations to all the nonlogical constants of L except G.[26] Given a possible two-valued (three-valued, four-valued) interpretation g of G in M,[27] let M + g be the two-valued (three-valued, four-valued) model that is just like M except that it assigns to G the interpretation g. We shall call models such as M that meet the two conditions stated above *ground* models of L.[28] As before, we shall call models such as M + g that interpret *all* the nonlogical constants of L *standard* models of L. We use Roman variables M, M', M_1, ... to range over ground models and script variables $\mathscr{M}$, $\mathscr{M}'$, $\mathscr{M}_1$, ... to range over standard models. We can now define the crucial notion of the jump operation ρ_M for a valuation scheme ρ.

2B.8 Definition ($\mathscr{L}_g$; Jump ρ_M) Let ρ be a valuation scheme, and let M $(= \langle D, I \rangle)$ be a ground model of L.

(i) If g is a possible interpretation of a one-place predicate, then $\mathscr{L}_g$ is the interpreted language $\langle L, M + g, \rho \rangle$.

(ii) The *jump* ρ_M is an operation on the possible interpretations g of a one-place predicate in M.[29] It is required to satisfy the condition that, for all d $\in$ D,

$$\rho_M(g)(d) = \begin{cases} \mathrm{Val}_{\mathscr{L}_g}(A) & \text{if d is (a code of) } A \\ f & \text{otherwise.} \end{cases}$$

2B.9 Definition (Fixed point) Let f be an operation on a set X. Then $x \in X$ is a *fixed point of* f iff f(x) = x.

The importance of fixed points arises from the following fact. Consider the jump ρ_M for a scheme ρ and the interpreted language $\mathscr{L}_g = \langle L, M + g, \rho \rangle$, where g is in the domain of ρ_M. Assuming that g(d) = f for all nonsentences d of L, the following equivalences hold:

---

[26] M leaves G uninterpreted. M is, therefore, a classical model of L minus G.

[27] So g $\in \{t, f\}^D$ (respectively: $\{t, f, n\}^D$, $\{t, f, n, b\}^D$).

[28] Whether a structure is a ground model for a language depends upon the predicate that is taken to play the role of G. Below we suppress this relativity to G whenever possible; we write as if G is fixed once and for all. Occasionally we shall refer to all the predicates of L except G as *ground predicates*—these are the predicates interpreted by the ground models.

[29] μ_M and κ_M are operations on $\{t, f, n\}^D$. Similarly, τ_M is an operation on $\{t, f\}^D$, and υ_M is an operation on $\{t, f, n, b\}^D$.

g is a fixed point of ρ_M

   iff $\rho_M(g) = g$,

   iff $\rho_M(g)(A) = g(A)$ for all sentences A of $\mathscr{L}_g$,

   iff $\mathrm{Val}_{\mathscr{L}_g}(A) = g(A)$ for all sentences A,   [definition of ρ_M]

   iff $\mathrm{Val}_{\mathscr{L}_g}(A) = \mathrm{Val}_{\mathscr{L}_g}(Gx, A)$ for all sentences A,   [definition of $\mathscr{L}_g$]

and

   iff G is a T-predicate for $\mathscr{L}_g$.   [Lemma 2B.2]

Since both sides of the equivalence

G is a T-predicate for $\mathscr{L}_g$ iff g is a fixed point of ρ_M

imply that $g(d) = \mathbf{f}$ for all nonsentences d of $\mathscr{L}_g$, the equivalence holds unconditionally. In short, *fixed points yield languages that contain T-predicates for themselves.*

Let us note some relationships between the fixed points of various schemes.

2B.10 Theorem (Fixed-point relationships)   Let M be a ground model of L.

(i) If $g \in \{\mathbf{t}, \mathbf{f}\}^D$, then for all schemes ρ ($\rho = \mu, \kappa, v$)

   $\tau_M(g) = \rho_M(g)$.

Hence, if g is a fixed point of τ_M, it is also a fixed point of ρ_M.

(ii) If $g \in \{\mathbf{t}, \mathbf{f}, \mathbf{n}\}^D$ then

   $\mu_M(g) \leq \kappa_M(g) = v_M(g)$.

Hence, all fixed points of κ_M are fixed points of v_M. (But they are not necessarily fixed points of μ_M. It can be shown, however, that above every fixed point of μ_M there is a fixed point of κ_M.)

Proof   (i) is an easy consequence of the first part of Theorem 2A.6. (ii) follows from the remaining two parts of the same theorem. (To show that above every fixed point of μ_M there is a fixed point of κ_M, use 2C.6.)   ∎

It is a remarkable property of the three- and four-valued schemes considered above that their jumps *always* have fixed points. Hence, given any one-place predicate G of these languages and any interpretation of the other nonlogical constants, one can always find an interpretation of G so that it is a T-predicate for the resulting language. This property does not hold for the classical scheme τ.

2B.11   Definition   (Fixed-point property)   A scheme ρ is said to have the *fixed-point property* iff for all languages L with a one-place predicate G and all ground models M of L the jump ρ_M has a fixed point.

2B.12   Theorem   (Indefinability Theorem V)   The classical scheme τ does not have the fixed-point property.

Proof   Let L be a language with a name b and let M be a ground model such that $I(b) = \sim Gb$. Then, τ_M does not have fixed points. For if g were a fixed point of τ_M, then G would be a T-predicate for $\mathscr{L}_g$, violating Theorem 2B.3. (Note that we could have used any of the earlier indefinability theorems to establish this one.)   ∎

2B.13   Theorem   (The Fixed-Point Theorem)   The schemes κ, μ, and υ have the fixed-point property.[30]

The proof of Theorem 2B.13 relies on a certain "monotonicity" of the jumps. Recall our earlier definitions (section 2A) that if D is the domain of a model then

$$D3 = \{t, f, n\}^D, \ D4 = \{t, f, n, b\}^D$$

and

$$\mathbf{D3} = \langle D3, \leq \rangle, \ \mathbf{D4} = \langle D4, \leq \rangle,$$

where for f, g $\in$ D3 (D4)

$$f \leq g \text{ iff } f(d) \leq g(d) \text{ for all } d \in D.$$

2B.14   Lemma   (Monotonicity of jumps)   For $\rho = \mu, \kappa, \upsilon$, the jump ρ_M is *monotone* in the sense that if f $\leq$ g then $\rho_M(f) \leq o_M(g)$.[31]

Proof   The lemma is a consequence of the monotonicity of the schemes (Theorem 2A.7). If f $\leq$ g then M + f $\leq$ M + g. Hence,

---

[30] Kripke (1975, 1976) showed that κ has the fixed-point property. Martin and Woodruff (1975) established this of μ, and Woodruff (1984), Visser (1984), and Bradley H. Dowden (1984) of υ.
[31] The lemma holds for the classical scheme τ also, but vacuously.

$\mathscr{L}_f \leq \mathscr{L}_g$.

By Theorem 2A.7, for any sentence A

$$\text{Val}_{\mathscr{L}_f}(A) = \text{Val}_{\mathscr{L}_f, s}(A) \leq \text{Val}_{\mathscr{L}_g, s}(A) = \text{Val}_{\mathscr{L}_g}(A).$$

where s is any assignment of values to the variables. (For the equalities we rely on Theorem 2A.8.) By the definition of the jump,

$\rho_M(f)(A) = \text{Val}_{\mathscr{L}_f}(A)$ and $\rho_M(g)(A) = \text{Val}_{\mathscr{L}_g}(A)$.

Hence, for all sentences A,

$\rho_M(f)(A) \leq \rho_M(g)(A)$.

We can now conclude that

$\rho_M(f) \leq \rho_M(g)$.   ■

Proof of Theorem 2B.13   We have noted that **D3** and **D4** are ccpos. (See Theorem 2C.4. In fact **D4** is a complete lattice.) By Lemma 2B.14, ρ_M ($\rho = \mu, \kappa, \upsilon$) is a monotone operation on these structures. Since every monotone operation on a ccpo has a fixed point (see Theorem 2C.8), ρ_M has a fixed point. This holds for all ground models M. Hence, μ, κ, and υ have the fixed-point property.   ■

Note that the argument given is general and does not depend on the details of the schemes. It works for any scheme that has the property of monotonicity. We can adopt a different semantics for the connectives, or we can add new types of logical constants to our languages, or even new "truth values." As long as the space of possible interpretations of a one-place predicate is a ccpo and the property of monotonicity is respected, the resulting scheme will have the fixed-point property.[32] The broad framework stays the same even if we shift to a semantical notion other than "truth" (e.g., "satisfaction," "definition," or "reference").

Monotonicity of the schemes, then, is sufficient to ensure that it has the fixed-point property. It is not, however, necessary. A counterexample is given in section 2E, where it is shown that a nonmonotonic truth-functional extension of the Weak Kleene scheme also has the fixed-point

---

[32] The classical jump τ_M is (vacuously) monotonic, but the above proof does not go through for it. The reason is that the relevant space is not a ccpo.

property. On the other hand, it can be shown that no such extension of the Strong Kleene scheme has this property.

2B.15 Problem Characterize the class of three-valued (four-valued) schemes that are truth-functional and have the fixed-point property.

2C Coherent Complete Partial Orders

In this section we shall study monotone operations on coherent complete partial orders. This study will reveal much about the fixed points of jump operations introduced in section 2B. Recall the definition of a coherent complete partial order given earlier.

2C.1 Definition (Consistent sets, ccpos) Let $\mathcal{X} = \langle X, \leq \rangle$ be a partial order (po) and let $Y \subseteq X$. We say, following Visser (1984, 1989),[33] that

(i) Y is *consistent* (in $\mathcal{X}$) iff each $\{u, v\} \subseteq Y$ has an upper bound in $\mathcal{X}$

and

(ii) $\mathcal{X}$ is a *coherent complete partial order* (*ccpo*) iff every consistent subset of X has a supremum.[34]

2C.2 Example (For ccpos) Every complete lattice is a ccpo. The simplest example of a structure that is a ccpo but not a lattice is **A3**:

An example of a structure that is not a ccpo is the following.

---

[33] Throughout this section we are heavily indebted to these two papers.
[34] Fitting (1986) studies monotone operations on posets in which (i) there is a least element, (ii) every chain has an upper bound, and (iii) every nonempty set with an upper bound has a least upper bound. These conditions are weaker than those on ccpos. We have chosen to work with ccpos because they reveal more about the structure of fixed points that interest us.

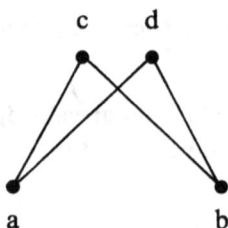

Here the set $\{a, b\}$ is consistent but does not have a supremum. For another example, the structure

is a ccpo but the structure

is not.

2C.3   Theorem   (Ccpo properties)   Let $\mathcal{X} = \langle X, \leq \rangle$ be a ccpo and let $x \in X$. Then:

 (i) $\mathcal{X}$ has a least element.

 (ii) Every nonempty subset of X has an infimum in $\mathcal{X}$.

 (iii) If $\mathcal{X}$ has a greatest element then $\mathcal{X}$ is a complete lattice.

 (iv) The structure $\mathcal{Y} = \langle Y, \leq \restriction Y \rangle$, where $Y = \{y \in X : x \leq y\}$, is a ccpo.

 (v) The structure $\mathcal{Z} = \langle Z, \leq \restriction Z \rangle$, where $Z = \{z \in X : z \leq x\}$, is a complete lattice.

 (vi) There is a maximal element of $\mathcal{X}$ that is greater than or equal to x.

Proof

   (i) $\varnothing$ is consistent and $\varnothing \subseteq X$. By the definition of ccpo, $\bigvee \varnothing$ exists. Since every member of X is an upper bound of $\varnothing$, $\bigvee \varnothing$ is less than every member of X. Hence, $\bigvee \varnothing$ is a least element of $\mathcal{X}$.

(ii) Let Y be a nonempty subset of X. Consider $Z = \{u \in X: u \text{ is a lower}$ bound of Y}. Since Y is nonempty, Z is consistent. Hence, $\bigvee Z$ exists. We now verify that $\bigvee Z$ is an infimum of Y.

Since every element of Y is an upper bound of Z and $\bigvee Z$ is the *least* upper bound of Z, we conclude that $\bigvee Z$ is a lower bound of Y. But every lower bound of Y is in Z. Hence, $\bigvee Z$ is the greatest lower bound of Y.

(iii) If $\mathscr{X}$ has a greatest element then $\bigvee \varnothing$ exists. Using (ii), we conclude that *every* subset of $\mathscr{X}$ has an infimum. It follows that $\mathscr{X}$ is a complete lattice.

(iv) Any subset U of Y that is consistent in $\mathscr{Y}$ is consistent also in $\mathscr{X}$. So U has a supremum u in $\mathscr{X}$. If $U \neq \varnothing$ then u is its supremum in $\mathscr{Y}$ also; otherwise x is its supremum in $\mathscr{Y}$.

(v) Any subset of Z is consistent in $\mathscr{X}$. Its supremum in $\mathscr{X}$ is also its supremum in $\mathscr{Z}$.

(vi) Let $Y = \{y \in X: x \leq y\}$. Then, by (iv), $\mathscr{Y} = \langle Y, \leq \restriction Y \rangle$ is a ccpo. We show using Zorn's lemma that there are maximal elements in $\mathscr{Y}$. These maximal elements are maximal also in $\mathscr{X}$ and are greater than x.

Let C be a chain in $\mathscr{Y}$. By definition, C is consistent in $\mathscr{Y}$. Hence, its supremum exists in $\mathscr{Y}$. We conclude that every chain has an upper bound in $\mathscr{Y}$. By Zorn's lemma it follows that there are maximal elements in $\mathscr{Y}$. ∎

We have seen that **A3** is a ccpo. The next theorem establishes that the possible three-valued interpretations of a predicate also constitute a ccpo.

2C.4 Theorem (Function-space ccpos) Let $\mathscr{X} = \langle X, \leq \rangle$ be a ccpo and let D be a set. Define the structure $\mathscr{X}^D = \langle X^D, \leq \rangle$ so that for all f, $g \in X^D$

$f \leq g$ iff for all $d \in D$, $f(d) \leq g(d)$.

Then:

(i) $\mathscr{X}^D$ is a ccpo.

(ii) If $\mathscr{X}$ is a complete lattice then $\mathscr{X}^D$ is also a complete lattice.

Proof

(i) Let $F \subseteq X^D$ be consistent in $\mathscr{X}^D$. We need to verify that F has a supremum in $\mathscr{X}^D$. For $d \in D$, set $F_d = \{x: x = f(d) \text{ for some } f \in F\}$. It is easily seen that F_d is consistent in $\mathscr{X}$. Hence, $\bigvee F_d$ exists. Define a function $f \in X^D$ so that $f(d) = \bigvee F_d$ for all $d \in D$. The function f is a supremum of F.

(ii) If $\mathscr{X}$ is a complete lattice, then it has a largest element (say x). Define $f \in X^D$ so that $f(d) = x$ for all $d \in D$. Clearly, f is the largest element of $\mathscr{X}^D$. We have already shown that $\mathscr{X}^D$ is a ccpo. So, by Theorem 2C.3(iii), $\mathscr{X}^D$ is a complete lattice. ∎

The second part of the above theorem shows that the possible four-valued interpretations of a predicate constitute a complete lattice.

2C.5 Definition (Sound, replete, fixed point) Let $\mathscr{X} = \langle X, \leq \rangle$ be a po, let $f: X \to X$ be an operation on X, and let $x \in X$. Then[35]

(i) x is *sound* (relative to $\mathscr{X}$ and f) iff $x \leq f(x)$.

(ii) x is *replete* (relative to $\mathscr{X}$ and f) iff $f(x) \leq x$.

(iii) x is a *fixed point* (of f in $\mathscr{X}$) iff $x = f(x)$.

2C.6 Theorem (Existence of fixed points in ccpos) Let $\mathscr{X} = \langle X, \leq \rangle$ be a po; let $x,y \in X$; and let f be an operation on X that is *monotone*, i.e., for all $u,v \in X$, $u \leq v$ implies that $f(u) \leq f(v)$. Then:

(i) If x is sound then there is a fixed point z such that $x \leq z$.

(ii) If x is sound, y is replete, and $x \leq y$ then there is a fixed point z such that $x \leq z \leq y$.

(iii) If y is replete then there is a fixed point z such that $z \leq y$.

Proof

(i) Let x be a sound element in $\mathscr{X}$. Consider the structure $\mathscr{Y} = \langle Y, \leq\!\upharpoonright Y \rangle$, where $Y = \{y: y$ is a sound element in $\mathscr{X}$ and $x \leq y\}$. We verify that $\mathscr{Y}$ is a ccpo. Let Z be a consistent subset in $\mathscr{Y}$. Then it is also a consistent subset in $\mathscr{X}$, and it has a supremum (say b) in $\mathscr{X}$. Clearly, $b \geq x$. Thus, to establish that b is a supremum of Z in $\mathscr{Y}$ it suffices to show that b is sound.

Let $z \in Z$. Then $z \leq b$. By monotonicity of f, $f(z) \leq f(b)$. Since z is sound, we conclude that $z \leq f(b)$. Thus, $f(b)$ is an upper bound of Z. As b is a least upper bound of Z, it follows that $b \leq f(b)$. That is, b is sound.

By Theorem 2C.3(vi), there are maximal elements in $\mathscr{Y}$. Let m be one such. As m is sound, $x \leq m \leq f(m)$. Monotonicity of f implies that $f(m) \leq f(f(m))$. So $f(m)$ is sound and belongs in the structure $\mathscr{Y}$. Maximality of m yields that $m = f(m)$: m is a fixed point $\geq x$.[36]

[35] In the definitions below we have followed the terminology of Woodruff (1984).
[36] Martin and Woodruff (1975) proved the existence of a fixed point of μ_M by an argument essentially similar to that just given.

(ii) Consider the structure $\mathscr{Z} = \langle Z, \leq^\restriction Z \rangle$, where $Z = \{z \in X: x \leq z \leq y\}$. $\mathscr{Z}$ is a ccpo (in fact a complete lattice) and $f^\restriction Z$ is a monotone operation on $\mathscr{Z}$. By (i), there is a fixed point of $f^\restriction Z$ in $\mathscr{Z}$. This is also a fixed point of f and lies between x and y.

(iii) Let y be replete and let b be the least element of $\mathscr{Z}$. Then $b \leq y$ and b is sound. So (ii) applies, yielding that there is a fixed point below y. ∎

Remark Monotone functions can be shown to have fixed points even in posets that satisfy a much weaker condition than the one imposed on ccpos. For instance, monotone operations on what Scott calls "complete" posets have fixed points. (A poset is *complete* iff all directed subsets of it have suprema, where a *directed* set is one that contains an upper bound for every pair of elements in it.) Weaker conditions than completeness suffice to establish the existence of fixed points also.

2C.7   Definition   (Set F(X, f) and structure $\mathscr{F}(\mathscr{X}, f)$ of fixed points)   Let $f: X \to X$ be an operation on $\mathscr{X} = \langle X, \leq \rangle$. Define

(i) $F(X, f) = \{x: f(x) = x\}$

and

(ii) $\mathscr{F}(\mathscr{X}, f) = \langle F(X, f), \leq^\restriction F(X, f) \rangle.$

2C.8   Theorem   (Visser's Fixed-Point Theorem)   If $f: X \to X$ is a monotone operation on a ccpo $\mathscr{X} = \langle X, \leq \rangle$, then

(i) $\mathscr{F}(\mathscr{X}, f)$ is a ccpo

and

(ii) if $\mathscr{X}$ has a largest element, $\mathscr{F}(\mathscr{X}, f)$ has a largest element also.

Proof

(i) It is easily seen that $\mathscr{F}(\mathscr{X}, f)$ is a po. Let Y be a consistent subset in $\mathscr{F}(\mathscr{X}, f)$. Then Y is consistent in $\mathscr{X}$ and $\bigvee Y$ exists in $\mathscr{X}$. For arbitrary $y \in Y$, we have $y \leq \bigvee Y$. So

$$y = f(y) \leq f(\textstyle\bigvee Y).$$

That is, $f(\bigvee Y)$ is an upper bound of Y. Hence, $\bigvee Y \leq f(\bigvee Y)$; i.e., $\bigvee Y$ is sound.

Now let $Z = \{z: z$ is a fixed point of f in $\mathscr{X}$ and $\bigvee Y \leq z\}$. Since $\bigvee Y$ is sound, Theorem 2C.6(i) yields that Z is nonempty. Consequently, $\bigwedge Z$ exists in $\mathscr{X}$. For arbitrary $z \in Z$, monotonicity of f implies that

$f(\bigwedge Z) \le f(z) = z.$

Thus, $f(\bigwedge Z)$ is a lower bound of Z. Therefore, $f(\bigwedge Z) \le \bigwedge Z$; i.e., $\bigwedge Z$ is replete.

But $\bigvee Y \le \bigwedge Z$. Theorem 2C.6(ii) applies, yielding a fixed point b between $\bigvee Y$ and $\bigwedge Z$. By definition of Z, $b \in Z$. So $b = \bigwedge Z$. I.e., b is a fixed point that is an upper bound of Y and a lower bound of Z (in $\mathscr{X}$). Hence, b must be a supremum of Y in $\mathscr{F}(\mathscr{X}, f)$.

(ii) Let $\mathscr{X}$ have a largest element. Then $F(X, f)$, the set of fixed points, is consistent in $\mathscr{X}$. Hence, $\bigvee F(X, f)$ exists. We can verify by an argument similar to that given in (i) above that $\bigvee F(X, f)$ is sound. Theorem 2C.6(i) implies that there is fixed point above $\bigvee F(X, f)$. This fixed point is the largest element of $\mathscr{F}(\mathscr{X}, f)$.   ∎

An immediate corollary of part (ii) of this theorem is Tarski's Fixed-Point Theorem.

2C.9   Theorem   (Tarski's Fixed-Point Theorem)   Let $\mathscr{X} = \langle X, \le \rangle$ be a complete lattice, and let f be a monotone operation on $\mathscr{X}$. Then $\mathscr{F}(\mathscr{X}, f)$ is a complete lattice.[37]

Proof   If $\mathscr{X}$ is a complete lattice, then $\mathscr{X}$ is a ccpo with a largest element. Hence, by parts (i) and (ii) of Theorem 2C.8, $\mathscr{F}(\mathscr{X}, f)$ is also a ccpo and has a largest element. So $\mathscr{F}(\mathscr{X}, f)$ is a complete lattice (Theorem 2C.3(iii)).

2C.10   Example $(\mathscr{F}(\mathbf{D3}, h))$ If $D = \{1, 2\}$, then $\mathbf{D3}\ (= \mathbf{A3^D})$ is the following ccpo:

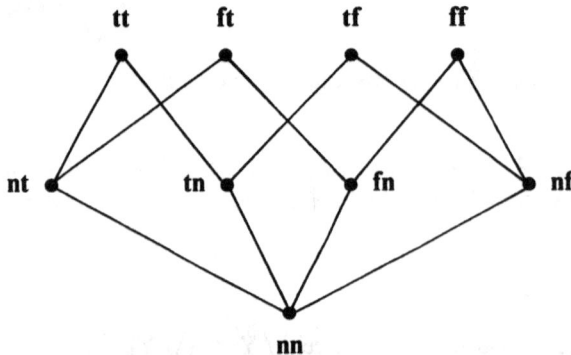

---

[37] This is also known, especially in the computer science literature, as the Knaster-Tarski Fixed-Point Theorem.

(Note: We are letting **xy** stand for the function g such that $g(1) = x$ and $g(2) = y$.) Let h be the following monotone operation on **D3**:

g	nn	nt	nf	tn	fn	tt	tf	ft	ff
h(g)	nn	nf	nt	tn	fn	tf	tt	ff	ft

Now the fixed-point structure $\mathscr{F}(\mathbf{D3}, h)$ is the following ccpo:

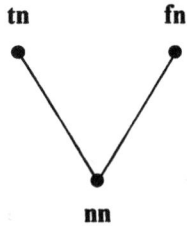

tn   **fn**

nn

Note that if we add a top element (say ∗) to the first structure diagrammed above and extend the definition of h to ∗ so that its monotonicity is preserved, the fixed-point structure would have to have a top element too. In fact ∗ would end up being the largest fixed point, for we have stipulated that **tt** ≤ ∗ and **ff** ≤ ∗. So the monotonicity of h requires that the following hold:

tf $= h(\mathbf{tt}) \leq h(∗)$,

ft $= h(\mathbf{ff}) \leq h(∗)$.

This is possible only if $h(∗) = ∗$.

The intrinsic elements of a ccpo are of special interest.[38]

2C.11 Definition (Set $I(\mathscr{X})$ and structure $\mathscr{I}(\mathscr{X})$ of intrinsic elements) Let $\mathscr{X} = \langle X, \leq \rangle$ be a ccpo.

(i) x is an *intrinsic element* in $\mathscr{X}$ iff, for all $y \in X$, $\{x, y\}$ is consistent in $\mathscr{X}$.

(ii) $\mathscr{I}(\mathscr{X}) = \langle I(\mathscr{X}), \leq \upharpoonright I(\mathscr{X}) \rangle$, where $I(\mathscr{X})$ is the set of intrinsic elements in $\mathscr{X}$.

2C.12 Theorem (Intrinsic elements) Let $\mathscr{X} = \langle X, \leq \rangle$ be a ccpo.

(i) Then $\mathscr{I}(\mathscr{X})$ is a complete lattice. Hence, there is a largest intrinsic element, $i(\mathscr{X})$, in $\mathscr{X}$.[39]

[38] In the context of truth theory these were first defined by Kripke (1975).
[39] This was noted by Kripke (1975).

(ii) Let M be the set of maximal elements in $\mathscr{X}$. Then $i(\mathscr{X}) = \bigwedge M$.[40]

Proof

(i) Let $Y \subseteq I(\mathscr{X})$. Y is a set of intrinsic elements, so it is consistent and it has a supremum (say b) in $\mathscr{X}$. We verify that b is intrinsic. This will establish that b is a supremum of Y in $\mathscr{I}(\mathscr{X})$.

Consider an arbitrary $x \in X$. $Y \cup \{x\}$ is consistent (since Y consists only of intrinsic elements) and has a supremum (say z) in $\mathscr{X}$. Now z is an upper bound of Y, and hence $z \geq \bigvee Y = b$. But $z \geq x$. So z is an upper bound of $\{b, x\}$. Thus, $\{b, x\}$ is consistent. Since x is arbitrary, it follows that b is intrinsic.

(ii) Let $m \in M$. As $i(\mathscr{X})$ is intrinsic, $\{i(\mathscr{X}), m\}$ is consistent. Hence, $i(\mathscr{X}) \leq m$. Thus, $i(\mathscr{X})$ is a lower bound of M and $i(\mathscr{X}) \leq \bigwedge M$. We next verify that $\bigwedge M$ is intrinsic. This implies that $\bigwedge M \leq i(\mathscr{X})$, thus yielding the desired $i(\mathscr{X}) = \bigwedge M$.

Let $x \in X$. There is a maximal element m of $\mathscr{X}$ above x (Theorem 2C.3(vi)). So $x \leq m$ and $\bigwedge M \leq m$. We conclude that $\bigwedge M$ is consistent with every element of X. That is, $\bigwedge M$ is intrinsic.   ∎

2C.13 Example (Intrinsic elements) In each of the structures illustrated in Example 2C.10 there is only one intrinsic element, namely **nn**.

This completes our exposition of ccpos and of monotone operations on them. Let us now gather together what we can learn from all this about the fixed points of υ_M, κ_M, and μ_M.

- Concerning υ_M: We have seen that the possible four-valued interpretations of G, **D4**, constitute a complete lattice. As υ_M is a monotone operation on **D4**, Tarski's Fixed-Point Theorem tells us that the fixed points of υ_M exist and themselves form a complete lattice. The notion of intrinsicness is not interesting within the context of complete lattices, for every element is intrinsic by definition.

- Concerning κ_M: By Lemma 2B.14, κ_M is a monotone operation on the ccpo **D3**. Hence, by Visser's Theorem (2C.8), κ_M has fixed points and the fixed-point structure $\mathscr{F}(\mathbf{D3}, \kappa_M)$ is a ccpo. The properties of ccpos established in Theorem 2C.3 imply that there is a least fixed point of κ_M. (Kripke calls sentences that are assigned a value **t** or **f** by the least fixed

---

[40] Visser attributes this result to Manna and Shamir (1976).

point *grounded sentences.*[41]) Further, below every fixed point there is a complete lattice of fixed points (Theorem 2C.3(v)), and above every fixed point there is a ccpo of fixed points (Theorem 2C.3(iv)). Maximal fixed points exist above every fixed point, and every nonempty set of fixed points has an infimum in $\mathscr{F}(\mathbf{D3}, \kappa_M)$ (Theorem 2C.3, points (vi) and (ii) respectively). The intrinsic elements of $\mathscr{F}(\mathbf{D3}, \kappa_M)$—also called the *intrinsic fixed points of* κ_M—constitute a complete lattice (Theorem 2C.12(i)). The least fixed point is also the least intrinsic fixed point. Although in general there is no assurance that κ_M has a largest fixed point, it does have a largest intrinsic fixed point. This fixed point is also the infimum (in $\mathscr{F}(\mathbf{D3}, \kappa_M)$, not necessarily in **D3**) of the set of maximal fixed points (Theorem 2C.12(ii)).

• Concerning μ_M: All the claims made above for κ_M hold for μ_M.

It would be desirable to illustrate these facts with some examples. In attempting to do this we face the difficulty that, even for relatively simple ground models M, the jump operations κ_M, μ_M, and υ_M are complex. The source of the complexity is the quantifiers. Their presence in the language makes the calculation of truth and falsity a complicated affair, and this in turn makes it difficult to survey the fixed points of the jumps. In the next section we develop a technique that enables us to bypass this problem in some special cases.

2D   The Transfer Theorem

The idea underlying the upcoming Transfer Theorem is to reduce the problem of determining the fixed points of a jump operation to a calculation in propositional logic. This cannot be done in all cases, but the cases in which it can be done are varied enough to provide us with a rich source of examples.

Consider a language whose logical resources are those of propositional logic (so it has no quantifiers or variables) and which has only one predicate G and some names N. We shall identify such a language with the set of its names N.

---

[41] For an intuitive characterization of groundedness see the quotation from Kripke given at the beginning of section 6A. Herzberger 1970a is an early discussion of the notion.

A *two-valued* (*three-valued, four-valued*) *interpretation* for N is a function v that assigns to each atomic sentence Ga of N one of the truth values from the set

$\{t, f\} (\{t, f, n\}, \{t, f, n, b\})$.

Given an interpretation v and a valuation scheme ρ, we can calculate in the usual way the semantic value of any sentence of N.

A *reference list* R for N is a function that assigns to each name in N a sentence of N. For example, if $N = \{a, b\}$ then a possible reference list R' for N is

R$'(a) = \sim Ga$,

R$'(b) = (\sim Ga \ \& \ Gb)$.[42]

Given a reference list R for a propositional language N, we define as follows a jump operation ρ_R on the possible interpretations of the atomic sentences Ga, $a \in N$. Let v be a possible interpretation. Then, for all names $a \in N$,

$[\rho_R(v)](Ga) =$ the value of the sentence R(a) relative to the interpretation
                    v and the scheme ρ.

Here we use the notation ρ_R because of its analogies with the jump ρ_M introduced in section 2B, and indeed the Transfer Theorem below will establish explicit connections. Note that R here plays the role of "ground model for N." The resources of N are so restricted that a ground model need only specify the denotations of the names in N. And v plays the role of "interpretation of G." It specifies whether G is true or false of all the relevant objects (i.e., the denotations of the names in N). ρ_R and ρ_M are fundamentally alike. The differences between them are all due to the differences in the resources of the languages with which they are concerned.

If v is a fixed point of ρ_R, then for all $a \in N$

$v(Ga) =$ the value of R(a) in v relative to the scheme ρ.

Hence, G behaves like a T-predicate over sentences denoted by the names in N.

---

[42] If we imagine the G as invisible in a reference list, we arrive at Visser's (1984) *stipulations*. Note that, whereas reference lists give the denotations of the names in a language, Visser's stipulations are meant to fix the meanings of atomic sentences.

It is easy to determine (at least for finite reference lists R) whether ρ_R has fixed points, and if it does have them it is easy to determine fully the structure of the fixed points.

2D.1 Example (Fixed Points of $\kappa_{R'}$) Let $N = \{a,b\}$ and consider the reference list R' for N given above:

$R'(a) = \sim Ga,$

$R'(b) = (\sim Ga \ \& \ Gb).$

N has nine three-valued interpretations forming a structure that can be pictured as follows:

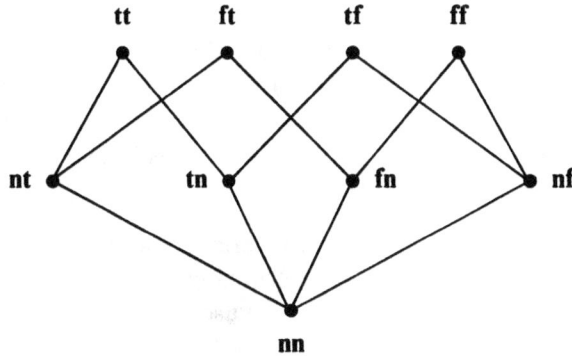

In this diagram (and also in others below) **xy** stands for the interpretation v such that v$(Ga) = $ **x** and v$(Gb) = $ **y**.

We can calculate the truth values of $\sim Ga$ and $(\sim Ga \ \& \ Gb)$ in each of the nine interpretations relative, say, to the Strong Kleene scheme κ. The calculations for a few interpretations are given in the following table:

Ga	Gb	$\sim Ga$	$(\sim Ga \ \& \ Gb)$
n	n	n	n
t	n	f	f
f	f	t	f

These calculations establish that

$\kappa_{R'}(\text{nn}) = \text{nn}; \ \kappa_{R'}(\text{tn}) = \text{ff}; \ \kappa_{R'}(\text{ff}) = \text{tf}.$

The full table for $\kappa_{R'}$ can be calculated similarly:

v	nn	nt	nf	tn	fn	tt	tf	ft	ff
$\kappa_{R'}(v)$	nn	nn	nf	ff	tn	ff	ff	tt	tf

This table reveals that $\kappa_{R'}$ has two fixed points, and that these form the structure

nf

nn

Observe that the structure displayed in the first figure above is a ccpo, and that $\kappa_{R'}$ is a monotone operation on it. Observe also that the fixed points of $\kappa_{R'}$ form a ccpo. This is an instance of the general fact that the fixed points of a monotone operation on a ccpo themselves constitute a ccpo (Visser's Fixed-Point Theorem (2C.8)).

The problem of determining the fixed points for certain quantificational languages can be reduced to the problem of determining the fixed points for certain reference lists. The next two notions are useful in articulating this connection.

2D.2 Definition (X-neutrality) Let M $(= \langle D, I \rangle)$ be a ground model for a language L with a distinguished predicate G (so G is not in the domain of I), and let $X \subseteq D$.

(i) The interpretation of a name a is X-*neutral* in M iff $I(a) \notin X$.

(ii) The interpretation of an n-place ground predicate F is X-*neutral* in M iff for all $d_i, d_i' \in X$ $(1 \le i \le n)$

$$I(F)(d_1, \ldots, d_i, \ldots, d_n) = I(F)(d_1, \ldots, d_i', \ldots, d_n).$$

(iii) The interpretation of an n-place function symbol f is X-*neutral* in M iff the range of $I(f)$ does not contain any member of X and for all d_i, $d_i' \in X$ $(1 \le i \le n)$

$$I(f)(d_1, \ldots, d_i, \ldots, d_n) = I(f)(d_1, \ldots, d_i', \ldots, d_n).$$

Intuitively, the interpretation of a constant is X-neutral iff it does not make any distinctions among the members of X. The notion of X-neutrality extends to standard models in the obvious way.

The next notion we need to define is that of a quantificational enrichment of a reference list. The key idea is that a quantificational enrichment generally contains no vicious reference beyond that found in the reference list.[43]

2D.3 Definition (Quantificational enrichment) Let M $(= \langle D, I \rangle)$ be a ground model for a language L with a distinguished predicate G, and let S be the set of sentences of L. M is a *quantificational enrichment* of a reference list R for N iff the following conditions hold:

(i) $S \subseteq D$.

(ii) The names of L include those in N.

(iii) L contains for each sentence A a quotational name 'A'. The interpretation I assigns to the name 'A' the sentence A.

(iv) If $a \in N$ then $I(a) = R(a)$.

(v) The interpretations of all the names other than the quotational names and the names in N, all the function symbols, and all the ground predicates of L are S-neutral.

We can now state the main theorem.

2D.4 Theorem (Transfer Theorem) Let R be a reference list for a language N and let M be a quantificational enrichment of R. Then there is an isomorphism F between the fixed points of ρ_R and those of ρ_M ($\rho = \kappa, \mu, \upsilon, \tau$) such that for all atomic sentences Ga of N and fixed points v of ρ_R

$$v(Ga) = F(v)(Ga),$$

provided that if ρ is not classical then there is a name a in N such that $R(a) = \sim Ga$.

Proof See the addendum to section 6A.

Remark A much stronger version of this theorem can be proved also. The final proviso and the conditions on quantificational enrichment can

---

[43] Example 2D.6 is the reason for the qualification 'generally'.

be weakened considerably. The theorem can also be extended to cover other schemes.

2D.5   Example   (T-predicate for arithmetic)   Let L_0 be a language containing the arithmetical constants *Num* (for natural number), 0, ', +, and · but in which the latter three are treated as relations rather than as functions. Suppose that L_0 has in addition a one-place predicate G, quotational names 'A' for each of its sentences A, and a name a.

Consider a ground model M_0 ($= \langle D_0, I_0 \rangle$) for L_0 in which the arithmetical constants and the quotational names receive their intended interpretations and

$$I_0(a) = \perp.   \text{ (Recall that } \perp \text{ is The False.)}$$

Problem: Can we find an interpretation g for G so that G is a T-predicate for the classical language $\mathscr{L}_g = \langle L_0, M_0 + g, \tau \rangle$? In other words, does the jump τ_{M_0} have fixed points?

Solution: Since M_0 is a quantificational enrichment of the reference list R_0 for the language $\{a\}$, where $R_0(a) = \perp$, we need only examine the jump τ_{R_0}. It is obvious that τ_{R_0} has exactly one fixed point. Hence, by the Transfer Theorem, so does τ_{M_0}.

Remarks

(i) For each sentence A of L_0, the biconditional $G('A') \leftrightarrow A$ is true in the fixed-point language $\mathscr{L}_g$: If A is true in $\mathscr{L}_g$, then g(A) = t, since g is a fixed point. So G is true of A. It follows that $G('A')$ is also true in $\mathscr{L}_g$, making the biconditional true. Similarly if A is false in $\mathscr{L}_g$.[44]

(ii) Since g is the unique fixed point of τ_{M_0}, g is the only interpretation that makes the above biconditionals true.[45] Hence, the Signification Thesis holds in this case; the biconditionals fix a unique interpretation for the truth predicate.

(iii) $\mathscr{L}_g$ has a truth predicate for itself—even though it contains arithmetic and, consequently, by Tarski's Indefinability Theorem,[46] cannot define the set of Gödel numbers of its truths. This situation is possible because the Gödel numbering is not definable *in* the language.

---

[44] $\mathscr{L}_g$ meets the conditions on semantical closure stated in section 8 of Tarski 1944. Yet, contrary to Tarski's claim, it contains its own truth predicate. (The existence of classical languages containing their own truth predicates was first proved in section 2 of "Truth and Paradox.")

[45] Assuming that G is to be false of nonsentences.

[46] Actually, we need an extended version of the theorem.

2D.6 **Example** (Need for proviso on the Transfer Theorem) Consider again the reference list R_0 from the previous example. Now each of μ_{R_0} and κ_{R_0} has exactly one fixed point. But it can be shown that each of μ_{M_0} and κ_{M_0} has two fixed points. In one the sentence $(\forall x) \sim (Gx \,\&\, \sim Gx)$ has the value **n**; in the other it has the value **t**. Hence, the Transfer Theorem will fail if the final proviso in it is dropped. The proviso is necessary for the scheme v also: The jump v_{R_0} has one fixed point, but v_{M_0} has three.

2D.7 **Example** (Exactly $p + 1$ fixed points) For each $p \geq 0$, consider a language $N_p = \{a, b_1, \ldots, b_p\}$ and a reference list R'_p satisfying the following conditions:

$$R'_p(a) = \sim Ga,$$

$$R'_p(b_i) = (Gb_1 \vee \sim Gb_1) \,\&\, \ldots \,\&\, (Gb_i \vee \sim Gb_i) \quad [= A_i, \text{ say}].$$

It is not hard to show that $\kappa_{R'_p}$ has exactly $p + 1$ fixed points, which form the following structure:

f_p

●

.

.

.

f_1 ●

│

│

●

f_0

Here f_i ($0 \leq i \leq p$) represents a fixed point in which Ga is **n**, and in which Gb_j is **t** if $0 < j \leq i$ and is **n** otherwise. [Sketch of proof: The reference list R'_p is so constructed that no sentence Gb_i can be false in a fixed point of $\kappa_{R'_p}$, for this would require a conjunct of A_i to be false (which is impossible). Further, if Gb_i is true in a fixed point then it follows that Gb_j is true for all $j \leq i$, but it is possible for Gb_k ($k > i$) to be neither true nor false.] By the Transfer Theorem we conclude that for each $p \geq 0$ there is a ground model M'_p such that $\kappa_{M'_p}$ has exactly $p + 1$ fixed points. Quantificational enrichments of R'_p suffice to establish a similar claim for μ.

Remark If R is a reference list over a denumerable $N = \{a, b_1, \ldots, b_i, \ldots\}$ in which each b_i ($1 \leq i$) denotes A_i, then the jumps μ_R and κ_R have $\aleph_0$

many fixed points. Consequently, ground models M exist for which the number of fixed points of κ_M and μ_M is $\aleph_0$. Further, using a reference list that has denumerably many Truth Tellers,[47] we can prove the existence of models with continuum many fixed points. Conclusion: *If the Continuum Hypothesis is true, then for any cardinal* m, $1 \le m \le 2^{\aleph_0}$, *there is a ground model* M *such that the cardinality of the fixed points of* μ_M (κ_M) *is* m. The claim can be slightly strengthened for the classical jump; there are also models with no fixed points. For the scheme v, the claim has to be weakened; there are no models with exactly one fixed point.

2D.8 Example (Fixed-point structures)   *An exercise:* Construct a model M whose fixed points in the Strong Kleene scheme exhibit the following structure.

Solution   A little experimentation shows that the fixed points of κ_{R_1} form this structure if R_1 is defined as follows:

$R_1(a) = \sim Ga,$

$R_1(b) = Gb.$

κ_{R_1} has three fixed points, **nn**, **nt**, and **nf**, and they exhibit the structure displayed above. Thus, for any quantificational enrichment M of R_1, the fixed points of κ_M also exhibit the same structure.

Another Exercise   What reference list yields fixed points with the following structure?

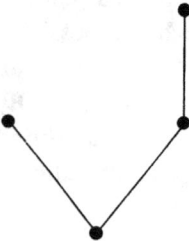

---

[47] More precisely, the reference list makes Gb_j the denotation of the name b_j ($1 \le j$).

Solution   The following reference list R_2 succeeds:

$R_2(a) = \sim Ga,$

$R_2(b) = Gb,$

$R_2(c) = (\sim Gb \vee \sim Gc) \mathbin{\&} (Gc \vee \sim Gc).$

Remarks

(i) The fixed-point structures constructed above illustrate several general principles, including the following:

(a) μ_M, and κ_M always have a unique least fixed point.

(b) μ_M and κ_M always have maximal fixed points but do not necessarily have a largest fixed point. In fact, maximal fixed points exist above every fixed point.

(c) Below every fixed point is a complete lattice of fixed points, and above it is a ccpo of fixed points.

These are all immediate consequences of Visser's Fixed-Point Theorem (2C.8).

(ii) In the two structures of Example 2D.8 there is only one intrinsic fixed point (i.e., a fixed point that is consistent with all other fixed points). On the other hand, in the structure displayed in Example 2D.7 every fixed point is intrinsic. Intrinsic fixed points always form complete lattices (Theorem 2C.12). Consequently, there is always a largest intrinsic fixed point. In the two structures of our Example 2D.8, the largest intrinsic fixed point is also the least fixed point.

(iii) The above examples are illustrative of a general fact established by Visser, and independently by Wim Blok and Joel Berman. They have shown that for any finite ccpo one can construct a reference list R whose fixed points in the Strong Kleene scheme form that structure.

2D.9   **Example**   (Fixed-point structure in υ_M)   If M is a quantificational enrichment of the reference list R_1 given in the previous example, then the fixed points of υ_M form a lattice isomorphic to the following:

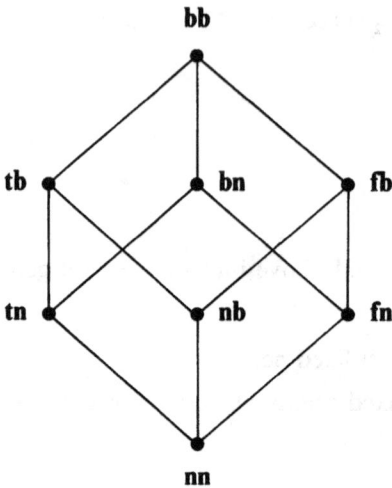

Remarks

(i) The fixed points of υ_M always form a complete lattice (Tarski's Fixed-Point Theorem). Hence there is always a least and a largest fixed point of υ_M.

(ii) Every fixed point of κ_M is also a fixed point of υ_M (Theorem 2B.10(ii)). Every dual of a fixed point of υ_M is again a fixed point of υ_M (where a dual is obtained by switching **n**'s and **b**'s).[48] In the above example, **nb** and **bn** are dual, as are **tn** and **tb**. Since κ_M always has a nonclassical fixed point, υ_M always has two or more fixed points.

2E   The Extended Weak Kleene Scheme

We will show here that a nonmonotonic extension of the Weak Kleene Scheme has the fixed-point property.[49]

Let us extend the Weak Kleene language by adding to it a unary connective ↓ whose semantics is given by the following table:

---

[48] See Visser 1984 and Woodruff 1984 for a proof and for more information on the fixed points of υ_M.

[49] The proof of this fact may be omitted without loss of continuity.

$\downarrow$	
t	**f**
f	**f**
n	**t**

For mnemonic value rather than as a philosophical point, we might read $\downarrow A$ as saying that A is neither true nor false.

We define in the usual way the notion of semantic value, $\text{Val}^+_{\mathscr{M},s}(X)$, and the jump operation, μ^+_M, for the extended language (see Definitions 2A.4 and 2B.8). Clearly, μ^+_M is not monotone; however, as we will now show, it has fixed points.

2E.1   Theorem   (Fixed points in nonmonotonically extended μ)   In all ground models M, μ^+_M has at least one fixed point.[50]

Proof   The following property of the Extended Weak Kleene language is crucial to the proof: The class of sentences that are neither true nor false in a standard model is determined entirely by the range of application of the predicates. It does not depend on how the range of application is carved up into extension and anti-extension. Furthermore, this class remains the same even if we give a strongly deviant (e.g., non-truth-functional) semantics for $\downarrow$. The only condition is that no formula of the form $\downarrow A$ be evaluated as **n**. Let us make this idea a little more precise.

We define a deviant notion of semantic value, $\text{Val}^*_{\mathscr{M},s}$, by following the standard definition (cf. Definition 2A.4) in all respects except one: We let the value of a formula of the form $\downarrow A$ be determined by an arbitrarily chosen *stipulation* N, where N is a function whose range is included in $\{\mathbf{t}, \mathbf{f}\}$ and whose domain is the set of pairs of formulas and assignments. The clause for $\downarrow A$, then, is

$$\text{Val}^*_{\mathscr{M},s}(\downarrow A, N) = N(A, s).$$

The fundamental relationship between the deviant and the standard notion of semantic value is transparent enough:

(1)   If for all formulas B we have $\text{Val}^+_{\mathscr{M},s}(B) = \mathbf{n}$ iff $N(B, s) = \mathbf{t}$, then
$\text{Val}^+_{\mathscr{M},s}(A) = \text{Val}^*_{\mathscr{M},s}(A, N)$.

---

[50] The theorem was stated but not proved in Gupta and Martin 1984, though it can be proved using the technique introduced there. The proof below proceeds along somewhat different lines.

Let $\mu^*_{M,N}$ be the deviant jump rule defined on the basis of $\text{Val}^*_{\mathscr{A},s}(A, N)$. And let us say, for f, $g \in D3$, that f is **n-equivalent** to g (f $\approx$ g) iff, for all $d \in D$, $f(d) = \mathbf{n}$ iff $g(d) = \mathbf{n}$. It can be shown that if f $\approx$ g then, for all stipulations N, formulas A, and assignments s,

(2) $\text{Val}^+_{M+f,s}(A) = \mathbf{n}$ iff $\text{Val}^+_{M+g,s}(A) = \mathbf{n}$
$\qquad\qquad$ iff $\text{Val}^*_{M+f,s}(A, N) = \mathbf{n}$.

Hence, it follows that if f $\approx$ g then for all stipulations N and N'

(3) $\mu^+_M(f) \approx \mu^+_M(g) \approx \mu^*_{M,N}(f) \approx \mu^*_{M,N'}(f)$.

Note that $\mu^*_{M,N}$ is monotone and, consequently, has fixed points. It is possible, however, that none of these are fixed points of μ^+_M. The problem is that N may not give the right information about what is neither true nor false relative to any fixed point of $\mu^*_{M,N}$. Fortunately, there is a way of solving this problem. The idea is this: Using the least fixed point, say f, of $\mu^*_{M,N}$, we construct a new stipulation N' so that

(4) $N'(A, s) = \begin{cases} \mathbf{t} \text{ iff } \text{Val}^*_{M+f,s}(A, N) = \mathbf{n} \\ \mathbf{f} \text{ otherwise.} \end{cases}$

Since $\mu^*_{M,N'}$ is monotone, it also has fixed points. For some of these fixed points the problem mentioned above may well arise again, but in virtue of the special properties of the Extended Weak Kleene scheme we can show that there is at least one fixed point for which the problem does not arise.

Let X be the set of functions g such that

(i) g is sound for $\mu^*_{M,N'}$; i.e., g $\leq \mu^*_{M,N'}(g)$

and

(ii) there is an h such that h is sound for $\mu^*_{M,N}$ and g $\approx$ h and h $\leq$ f.

We show first (a) that X has maximal elements (relative to $\leq$) and (b) that X is closed under $\mu^*_{M,N'}$.

(a) X has maximal elements: Consider an arbitrary chain $C \subseteq X$. We claim that its supremum $\bigvee C \in X$. It is easy to see that $\bigvee C$ satisfies condition (i). We need only show that condition (ii) is also met. Define

$C' = \{h\colon h$ is sound for $\mu^*_{M,N}$ and h $\leq$ f and there is a $g \in C$ such that
$\qquad\qquad\qquad\qquad\qquad\qquad\qquad\qquad\qquad\qquad\qquad g \approx h\}$.

It is routine to verify that $\bigvee C'$ meets all the conditions on h in (ii). Hence, by Zorn's Lemma, X has maximal elements.

(b) X is closed under $\mu_{M,N'}^*$: If $g \in X$, then $\mu_{M,N'}^*(g)$ must be sound since g is. This takes care of (i). For (ii), let h be a function such that h is sound for $\mu_{M,N}^*$ and $g \approx h$ and $h \leq f$. Then it can be verified that $\mu_{M,N}^*(h)$ is sound for $\mu_{M,N}^*$ and $\mu_{M,N'}^*(g) \approx \mu_{M,N}^*(h)$ and $\mu_{M,N}^*(h) \leq f$. (For the middle conjunct we appeal to (3).) Consequently, (ii) holds for $\mu_{M,N'}^*(g)$.

Let g be a maximal element of X. By definition of X,

$$g \leq \mu_{M,N'}^*(g).$$

Since X is closed under $\mu_{M,N'}^*$,

$$\mu_{M,N'}^*(g) \in X.$$

As g is maximal, it cannot be strictly less than $\mu_{M,N'}^*(g)$. Hence,

$$g = \mu_{M,N'}^*(g).$$

That is, g is a fixed point of $\mu_{M,N'}^*$. We now show that it is also a fixed point of μ_M^+. First we establish that $f \approx g$.

Since $g \in X$, we know by condition (ii) on the definition of X, that there is an h such that h is sound for $\mu_{M,N}^*$ and $g \approx h$ and $h \leq f$. Since g is a fixed point of $\mu_{M,N'}^*$, we conclude in virtue of (3) that

$$h \approx g = \mu_{M,N'}^*(g) \approx \mu_{M,N}^*(h).$$

This together with the soundness of h yields

$$h = \mu_{M,N}^*(h).$$

As f is the least fixed point of $\mu_{M,N}^*$, we conclude that $f = h$, and thus that $f \approx g$.

The n-equivalence of f and g entitles us to the following:

$$Val_{M+g,s}^+(A) = \mathbf{n} \text{ iff } Val_{M+f,s}^+(A) = \mathbf{n} \qquad\qquad \text{[by (2)]}$$

$$\text{iff } Val_{M+f,s}^*(A, N) = \mathbf{n} \qquad\qquad \text{[by (2)]}$$

$$\text{iff } N'(A, s) = \mathbf{t} \qquad\qquad \text{[by definition of N']}$$

We now appeal to (1) to deduce that for all formulas A

$$Val_{M+g,s}^+(A) = Val_{M+g,s}^*(A, N').$$

As g is a fixed point of $\mu_{M,N'}^*$, it is also a fixed point of μ_M^+.   ∎

3 Fixed Points and the Signification of Truth

The discovery of fixed points has created a new hope of gaining a semantic understanding of the concept of truth. Fixed points yield languages that contain their own truth predicates—predicates that agree perfectly with what, on semantic reflection, is found to be true (and what false) in the language. These predicates conform to the demands of Convention T:[1] They satisfy the Tarski biconditionals, and their signification is completely determined by the biconditionals.[2] Where earlier theories had seen only incoherence, inconsistency, and ambiguity in the concept of truth, the fixed-point approach promises natural and attractive models. The hope is inevitable that the semantic interpretation of our ordinary notion of truth takes the form of a fixed point. This hope will be critically examined in this chapter. It will be argued that fixed points are correct interpretations of truth not in general but only under very special conditions—conditions that can intuitively be characterized as those in which there is no vicious reference in the language.

3A The Proper Interpretation of Fixed Points

Let us begin by observing a curious feature of fixed points. In *any* fixed-point language $\mathscr{L}_g$ $(=\langle L, M + g, \rho \rangle)$ the predicate G is coextensive with truth, yet sometimes these languages are possible *only if G does not mean truth*. Similarly, although the Signification Thesis holds for *any* fixed-point language, sometimes this is so precisely because the T-predicate does not *mean* truth.[3] Let us clarify these claims through an example.

Consider a classical language $\mathscr{L}_{g_1}$ $(=\langle L, M + g_1, \tau \rangle$; g_1 a fixed point of τ_M) in which there is no vicious reference except that a name b denotes the sentence Gb. Suppose that the ground model M of L is a quantificational enrichment of a reference list R defined on $\{b\}$ so that $R(b) = Gb$. It is easily verified that τ_R has exactly two fixed points. Hence, by the Transfer Theorem, the jump for the quantificational enrichment M, τ_M, also has two fixed points—say g_1 and g_2. In one of these, say g_1, the sentence Gb is true; in the other, g_2, it is false.

The language $\mathscr{L}_{g_1}$ is clearly possible. We can coherently imagine a world w inhabited by a community $\mathscr{C}$ whose language L has the syntax repre-

---

[1] More precisely, the Signification Thesis (see p. 31).
[2] As will become clear below.
[3] This claim will be discussed in section 3C.

sented by L. We can imagine further that the meanings of L's logical constants are given by the usual classical rules, and that the meanings of the nonlogical constants are such that their extensions in w are as represented in the model $M + g_1$. In short, we can coherently imagine that extensional information about L is correctly represented by $\mathscr{L}_{g_1}$.[4] Since g_1 is a fixed point of τ_M, G is coextensive with the concept "true in L." We want to claim, however, that G in L cannot mean "true sentence of L."

From now on it will prove useful to say that a predicate is a *truth predicate* for a language L iff it *means* "true in L." In contrast, a predicate is a T-predicate for L iff it is coextensive with truth for L. "Truth predicate" is an intentional notion: We cannot in general determine whether an expression is a truth predicate for L without examining its meaning in L. "T-predicate," on the other hand, is an extensional notion: Extensional information about L is sufficient to determine whether a predicate is a T-predicate for the language.[5] Our claim, then, is that in the situation imagined above, although G is a T-predicate for the community's language, it cannot be its truth predicate.[6]

Compare two hypotheses concerning the meaning of G in L. On the first hypothesis, it expresses the concept "is a sentence that the computer XYZ is programmed to produce." This hypothesis is consistent with the story narrated above; we need only imagine that in w (the world the community inhabits) the computer XYZ is programmed to produce all and only the

---

[4] For some purposes the language L can be identified with $\mathscr{L}_{g_1}$. However, for our purposes here it is crucial to distinguish between them. Intentional aspects of L will be of crucial importance in our argument, whereas the set-theoretic construct $\mathscr{L}_{g_1}$ ignores these completely.

In our terminology, L ranges, as before, over languages construed syntactically. More precisely, it ranges over a set-theoretic construct that carries syntactic information about the language. $\mathscr{L}$ ranges, again as before, over constructs that carry extensional information about the language. Denotations of names, extensions of predicates, etc., can be recovered from $\mathscr{L}$, but not from L. Finally, L ranges over languages construed intentionally (i.e., over constructs that carry information about what the names, predicates, and function symbols of the language mean); L does not carry extensional information about the language.

[5] We mean to restrict ourselves to languages of the sort we introduced in section 2A. We are ignoring modal and other nonextensional languages.

The fact that we have, following common practice, called set-theoretic constructs such as $\mathscr{L}_g$ 'languages' may create the impression that the notion "truth predicate for $\mathscr{L}_g$" makes sense. But it does not, for $\mathscr{L}_g$ does not represent the meanings of the constants, only extensions. Note, however, that it does make sense to speak of "T-predicate for $\mathscr{L}_g$," as this requires only extensional information.

[6] The first argument given below for this claim is a revised version of one we gave in "A note on extension, intension, and truth" (1987). Another argument will be given in section 3C.

true sentences of $\mathscr{L}_{g_1}$.[7] Since g_1 is a fixed point of τ_M, G ends up being coextensive with "true in L."[8] Compare this coherent hypothesis with a second according to which G means "true in L." With this hypothesis it is not clear that the signification of G should be g_1, and consequently it is not clear that this hypothesis coheres with our earlier story.

Before arguing that the hypothesis does not cohere with the earlier story, we note a puzzle that it creates: On the first hypothesis the sentence Gb says of itself that it is a sentence that the computer XYZ is programmed to produce, and it is true in w because in w the computer is indeed programmed to produce Gb. There is no mystery as to why Gb is a true sentence of the language. On the second hypothesis Gb says of itself that it is true and, thus, is like the Truth Teller in English: "This very sentence is true." We can—in some sense of 'can'—say that the Truth Teller is true, and we can also say that it is not true. But there is little to choose between these options. Both are equally arbitrary. On the hypothesis that G expresses truth, we then have this puzzle: How is it that the Truth Teller is true and not false in L? What facts about the community's language and the world the community inhabits make the Truth Teller true? This puzzle, we hope, encourages some skepticism about the coherence of the second hypothesis. It does not *prove* that the hypothesis is incoherent. We now argue that the hypothesis conflicts with a basic feature of truth, a feature we call *the supervenience of the signification of truth*. It is related to, but distinct from, Ramsey's Redundancy Theory of Truth.

It has often been remarked that the sentence "'snow is white' is true" says nothing more nor less than the sentence 'snow is white'—that 'is true' is eliminable from and redundant in the first sentence. Whether this observation can be extended to all sentences depends on the logical resources of the language. If the language has propositional variables and quantifiers, then the redundancy thesis could well be true. But if such quantification is not available and the language has ordinary first-order quantifiers, the redundancy claim cannot hold for all the occurrences of 'true'. Nevertheless, even here the following kind of redundancy does obtain: *To evaluate the sentences of a first-order language that contains its own truth predicate*

---

[7] The reader may worry that the truths of $\mathscr{L}_{g_1}$ may not be r.e. The worry can be removed by assuming that the ground model M is simple. One extreme possibility here is that there are no nonlogical constants in the language aside from G.

[8] In his autumn 1982 seminar on Truth, which Gupta attended, Kripke discussed similar examples containing empirical predicates with fixed-point interpretations.

one does not need the semantic interpretation of the truth predicate. For example, suppose we wish to determine the semantic status of a sentence such as

(1) $(\forall x)(Fx \to Gx)$.

Suppose we are given the domain of quantification and the extension of F. Suppose also that F is true of only one object in the domain: the sentence Hd. Now, to determine the semantic status of (1) we would need to know the extension of G in the language. This is so *except* when G is a truth predicate for the language. In this case the status of (1) is entirely determined by the interpretations of F, H, and d. More generally, the point is that if a first-order extensional language contains a truth predicate G for itself, then the status of all the sentences of the language is entirely determined by the interpretation (more precisely, the extensional signification) of the G-free part. The signification of G, whatever it be, supervenes upon the signification of the G-free part.[9] We are calling this feature "the supervenience of the signification of truth".[10] In reference to the community $\mathscr{C}$ imagined earlier, this feature implies that if G is a truth predicate for L then its signification is fixed by that of the G-free part, i.e., by the ground model M.[11]

[9] This idea was built into the very formulation of the problem of truth and paradox in chapter 1. See p. 32.

[10] In section III of "Truth and paradox" it was called "the reducibility of truth." Michael Kremer suggested to us the appropriateness of the term 'supervenience'. The suggestion is valuable, for it underlines the similarities of the claim made here to others familiar from the philosophy of mind and the philosophy of social sciences. We have only one qualm about using Kremer's terminology: The notion of supervenience in these other areas has never been clearly explained, and all attempts at an explanation have run into difficulties. (A good survey of these attempts can be found in Teller 1983.) The chief difficulty appears to be this: The claim of supervenience of (e.g.) the mental over the physical is that if the physical facts are the same then so also *must* be the mental facts. The difficulty arises over the force of the 'must'. It is not easy to specify precisely what range of possible situations is meant to be covered by this modality. We wish to emphasize that such difficulties do not arise for the thesis put forward above. If G is a truth predicate, then its signification is fixed by the interpretation of the G-free part in *all* possible situations. More formally, its signification is a function of the ground model M. This holds even though occurrences of the truth predicate are not eliminable from the language.

[11] The supervenience described above is a special case of a much more general feature of truth. Suppose that $L_1, ..., L_n$ are languages that contain truth predicates for each other. (One extreme possibility here is that they form the bottom part of a Tarski hierarchy. At another extreme, each may contain truth predicates for all the others.) Then, to determine the semantic status of the sentences of $L_1, ..., L_n$, one does not need the significations of the truth predicates. These are redundant once the interpretations of the other constants of $L_1, ..., L_n$ are fixed.

Supervenience does not hold, in general, of T-predicates, but only of truth predicates.

Let us suppose, for *reductio*, that our second hypothesis is coherent—that there is a possible situation w_1 in which G means truth in the community's language L and in which the significations of L's constants are given by $M + g_1$. Now, if w_1 is a possible situation, then so also must be a situation w_2 in which G means truth but in which the significations of the constants are given by $M + g_2$. (Recall that g_1 and g_2 are the fixed points of τ_M.) The two situations envisaged are exactly parallel. The only difference between them is that in one the Truth Teller turns out to be true and in the other it turns out to be false. Neither of these consequences is any worse than the other. However, the supervenience feature discussed above is inconsistent with the thesis that both the situations w_1 and w_2 are possible. The G-free part of the language has the same interpretation in w_1 and w_2; it is as given in the ground model M. Supervenience now yields that the significations of the truth predicate in w_1 and w_2 must be the same.[12] But they are not. We conclude that the supervenience of truth and the symmetry of w_1 and w_2 imply that neither of the situations is possible.

Two objections to this argument deserve to be considered before we proceed any further. First, it may be objected that w_1 and w_2 are possible on the grounds that the community $\mathscr{C}$ may stipulate in w_1 (w_2) that the Truth Teller is true (false).[13] This objection grants the validity of our argument but denies its major premiss: supervenience.[14] For if w_1 and w_2 are possible then the supervenience claim must be false. The second objection also grants the validity of the argument but questions the remaining premiss: the symmetry of w_1 and w_2. It may be argued that the Truth Teller is false.[15] And if it is false then the symmetry assumption is incorrect.

Our response to the first objection is that it begs the question by supposing that the community can coherently stipulate the truth value of the Truth Teller.[16] It is possible for the community to adopt various linguistic

---

[12] Supervenience of G, as we understand it, implies that if the constants of the language mean the same in worlds w and w' and if the significations of the G-free parts are also the same in w and w' then so also are the significations of G.

[13] Woodruff suggested this objection. He does not necessarily endorse it.

[14] Kremer (1986, 1989) offers an objection to supervenience, but it appears to us to be flawed. The objection is overcome once it is noted that supervenience holds only for truth predicates and not, as already remarked, for T-predicates.

[15] This idea has found advocates in the literature. The idea that the Truth Teller is true has not, as far as we know.

[16] And does so in an objectionable way. We insert this qualification for those readers who think, following John Stuart Mill, that all good arguments are circular and, thus, beg the question.

conventions and stipulations that force the *sentence Gb* to be (say) true, but it does not follow that in virtue of these stipulations the *Truth Teller* is true. This would follow only if it could be shown that *G* expresses truth in the language—something that is at issue here. It seems to us that if the community were to make special stipulations that force *Gb* to be true then *G* would not express the same concept as that expressed by our word 'true', for then the rules governing *G* in the community's language would not be the same as the rules governing our word 'true'. We can grant that *G* may express a concept very like truth, and it may even serve many of the functions that the concept of truth serves in our language;[17] still *G* would not express our ordinary notion of truth. Analogously, a predicate that is not at all vague cannot express the concept expressed by our word 'red'. It might express a concept very like "red," but it would not be identical to "red." The very precision of the concept is an argument against the identity.[18]

In response to the second objection we note that our original claim— that w_1 is impossible—must be granted by anyone who denies symmetry and holds that the Truth Teller is false. Supervenience implies that if the interpretation of the *G*-free part of the language is given by M and if *G* is a truth predicate, then its signification must be given by g_2. As the signification of *G* in w_1 is g_1, it follows that *G* is not a truth predicate in w_1.

By similar reasoning, if it is held that the Truth Teller is true, then w_2 is not a possible situation. Hence, even if symmetry be denied, it must be admitted that one of w_1 and w_2 is not possible. The role of symmetry in our argument is minimal. It allows us to assert that *both* w_1 and w_2 are impossible.[19] It is not needed to establish the existence of the phenomenon claimed earlier: *Even though any fixed-point language contains a T-predicate G for itself, sometimes these languages are possible only if G does not mean truth.*[20]

---

[17] Actually, the apparent similarity of the two concepts is due to the simplicity of the situation imagined. In a more realistic situation the community would need to stipulate truth values for an infinity of sentences that are like the Truth Teller (including the contingent Truth Tellers) and the sentences that depend upon them. These stipulations are bound to be complicated. In addition, it can be doubted whether the resulting concept would be adequate for the functions served by our notion of truth. Certainly it will not share the simplicity (and the beauty) of our notion.

[18] We do not mean to suggest by this analogy that the notion of truth is vague with respect to the Truth Teller.

[19] The argument given in section 3C for this claim does not rely on symmetry.

[20] This conclusion appears to be inconsistent with the opening paragraph of Martin and Woodruff 1975.

The example given above shows that, even within an extensional perspective, "T-predicate" and "truth predicate" invoke different procedures, different points of view. To determine whether G is a T-predicate, we take the signification of G *as given* and using that signification we see whether G is coextensive with truth. If it is, then G is a T-predicate; otherwise it is not. But when we entertain the hypothesis that G is a truth predicate, no interpretation of G is taken as given (because of the supervenience feature). We determine which sentences are true and which sentences are not true on the basis of the G-free part alone. Sometimes the two ways of proceeding give the same result. Sometimes, as in the example constructed above, they do not. It is this that gives rise to fixed-point languages that are possible only if G does not mean truth.

The proper intuitive meaning of a fixed point is this: We know that if g is a fixed point of ρ_M then G is a T-predicate for $\mathscr{L}_g$ ($= \langle L, M + g, \rho \rangle$). What this means is that *if* $M + g$ gives the significations of the constants of the language—in particular, *if* the signification of G is given by g—then G will be a T-predicate for the language. It does not follow from this that if G had *meant* truth then its signification would be g. Sometimes, as we have seen above, G can have this signification only if it does not mean truth. The fact that fixed points invariably yield T-predicates does not mean that they are always acceptable interpretations of truth predicates.

3B Expressive Incompleteness and Hierarchies

A theory of truth, if it is to preserve the property of supervenience, must specify a unique interpretation for truth for each collection of nonsemantic facts. One fundamental decision facing the theory concerns the *form* that this interpretation should take. The seminal work of Kripke, Martin, and Woodruff has shown that one attractive option is provided by the fixed points of the various three- and four-valued schemes. Many theories are possible within this general framework. But none of these authors commits himself to any particular theory. Even their commitment to the general framework of fixed points can be doubted. Kripke prefaced his presentation of fixed-point theories as follows: "I do not regard any proposal, including the one to be advanced here, as definitive in the sense that it gives *the* interpretation of the ordinary use of 'true'...."[21] However,

---

[21] Kripke 1975, p. 63. We are unclear on the reference of Kripke's phrase 'the one to be

most if not all commentators have read these works as recommending the general framework.[22] In any case, the framework is sufficiently plausible and interesting to warrant close examination.

At least from an abstract point of view, a proper infinity of fixed-point theories is possible. Any arbitrary function that assigns to each ground model a unique fixed point represents a possible theory. Even if we ignore the more implausible of these, many theories remain—each exhibiting its own distinctive virtues. A full assessment of fixed-point theories is a large undertaking. It requires us to decide, in the first place, whether the pathological sentences such as the Liar and the Truth Teller should be seen as generating truth-value gaps or truth-value gluts (i.e., whether these sentences should be regarded as neither true nor false or both true and false). After the settling of this issue we would need to assess the comparative merits of the various schemes for handling the gaps (or the gluts, or both) and the comparative merits of the various fixed points. For the sake of conciseness we forgo this type of detailed investigation.[23] Instead we shall discuss in this and the next section some common problems that confront all fixed-point theories. The principal problem to be discussed in this section is connected to the phenomenon of expressive incompleteness of fixed-point languages. We begin with a brief review of some basic facts concerning this phenomenon.

Consider the Tarski biconditionals for, say, a Strong Kleene language L whose interpretation is given by a fixed-point structure $\mathscr{L}_g$ ($= \langle L, \mathrm{M} + \mathrm{g}, \kappa \rangle$). We notice that the biconditionals of the form

(1) $G(`A') \leftrightarrow A$

are not always true in L. The reason is that by the definition of $\leftrightarrow$,

$$A \leftrightarrow B =_{\mathrm{Df}} (A \ \& \ B) \vee (\sim A \ \& \ \sim B),$$

advanced here'. Does it refer to the particular theory—the least fixed point of the Strong Kleene scheme—presented in the most detail by him, or does it refer to the general framework of fixed-point theories? How far Kripke's agnosticism extends depends partly on how we answer this question.

[22] See, for example, Hawthorn 1983, Hellman 1985, and Visser 1989. This reading, it seems to us, is natural and justified. Martin and Woodruff (1975, p. 47) take the existence of fixed points to show that a language can express its own truth-*concept*. Kripke (1975, note 29) talks of the least fixed point as an interpretation that is "natural in many respect."

[23] See, however, Gupta 1982, Hawthorn 1983, and Hellman 1985 for criticisms of some important fixed-point theories—in particular, of theories that interpret truth via the least fixed point or the largest intrinsic fixed point of μ, κ, or the supervaluational schemes.

the value of $(A \leftrightarrow B)$ is **n** if both A and B are **n**. Hence, if A is neither true nor false, then G must be neither true nor false of A (since the interpretation of G is a fixed point). Consequently, (1) is also neither true nor false. This shows not that there is a problem with the Tarski biconditionals but that the 'iff' in them is not to be read as $\leftrightarrow$. How else can it be read? Since we are concerned with the weak notion of truth in a three-valued language, one plausible reading of the 'iff' is via the Łukasiewicz biconditional $\equiv$, whose semantics is as follows:[24]

$\equiv$	t	f	n
t	t	f	n
f	f	t	n
n	n	n	t

Note that $(\mathbf{n} \equiv \mathbf{n}) = \mathbf{t}$. So the problem mentioned for $\leftrightarrow$ does not arise with $\equiv$: Fixed-point interpretations make the Tarski biconditionals true on the Łukasiewicz reading of the 'iff'. Note also that $(\mathbf{t} \equiv \mathbf{f}) = \mathbf{f}$. Hence $\equiv$ is not monotonic. Since all connectives definable in the Weak and Strong Kleene schemes are monotonic, it follows that $\equiv$ is definable in neither scheme. Similarly, the four-valued analogue of the Łukasiewicz biconditional (for which $\mathbf{b} \equiv \mathbf{b} = \mathbf{t}$ holds) is not definable in v. Hence, the Tarski biconditionals cannot be formulated in any of the three- and four-valued languages introduced above.[25] This lack of expressive power is not accidental:

3B.1 Theorem Any three-valued scheme ρ that contains the connective $\equiv$ does not have the fixed-point property: Ground models M can be found for which the jump ρ_M does not have any fixed points.

Proof Choose a model M so that there is

(i) a sentence A that is false in M,

(ii) a name b that denotes $(A \equiv Gb)$,

(iii) a name c that denotes $(Gb \equiv Gc)$.

---

[24] There is one other plausible truth-functional reading of the 'iff'. By this reading, $(v \text{ iff } v') = \mathbf{t}$ if $v = v'$; $(v \text{ iff } v') = \mathbf{f}$ otherwise. The arguments given below go through on this reading also.
[25] That this holds also for the Extended Weak Kleene scheme of section 2E is a consequence of the next theorem.

Suppose, for *reductio*, that ρ_M has a fixed point g. Then *Gb* must have the value **n** in it, for *Gb* is Liar-like. A contradiction can now be deduced from any hypothesis concerning the value of *Gc* in g: If it is **t** or **f** then $(Gb \equiv Gc)$ is evaluated as **n** and so *Gc* must be **n** in g; if it is **n** then $(Gb \equiv Gc)$ is evaluated as **t** and so *Gc* must be **t** in g.   ■

3B.2   Corollary   A three-valued scheme whose only connective is $\equiv$ fails to have the fixed-point property.

A similar argument shows that a scheme that has *exclusion negation* $\bar{A}$ will also fail to have the fixed-point property. The semantics for exclusion negation is as follows:

A	$\bar{A}$
t	f
f	t
n	t

Note that exclusion negation $\bar{A}$ is just like *choice* negation $\sim A$ except that, whereas $\sim\mathbf{n} = \mathbf{n}$, $\bar{\mathbf{n}} = \mathbf{t}$.

A parallel claim holds for the four-valued schemes. The analogues of $\equiv$ and $\bar{A}$ are not expressible in any four-valued scheme with the fixed-point property. More generally, *any* n-valued scheme, if it has the fixed-point property, is bound to be *logically incomplete* in the sense that some n-valued truth function will not be expressible in it. From this viewpoint, the failure of the classical scheme to have the fixed-point property is to be explained by its *logical richness*, i.e., by the fact that all two-valued truth functions are expressible in it. Three- and four-valued languages that are logically rich also fail to have the property. And, if we allow the weakening of logical resources, then, in parallel to the three- and four-valued cases, two-valued schemes can be found that have the fixed-point property.

3B.3   Theorem   The positive fragment of the classical scheme, whose logical resources consist of $=$, &, $\vee$, $\forall$, and $\exists$, has the fixed-point property.[26]

Proof   Let M $(= \langle D, I \rangle)$ be a ground model and let τ_M^+ be the jump for the positive fragment (Definition 2B.8). It can be shown that τ_M^+ is monotone under the following ordering of $\{t, f\}^D$:

---

[26] We are unclear who should receive the credit for this theorem: Fitch? Myhill? Gilmore?

$f \leq g$ iff, for all $d \in D$, $f(d) = t$ implies that $g(d) = t$.

That is, τ_M^+ is a monotone operation on $\langle \{t, f\}^D, \leq \rangle = \langle \{t, f\}, \leq \rangle^D$, where the truth values are ordered thus:

t

●

|

|

●

f

But $\langle \{t, f\}, \leq \rangle$ is a complete lattice. Hence so also is $\langle \{t, f\}, \leq \rangle^D$ (Theorem 2C.4(ii)). By Tarski's Fixed Point Theorem (2C.9), τ_M^+ has a fixed point.   ∎

Irrespective of whether we consider classical or nonclassical schemes, then, only logically incomplete schemes have the fixed-point property. Notice another related phenomenon: Consider a scheme ρ that has the fixed-point property. Languages based on ρ can contain their own T-predicates, i.e., predicates that are extensionally equivalent to the *weak* notion of truth. It can be shown, however, that there are related semantical notions that these languages cannot contain. Thus, the positive fragment of the classical scheme cannot contain its own falsity predicate;[27] the Strong Kleene scheme cannot—but the Weak scheme can—contain its own "neither true nor false" predicate;[28] and neither scheme can contain a predicate for its own "strong truth," i.e., a predicate that is true of all the truths and false of all the rest. Further, no syntactically rich three-valued language (even if it has no connectives or quantifiers at all) can contain its own "strong-falsity" predicate, i.e., a predicate that is true of the false sentences and false of all the rest. All these claims of indefinability, and others like them, can be established by means of variants of the Liar argument. Illustration: The argument for the last indefinability claim is this. Suppose F is a strong-falsity predicate. Then a sentence that says "I

[27] When we say that a scheme ρ cannot contain a semantic concept C we mean that languages based on the scheme ρ cannot always contain a predicate extensionally equivalent to C. More precisely still, we mean that the jump operation for C relative to ρ (defined in the manner of Definition 2B.8) does not always have a fixed point.

[28] This was first observed by John Hawthorn (1983). See also McCarthy 1985 for some indefinability results for the Strong Kleene languages.

am F" can have none of the values **t**, **f**, and **n**. For, if it has the value **f** then since F is a strong-falsity predicate its value should be **t**; similarly, if it has the value **t** or **n** then its value should be **f**.

There are many versions of the Liar argument, but their fundamental lesson is the same. They show that there is a problem when the combination

Logical richness + Syntactic richness + Semantic richness

is present in a language. It is intuitively obvious that the problem will not arise if the power of the language is suitably weakened in any of the three dimensions: logical, syntactic, and semantic. The definability theorems we have seen capture this intuitive point in a formal way. Different ways of blocking the construction of the Liar sentence yield different types of definability theorems, just as different ways of constructing it yield different types of indefinability theorems.

The most direct way of blocking the construction of Liar sentences is to restrict the syntactic resources of the language. Corresponding to this way is one type of definability theorem. We have seen an instance of this type in chapter 2: A syntactically weak classical language can contain its own T-predicate (Example 2D.5). Another example: It can be shown that a Strong Kleene language, if it is syntactically weak, can contain both its T-predicate and its "neither true nor false" predicate. A second type of definability theorem is obtained by limiting the logical resources of the language. In this category fall the theorems of Kripke, Martin, and Woodruff (and also Theorem 3B.3). Here, too, the resources for formulating the problem sentences are absent. To be sure, one can formulate, for any predicate G, a self-referential sentence that says "I am not G." But here 'not' must be read as expressing choice negation (*not* exclusion negation), and G can stand only for the weak notion of truth (*not* the strong one). There are appearances of the Liar here, but they deceive. The third and final type of definability theorem arises by weakening the semantic resources of the language, and also by weakening the conditions on semantic concepts. For example, it can be shown that even syntactically and logically rich classical languages can have predicates that are like truth. These predicates do not satisfy all the Tarski biconditionals, but they satisfy a great many.[29]

---

[29] There are indefinability results of this type also. The best known is Richard Montague's (1963) result that a syntactically rich classical language contains no predicate that satisfies

In summary: If predicates of a language are interpreted in the traditional way (i.e., as two-, or three-, or n-valued), then some combinations of logical, syntactic, and semantic richness are possible and some are not. The definability and indefinability theorems we have seen are a few signposts that serve to demarcate the realm of the possible combinations from that of the impossible ones. One qualification on these theorems deserves to be stressed: They all concern *languages whose predicates have traditional semantics.*

Before we discuss some of the problems facing fixed-point theories, we would like to make a few preliminary remarks.

(i) Our concern is exclusively with the *descriptive* problem posed by the paradoxes, and it is from *this* viewpoint that we shall criticize fixed-point theories. Consequently, the problems to be raised—even if they prove to be devastating, which we doubt they will—do not touch the relevance and importance of these theories for the *normative* problem raised by the paradoxes, i.e., the problem of designing paradox-free languages.

(ii) A fixed-point theory, as we understand the term, respects the supervenience of truth. It specifies a scheme ρ, and for each ground model M it specifies a unique fixed point of ρ_M as the interpretation of truth in M. Since this is a common reading of fixed-point theories, and since supervenience seems to us to be a feature of truth, we feel justified in reading fixed-point theories in this way. Still, the possibility remains open that other theories of truth can be built using fixed points. The criticisms to be made will not necessarily apply to these alternative theories.

(iii) We shall return to the fixed-point theories on several occasions below (especially in the final section of chapter 4). The remarks in the present section should not be taken to be our final word on the topic. Later discussions and our positive views may help clarify the worries expressed here.

The first problem we wish to discuss concerns the notion of implication yielded by fixed-point theories. Given a fixed-point theory $\mathscr{F}$, let $\mathscr{F}_M$ be the interpretation of truth in M according to $\mathscr{F}$. A natural explanation of "implies in $\mathscr{F}$," then, is as follows. (It is modeled on Definition 2A.15.)

---

conditions considerably weaker than the Tarski biconditionals. No arithmetical predicate, for example, satisfies the syntactic analogues of the theorems of the modal system T. For further results along these lines see Thomason 1980 and McGee 1985. Friedman and Sheard 1987 is a particularly thorough and valuable study.

3B.4 Definition   Let Γ be a set of sentences and A any sentence. Then Γ *implies A according to the fixed-point theory* $\mathscr{F}$ (symbolically, $\Gamma \models^{\mathscr{F}} A$) iff, for all languages L whose sentences include A and the members of Γ and all ground models M for L,

(i) A has the value **t** in $\mathscr{F}_M$ if all members of Γ have the value **t** in $\mathscr{F}_M$

and

(ii) some member of Γ has the value **f** in $\mathscr{F}_M$ if A has the value **f** in $\mathscr{F}_M$.[30]

It is a pleasant feature of fixed-point theories that they validate the inferences

$A \models^{\mathscr{F}}$ 'A' is true

and

'A' is true $\models^{\mathscr{F}} A$.[31]

In some other respects, however, the notion of implication they yield is at once too narrow and too broad. It is too narrow because the theory is forced to depart from the classical scheme τ (as τ does not have the fixed-point property) and to postulate truth-value gaps or gluts (or both) for the pathological sentences. As a result, it is bound to invalidate some of the classical laws (see Example 2A.16).[32] The notion is also too broad,

---

[30] Kremer (1986, 1989) has observed that if the notion of implication is defined for a fixed language L then compactness will not hold. This is our motivation for quantifying over all languages in the above definition. There are other ways of getting around the problem (Kremer 1986, 1989).

[31] We are assuming here (and below) that the quotational names 'A' have their standard interpretations in all models. Thus, the intuitive notion that "$\models^{\mathscr{F}}$" is meant to represent is that of "implication in virtue the meanings of 'true' and of the quotational names."

[32] Kripke (1975, note 18, pp. 64–65) expresses impatience with such objections: "I have been amazed to hear my use of the Kleene valuation compared occasionally to the proposals of those who favor abandoning standard logic "for quantum mechanics".... Nor should it be said that "classical logic" does not generally hold.... *If* certain sentences express propositions, any tautological truth function of them expresses a true proposition.... [C]onventions for handling sentences that do not express propositions are not in any philosophically significant sense "changes in logic".

In response to this, observe first that the implication relation, even between sentences that *do* express propositions, is not the same as the classical one. The classically valid implication "snow is white, therefore what Jones said is either true or untrue" fails even though the conclusion may express a proposition (it may be grounded). Second, insofar as the theory of truth is directed toward the descriptive problem, it should preserve (as far as possible) our ordinary ways of reasoning with sentences containing 'true', *including* pathological ones. Therefore, the observation that a theory does not accord with our ordinary ways of reason-for it results in implication relationships between various pathological sentences—relationships that are highly counterintuitive. For example, if $\mathscr{F}$ interprets truth via the least (or the largest intrinsic) fixed point of the Strong Kleene scheme, then a Truth Teller implies a Liar sentence:

$a =$ 'a is true', $b =$ 'b is not true', a is true $\models^{\mathscr{F}} b$ is not true.[33,34]

This particular relationship does not hold if the theory $\mathscr{F}$ always chooses maximal fixed points in which the Truth Teller is true, but such an $\mathscr{F}$ validates the following:

$a =$ 'a is true', $b =$ 'b is not true', a is not true $\models^{\mathscr{F}} b$ is not true.

As a final example, note that both implications hold if $\mathscr{F}$ is based on the largest fixed point of v.[35]

Any theory, unless it declares the notion of truth to be inconsistent, will yield a notion of implication that deviates at least a little from our raw intuitions. The trouble with the fixed-point theories is that the notions they yield differ substantially from our intuitive judgments. Even this would not be damaging if no better theories were possible. However, theories that preserve much more of our ordinary reasoning can be constructed.[36] It is because of this that the lack of fit between the phenomena and the consequences of the fixed-point theories is a problem for them.

Another respect in which fixed-point theories seem to us to be descriptively inadequate concerns their treatment of the pathological sentences. These theories assign definite semantic values to pathological sentences; for example, some hold the Liar to have the value **n** whereas others declare its value to be **b**. This raises a problem not only because neither value seems better than the other but also because the fixed-point theories are

ing is, if correct, a legitimate objection to the theory. The exact force of the objection will depend on how far it is possible for a theory to capture our ordinary reasonings. (We agree with Kripke that the comparison to "quantum mechanics" is not an apt one and that it is inappropriate in the present context to talk of "changes in logic.")

[33] This was first observed by Kremer (1986) and Visser (1989).

[34] Problem 3B.5: Is the notion $\models^{\mathscr{F}}$ axiomatizable, where $\mathscr{F}_M =$ the least (the largest intrinsic) fixed point of κ_M?

[35] These implications may fail if $\mathscr{F}$ assigns different values to Ga (and to $\sim Gb$) in different ground models. But then the theory will violate the local determinability of truth stated in section 3C below.

[36] None of the problem inferences given above hold in the theories based on the systems $S^{\#}$ and S^{*} of section 5D.

able to assign a definite value to the Liar only by reading it in a new way—a way different from the original reading that yielded the intuition of paradoxicality. The Liar sentence, 'This sentence is not true', is intuitively paradoxical if we take the possible values for sentences to be t and f. It remains intuitively paradoxical if the possible values for the sentences are extended to include n (and b), provided that 'not' is read as exclusion negation. The fixed-point theories are forced to read the negation as choice negation, for only on this reading is it possible to assign the sentence a definite value. However, so read, it ceases to be intuitively paradoxical.[37] An adequate solution to the descriptive problem should not provide new readings for sentences; instead, it should capture and explain the behavior of sentences on their original readings. The essential thing about the Liar appears to be its instability under semantic evaluation: No matter what we hypothesize its value to be, semantic evaluation refutes our hypothesis. A theory of truth ought to capture *this* intuition. It should provide a way of distinguishing sentences that exhibit this behavior from those that do not, and it should explain *why* certain sentences behave in this way.

Kripke (1975) does provide a definition of one interesting class of pathological sentences: He defines a sentence A to be *paradoxical* under conditions M (relative to κ) iff A has the value n in all fixed points of κ_M. And it may be possible to give definitions of other types of pathological sentences along parallel lines.[38] Even if we put aside worries about the descriptive adequacy of these definitions, there is a problem here: The definitions require one to quantify over *all* fixed points of a scheme, but only one of these is assigned by the theory as the interpretation of truth.[39] We are therefore owed an account of why fixed points other than the one picked out by the theory are relevant to explaining the behavior of sentences containing 'true'.

The final problem we shall discuss arises from the phenomenon of expressive incompleteness, treated above. The problem concerns the gap

---

[37] Similarly, the addition of new values does not make it more intuitive to assign a definite status to the Truth Teller. Within a three-valued context all three values t, f, and n are possible for the Truth Teller. And it is just as arbitrary to pick one of these as its value as it is to pick one of t and f in the classical case.

[38] An example: Truth-Teller-like sentences of M (relative to κ) may be defined as those that never have the value n in a maximal fixed point and whose value is t in some fixed points and f in some others.

[39] Visser (1989) makes this point in his discussion of Kripke's iterative picture.

between the expressive power of the original language we are theorizing about and the expressive power of languages yielded by fixed-point theories. Recall the phenomenon that prompted our inquiry: that we can use the notion of truth effectively even in languages that are logically and syntactically rich. We have clear intuitions about which sentences of these languages are true (and which false) under various conditions. To be sure, there are sentences with vicious reference in them that are perplexing to us. Even here, however, we can figure out which sentences are problematic and in which ways. These intuitions are not confined to classical languages. We can add truth (and other semantic notions, e.g. "reference") to *any* language—two-, three-, or n-valued—and we can make parallel judgments about the behavior of its various sentences. It is *this* phenomenon that we are trying to understand. If our concerns were normative, we might happily trade some expressive resources for a guarantee of freedom from paradox; with the descriptive problem, however, this option is not available to us.

We want to emphasize that the problem we are raising is *not* that fixed-point theories do not yield "universal" languages (whatever these may be), nor is it that there is a gap between the resources of the object language and those of the metalanguage. (This kind of objection is sometimes lodged against fixed-point theories. We shall argue in chapter 7 that it is of little weight.) The problem we are raising is that there is a gap between the resources of the language that is the original object of investigation and those of the languages that are amenable to fixed-point techniques.[40] The problem is: How are we to bridge *this* gap?

There are two broad strategies that can be followed in response to this question:

- It can be argued that, despite appearances, natural languages are incomplete in certain specified ways—that certain sentences which appear meaningful are in fact meaningless.
- The problematic resources might be accommodated through the use of hierarchies.

---

[40] This is a particularly important problem not only for fixed-point theories as we have defined them, but also for several variant theories that might be constructed using fixed points—e.g., for those in which the signification of truth in M is taken to be the class of all the fixed points of κ_M (or μ_M or υ_M).

The two strategies are not mutually exclusive. A theory might accommodate some resources through the hierarchy approach and might explain some others away using the first approach. Nor are these strategies new. All traditional theories have relied on them. Russell's Ramified Type Theory uses the first strategy on phrases such as 'all propositions' ('all properties') that quantify unrestrictedly over the universe of propositions (properties), and it tries to accommodate, through a ramified hierarchy of variables, some uses of these expressions that it deems unproblematic.[41] A Tarskian theory uses the first strategy on certain global uses of 'true' and tries to accommodate others through a hierarchy of truth predicates (see, for instance, Burge 1979).

The fixed-point approach, if it is to offer plausible theories, will have to rely on both strategies. Exclusive reliance on the first strategy would require a fixed-point theorist to argue that although pathological sentences create gaps (or gluts, or both), certain related logical and semantic notions (e.g., the Łukasiewicz biconditional, exclusion negation, and strong truth) cannot be present in natural languages—an argument that, in our opinion, is difficult to construct. The fixed-point theorist must appeal to hierarchies to explain the richness of language.[42] This would not eliminate the need for the first strategy, but it would put less of a burden on it.

The most direct way to accommodate the missing resources, such as the Łukasiewicz biconditional and exclusion negation, is through a hierarchy of the following sort. Each language $\mathcal{L}_n$ of the hierarchy contains a new truth predicate T_n interpreted via, say, the least fixed point of κ for $\mathcal{L}_n$. To ensure that the fixed points exist, the problematic resources (such as the Łukasiewicz biconditional) must not interact with the truth predicate. This is achieved by having a hierarchy of logical notions: The Łukasiewicz biconditional of level n can only combine with truth predicates with index less than n. The resulting hierarchy is more complex than the Tarskian one, but in at least one respect it is more natural. In the Tarskian hierarchy each iteration of the truth predicate forces one to move to a higher level. Not so in the hierarchy just sketched; here the two occurrences of the truth predicate in the sentence "'snow is white' is true' is true" can be viewed as having the same level.

---

[41] See Russell 1908 and Whitehead and Russell 1910. Hazen 1983 contains a good account of Ramified Type Theory.
[42] Kripke (1975) recognizes the necessity of hierarchies and suspects that it causes problems. On page 80 he writes: "The necessity to ascend to a metalanguage may be one of the weaknesses of the present theory. The ghost of the Tarski hierarchy is still with us."

One can gain this advantage and yet avoid a hierarchy of logical notions if one is willing to interpret the predicates T_n not as truth for $\mathscr{L}_n$ (or for $\mathscr{L}_{n-1}$) but as only "truth-like" for $\mathscr{L}_n$. Burge (1979) and Parsons (1983b) have constructed a hierarchy with these features. They avoid hierarchies of logical notions by following Tarski and working with a classical language. (One could have worked equally with an expressively rich three-valued language.) Because of expressive richness, the interpretation of T_n cannot be, as in the hierarchy above, a fixed point for $\mathscr{L}_n$. Further, if automatic shifting of levels in iterations of truth is to be avoided, the interpretation of T_n cannot be, as in Tarski, the truths of $\mathscr{L}_{n-1}$. Burge and Parsons interpret T_n via the *closure* of the minimal fixed point of κ, where a closure is obtained by letting all objects that have the value **n** be in the antiextension of T_n.[43] T_n so interpreted is *like* truth for $\mathscr{L}_n$ but is not identical to it (by Tarski's Indefinability Theorem). Hierarchies using fixed points can be constructed in many other ways also.

In our view, hierarchies, whether they are constructed using fixed points or otherwise, do not provide a promising approach to the descriptive problem. Our reasons, briefly, are these: No matter how one constructs the hierarchy, one has to argue that certain sentences containing global uses of 'true' do not mean what they seem to mean. Some such sentences, it is true, can be accommodated through the use of schematic indices (i.e., Russell's [1908] distinction between 'all' and 'any'). Thus, a sentence such as 'God knows all truths' can be explained as 'every truth$_i$ is known by God', where i can have as its value any index. But one cannot get the proper reading of 'God does not know all truths'. What this sentence seems to be saying must be relegated (or elevated) to the realm of the unsayable.

The main difficulty with the approach is that it requires one to construct a *theory of levels*, a theory that would specify the level of each occurrence of the truth predicate in a sentence. Recall that our goal is to interpret a language with a truth predicate for itself, a predicate that has no indices attached to it. But a hierarchy, however constructed, provides only an interpretation for the indexed predicates T_n. To gain an interpretation of the original language, we need a theory that will tell us which T_n's correspond to which occurrences of the truth predicate in the original language.

---

[43] For a more precise account see Parsons 1983b. This type of mixing of logics produces interesting results; see Feferman 1984 and Gilmore 1974.

We need, in other words, a theory of levels. Thus, on the hierarchy approach the descriptive problem of constructing a theory of truth reduces to that of constructing a theory of levels. The main difficulty with the approach is that the theory of levels appears to be at least as difficult to construct as the theory of truth.[44] The reduction the approach offers is spurious. It does not make our task any easier.[45]

3C The Signification Thesis

We argue in this section that the Signification Thesis (p. 31) poses a problem for fixed-point theories.

Recall the example discussed in section 3A. There we imagined a world w inhabited by a community $\mathscr{C}$, extensional information about whose language L is given by the structure $\mathscr{L}_{g_1}$ ($= \langle L, M + g_1, \tau \rangle$). $\mathscr{L}_{g_1}$ was so defined that M is a quantificational enrichment of a reference list R on $\{b\}$ satisfying the condition $R(b) = Gb$, and g_1 is one of the two fixed points of τ_M (the other being g_2).

Let us examine the behavior of the Tarski biconditionals under each of the two hypotheses, discussed above, concerning the meaning of G in L. According to the first hypothesis, G means "is a sentence that the computer XYZ is programmed to produce"; according to the second it means "true sentence of L." Under the first hypothesis, the biconditional for Gb is (1).

(1)   'Gb' is a true sentence of L iff 'Gb' is a sentence that the computer XYZ is programmed to produce.[46]

Note that the biconditional does not contain 'true' or any other semantic term on the right-hand side. It fixes in a completely unproblematic way the conditions under which the sentence Gb falls under the English predicate 'true in L': It falls under the predicate in all worlds in which the

---

[44] See section 4 of Gupta 1982 for some reasons why this is so. For an attempt to construct a theory of levels, see Koons 1987.

[45] Parsons (1974b, 1983b) and Burge (1979) have argued that the level of the truth predicate is a pragmatic matter and so falls outside the domain of the semantics of truth. We are unconvinced by their argument. The interpretations of sentences containing the truth predicate do not seem to us to vary with the context of use (assuming that there are no context-sensitive elements in the ground language). See Gupta 1982 for a discussion of this point.

[46] We assume that the quotational name 'Gb' is the proper translation in English of the term b of L. The assumption is convenient but inessential to our argument.

computer XYZ is programmed to produce the marks 'Gb'; in all other worlds it does not. The Tarski biconditionals for the other sentences of L exhibit similar behavior. They determine in an unproblematic way the conditions under which the various sentences are true. Hence, the totality of the biconditionals fixes a classical signification for the predicate 'true in L'.[47] Under the first hypothesis, the Signification Thesis holds.

Compare this situation with what happens under the second hypothesis. Since by this hypothesis G means "true sentence of L," the biconditional for Gb is (2).

(2)   'Gb' is a true sentence of L iff 'Gb' is a true sentence of L.

In contrast to (1), this biconditional *does* contain 'true' on the right-hand side and says nothing substantive about the conditions under which Gb falls under the predicate 'true in L'. The biconditional is a mere tautology; its two sides are identical. The problem persists when we consider the totality of L's biconditionals. These biconditionals do not determine a unique classical signification for 'true in L'. If the facts are as in w, there are two classical significations, g_1 and g_2, that satisfy them. Since it is assumed that the signification of G in w is g_1 and since the second hypothesis takes G to mean truth, it follows that the second hypothesis implies that the Signification Thesis is false. By contraposition we conclude that the Signification Thesis implies that G cannot mean truth.

A few remarks concerning this argument:

(i) It establishes the same conclusion as the argument given in section 3A but without the premiss of symmetry. We are able to dispense with symmetry because we now rely on a premiss (the Signification Thesis) that is much stronger than the key premiss of the earlier argument (Supervenience). Supervenience puts only a very abstract constraint on the semantics of truth. It rules out the possibility that, relative to the same nonsemantic facts, truth sometimes has one signification and sometimes another. It puts no restrictions on what the signification should be. The signification can be anything. It can even make everything true, or everything false. Hence, Supervenience by itself does not imply that G in L cannot mean 'true in L'. The Signification Thesis, on the other hand, does imply this. It requires not only that the signification be a function of the nonsemantic facts but also that it be completely determined by the Tarski

---

[47] Assuming as always that nonsentences are not true.

biconditionals. It thus puts a strong constraint on what the signification of truth in a given situation can be.

(ii) The argument allows that *every* fixed point is a possible interpretation of 'true in L'. If the meaning of G is of the sort postulated in the first hypothesis then any fixed point g can be the interpretation of G and, consequently, g is a possible interpretation of the predicate 'true in L'. What the argument shows is that, for some fixed points g, 'true in L' cannot be in L itself (as that violates the Signification Thesis);[48] thus the truth predicate can only belong to a distinct metalanguage. Hence, although every fixed point is a possible interpretation of 'true in L', yet some fixed points can be interpretations of this predicate only if the predicate is not in L.[49]

(iii) The above considerations, if they are sound, yield intensional versions of indefinability theorems. The indefinability theorems of section 2B were all extensional: They established of predicates of certain kinds of classical languages that they are not *extensionally* equivalent to truth. We now see that, although certain classical languages may contain a predicate coextensive with their own truth, it can sometimes be shown that the predicate is *intensionally* nonequivalent to truth. The extensional type of indefinability theorem entitles us to conclude that a classical predicate G is not coextensive with truth if the language has, for example, Liar-like self-reference for G. The intensional type of indefinability theorem, on the other hand, entitles us to conclude that G is not intensionally equivalent to truth if the language has Truth-Teller-like self-reference for G. Both types of theorems can be seen as relying on the Signification Thesis: In both cases the signification of G is not fixed by the Tarski biconditionals. In the first case this is so because *no* classical interpretation makes the Tarski biconditionals true, and in the second case it is so because *too many* do.[50]

(iv) The argument given applies to nonclassical languages also. Let ρ be any scheme, and let the extensional information about a language L be

---

[48] Note that the Signification Thesis holds trivially if L does not contain its own truth predicate. In this case the status of the right-hand side of the Tarski biconditionals for L is completely determined by the nonsemantic facts and, hence, so also is the extension of 'true in L'. If L contains its own truth predicate, however, then the notion "true in L" will appear in the right-hand sides of the biconditionals and as a result, as we saw above, more than one extension for 'true in L' may satisfy these biconditionals.

[49] Languages of the following sort also exist: The language has two (coextensive) T-predicates for itself, yet only one of the predicates can mean truth.

[50] Assuming that the Truth Teller is the only vicious reference in the language.

given by the structure $\mathscr{L}_g (= \langle L, M + g, \rho \rangle$, g a fixed point of ρ_M). We can show as before that if ρ_M has more than one fixed point then G cannot mean truth, for if it did then, as each fixed point of ρ_M would satisfy the Tarski biconditionals for L,[51] the Signification Thesis would be violated. By contraposition we can conclude that

(3) If G is a truth predicate for a language L based on the scheme ρ then the interpretation of G relative to a ground model M can be a fixed point of ρ_M only if ρ_M has a unique fixed point.

The difficulty the Signification Thesis creates for the fixed-point theories should now be plain. No matter which scheme ρ $(= \mu, \kappa, \upsilon)$ the fixed-point theorist picks, there are bound to be ground models M in which the jump ρ_M has more than one fixed point (see Example 2D.7).[52] Hence, the interpretation the fixed-point theorist assigns to the truth predicate will violate condition (3) and, thus, will violate the Signification Thesis.

Can we evade this difficulty by shifting to another scheme? Is there a three- or four-valued scheme ρ whose jump always has a unique fixed point? If the notion of scheme is given a very general explanation, these questions may well have a positive answer. However, any such scheme would have to be very unnatural. First, ρ cannot be normal in the sense of section 2A. If it is, then the fixed points of τ_M will also be fixed points of ρ_M (see Theorem 2B.10(i)). Since there are ground models M in which τ_M has more than one fixed point, it will follow that ρ_M too will sometimes have more than one fixed point. Second, ρ cannot be monotonic, for, given any monotonic scheme ρ, one can always find ground models M in which the jump ρ_M has more than one fixed point.[53]

Can we evade the difficulty by shifting to a notion other than that of weak truth? Could it be that the argument goes through because of some peculiarity of this notion? Perhaps the difficulty does not arise for a richer notion, such as "satisfaction"? Some parts of the above argument, it is true, do not go through for "satisfaction." Logically rich languages, though they can contain their own truth predicates, cannot contain their

---

[51] We are assuming here that *if* the interpretation of truth is given by a fixed point *then* the 'iff' in the biconditionals may be read as the Łukasiewicz biconditional (or, for the four-valued semantics, something analogous).

[52] The same holds of the Extended Weak Kleene scheme of section 2E.

[53] We are assuming that predication is treated in the natural way. If so, then any model M in which there is Truth-Teller-type self-reference does the job. See Theorem 2C.6.

own satisfaction-predicates.[54] In other words, the jump for the notion of satisfaction for a logically rich language never has fixed points. However, if we weaken logical resources so that this jump does have fixed points, we find that there are conditions under which it has more than one (assuming as before that the scheme has some natural properties). So the essential difficulty posed by the Signification Thesis remains.

Can we evade the difficulty by shifting to another reading of 'iff' in the Tarski biconditionals? We have assumed in the above argument that the 'iff' may be read in the Łukasiewicz way (so $(\mathbf{n}$ iff $\mathbf{n}) = \mathbf{t}$, $(\mathbf{b}$ iff $\mathbf{b}) = \mathbf{t}$, etc.).[55] This reading seems to us to be natural and correct *once one opts for the fixed-point semantics*. Furthermore, any reading of the 'iff' that preserves the Signification Thesis on this semantics is bound to be unusual, for any such reading would have to be highly intentional. Consider two alternative fixed-point significations of truth across possible worlds. On both alternatives, the two sides of the Tarski biconditionals receive the same truth values in all the worlds. Yet, if the Signification Thesis is to be saved, only one of them can make the biconditionals true.

The problem that the Signification Thesis poses for a traditional semantics for truth and related notions can be summarized thus. If we view the interpretations of these notions as two-, three-, or n-valued and read the 'iff' in the most natural way suggested by the semantics, we have the following dilemma:

(i) If the language is rich in logical and semantic resources then there will be conditions under which no fixed points exist. Hence no possible interpretation of truth (and other notions) satisfies the biconditionals (and their analogues).

(ii) If the language is weak in logical or semantic resources then there will be conditions under which there is more than one fixed point. Hence too many interpretations of truth (and other notions) satisfy the biconditionals (and their analogues).

[54] This can be shown by applying a Grelling-type argument to the formula 'x is not satisfied by x', with 'not' read in the manner of exclusion negation. Then, this predicate is satisfied by itself iff it is not satisfied by itself.

[55] Hence, as we saw in section 3B, the biconditionals will not be expressible in the language L to which the truth predicate is added. The Signification Thesis still creates a problem, however: If the interpretation of the truth predicate in L is taken to be a fixed point, then more than one interpretation satisfies the Tarski biconditionals *as they are formulated in the metalanguage*.

In either case traditional semantics assigns interpretations that violate the Signification Thesis.

This argument, we recognize, is only as strong as one's commitment to the Signification Thesis. Some may read it as a refutation not of traditional semantics but of the Signification Thesis. The reason *we* do not read it in this way is that we think the Signification Thesis can be preserved by a natural, though nontraditional, semantics (see chapter 4). The Signification Thesis captures a basic intuition about the notion of truth: that the whole meaning (i.e., the intension) of truth is determined by the Tarski biconditionals. That this intuition be preserved was one of the two desiderata that we put on a theory of truth (p. 32). Fixed-point theories, unfortunately, fail to satisfy this desideratum. We take this failure as an argument against them.

We have argued that the interpretation of 'true in *L*' in *L* cannot *always* be a fixed point. Let us now try to isolate more precisely the conditions under which the interpretation of the truth predicate can be a fixed point, and the conditions under which it cannot. Our earlier results entitle us to the following claim for classical languages.

(4)   If *G* means truth in a language *L* then it has a classical interpretation relative to M only if τ_M has a unique fixed point.

It is tempting to strengthen (4) by reading a biconditional in place of the second conditional:

(5)   If *G* means truth in *L* then it has a classical interpretation relative to M *if* and only if τ_M has a unique fixed point.

Unfortunately, this strengthening is incorrect. There are models M for which τ_M has a unique fixed point but this fixed point is intuitively not the correct interpretation for truth.

An example: Let *L* be a language whose extensional information is given by $\mathscr{L}_g$ ($= \langle L, M + g, \tau \rangle$). Suppose that M is a quantificational enrichment of a reference list R defined on $\{a, b\}$ so that

$$R(a) = Ga$$

and

$$R(b) = (Gb \to Ga).$$

It is easily verified that τ_R has exactly one fixed point. By the Transfer Theorem, τ_M also has exactly one fixed point, say g. We want to argue that here too G cannot mean "true in L." Note that since the Tarski biconditionals for L are satisfied only by g, the claim that G means truth does not conflict with the Signification Thesis. It does conflict, however, with another property of truth, a property we shall call "local determinability."

The property of *local determinability* is easy to explain but difficult to define precisely. The intuitive idea is this: When we wish to determine the truth or falsity of a sentence, we are not necessarily required to determine the significations of *all* the names, predicates, and function symbols in the language. We need only determine the significations of a limited number of these constants. Thus, if we wish to determine the truth value of the sentence 'Jones is a good philosopher' we need only discover the denotation of 'Jones' and the extension of 'is a good philosopher'. The significations of such constants as 'is on display in' and 'the Museum of Modern Art' are entirely irrelevant. In general, a certain limited number of nonlogical constants are relevant to determining the truth or falsity of a sentence. These nonlogical constants, we say, constitute the *dependency range* of the sentence. The difficulty in giving a precise formulation of the local determinability property lies in the definition of dependency range. The dependency range of a sentence that does not contain the truth predicate is easy to define: It consists of all the nonlogical constants that occur in the sentence. Further, the dependency range of certain sentences containing 'true' is easily specified. The dependency range of the sentence '"Jones is a good philosopher" is true' is the same as the dependency range of 'Jones is a good philosopher' and consists of 'Jones' and 'is a good philosopher'. The problem arises when we come to quantified sentences such as 'every sentence in that book is true'. Intuitively, the dependency range of this sentence is a function of the sentences that are found in the book in question. If we assume that the book is very short and contains only one sentence, 'Jones is a good philosopher', then the dependency range of 'every sentence in that book is true' consists of 'is a sentence in', 'that book', 'Jones', and 'is a good philosopher'. It is difficult to frame a general definition that gives intuitively correct results in this and other similar cases. Fortunately, for our purposes here we need the notion of dependency range only for the quantifier-free fragment of the language, for which the notion not only is perfectly clear but also has an easy definition.[56]

---

[56] The notion may be defined as follows: Let A be a quantifier-free sentence, and let G be the

Local determinability of truth is a local and stronger version of super-venience. Supervenience puts a broad global constraint on the significa-tion of truth. It requires that the status of a sentence stay the same if the interpretation of *all* the nonlogical constants of the language (aside, of course, from truth) is the same. Local determinability puts a similar con-straint but in a more fine-grained way. It requires that the status of a sentence be the same if the constants in its dependency range have the same interpretation. Local determinability implies supervenience, but not conversely. Note that we can obtain in a parallel way a local version of the Signification Thesis. This version states that the status of a sentence is determined by the Tarski biconditionals for a limited number of sentences: those on which the sentence in question depends.[57] The relationships be-tween the four theses are as follows, where arrows represent implication:

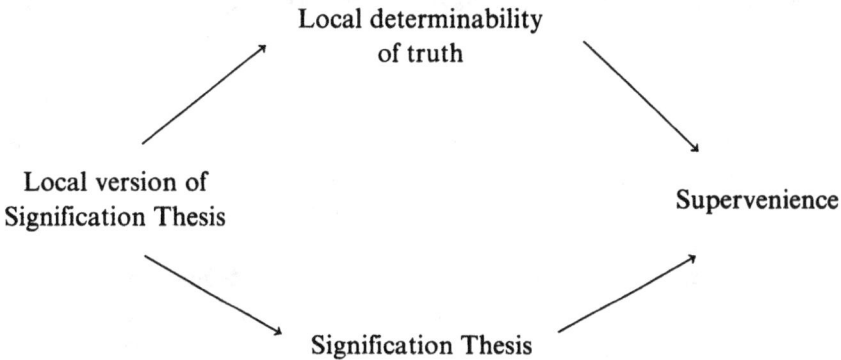

Local determinability
of truth

Local version of
Signification Thesis

Supervenience

Signification Thesis

Let us return to the example. Suppose that G means truth. Since a denotes Ga, the dependency range of Ga consists only of a. Local deter-minability requires that in any model in which the denotation of a is the same (viz., Ga) the status of Ga also be the same (viz., true). However, if we consider a model M' just like M except that in M' the denotation of b is $Gb \rightarrow \sim Ga$, we find that the classical jump again has exactly one fixed point and in it Ga is false. By symmetry, if G can mean truth in the first

truth predicate. We say that A *immediately depends on* B iff either $A = B$ or B is a sentence that is the denotation of some name c and Gc is a subformula of A. Let us define A *depends on* B to mean that A immediately depends on B or A immediately depends on some sentence that itself immediately depends on B or.... (This can be made precise via Frege's definition of the ancestral of a relation.) A nonlogical constant is in the *dependency range* of A iff it is distinct from G and occurs in some sentence on which A depends.
[57] A still more general formulation of these theses, along the lines of note 11 of section 3A, is also possible.

case, it can also mean truth in the second.[58] But this violates local determinability, for the status of Ga ends up depending on the denotation of an
irrelevant constant *b*—a constant outside the dependency range of *Ga*.[59]

Experimentation with the classical jump τ_M shows that when there is no
vicious reference in the language (relative to M) τ_M has a unique fixed
point. The example just constructed shows that the converse is not true:
Sometimes τ_M has a unique fixed point even though the language has some
types of vicious reference. This suggests the following modification of thesis (5):

(6)   If *G* means truth in *L* then its interpretation relative to a ground
      model M is the unique fixed point of τ_M iff there is no vicious
      reference in *L* under M.

The demand that this thesis puts on a theory of truth, it seems to us, is a
plausible one. It captures the intuition that if there is no vicious reference
in the language then our ordinary ways of working with the concept of
truth are unproblematic and, consequently, the interpretation of truth
should be classical. Admittedly, the thesis is vaguer than (5), for no precise
definition of vicious reference has been given and none is easily forthcom-
ing. Still the thesis is useful, since in many cases one can tell intuitively
whether a language has vicious reference or not.[60]

The example given above shows a surprising inadequacy of the Tarski
biconditionals *when they are interpreted in the usual way*, i.e., when the
'iff' is read as material equivalence. It shows that there are conditions
under which the biconditionals determine a unique extension for truth
but this extension is not correct.[61] Hence, the Tarski biconditionals
are sometimes wrong even from the *extensional* point of view. This
curious inadequacy of the biconditionals does not seem to have been
noticed before.[62]

---

[58] The symmetry assumption can be eliminated in ways parallel to those given earlier. In
particular, it is not needed if one argues from the local version of the Signification Thesis.

[59] If one attempts to satisfy local determinability by suggesting that *G* can mean truth only
in the first case but not in the second, then the second example refutes (5).

[60] Theories based on the least fixed points of the schemes μ, κ, and υ fail to satisfy (6). The
least fixed points of these schemes are never classical.

[61] This confirms the conclusion of Spade (1975).

[62] The example does not call into question the Signification Thesis. All it shows is that the
'iff' in the biconditionals may not always be read as material equivalence.

4 The Revision Theory: An Informal Sketch

The key to the proper resolution of the problem of truth and paradox lies, in our view, in the theory of definitions. The behavior of the concept of truth, both ordinary and pathological, is strikingly similar to that exhibited by certain kinds of definitions. Reflection on these definitions reveals, we believe, a key clue to the proper account of the meaning of truth. Let us begin by observing some of the similarities between the two.

Consider the definition

(1) x is $G =_{Df} x$ is F or x is both H and non-G,

where F and H are some clear and well-understood predicates. In this definition the *definiens*

x is F or x is both H and non-G

contains the *definiendum* G.[1] Hence, the definition is circular and, by traditional doctrines, illegitimate. Before we dismiss it altogether, however, let us look more closely at its behavior. Its most striking feature, and a principal reason for its traditional dismissal, is that it is *creative*: In conjunction with the usual rules of inference, it implies substantive and possibly absurd claims about F and H. Suppose, for *reductio*, that

(2) x is non-F and x is H.

Suppose further that

(3) x is G.

The traditional logical rules for definitions allow that, given a definition of the form

(4) x is $G =_{Df}$ ——— x ———,[2]

one can infer the definiens

(5) ——— x ———

from the definiendum

---

[1] Sometimes we speak of 'x is G' as the definiendum also.
[2] For simplicity we confine ourselves to definitions of one-place predicates. The points made below carry over in the most straightforward way to definitions of many-place predicates, names, and expressions of other logical categories.

(6) *x* is *G*;

and, conversely, one can infer (6) from (5). Let us call the first rule *Definiendum Elimination* (DfE), and the second *Definiendum Introduction* (DfI). Using DfE, we deduce from (3) that

x is *F* or *x* is both *H* and non-*G*.

This in conjunction with (2) implies by the rules of propositional logic that *x* is non-*G*. Thus, from the hypothesis (3) we have deduced its negation. Hence, (2) implies that

(7) *x* is non-*G*.

By propositional logic, (2) and (7) yield

x is *F* or *x* is both *H* and non-*G*.

Applying DfI to this gives

(8) *x* is *G*.

Thus, the contradictory conclusions (7) and (8) follow from (2). Hence, definition (1) allows us to prove *a priori* that all *H*'s are *F*'s. If we let *H* be "identical to itself" and *F* be "identical to the One," we can prove *a priori* the doctrine of Monism.

The reader may have noticed that this argument bears a striking resemblance to the argument in the Epimenides paradox. In the latter, as in the former, we deduce on purely logical grounds a contradiction from a contingent hypothesis. (In the Epimenides paradox, the hypothesis is that Epimenides the Cretan says "All Cretans are liars" and all other Cretan utterances are false.) The role played in the former argument by the rules DfI and DfE is played in the latter by the rules *Truth Introduction* (TI) and *Truth Elimination* (TE).

$$\frac{A}{\text{'}A\text{' is true}} \text{ TI} \qquad \frac{\text{'}A\text{' is true}}{A} \text{ TE}$$

There is another way of bringing out the similarities between the two cases. Let us view the rules for truth, TI and TE, as procedures for determining whether a sentence is true or not. To determine the status of '*A* is true' they direct us to determine the status of *A*; to determine the status of

'A is not true' they direct us to not-A. These "reductions" can be represented diagrammatically as follows:

'A' is true   'A' is not true

$\downarrow$ $\downarrow$

A not-A

The rules for definitions, DfI and DfE, can similarly be viewed as procedures for determining whether an object is G:

t is G t is not G

$\downarrow$ $\downarrow$

——t——   not [——t——]

Suppose we try to determine of an object (say a) which is both non-F and H whether it is G. Definition (1) directs us to determine whether a is F or a is both H and non-G. Since a is known to be non-F and H, the problem reduces to determining whether a is non-G. So:

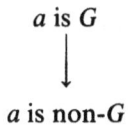

a is G

$\downarrow$

a is non-G

But when we apply the procedure to 'a is non-G', we are directed to determine whether

not [a is F or a is both H and non-G].

Again, since a is non-F and H, this holds if and only if a is G. So:

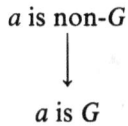

a is non-G

$\downarrow$

a is G

We thus enter an unending loop: 'a is G' reduces to 'a is non-G', and this in turn reduces back to 'a is G'. The same kind of thing happens with the Epimenides sentence: To determine whether it is true, the rules direct us to first determine whether it is not true; and they reduce the second task in turn to the first. In both cases we obtain the parallel patterns displayed below. (Here E denotes the Epimenides sentence.)

a is G	E is true
↓	↓
a is non-G	E is not true
↓	↓
a is G	E is true
↓	↓
a is non-G	E is not true
⋮	⋮

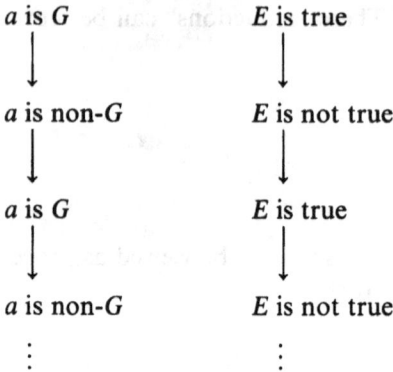

Definition (1) does not exhibit any Truth-Teller-like phenomenon.[3] Definitions that do are easy to construct, however. If we change the clause 'x is non-G' in the definiens of (1) to 'x is G', then 'a is G' behaves like a Truth-Teller on all objects a that are both non-F and H. To determine the status of 'a is G' we are led by the rules back to the very same starting point: 'a is G'. The "reduction sequence" for 'a is G' and that for 'TT is true' (here TT is the Truth-Teller) are exactly parallel and look like this:

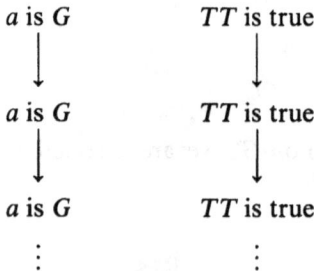

a is G	TT is true
↓	↓
a is G	TT is true
↓	↓
a is G	TT is true
⋮	⋮

Notice that the new definition does not exhibit any Liar-like phenomenon. Definitions that exhibit both kinds of pathologicality do, however, exist; (9) is an example.

(9) x is G $=_{\text{Df}}$ either (x is F and H) or (x is F and non-H and G) or (x is non-F and H and non-G).

By this definition 'a is G' behaves like a Truth-Teller if a is both F and non-H. It behaves like the Liar if a is non-F and H. These examples and others like them lend support to the thesis that *every kind of pathological*

[3] That is, the kind exhibited by sentences such as "This very sentence is true."

behavior that the concept of truth exhibits can be mirrored in concepts with
circular definitions.

The similarities between concepts with circular definitions and the concept of truth are not confined to the pathological. Much as the rules for
truth imply that 'true' is unproblematic over a range of sentences, the rules
for definitions imply that a circular concept G is unproblematic over a
range of objects. Suppose we want to determine whether an object b is G
in the sense of (9). Rules for definitions direct us to determine whether

(10) either (b is F and H) or (b is F and non-H and G) or (b is non-F
      and H and non-G).

If b is F and H, then (10) holds and we can conclude unproblematically
that b is G. On the other hand, if b is neither F nor H then (10) fails to hold
and we can conclude that b is not G. So by definition (10) G is unproblematic over objects that are either both F and H or neither F nor H. (Note
that by definition (1) G is unproblematic over objects that are either F or
non-H.)

Concepts with circular definitions, then, behave in ways that are remarkably similar to the behavior of the concept of truth. They exhibit the
same kinds of pathological behavior as truth. And like truth, they can be,
and usually are, unproblematic over a range of cases.[4] These similarities
suggest, first, that the outright rejection of circular definitions in logic may
be too precipitous, for their behavior is very much like that of a concept
the use of which we *do* accept and *want* to accept. Perhaps a more general
logic of definitions is possible that will show us how to make sense of, and
work with, circular definitions. Second, the similarities suggest that the
perplexing behavior of the concept of truth might be explainable as arising
from some circularity in its definition. Our aim in this essay is to argue
that these suggestions are more than mere possibilities, that they are close
to actuality.[5] The logics of circular definitions and of truth, in our view,
illuminate and support one another.

---

[4] The parallelism between the two extends further. The theoretical moves that have been
made in response to the pathological behavior of truth can all be made with respect to
circular concepts. For example: (i) One can put forward an Inconsistency View of such
concepts. (ii) One can argue that pathological sentences containing circular predicates do not
express propositions. (iii) One can attempt to develop a Hierarchy View by which each
circular predicate is viewed as systematically ambiguous. (iv) One can opt for a three- or
four-valued approach and interpret these predicates via various fixed-points.... In fact, the
entire history of the Liar paradox can be mimicked in the context of circular definitions.
[5] It is not our aim, however, to argue that all strictures against circular definitions must be

II

Let us see whether a logical theory of definitions can be constructed that would do justice to both the occasional pathologicality and the content of circular definitions. Such a theory should try to specify

- the meaning that definitions, circular ones included, ascribe to their respective definienda

and

- logical rules for working with definitions.

Let us begin with the first of these tasks.

Let us accept the natural idea that a definition fixes completely the meaning of its definiendum. Our problem is to say how we should think of this *meaning*. As far as noncircular definitions are concerned, there is no difficulty if we accept the traditional account. The meaning of a predicate, by this account, is a rule that gives the extension of the predicate in all possible situations. Or, equivalently, the meaning determines the conditions for the predicate's applicability. For example, the meaning of 'red', by the traditional account, is a rule that determines the conditions under which an object counts as red. Now, a noncircular definition enables us to calculate the extension of the definiendum once we are given the extensions of the terms in the definiens.[6] Hence, by the traditional account of meaning, it explains the meaning of the definiendum on the basis of the meanings of the terms in the definiens. There is a problem with the traditional account, however, if we want to preserve the idea that a circular definition *also* fixes the meaning of its definiendum. A circular definition does not in general enable us to determine the extension of its definiendum. Like all definitions, it does provide a rule for determining this extension, once the extensions of *all* the terms in the definiens are given. The problem is that, as the definiendum occurs in the definiens, to apply this rule we need to know the very thing we are trying to determine, namely

relaxed. In certain contexts it may well be advisable to avoid circular definitions, for these definitions are more difficult to work with than the noncircular ones, and it is easy to fall into error and paradox in their use. This does not mean that circular definitions are logically illegitimate. Nor that they are not the proper tool if we aim at a *description* of some of our ordinary concepts.

[6] Here and below we assume for simplicity that the definition is formulated in an extensional two-valued language. Parallel things can be said for definitions formulated in other languages.

the extension of the definiendum. To capture the meaning that a circular definition ascribes to its definiendum, we need to think of meaning in a different way.

A circular definition, though it may not determine the extension of the definiendum, does provide a rule that can be used to calculate what the extension should be *once we make a hypothesis concerning the extension of the definiendum.* This is the key, in our view, to the problem of meaning before us. The meaning a circular definition ascribes to its definiendum, we wish to suggest, should be viewed as having a *hypothetical* character. It does not determine the conditions of applicability of the definiendum absolutely, but only hypothetically. We cannot pick a set and say that it is the extension of the definiendum. We can say only that it should be the extension *if* such-and-such other set is supposed to be the extension. Let us clarify this idea through an example.

Consider again definition (9):

(9) x is G $=_{Df}$ either (x is F and H) or (x is F and non-H and G) or (x is non-F and H and non-G).

Suppose that the relevant facts are as follows. We shall call this collection of facts 'M'.

(11)   The set of objects in the universe or the domain of discourse (more briefly, D) = $\{\mathbf{a}, \mathbf{b}, \mathbf{c}, \mathbf{d}\}$;

the extension or interpretation of F (more briefly, I(F)) = $\{\mathbf{a}, \mathbf{b}\}$;

I(H) = $\{\mathbf{a}, \mathbf{c}\}$; I($a$) = $\mathbf{a}$; I(b) = $\mathbf{b}$; I(c) = $\mathbf{c}$; I(d) = $\mathbf{d}$.

We can determine the extension of G on the basis of (9) *if* we are given the extensions of all the terms in the definiens. The difficulty (as we noted above) is that since G occurs in the definiens, we already need to know the extension of G in order to determine the extension of G. Suppose, however, that we make an arbitrary hypothesis concerning the extension of G. Suppose, for example, that

(12)   I(G) = $\varnothing$.

We can now apply definition (9) to determine which objects fall in the extension of G, relative to our hypothesis. We need only determine which objects satisfy the following definiens:

Either (x is F and H) or (x is F and non-H and G) or (x is non-F and H and non-G).

It can be verified that these are $\mathbf{a}$ and $\mathbf{c}$. Hence, if we suppose the extension of G to be $\emptyset$, then the definition dictates that the extension of G should be $\{\mathbf{a}, \mathbf{c}\}$. Another example: If we suppose that the extension of G is the universe D, then the extension of G is calculated to be $\{\mathbf{a}, \mathbf{b}\}$. Similar calculations can be done for all possible hypotheses concerning the extension of G.

Definition (9) thus determines a function $\delta_{D,M}$ that takes as input a hypothetical extension X for G and yields as output $\delta_{D,M}(X)$, the set the definition declares as the resulting extension of G.[7] In the above example the function $\delta_{D,M}$ is very simple. It is fully specified by the following rules:

If $\mathbf{b} \in X$ and $\mathbf{c} \in X$ then $\delta_{D,M}(X) = \{\mathbf{a}, \mathbf{b}\}$.

If $\mathbf{b} \in X$ and $\mathbf{c} \notin X$ then $\delta_{D,M}(X) = \{\mathbf{a}, \mathbf{b}, \mathbf{c}\}$.

If $\mathbf{b} \notin X$ and $\mathbf{c} \in X$ then $\delta_{D,M}(X) = \{\mathbf{a}\}$.

If $\mathbf{b} \notin X$ and $\mathbf{c} \notin X$ then $\delta_{D,M}(X) = \{\mathbf{a}, \mathbf{c}\}$.

Observe that

$\mathbf{c} \in X$ iff $\mathbf{c} \notin \delta_{D,M}(X)$.

Hence, for all inputs X,

$\delta_{D,M}(X) \neq X;$

i.e., no X is a fixed point of $\delta_{D,M}$.[8] No matter what we hypothesize the extension of G to be, our calculation reveals that it should be different. So definition (9) does not yield an extension for G. But it does yield a function, $\delta_{D,M}$, that tells us "extension under various hypotheses." This function, we want to suggest, captures the key semantical information about G. It is the basis on which the behavior of G, both ordinary and pathological, can be understood.

Even though a circular definition ascribes to its definiendum a meaning with a hypothetical character, still this meaning can enable us to make

---

[7] The function $\delta_{D,M}$ depends not only on the facts M but also on the definition D given for G. D in our example is (9).

[8] An object x is a *fixed point* of a function f iff f(x) = x (Definition 2B.9).

categorical judgments in some cases. For example, if under all possible hypotheses a definition yields that an object falls under the definiendum G, then the definition implies categorically that the object is G. Thus, definition (9) implies that $\mathbf{a}$ is G in the situation M. The main problem before us is to state precisely *how the transition from the merely hypothetical to the categorical is to be made*. We shall consider several ways of solving this problem in chapter 5. Here we sketch one that, though flawed, is simple and motivates some key ideas. We call the resulting semantical system S_0.

A central idea in our approach is to view the function $\delta_{D,M}$ that is supplied by a circular definition D as a *rule of revision*. Its application to a hypothetical extension X results in a set $\delta_{D,M}(X)$ that is a *better candidate for the extension of G, according to the definition, than X*.[9] Repeated applications of $\delta_{D,M}$ result in a sequence of better and better candidates for the extension of G. To determine what categorical judgments can be made we should look at such sequences. Define

$$\delta_{D,M}^0(X) = X$$

and

$$\delta_{D,M}^{n+1}(X) = \delta_{D,M}(\delta_{D,M}^n(X)).$$

Example: If D is the definition (9), M is as given in (11), and X is $\varnothing$, then the repeated applications of $\delta_{D,M}$ yield the following sequence of revisions:

$$\delta_{D,M}^0(X) = \varnothing,$$

$$\delta_{D,M}^1(X) = \{\mathbf{a}, \mathbf{c}\},$$

$$\delta_{D,M}^2(X) = \{\mathbf{a}\},$$

$$\delta_{D,M}^3(X) = \{\mathbf{a}, \mathbf{c}\},$$

$$\delta_{D,M}^4(X) = \{\mathbf{a}\},$$

$$\vdots$$

If X is the universe $\{\mathbf{a}, \mathbf{b}, \mathbf{c}, \mathbf{d}\}$, then we obtain this revision sequence:

$$\delta_{D,M}^0(X) = \{\mathbf{a}, \mathbf{b}, \mathbf{c}, \mathbf{d}\},$$

$$\delta_{D,M}^1(X) = \{\mathbf{a}, \mathbf{b}\},$$

---

[9] Or, at least, it is as good a candidate as X. Henceforth, we shall omit this qualification; 'better than' should be understood as meaning "better than or at least as good as."

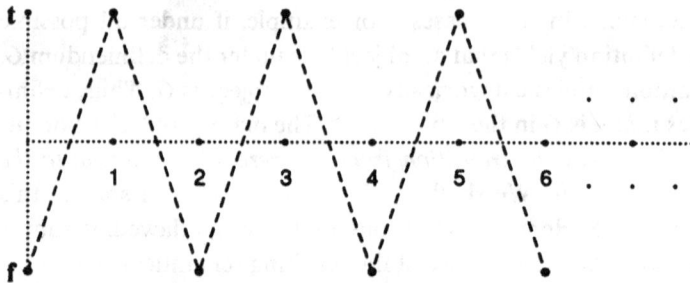

Figure 4.1

$$\delta_{D,M}^2(X) = \{a, b, c\},$$

$$\delta_{D,M}^3(X) = \{a, b\},$$

$$\delta_{D,M}^4(X) = \{a, b, c\},$$

$$\vdots$$

Let $M + X$ be the situation M together with the hypothesis that the extension of G is X. We shall say that a sentence is *true* (respectively, *false*) in $M + X$ iff it is true (respectively, false) in M relative to the hypothesis that the extension of G is X. Examples: The sentence 'a is G' is false in $M + \varnothing$, but true in $M + \delta_{D,M}^n(\varnothing)$, for all $n > 0$. The sentence

a is H but c is G [$= C$, say]

is true in $M + \delta_{D,M}^n(\varnothing)$ if n is odd, and false if n is even. The behavior of C in the revision sequence generated by $\varnothing$ can be pictured as in figure 4.1. (In this picture the stages of revision are plotted along the x axis and the truth value of C along the y axis.) In the same way, we can determine the behavior of C relative to all other hypotheses. A little reflection reveals that the revision pattern for C will always be either as in figure 4.1 or as in figure 4.2, depending on whether c does not or does belongs to the initial extension assigned to G. A sentence that behaves in this way—i.e., one whose truth value oscillates in the revision sequence generated by *each* hypothesis—is said to be *paradoxical in* S_0.

Contrast the behavior of C with that of 'a is G'. This latter sentence may be false at the initial stage of revision but is true at all later stages *irrespective of the initial hypothesis of revision*. Such a sentence is *categorically*

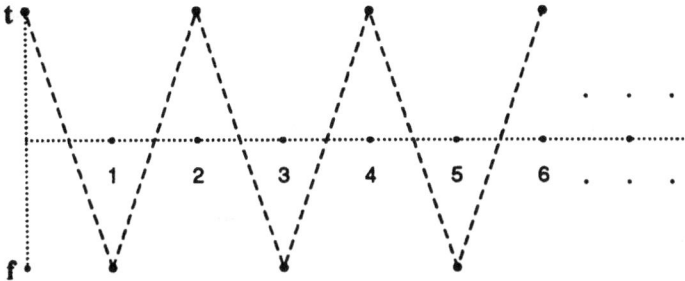

Figure 4.2

assertible (or, in the technical terminology we shall adopt, *valid in* S_0). The precise definition of this important notion is as follows:

(13) A sentence A is *valid in* M (*relative to* the definition D *in* the system S_0) iff there is a natural number p such that, for all $q \geq p$ and all subsets X of the universe, A is true in $M + \delta^q_{D,M}(X)$.[10] We say that A is *categorical in* M iff either A or its negation is valid in M; A is *pathological in* M iff it is not categorical in M.

A is valid in M, then, if its semantic evaluation displays in the revision process a pattern of the kind shown in figure 4.3. Observe the following equivalence. The definition of validity we will adopt in section 5A will be based on it.

(14) A is valid in M relative to D in S_0 iff there is a natural number p such that, for all subsets X of the universe, A is true in $M + \delta^p_{D,M}(X)$.

Let us see how the above distinctions work in the context of a richer example. Let D be the following definition:

(15) x is $G =_{Df}$ (x is F and every object y such that yRx is G) or (x is non-F
      and H and non-G).

Suppose the facts M are now as follows:

---

[10] A variant notion of validity deserves to be noted. Its definition is the same as that just given except that the quantifier 'all subsets X' has wider scope. More precisely: A is valid in this sense iff for all subsets X of the universe there is a natural number p such that, for all $q \geq p$, A is true in $M + \delta^q_{D,M}(X)$. This variant notion gives us a larger class of validities. We do not know whether the resulting logic is axiomatizable.

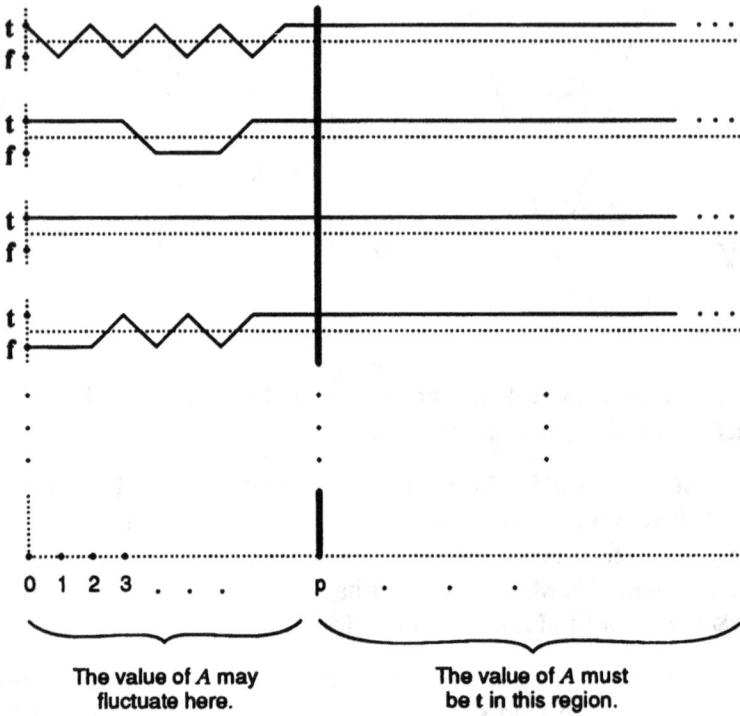

Figure 4.3

$D = A \cup B \cup \{c, d\}$, where

$\quad A = \{a_0, a_1, a_2, \ldots, a_i, \ldots\}$

$\quad B = \{b_0, b_1, b_2, \ldots, b_i, \ldots\}$;

$I(F) = A \cup \{c\}$;

$I(H) = \{d\}$;

$I(R) = \{\langle x, y \rangle : (x = y = c) \text{ or } (x = a_i \text{ and } y = a_j \text{ and } i < j)\}$;

$I(a_i) = a_i$; $I(b) = b_2$; $I(c) = c$; $I(d) = d$.

It can be verified that now the rule of revision $\delta_{D,M}$ has the following properties:

$\mathbf{a}_i \in \delta_{D,M}(X)$ iff, for all $j < i$, $\mathbf{a}_j \in X$.

$\mathbf{b}_i \notin \delta_{D,M}(X)$.

$\mathbf{c} \in \delta_{D,M}(X)$ iff $\mathbf{c} \in X$.

$\mathbf{d} \in \delta_{D,M}(X)$ iff $\mathbf{d} \notin X$.

Calculation shows that, for any i, 'a_i is G' is valid, since after the ith stage of revision the sentence is always true. After the first stage of revision 'b is G' is false. Hence it and its negation are categorical. The sentences 'c is G' and 'd is G' are pathological. The truth value of the latter invariably oscillates in the revision process. Hence it counts as paradoxical. The former behaves like the Truth Teller. If **c** is hypothesized as falling in the extension of G, then the truth value of 'c is G' stabilizes as true; otherwise it stabilizes as false.

The system S_0 will be studied in sections 5A and 5B. We shall see that it does not provide a fully satisfactory account of circular definitions. Its principal flaw is that it attributes to circular definitions much too weak a content (see Example 5A.17).[11] This flaw can be removed, as we shall see in sections 5C and 5D, by considering transfinite applications of the revision rule. Although the later developments will make the theory technically more complex, the fundamental semantical ideas will remain the same. These ideas can be summarized as follows.

A circular definition is to be viewed as attributing to its definiendum G a meaning with a hypothetical character. It does not give the conditions for G's applicability absolutely, only hypothetically. It does not give a rule of application for G; it gives only a rule of revision—a rule that, applied to a hypothetical extension, gives a better candidate for the extension of G. The transition from the hypothetical to the categorical is made by considering the sequences of revisions that are generated through repeated applications (possibly transfinite) of the revision rule to all hypotheses. In this transition lies the source of the definiendum's behavior, both ordinary and pathological. In the ordinary cases the revision rule results in the same determinate judgments irrespective of the hypothesis we consider. In the pathological cases this fails to happen for a variety of reasons. And this variety corresponds to the variety of pathological behavior.

---

[11] Some may also regard S_0 as too strong in one respect. (See Example 5A.19.)

III

Let us now turn to the second of our two tasks: to try to specify the logical rules governing definitions. A good place to begin is with modifications of DfI and DfE. The modifications are necessary because, as we saw at the outset, DfI and DfE yield contradictions when applied to certain circular definitions; our goal, however, is to develop a logical theory on which all circular definitions count as legitimate. How, then, should DfI and DfE be modified? The semantical scheme sketched above suggests a natural answer. We notice that if the definiens,

$A(x, G)$,

holds of an object x at a revision stage i, then the definiendum,

x is G,

holds at the revision stage i + 1. Similarly, if the definiendum holds at i + 1, then the definiens must hold at i. This suggests that when applying DfI and DfE we should keep track of the stages of revision. This can be done by associating an integer index (positive or negative) with each step in a derivation. Application of a rule for definitions will result in a conclusion with an index one above or one below that of the premiss. The modified versions of DfI and DfE are as follows:

$$\frac{A(t, G)^i}{[t \text{ is } G]^{(i+1)}} \text{ DfI}_r \qquad \frac{[t \text{ is } G]^i}{A(t, G)^{(i-1)}} \text{ DfE}_r.$$

Note that stages are indicated by integer superscripts on formulas.

The logical rules for the connectives are classical with the proviso that their application requires that the premisses and the conclusion have the same indices. This reflects the semantical idea that at each stage i of revision the definiendum has a classical extension and, hence, classical logic can be used to infer what holds at i. Thus, in order for *modus ponens* to be applied, the two premisses A and 'if A then B' must have the same index i, and the conclusion deduced will also have the index i. To prove 'if A then B' with index i by *Conditional Proof*, we need to prove B^i from the hypothesis A^i. The calculus has only one special rule, *Index Shift*, that allows arbitrary shifting of the index of a formula so long as there are no occurrences of the definiendum G in it. This is motivated by the fact that the truth value of a *G*-free sentence remains the same throughout the revision process. Let C_0 be the logical calculus whose rules are

DfI$_r$ + DfE$_r$ + Index Shift + Classical Logic.

(A fuller statement can be found in section 5B.) A sentence *A* is *deducible in C_0 from a definition D* iff a derivation of A^0 can be constructed in C_0 from *D*. Since the correctness of a derivation is preserved under uniform shifting of indices, if A^i can be deduced for one index i then it can be deduced for any index i.

We give one simple example of a derivation in C_0. Consider again definition (1):

x is *G* =$_{Df}$ *x* is *F* or *x* is both *H* and non-*G*.

We can prove from it that all *F*'s are *G*'s:

(i)	$(x \text{ is } F)^0$	[Supposition]
(ii)	$(x \text{ is } F)^{-1}$	[Index Shift, (i)]
(iii)	$(x \text{ is } F \text{ or } x \text{ is both } H \text{ and non-}G)^{-1}$	[Propositional Logic, (ii)]
(iv)	$(x \text{ is } G)^0$	[DfI$_r$, (iii)]
(v)	$(\text{if } x \text{ is } F \text{ then it is } G)^0$	[Conditional Proof, (i)–(iv)]
(vi)	$(\text{all } F\text{'s are } G\text{'s})^0$	[Universal Generalization, (v)]

By the revision scheme given above, 'all *F*'s are *G*'s' is categorically assertible under all conditions M; hence, the implication holds from the semantical viewpoint also. On the other hand, since 'all *H*'s are *F*'s' is not so assertible, the definition does not semantically imply 'all *H*'s are *F*'s' Nor can this sentence be derived in C_0. Its earlier proof on the basis of DfI and DfE does not go through because of the presence of indices. (In particular, if we hypothesize (2) with index 0 and (3) with index 1 then we can prove the negation of (3) not with index 1 but with index 0. As a result the derivation of (7) from (2) breaks down.)

The calculus C_0 will be studied in chapter 5. Here we briefly note some of its more important properties. First, the calculus can be shown to be sound and complete with respect to the semantics given above. See section 5B for a sketch of the proof. Second, as a consequence of the soundness of the calculus, circular definitions are not creative in C_0; and as a consequence of completeness, they are not barren either. The definitions are not creative in the sense that they do not enable us to prove essentially new things (i.e., new things that do not involve the definienda). They are not barren in the sense that at least some claims about the definienda can be established. Third, the indices employed in the calculus are important only in the context of *hypothetical* reasoning. Within categorical contexts, they can be dispensed with; one can work with DfI and DfE unmodified. This is a consequence of the fact that a uniform shifting of indices preserves the correctness of derivations. Fourth, the indices are dispensable in all contexts if the definition in question is noncircular. This is a consequence of Index Shift, which allows the following derivation to be constructed:

(i) $(t \text{ is } G)^i$ [Supposition]

(ii) $A(t, G)^{i-1}$ [DfE_r, (i)]

(iii) $A(t, G)^{j-1}$ [Index Shift, (ii)]

(iv) $(t \text{ is } G)^j$ [DfI_r, (iii)]

Hence, if the definition is noncircular, indices on 't is G' can be shifted arbitrarily. It can be shown by induction that the same holds of all formulas. Thus, with noncircular definitions the indices do no work; they can be eliminated.

Traditional doctrine imposes two requirements on definitions: *noncreativity* and *eliminability*. According to the first requirement, essentially new things should not be provable through the use of definitions. According to the second, the definienda should always be, in principle, eliminable: For every statement containing the definienda, one should be able to produce an equivalent statement not containing them. The two requirements, it seems to us, are not of equal status (at least on certain sorts of definitions). The requirement of noncreativity ensures that definitions only fix meanings and do not conceal substantive assertions. Noncreativity is undoubtedly correct as a requirement on "pure" definitions, the only kind with which we are concerned. It would be strange indeed if one could prove the doctrine of Monism, say, from a definition of some irrelevant predicate G. Noncreativity is respected by all definitions, circular and noncircular, if they are used according to the rules sketched above. The requirement of eliminability, on the other hand, has nothing to do with the "purity" of definitions. It is *not* implied by the idea that definitions only fix meanings and do not involve substantive assertions. On the semantical theory given above, definitions only fix meanings of their definienda, but eliminability does not hold. Eliminability, we believe, is best viewed not as an absolute requirement but as a relative one, one that can be met in varying degrees. The degree of eliminability required of a definition depends upon the context in which the definition is used.[12]

The theory of definitions put forward here entails a few changes in our general conception of definitions, but it leaves our ordinary ways of working with noncircular definitions as they are. We can use DfI and DfE unmodified in the context of such definitions. And we can assign definite extensions to their definienda.[13] By accepting the logical theory proposed above, we do not lose anything; we can work with noncircular definitions in the usual way. But we do gain something: We can make sense of definitions that previously had to be ruled illegitimate.

The theory in its present formulation is admittedly much too simple to be entirely satisfactory. On two points especially improvements are needed. First, one would want to attribute greater content to circular definitions than that attributed so far. Second, one would want to allow systems of mutually interdependent definitions—i.e., systems in which a concept G, for example, is defined using $F, H, \ldots$, and F in turn is defined using $G, H, \ldots$. We believe that these improvements can be made (see chapter 5), though the resulting theory is necessarily more complex.

We hope that the simple theory sketched above, even though it is not completely satisfactory, succeeds in showing that logical and semantical frameworks in which circular definitions make sense are *possible*. The fact that these definitions are ruled illegitimate by traditional logic and semantics may be read as an argument not against the former but against the latter. Whether it should be so read depends on these important questions: (i) Are circular concepts useful in any way? (ii) Are any of our ordinary concepts circular? We want to answer both questions affirmatively. Concerning question (i): We shall show in section 5D that circular definitions increase the expressive power of the language (see Example 5D.19). Concerning question (ii): We want to argue—as the reader undoubtedly expects—that truth is a circular concept. This will be the principal goal of

---

[12] Another way of bringing out differences between the two requirements is this: To the extent that a candidate definition is creative, it goes beyond defining into stating. We may wish to accept speech acts that are mixed in that respect, but we should label them as mixed and not as merely definitions. To the extent that a candidate definition does not permit total eliminability, it is not doing all that we might have hoped. It is defective *in this respect*, but it is nonetheless a definition.

[13] This is so because the conditions of applicability of a definiendum G in a noncircular definition do not depend on any prior hypothetical extension for G. Hence, the rule of revision is a constant function and entitles one to speak of *the* extension of the definiendum.

the remainder of this chapter. Before we turn to this, we need to take care of some preliminary matters.

When a definition is put forward not as a stipulation but as a description of a preexisting concept, we can evaluate it from any one of three standards of adequacy: extensional equivalence, intensional equivalence, and cognitive synonymy. This point is familiar for noncircular definitions. What must be noted is that it also holds for circular ones. Imagine a situation M in which a community introduces a predicate G stipulatively through the following definition:

(16)   x is $G =_{Df}$ (x is F) or (a is G and $x = b$) or (x is non-F and H and non-G).

Imagine further that a linguist visits the community and, after some research, puts forward a definition that is just like the above except that in place of F it has an intensionally nonequivalent predicate, J. If F and J have the same extension in M, the linguist's definition will yield the same rule of revision in M as the original one, so the definition will be extensionally correct. But it will not be intensionally correct, since there will be possible situations in which the two definitions yield rules that differ in important ways. We can construct similarly examples in which a proposed circular definition is intensionally correct but fails to meet the stricter standard of cognitive synonymy.

For circular definitions, but not for noncircular ones, different grades of extensional and intensional equivalence can be distinguished. A definition may fail to be extensionally correct in the sense that it may not give the same rule of revision as the original stipulation. But it may be correct from a coarser extensional point of view. The definition may yield a rule of revision whose behavior is "essentially" the same as that yielded by the original stipulation. An example will clarify the point. Imagine a case like the one discussed above but in which a is F. Now the definition

(17)   x is $G =_{Df}$ (x is F or $x = b$) or (x is non-F and H and non-G)

yields a rule of revision different from that yielded by (16); the two rules assign different values to $\emptyset$. But despite this difference, their behavior is very similar. After the first application they generate identical revision sequences. Hence, they yield the same ordinary judgments and the same pathologies. By imposing weaker or stronger conditions on when revision rules count as being "essentially" the same, we obtain different grades of extensional adequacy. The highest grade demands that the revision rules be identical. The lowest grade settles for identity of classification into ordinary, paradoxical, etc. Numerous intermediate grades are possible.

A peculiar kind of confusion is possible when one is evaluating descriptive circular definitions. With noncircular definitions, all that is necessary for extensional adequacy (for example) is that the definiendum and the definiens have the same extension. This holds in a way for circular definitions too, but one must be careful. One needs to be aware of this sophistical trap: 'x is G' is certainly extensionally equivalent to itself. Hence, for any concept G, the following is an extensionally correct definition:

(18) x is $G =_{\text{Df}} x$ is G.

But by this definition 'x is G' is like the Truth Teller for all x! What has gone wrong?

Simply this: Two things that should be distinguished are run together by the argument. Extensional equivalence of the definiendum to the definiens is one thing, but extensional adequacy of the definition is an entirely distinct thing. The reason for the difference is that the role of the definiendum G is different in the two cases. In assessing extensional equivalence, occurrences of G are taken as having an antecedently specified interpretation. The definiendum and the definiens are extensionally equivalent if they have the same extension *given* the interpretation of G. But in assessing the adequacy of a definition, occurrences of G are not treated as having an antecedent interpretation. The interpretation of G is supposed to be fixed by the definition itself. Perhaps the following remark will help clarify matters: When evaluating extensional equivalence one treats G as a constant, but when evaluating extensional adequacy one treats it as a bound variable.

One final remark concerning nonstipulative definitions should be made before we turn to the concept of truth: Sometimes it is difficult to lay down a definition that is correct for *all* objects, but it is possible to put one forward that is correct (extensionally or in a stronger sense) for some restricted range of objects. An extreme case of this occurs when a definition is claimed correct only for one object. Such a definition would perhaps not be very interesting, but it is legitimate. We therefore allow as logically admissible *partial* definitions of the form

b is $G =_{\text{Df}} A(b, G)$,

where *b* is a name of some object. Such a definition lays down the conditions under which one particular object, *b*, is *G*.

IV

Tarski wrote of the T-biconditional that it "may be considered a partial definition of truth, which explains wherein the truth of ... one individual sentence consists."[14] This is exactly what we would like to say, provided that two qualifications from chapter 1 are kept in view: The notion of truth under discussion is the weak logical one, and definitions are to be evaluated by a standard no stricter than that of intensional equivalence (see pp. 20–29). One cannot say what Tarski says, however, and also accept his requirement that definitions be *formally correct*. Formal correctness rules out circular definitions, yet the partial definitions we obtain from the biconditionals may be circular. Suppose we read the biconditionals for "'snow is white' is true' and for 'everything Jones says is true' as partial definitions:

(19)   "Snow is white' is true' is true $=_{Df}$ 'snow is white' is true.

(20)   'Everything Jones says is true' is true $=_{Df}$ everything Jones says is true.

We find that the resulting definitions are circular since the definiens in each contains the word 'true'. In the first example the circularity is eliminable, but in the second it is not. There is thus a conflict between the two requirements Tarski accepts on a definition of truth, the requirement of formal correctness and that of material adequacy (Convention T). The latter demands that the definition be circular, while the former rules this out. It is a common strategy to resolve this conflict in favor of the formal correctness requirement. Let us instead explore the other alternative. Let us see what kind of theory results if we treat the biconditionals as Tarski suggested: as partial definitions of truth.

[14] Tarski 1944, section 4. In a similar vein, Peter Aczel and Solomon Feferman (1980) consider reading the unrestricted abstraction principle,

$z \in \{x: A(x)\}$ iff $A(z)$,

as definitional. However, as Feferman (1984) notes, it can be doubted whether the theory developed by Aczel and Feferman sustains this reading.

Suppose that the Tarski biconditionals for a language are the following:

s_1 is true $=_{\mathrm{Df}} A_1$

s_2 is true $=_{\mathrm{Df}} A_2$

s_3 is true $=_{\mathrm{Df}} A_3$

$$\vdots$$

As the definiens A_i may contain 'true', we need a hypothetical extension for 'true' before we can evaluate them.[15] Once such an extension is at hand, however, the biconditionals yield a judgment concerning *each* sentence, and thus produce a new revised extension for 'true'. They therefore determine a revision rule, τ_M, which we shall call the *Tarski jump* (sometimes we shall call it the *classical jump*). τ_M can be defined as follows:

Let M be the totality of relevant facts and U an arbitrary set. Then $s_i \in \tau_M(U)$ iff A_i holds in M under the hypothesis that the extension of 'true' is U, where A_i is the definiens in the partial definition of 's_i is true'.[16]

Another characterization of τ_M: It is the rule of revision yielded by the infinitistic circular definition

x is true $=_{\mathrm{Df}} (x = s_1$ and $A_1)$ or $(x = s_2$ and $A_2)$ or $(x = s_3$ and $A_3)\ldots$.

Let us see in a simple example what the rule of revision τ_M looks like. Consider a (first-order) fragment of English—call it L—whose logical resources are the following: *is* of predication and identity, *not, and, or, if ... then ..., every,* and *some.* Suppose that its nonlogical vocabulary, aside from *true*, consists of the following.

Names: **snow, Jones,** and quotational names for its sentences;

One-place predicate: **white**;

Two-place predicate: **says.**

Consider a situation M in which

---

[15] We remind the reader that we are restricting ourselves to extensional languages.
[16] The function τ_M defined here is the same as the one defined in section 2B except we now exploit the fact that in a two-valued extensional language the interpretation of a predicate can be identified with its extension. Note that in the above definition we are not being completely rigorous and precise.

D = {snow, Jones} ∪ the set of sentences of L;

I(*snow*) = snow; I(*Jones*) = Jones; and quotational names have their intended interpretations;

I(*white*) = {snow};

I(*says*) = {⟨Jones, *snow is white*⟩, ⟨Jones, *'snow is white' is true*⟩,
⟨Jones, *something Jones says is true*⟩}.

τ_M is a function that maps subsets of D into subsets of D. To determine what the value of τ_M is at $\varnothing$, say, we need to find out what sentences of L are evaluated true if we take I(*true*) = $\varnothing$. It is easily seen that under this hypothesis the following are true:

snow is white, 'snow is white' is not true, ''snow is white' is true' is not true, . . . , everything is untrue, everything Jones says is untrue, ...

$\tau_M(\varnothing)$ is the set consisting of the above sentences. Similarly,

$\tau_M(D)$ = {*snow is white, 'snow is white' is true, 'snow is not white' is true,*
. . . , Jones is true, everything is true, everything Jones says is true, . . .}.

The value of τ_M for other arguments U can be calculated in a similar way.

So, if the biconditionals are viewed as Tarski suggested, as partial definitions, then they dictate that the signification of truth is a rule of revision τ_M. This rule has numerous consequences concerning which sentences in which situations are unproblematic, which are pathological, and so on. One way to determine the adequacy of Tarski's suggestion is to compare these consequences to the observed behavior of 'true'. It turns out that the rule τ_M has some highly desirable properties that make it an attractive candidate for the signification of truth. We sketch below, in a rough and intuitive way, the most important of these properties. For more precise statements, and for proofs, see sections 6A–6C.

First, when we revise a hypothetical extension U for 'true' by repeated applications of τ_M, we find that under certain conditions—conditions that can roughly be characterized as those in which there is no vicious reference in the language—we reach a stage after which the revision rule ceases to revise. Repeated applications of τ_M produce a set that is left unchanged by the revision rule; we arrive at a fixed point V of τ_M. Further, *no matter with what hypothesis we choose to initiate the revision process, we end up in*

the same fixed point V.[17] Under these conditions τ_M displays perfect settledness and convergence. It displays *settledness* in the sense that in each
revision sequence the status of every sentence stabilizes at one value; none
is oscillating; equivalently, each revision sequence culminates in a fixed
point. It displays *convergence* in the sense that the status of a sentence is
always the same regardless of the hypothesis with which we begin a revision sequence. The initial arbitrariness of the hypothesis is completely
wiped out in the revision process.

This is illustrated in a simple way by the example given above. Some of
the arbitrariness of the initial hypotheses $\varnothing$ and D is removed by one
application of τ_M: $\tau_M(\varnothing)$ and $\tau_M(D)$ agree on *snow is white* and other
sentences that do not contain occurrences of *true*. Some of the arbitrariness remains, however, as is evident from the facts that

'snow is white' is not true $\in \tau_M(\varnothing)$

and

'snow is not white' is true $\in \tau_M(D)$.

Notice that these oddities are removed by the next application of the
revision rule. More generally, it is easy to see that for all U, if $n > 1$,

'snow is white' is true $\in \tau_M^n(U)$.

Thus, after the second application of τ_M, *'snow is white' is true* always
stabilizes in the revision process, and it stabilizes as true regardless of
the initial hypothesis. Similarly, the sentence *everything Jones says is true*
always stabilizes as true after three applications of τ_M. Sentences with
multiple embeddings of *true* within *true* take a little longer to settle down.
Nonetheless, it can be shown for this example, which is free of vicious
reference, that for every sentence there is a finite number after which its

---

[17] Conditions under which the revision rule behaves this way are called *Thomason* conditions
in section 6B. Since no precise definition of "vicious reference" is available, we cannot *prove*
the claim that the Thomason conditions consist of all and only those in which there is no
vicious reference in the language. Nonetheless, we can evaluate the claim by relying on our
intuitive judgments concerning the presence or absence of vicious reference. As many conditions that are intuitively free of vicious reference turn out to be Thomason conditions (and
conversely), we identify the two in the informal remarks below. But the reader should note
that this is one place where the theory's descriptive adequacy can be questioned. If there are
conditions that are intuitively free of vicious reference but which are not Thomason (or the
other way around), then that counts against the theory. Parallel remarks apply to similar
identifications below.

status is the same regardless of the initial hypothesis. (That this is so can be seen by consulting the proof of the Main Lemma in section 6A. It is a special feature of the present example that transfinite applications of the revision rule are not needed.) Note that simpler examples of perfect settledness and convergence can be found in the circular definitions given earlier. The revision rule for definition (1) behaves this way if all H's are F's, and that yielded by (9) does so if all and only F's are H's.

When there is no vicious reference in the language, the revision rule does not display any pathological behavior. It divides sentences into two sharply delimited classes: those to which 'true' applies and those to which it does not. It yields a particular set as the extension of 'true'.[18] In these special situations there is no difficulty if we think of the Tarski biconditionals and of the semantics of truth in the usual way. The extension to which the revision process converges is also the unique extension that makes the Tarski biconditionals true.

Second, if the only vicious reference in the language is due to the existence of a Truth Teller, then τ_M displays perfect settledness: The revisions always culminate in a fixed point; the status of every sentence stabilizes. But convergence fails: The fixed point reached depends on the initial hypothesis. The revision rule $\tau_{M'}$ behaves in this way if, for example, M' is a situation like M except that Jones says only one sentence:

(21) *Something Jones says is true.*

$\tau_{M'}$ has two fixed points, and the fixed point reached by revisions depends on the status of (21) in the initial hypothesis. If (21) is hypothesized as true, it stays true in the revision process; if it is hypothesized as false, it stays false.

Third, if the only vicious reference in the language is due to a Liar then settledness fails but convergence holds. The revision process never settles down; it ceaselessly revises the results of revision, changing forever its judgment on the Liar and related sentences. But it is convergent in the sense that the "patterns" of revisions we get do not depend upon the initial hypothesis. Consider a situation M* that is like M except that Jones says only one sentence, namely (22).

(22) *Something Jones says is not true.*

[18] This suggests that the desideratum (6) of section 3C may be met.

Table 4.1

	n =						
	0	1	2	3	4	5	...
Belongs to $\tau_{M^*}^n(U)$?	Yes	No	Yes	No	Yes	No	...

Intuitively (22) is like the Liar. And this intuitive feature is reflected in the revision process: The status of (22) oscillates between the true and the false.[19] Assuming that (22) belongs to U, we obtain the pattern shown in table 4.1. In contrast with the Truth Teller, the behavior of (22) does not depend on U; it oscillates on *all* hypotheses U.

Fourth, when the language has both kinds of vicious reference, the revision rule displays neither settledness nor convergence. The rule does, however, display settledness and convergence in a local way. On a range of sentences—sentences that can intuitively be characterized as nonpathological—it yields a definite verdict. (This happens, for example, on the grounded sentences as they are defined by Kripke. See Theorem 6C.1(iii).) Only on the pathological sentences do we get instability or divergence or both; only here does the rule fail to yield a categorical judgment.

In summary: If the Tarski biconditionals are read as partial definitions, then (i) truth must be a circular concept, (ii) its signification is a rule of revision and is completely determined by the biconditionals (the Signification Thesis is therefore preserved), and (iii) much of the behavior of the concept of truth, both ordinary and pathological, can be explained. The resulting theory thus promises to meet the two desiderata posited in chapter 1. Whether the theory deserves to be accepted can only be determined through detailed studies of the behavior of the revision rule in classical, and richer, languages. We report on some work along these lines in chapter 6, but much more needs to be done. The remainder of this chapter is devoted to some general comparative remarks that may help to clarify philosophical aspects of the theory.

---

[19] William Heytesbury, a fourteenth-century logician, defined an "insoluble sentence" as one such that, if "it signifies precisely as its words commonly pretend," then "from its being true it follows that it is false, and vice versa" (Spade 1974, p. 46). (Calvin Normore first drew our attention to Heytesbury's work.)

V

The view put forward here is in some respects similar to the Inconsistency View of Tarski and Chihara. It sees the paradoxes (and other pathological phenomena) as arising from the very nature of the concept of truth. And it takes the Tarski biconditionals to be descriptively adequate partial definitions of truth. The main difference between the two views is that according to the revision theory the principles governing truth are not inconsistent. The theory makes a distinction between two readings of the Tarski biconditionals. On one reading the 'iff' is read as definitional equivalence ($=_{Df}$); on the other it is read as material equivalence ($\leftrightarrow$):

(23) s_i is true $=_{Df} A_i$,

(24) s_i is true $\leftrightarrow A_i$.

It endorses the *definitional* biconditionals (23), but not the *material* biconditionals (24).

The two kinds of biconditionals differ greatly in their logic. The use of the former requires a shift in the index that marks revision stages in a derivation; the use of the latter does not. As a result, neither biconditional (generally) implies the other. For example, from the hypothesis that 's_i is true' holds at stage 1 we can conclude from (23) that A_i holds at stage 0, and conversely. But this does not entitle us to assert (24), for it requires that the premises and the conclusions have the same indices. (Only in very special situations will we be able to shift indices and deduce the material biconditional. We can do this if, for example, A_i does not contain any occurrences of 'true'.) Note that we can deduce everything from the material biconditional for the Liar, but not from its definitional biconditional. Let B be an arbitrary sentence and j an arbitrary stage. We can deduce B^j from the material biconditional for the Liar as follows:

(i)   (The Liar is true $\leftrightarrow$ the Liar is not true.)^i [Supposition][20]

(ii) (The Liar is true and not true.)^i [Propositional Logic, (i)]

(iii) (Everything is distinct from itself.)^i [Logic, (ii)][21]

---

[20] We have assumed that the standard name of the Liar is the same as the name used in the Liar sentence.
[21] We are relying on the fact that everything follows from a contradiction in classical logic. Note that the indices on the first three steps are the same.

(iv) (Everything is distinct from itself.)^j [Index Shift, (iii)]

(v) $(B)^j$ [Logic, (iv)]

However, the definitional biconditional for the Liar,

The Liar is true $=_{Df}$ the Liar is not true,

does not, in our theory, imply contradictions. This is a consequence of the soundness of the rules for definitions relative to the revision semantics.

Though the revision theory does not endorse all the instances of (24), it does accept many of them. For example, if a sentence A is categorical or is like the Truth Teller then the material biconditional for A turns out to be valid. Hence, when our concern is exclusively with such sentences the distinction between the two kinds of biconditionals is not so important. No difficulties result if in reasoning with them we ignore revision indices. Only for certain kinds of pathological sentences, such as the Liar, do we need to be more careful. Here the distinction between the two kinds of biconditionals enables us to accommodate tendencies that otherwise conflict with one another: (i) to accept the Tarski biconditional because it is definitional of truth and (ii) to reject the same biconditional because it is a contradiction.

The theory offered is similar in one important respect to those that follow the three-valued approach. Revision theory results in a tripartite division of sentences: sentences that are categorically assertible, those that are categorically deniable, and those that are pathological in one way or another. This is similar to what one finds in the three-valued approach; here some sentences are true, some others are false, and the remaining ones are neither true nor false.

The two approaches differ, however, in the accounts they give of the signification of truth. According to one the signification of truth is a rule of revision; it can be represented as a function from the power set of the domain into the power set of the set of sentences. According to the other the signification is a rule that divides objects into three classes; it can be represented as a function from the domain into the truth values $\{t, f, n\}$.[22] Equivalently, the signification can be represented by an ordered pair $\langle U, V \rangle$, where U is the extension and V the antiextension of 'true'.

[22] Here **t** stands for the value "The True," **f** for "The False," and **n** for "The Neither-True-Nor-False."

A consequence of this difference is the following. In the revision theory the distinction between the ordinary and the pathological sentences is explained *in terms* of the signification assigned to truth; in particular, it is explained as arising from the hypothetical character of the signification. In the three-valued approach, on the other hand, the explanation of the distinction is *external* to the signification of truth; it does not lie in the signification itself. In the three-valued approach one explains why the signification of truth is partial by relying on a *prior* explanation of what makes certain sentences pathological and, thus, neither true nor false. This structure is exemplified by theories of pathological sentences based on sortal incorrectness, presupposition failure, or ungroundedness.[23] The order of explanation in the revision theory is completely opposite. Here the signification of truth is used to explain the pathology of the relevant sentences; the latter is not used to explain the former. In the revision theory the signification of truth has a simple explanation: It is the way it is because the Tarski biconditionals are definitional of truth.

A related point: In the revision theory the signification of truth explains not only the distinction between the ordinary and the pathological but also finer distinctions among the pathological. It explains, among other things, why certain sentences are paradoxical, and why some others are like the Truth Teller and yet others dissimilar to both the Liar and the Truth Teller. The theory results not merely in a threefold division of sentences, but in a manyfold division. In the three-valued approach, however, the signification of truth does not even represent—let alone explain—this information.

Another source of differences between the two approaches is this: On the three-valued approach 'true' always has a definite extension and anti-extension, and pathological sentences are held to be neither true nor false. On the revision approach, 'true' has a definite extension and antiextension only when there is no vicious reference in the language; if vicious reference is present then there is no such thing as *the* extension or antiextension of truth. On the revision theory the pathological sentences do not turn out to be neither true nor false, for if the revision process does not give a definite verdict with respect to A then it does not do so with respect to 'A is not true' (or 'A is not false'). So to say of a pathological sentence that it is not true (or not false) is to say something that is itself pathological.

Since the three-valued approach declares the pathological sentences to be neither true nor false, there are problems in applying it to certain

---

[23] See Martin 1967, 1968, 1970b; van Fraassen 1968, 1970a; Kripke 1975.

nonclassical languages. Suppose we are trying to understand the behavior of the (weak, logical) notion of truth in a language L that is otherwise three-valued (say because of the presence of nondenoting singular terms). Suppose that L has the *Exclusion Liar*, i.e., a Liar-like sentence in which 'not' is understood in the sense of exclusion negation $\bar{A}$:

A	$\bar{A}$
t	f
f	t
n	t

What should one say of the Exclusion Liar on the three-valued approach? We cannot say that it is neither true nor false, for then the Exclusion Liar is evaluated true. We obviously cannot say that it is true or that it is false. Should we say then that it is neither true, nor false, nor neither true nor false? Such perplexities do not arise on the revision approach. *The approach applies easily and naturally to any language, classical or nonclassical, with or without the Exclusion Liar.* Fix the semantics for the ground language (i.e., the language minus the truth predicate) in any way. The signification of truth will always be the rule of revision yielded by the Tarski biconditionals, and the behavior of the pathological and the nonpathological sentences will be explained in the usual way by this rule. If we apply this obvious strategy to the Exclusion Liar, we find that it behaves as we would want: Its value oscillates in all revision sequences; it is paradoxical.

Perhaps the three-valued approach is best viewed as an *instance* of a general strategy for giving the logic and the semantics of truth. The strategy is to extend the *logical space* of the ground language (i.e., to countenance more possibilities than those recognized in the ground language). Thus, if we are attempting to give the semantics of a truth predicate for a classical ground language, this strategy directs us to expand the space of possible values of sentences from $\{t, f\}$ to $\{t, f, n\}$. If the ground language is three-valued to begin with, the possible values will be extended to four or more. Other nonclassical languages would be handled in a parallel way.[24] One consequence of following this strategy is that one will need to

---

[24] The strategy may exhibit a peculiar kind of instability. Suppose the truth predicate is always interpreted as the least fixed point in the extended space. Begin with a classical ground language, and extend it to a three-valued language L that contains its own truth

decide how the connectives and quantifiers will behave in the presence of the new "semantic value." The existing three-valued theories decide this along different lines—their decisions typically depend on the accounts they give of the pathological sentences. For example, three-valued theories that view the pathological sentences as meaningless tend to favor the Weak Kleene scheme, those that rely on their ungroundedness incline toward the Strong Kleene scheme, and so on.

In the revision approach, in contrast, the addition of a truth predicate to a language does not disturb the logical structure of the language in any way. The logical space of the ground language is not extended. No decisions have to be taken concerning the logic and semantics of the connectives and the quantifiers; these are entirely determined by the ground language. As a result, the principles of reasoning that are valid in the ground language are valid also in the extended language.[25] This is not guaranteed if one follows the strategy exemplified by the three-valued approach.

The theory of truth sketched above is a consequence of combining a general theory of definitions and Tarski's suggestion that the biconditionals be viewed as partial definitions. Tarski's suggestion brings out clearly the circularity in the notion of truth; the general theory of definition shows us how to make logical and semantic sense of this circularity. What distinguishes our theory from earlier ones is precisely this: Instead of denying or trying to get around the obvious circularity of the notion of truth, we build on it and exploit it. We have tried to show that once the circularity of truth is recognized, a great deal of its behavior begins to make sense. In particular, from this viewpoint, the existence of the paradoxes seems as natural as the existence of the eclipses. The paradoxes no longer appear as ominous indications of an incoherence in our conceptual scheme. Instead, they appear to be a natural outcome of the revision character of the concept of truth, much as eclipses are a natural outcome of the motions of the earth

predicate (say G). The interpretation of G, by hypothesis, is a fixed point in the three-valued space. But if we now take L as the ground language and ask what the interpretation of truth should be, the strategy will force us to extend logical space again. There is no guarantee that the least fixed point of the three-valued space will also be the least fixed point of the extended space. Hence, the interpretation of truth obtained through one application of the strategy may be ruled out by the next application.

[25] What are affected are the rules for truth. In applying them we need to take account of their revisionary character.

and the moon. We may, if we wish, continue with our old ways of talking and call the paradoxes 'pathological', but now there should not be any connotation of disease or a suggestion of a need for elimination. Once we understand the paradoxes better, we see a need to eliminate not *them* but only our preconceptions concerning the workings of our language in general and the concept of truth in particular.

5 A General Theory of Definitions

We turn now to the construction of a general theory of definitions, a theory that will recognize and make sense of systems of mutually interdependent definitions. In chapter 6 we shall apply the resulting ideas to the theories of truth and of some other concepts.

Let $\mathcal{L}$ $(= \langle L, M, \tau \rangle; M = \langle D, I \rangle)$ be an interpreted classical language (see pp. 44–45), and consider a set $\mathcal{D}$ of definitions that adds some (possibly infinitely many) new predicates to $\mathcal{L}$.[1] By the *definienda* we understand the predicates newly defined in $\mathcal{D}$. Let L^+ be the extended language —syntactically construed—that results from adding the definienda to L. Note that $\mathcal{D}$ contains for each n-place definiendum G a unique definition of the form

(1) $\quad G(x_1, \ldots, x_n) =_{\mathrm{Df}} A_G(x_1, \ldots, x_n),$

where $x_1, \ldots, x_n$ are distinct variables and A_G is a formula of L^+ whose free variables are $x_1, \ldots, x_n$.[2] (Note that A_G may contain occurrences of some definienda, including G itself.) Let $\mathcal{L}^+$ be the extended language construed semantically. The critical point concerning $\mathcal{L}^+$ is that the semantic status of each of its expressions is fully determined by $\mathcal{L}$ and $\mathcal{D}$; nothing else need be supplied except a semantical system explaining how the information in $\mathcal{L}$ and $\mathcal{D}$ is to be used.[3]

We shall develop more than one such semantical system. Each, however, is based on a rule of revision $\delta_{\mathcal{D}, \mathcal{L}}$ that arises from the ground language $\mathcal{L}$ and the definitions $\mathcal{D}$. It will be convenient to view $\delta_{\mathcal{D}, \mathcal{L}}$ as an operation on the set of functions

$$\bigcup_n (\{G: G \text{ an n-place definiendum of } \mathcal{L}^+\} \times D^n) \to \{\mathbf{t}, \mathbf{f}\}.$$

Members of this set will be called *hypotheses*. Because of the possibility of criss-cross circularity, it is not enough to have separate rules of revision for each definiendum, each with its own hypothesis. A hypothesis must instead award an interpretation to each definiendum *simultaneously*, for in the most general case the rule of revision requires all this information

---

[1] For simplicity we restrict ourselves to definitions of predicates. It is an easy exercise to extend the theory given to definitions of function symbols and names, and to definitions formulated in many nonclassical languages (including those based on μ, κ, and υ).

[2] It is possible to relax these conditions, but we shall not do so in this work.

[3] Note that $\mathcal{L}^+$ is *not* a classical language in the sense of section 2A. We may, if we wish, identify $\mathcal{L}^+$ with the ordered pair $\langle \mathcal{L}, \mathcal{D} \rangle$, since this pair carries all the information needed by the semantical system for the evaluation of the expressions of $\mathcal{L}^+$.

in order to yield a fresh interpretation for any of the definienda. Given
a hypothesis h, we construct as before a classically interpreted language

$$\mathscr{L}_h \, (= \langle L^+, M + h, \tau \rangle; \, M + h = \langle D, I' \rangle)$$

in which each n-place definiendum G is interpreted according to the rule

$$I'(G)(\bar{d}) = h(G, \bar{d}) \quad \text{for all } \bar{d} \in D^n$$

and the interpretations of the other constants are as in $\mathscr{L}$. $\mathscr{L}_h$ yields revised interpretations for the definienda: The new interpretation of each
G will be the signification X_G of its definiens A_G in $\mathscr{L}_h$ (see Definition
2A.9(iii)). Thus, the revision rule $\delta_{\mathscr{D}, \, \mathscr{L}}$ is an operation such that

$$\delta_{\mathscr{D}, \, \mathscr{L}}(h)(G, \bar{d}) = X_G(\bar{d}).$$

The central problem in giving a semantics for $\mathscr{L}^+$ is to show how *categorical* judgments can be made on the basis of the *hypothetical* information
provided by the rule $\delta_{\mathscr{D}, \, \mathscr{L}}$.

A satisfactory solution to this problem must satisfy two competing desiderata. On the one hand, it should attribute to the definienda a rich
content. On the other, the content attributed should not be so rich as to
violate the *conservativeness* of definitions. We shall see in the next section
that it is easy to construct natural theories that satisfy either of the two
desiderata—difficulties arise only when we attempt to satisfy both. In
subsequent sections we develop two ways in which the demands of content
and those of conservativeness can be met simultaneously.

Throughout this chapter we will assume the definitions and notational
stipulations introduced above. In particular, we will assume that $\mathscr{D}$ is a
system of definitions added to the language $\mathscr{L}$ $(= \langle L, M, \tau \rangle; \, M = \langle D, I \rangle)$,
that G is an arbitrary n-place definiendum of L^+, that definition (1) be-
longs to $\mathscr{D}$, and that $\mathscr{D}$ and $\mathscr{L}$ yield the rule of revision $\delta_{\mathscr{D}, \, \mathscr{L}}$. Instead of
$\delta_{\mathscr{D}, \, \mathscr{L}}$, we often write $\delta_{\mathscr{D}, M}$, thus highlighting the parameters we shall most
wish to vary.

We shall present in this chapter a variety of semantical systems,

$$S^{\#}, S^*, S_0, S_1, \ldots, S_n, \ldots,$$

that are designed to show how the rule of revision $\delta_{\mathscr{D}, M}$ endows the definienda of $\mathscr{D}$ with content. The systems S_n $(n \geq 0)$ will be studied in sections
5A and 5B. These systems, although conceptually deficient in ways that we
shall point out, are especially easy to understand and are also more tracta-

ble from the proof-theoretic point of view. The systems $S^{\#}$ and S^{*} will be introduced in section 5D. These require certain auxiliary concepts for their exposition, concepts that will be introduced in section 5C.

5A The Semantical Systems S_n

Given a revision rule $\delta_{\mathscr{D},M}$ and a member h of its domain, set

$$\delta_{\mathscr{D},M}^{0}(h) = h$$

$$\delta_{\mathscr{D},M}^{n+1}(h) = \delta_{\mathscr{D},M}(\delta_{\mathscr{D},M}^{n}(h)).$$

5A.1 Definition (n-reflexive hypothesis) A hypothesis h is n-*reflexive* on $\mathscr{D}$ in M (also, *for* $\delta_{\mathscr{D},M}$) iff $\delta_{\mathscr{D},M}^{n}(h) = h$.[4]

The crucial notion of validity is defined as follows (see pp. 122–123).

5A.2 Definition (Validity) Let A be a sentence of $\mathscr{L}^{+}$. Then,

(i) A is *valid on $\mathscr{D}$ in M in the system* S_n (notation: $M \models_{n}^{\mathscr{D}} A$) iff there is a natural number p such that, for all n-reflexive hypotheses h, A is true in $M + \delta_{\mathscr{D},M}^{p}(h)$.[5]

(ii) A is *valid on $\mathscr{D}$ in* S_n (notation: $\models_{n}^{\mathscr{D}} A$) iff, for all classical models M of L, $M \models_{n}^{\mathscr{D}} A$.

Remark For $n > 0$, we have

$M \models_{n}^{\mathscr{D}} A$ iff, for all n-reflexive h, A is true in $M + h$.

This is a consequence of the fact that if h is n-reflexive ($n > 0$) then, for all p,

$$\delta_{\mathscr{D},M}^{p}[\delta_{\mathscr{D},M}^{(np)-p}(h)] = h$$

and $\delta_{\mathscr{D},M}^{(np)-p}(h)$ is n-reflexive.

5A.3 Example (Validity) Consider a system $\mathscr{D}$ that consists of the definition

$Gx =_{Df} x = a \lor (x = b \ \& \ Fx \ \& \ \sim Gx).$

---

[4] Thus, 1-reflexive hypotheses are fixed points of $\delta_{\mathscr{D},M}$; 2-reflexive ones cycle in period 2; and so on. Every hypothesis is 0-reflexive.

[5] We sometimes read "$M \models_{n}^{\mathscr{D}} A$" as "$A$ is n-*valid on $\mathscr{D}$ in* M." Similarly for "$\models_{n}^{\mathscr{D}} A$" below.

The formulas

$$Ga, \quad (a \neq b \;\&\; \sim Fb) \rightarrow \;\sim Gb, \quad \forall x(Gx \rightarrow x = a \vee x = b)$$

are valid in all S_n. However, the formula

$$a \neq b \rightarrow \;\sim Gb$$

is valid in S_{2n+1} but not in S_{2n} ($n \geq 0$).

It turns out that the valid sentences of S_n are characterized by simple calculuses. Recall the calculus C_0 introduced in chapter 4. It consists of classical logic plus three special rules: DfI_r, DfE_r, and Index Shift. Let C_n be the calculus $C_0 + IS_n$, where IS_n is the rule that allows us to infer the indexed formula[6] $A^{(i+n)}$ from $A^{(i)}$, and conversely. A fuller statement of the rules of C_n can be found in section 5B.

5A.4   Definition   (Deducible; theorem)

(i) $B^{(j)}$ is *deducible in* C_n *on the basis of* $\mathscr{D}$ *from* a set Γ of indexed formulas (notation: $\Gamma \vdash_n^{\mathscr{D}} B^{(j)}$) iff there is a derivation of $B^{(j)}$ in C_n on the basis of $\mathscr{D}$ from some indexed formulas $A_1^{(i_1)}, \ldots, A_m^{(i_m)}$ that belong to Γ.

(ii) B is *deducible in* C_n *on the basis of* $\mathscr{D}$ *from* a set X of formulas (notation: $X \vdash_n^{\mathscr{D}} B$) iff there are formulas $A_1, \ldots, A_m \in X$ such that $A_1^{(0)}, \ldots, A_m^{(0)} \vdash_n^{\mathscr{D}} B^{(0)}$.[7] A is a *theorem of* C_n *relative to* $\mathscr{D}$ iff A is a sentence such that $\vdash_n^{\mathscr{D}} A$.

5A.5   Definition   (Relationships between systems)

(i) $C_m \leq S_n$ iff, for all definitions $\mathscr{D}$, all theorems of C_m are valid sentences of S_n. The notions $S_m \leq S_n$, $S_m \leq C_n$, and $C_m \leq C_n$ are understood analogously.

(ii) $C_m \equiv S_n$ iff $C_m \leq S_n$ and $S_n \leq C_m$; analogously for $C_m \equiv C_n$ and $S_m \equiv S_n$.

(iii) $S_m < S_n$ iff $S_m \leq S_n$ but not $S_n \leq S_m$; analogously for $C_m < C_n$, $S_m < C_n$, and $C_m < S_n$.[8]

---

[6] We may think of an indexed formula as an ordered pair $\langle A, i \rangle$ consisting of a formula A and an index i.

[7] This abbreviates the claim $\{A_1^{(0)}, \ldots, A_m^{(0)}\} \vdash_n^{\mathscr{D}} B^{(0)}$.

[8] The notions $\leq$, $\equiv$, and $<$ will sometimes be used to express relationships between systems other than C_m and S_n. In such contexts, these notions should be understood in a way parallel to that given above.

5A.6 Theorem (Soundness and Completeness Theorems) For all $n \geq 0$,

(i) $C_n \leq S_n$

and

(ii) $S_n \leq C_n$.

Proof See section 5B. ∎

It is an important feature shared by all systems S_n that they agree with the classical theory on ordinary definitions. The next two theorems articulate this point.

5A.7 Definition (Ordinary definitions) Let G and G_1 be definienda of L^+.

(i) *G depends on G_1* (in $\mathscr{D}$) iff the definiens of G contains an occurrence of G_1.

(ii) The definition of G_1 (in $\mathscr{D}$) is *ordinary* (we say also that G_1 is *ordinary*) iff G_1 has no infinitely descending sequence of dependencies, i.e., there are no definienda G_2, G_3, ... such that, for all $n \geq 1$, G_n depends on G_{n+1}. If G_1 is ordinary then the *rank* of G_1 (in $\mathscr{D}$) is the length of a maximally long sequence of dependencies for G_1. (Since the definiens are always finite, every ordinary G_1 is bound to have a rank.)

(iii) $\mathscr{D}$ is *ordinary* iff each G defined in $\mathscr{D}$ is ordinary.

5A.8 Definition (Regular definitions) $\mathscr{D}$ is *regular in* S_m iff, for all models M, (i) $\delta_{\mathscr{D},M}$ has an m-reflexive hypothesis and (ii) for each n-place definiendum G there is a number p such that

(1) for all m-reflexive hypotheses h and h' and all $\bar{d} \in D^n$,
$\delta^p_{\mathscr{D},M}(h)(G,\bar{d}) = \delta^p_{\mathscr{D},M}(h')(G,\bar{d})$.

5A.9 Theorem (Behavior of regular definitions) Let $\mathscr{D}$ be regular in S_m, let M be an arbitrary model, and let A be a sentence of $\mathscr{L}^+$. Then:

(i) $\delta_{\mathscr{D},M}$ has a unique 1-reflexive hypothesis h.

(ii) $M \models^{\mathscr{D}}_n A$ iff A is true in $M + h$.

Proof

(i) Construct h as follows: Since $\mathcal{D}$ is regular, there is, for every G, a number p such that (1) holds. For the duration of this proof call the least such p *the number of* G. Pick an arbitrary m-reflexive hypothesis h' and set

$$h(G,\bar{d}) = \delta^p_{\mathcal{D},M}(h')(G,\bar{d}),$$

where p is the number of G. Let q be a number $\geq$ the numbers of all the definienda occurring in the definiens A_G of G.[9] Observe that $M + h$ and $M + \delta^q_{\mathcal{D},M}(h')$ agree on all the constants occurring in A_G. Hence, A_G is true of an n-tuple $\bar{d}$ in one of these models iff it is true in the other. We have

$$\delta_{\mathcal{D},M}(h)(G,\bar{d}) = \delta^{q+1}_{\mathcal{D},M}(h')(G,\bar{d}) = \delta^p_{\mathcal{D},M}(h')(G,\bar{d}) = h(G,\bar{d}).$$

Thus, h is 1-reflexive. In view of (1), $\delta_{\mathcal{D},M}$ has a unique 1-reflexive hypothesis.

(ii) The argument here is similar to the one just given. Suppose B is a true in $M + h$. Since only finitely many definienda occur in B, there is a number $q \geq$ the numbers of all the definienda in B. Let h' be an arbitrary m-reflexive hypothesis. $M + h$ and $M + \delta^q_{\mathcal{D},M}(h')$ agree on the interpretations of all the constants occurring in B. Hence, B is true in $M + \delta^q_{\mathcal{D},M}(h')$. Thus, $M \models_m^{\mathcal{D}} B$. The converse is immediate. ∎

Remark It is easily verified that $\mathcal{D}$ is regular in S_m (m > 0) iff in all models M there is a unique m-reflexive hypothesis. Observe also that if $\mathcal{D}$ is regular in S_0 then it is regular in all S_m.

5A.10 Theorem (Behavior of ordinary definitions) If $\mathcal{D}$ is ordinary then $\mathcal{D}$ is regular in S_0 and, hence, in all S_n.

Proof Let $\mathcal{D}$ be ordinary, and let M be an arbitrary model. One can show by induction on p that, for all definienda G of rank p, all hypotheses h and h', and all $\bar{d} \in D^n$,

$$\delta^{p+1}_{\mathcal{D},M}(h)(G,\bar{d}) = \delta^{p+1}_{\mathcal{D},M}(h')(G,\bar{d}).$$

Hence, $\mathcal{D}$ is regular in S_0. ∎

Remark The above two theorems imply that all systems S_n treat ordinary definitions identically and in a manner that agrees with our ordinary practices. For, if $\mathcal{D}$ is regular in S_n, then, in all models M, $\delta_{\mathcal{D},M}$ has a

---

[9] If there are no definienda occurring in A_G, let q = 0.

unique 1-reflexive hypothesis h, and "validity in M" coincides with "truth in M + h." Thus the systems treat the definienda of regular definitions as though they had definite extensions. Further, given any definition

(2) $G(x_1,\ldots,x_n) =_{Df} A_G(x_1,\ldots,x_n)$

in $\mathscr{D}$, the universal closure of

(3) $G(x_1,\ldots,x_n) \leftrightarrow A_G(x_1,\ldots,x_n)$

is valid in S_n. Consequently, the systems S_n allow us to reason with regular definitions in the usual way.

All ordinary definitions are regular, but the converse fails because of trivial counterexamples: The definiens of a regular definition of G may contain only vacuous occurrences of G. (The definiens may be logically equivalent to a G-free formula.) There are, however, nontrivial counterexamples also.

5A.11 Example (Nonordinary regular definitions) Let $\mathscr{D}$ consist of just one definition:

$Gx =_{Df} [x = a \ \& \ (Ga \vee Gb)] \vee [x = b \ \& \ \sim Ga \ \& \ \sim Gb].$

The definiens here is not logically equivalent to any G-free formula. But it can be shown that for all M, all hypotheses h, h', and all $d \in D$,

$\delta^2_{\mathscr{D},M}(h)(G,d) = \delta^2_{\mathscr{D},M}(h')(G,d).$

It follows that $\mathscr{D}$ is regular in S_0.

Every definition regular in S_n is regular in S_1, but again the converse is not true:

5A.12 Example (Regular in S_{2n+1} but not in S_{2n}) Suppose $\mathscr{D}$ consists of just

$Gx =_{Df} [x = a \ \& \ Ga] \vee [x = b \ \& \ (Ga \vee \sim Gb)].$

$\mathscr{D}$ is regular in S_{2n+1}, but not in S_{2n}. (This is analogous to the example given on p. 109.)

Beth's Definability Theorem shows that regular definitions (even nonordinary ones) satisfy the requirement of eliminability. Suppose that $\mathscr{D}$ is regular in S_n. Let X be the set that contains, for each definition (2) in $\mathscr{D}$, the universal closure of (3). Since $\mathscr{D}$ is regular in S_n, it is regular in S_1. Hence, in every M there is a unique 1-reflexive hypothesis, and this hypothesis provides the only interpretation of the definienda that satisfies the sentences in X. By Beth's Theorem, X logically implies an "explicit definition" for each of the definienda G (i.e., it implies a universal closure of a formula of the form (3) in which the right-hand side contains no occurrences of the definienda). But sentences in X are valid in S_n. Hence, so also are these explicit definitions. It follows that the requirement of eliminability is satisfied. Illustration: The definition given in Example 5A.11 implies in all systems S_n that

$$\forall x(Gx \leftrightarrow x = a).$$

But the definition given in Example 5A.12 implies only in S_{2n+1} that

$$\forall x[Gx \leftrightarrow (x = a \lor x = b)],$$

which guarantees eliminability. This implication fails to hold in S_{2n} (where $\mathscr{D}$ is not regular).

On irregular definitions S_n may fail to respect not only the traditional demand of eliminability but also, if $n > 0$, the demand of conservativeness. This is, from our perspective, a damaging flaw.

5A.13 Definition (Weak and strong conservativeness)

(i) System S_n is *strongly conservative* iff, for all definitions $\mathscr{D}$, all models M, and all sentences A of L (so A contains no occurrences of the definienda), if $M \overset{\mathscr{D}}{\underset{n}{\models}} A$ then A is a true sentence of $\mathscr{L}$ $(= \langle L, M, \tau \rangle)$.

(ii) System S_n is *weakly conservative* iff, for all definitions $\mathscr{D}$ and all sentences A of L, if $\overset{\mathscr{D}}{\underset{n}{\models}} A$ then A is classically valid.

5A.14 Example (Conservativeness) Let $n > 0$ and let $a_1, \dots, a_n$ be distinct names. Define B_1 to be the formula

$$x = a_1 \ \& \bigwedge_{1 \leq j \leq n} \sim Ga_j.^{10}$$

---

[10] The notation

$$\bigwedge_{1 \leq j \leq n} \sim Ga_j$$

abbreviates

$$\sim Ga_1 \ \& \ \sim Ga_2 \ \& \cdots \& \ \sim Ga_n.$$

Similarly for $\bigvee$. (We will let the context disambiguate when $\bigwedge$ and $\bigvee$ are used syntactically and when they are used for operations on ccpos.)

For $2 \leq i \leq n$, define B_i to be the formula

$$x = a_i \ \& \left(\bigwedge_{1 \leq j < i-1} \sim Ga_j\right) \& \ Ga_{i-1} \ \& \left(\bigwedge_{i \leq j \leq n} \sim Ga_j\right).$$

Let $\mathcal{D}_n$ consist of only one definition:

$$Gx =_{\mathrm{Df}} B_1 \vee \ldots \vee B_n.$$

For example, $\mathcal{D}_1$ consists of the definition

$$Gx =_{\mathrm{Df}} x = a_1 \ \& \sim Ga_1,$$

and $\mathcal{D}_2$ of

$$Gx =_{\mathrm{Df}} (x = a_1 \ \& \sim Ga_1 \ \& \sim Ga_2) \vee (x = a_2 \ \& \ Ga_1 \ \& \sim Ga_2).$$

Let $a_1, \ldots, a_n$ denote distinct objects in a model M. Then the revision rule generated by $\mathcal{D}_n$ has no m-reflexive hypotheses ($0 < m \leq n$). Hence, the sentence A_n,

$$\left[\bigvee_{1 < j \leq n}\left(\bigvee_{1 \leq i < j} a_i = a_j\right)\right] \vee \perp,$$

is valid in S_m ($0 < m \leq n$). But as $\delta_{\mathcal{D}, M}$ has $(n + 1)$-reflexive hypotheses, this validity does not hold in S_{n+1}.

5A.15   Theorem   (Conservativeness)

(i) S_0 is strongly conservative.

(ii) S_n ($n > 0$) is not even weakly conservative.[11]

Proof (i) is an immediate consequence of the definition of validity, and (ii) is an immediate consequence of Example 5A.14.   ∎

The systems S_n ($n > 0$) tend to be weaker and *more* conservative as n increases.

5A.16   Theorem   (Relationships between systems)

$$S_0 < S_{m \cdot n} < S_n < S_1 \quad (m, n > 1).$$

---

[11] In section 5B we construct a system that is weakly, but not strongly, conservative.

Proof Let $m, n > 1$. Then, all 1-reflexive hypotheses are n-reflexive; all n-reflexive hypotheses are $(m \cdot n)$-reflexive; and these, in turn, are 0-reflexive. Thus,

$$S_0 \leq S_{m \cdot n} \leq S_n \leq S_1.$$

The remaining components of the theorem can be established using Example 5A.14. For instance, to show that $S_n \leq S_{m \cdot n}$ fails we consider the definition $\mathcal{D}_{(m \cdot n) - 1}$. Relative to this definition, $A_{(m \cdot n) - 1}$ is valid in S_n but not in $S_{m \cdot n}$.   ∎

Remark Example 5A.14 shows also that the above theorem gives a complete account of the relationships between the systems: If $m > n > 1$ and n does not divide m, then neither $S_n \leq S_m$ nor $S_m \leq S_n$.

System S_0 has the virtue that it is strongly conservative. The problem with it, as the next example shows, is that it is logically weak—it ascribes less content to the definienda than is desirable. Systems S_n ($n > 0$), on the other hand, ascribe a rich content to the definienda but fail to be conservative. What we want is a system that is both strongly conservative and logically rich. The construction of such a system is one of the principal goals of this chapter.

5A.17   Example (Weakness of S_0) Let the nonlogical resources of the language *L* consist of a name 0, a one-place function ′ ("the successor of"), and a two-place relation $<$. Let *AX* be the conjunction of axioms stating that $<$ is a strict linear order[12] and the following:

$\forall x \sim (x < 0),$

$\forall x (x < x' \ \& \ \forall y (x < y \rightarrow y = x' \lor x' < y)).$[13]

Let *G is closed* abbreviate the formula

(4) $\forall x [\forall y (y < x \rightarrow Gy) \rightarrow Gx],$

and let $\mathcal{D}$ consist of the definition

$Gx =_{Df} [G \text{ is closed} \ \& \ x = x] \lor [\sim (G \text{ is closed}) \ \& \ \forall y (y < x \rightarrow Gy)].$

---

[12] These axioms state that $<$ is irreflexive, transitive, and connected [$\forall x \forall y (x < y \lor x = y \lor y < x)$].

[13] To increase readability, we follow the standard practice of writing x' in place of $'(x)$.

The revision rule $\delta_{\mathscr{D},M}$, where M is a model of AX, works in the following way: If the hypothetical interpretation of G satisfies the condition of closure (i.e., (4)), then the revised interpretation makes G true of all the objects in the domain. This new interpretation satisfies closure and is therefore a fixed point of $\delta_{\mathscr{D},M}$. If, on the other hand, the hypothetical interpretation h does not satisfy closure, there will be a unique element d of the domain that satisfies

$$\forall y(y < x \rightarrow Gy)$$

but not Gx (in M + h). The rule $\delta_{\mathscr{D},M}$ revises the interpretation h so that d and everything less than it falls in the extension of G. Another application of $\delta_{\mathscr{D},M}$ adds the successor of d to the extension, and another *its* successor, and so on. Hence, for such an h there is no natural number p such that

$$\forall x Gx \text{ is true in M} + \delta_{\mathscr{D},M}^{p}(h).$$

Thus, the claim

$$\models_{n}^{\mathscr{D}} AX \rightarrow \forall x Gx$$

fails if n = 0; it holds, however, for all n > 0. Note that $\mathscr{D}$ counts as regular in all S_n (n > 0) but not in S_0.

A variant of this example shows that the "limit" of systems S_n (n > 0), though it ascribes to the definienda a rich content, is not adequate either. The limit system is not weakly conservative:

5A.18 Example (Nonconservativeness of the limit)   Let L, M, and AX be as in the previous example, and let us change the definition in $\mathscr{D}$ just a little:

$$Gx =_{Df} [G \text{ is closed } \& x \neq x] \vee [\sim(G \text{ is closed}) \& \forall y(y < x \rightarrow Gy)].$$

The revision rule $\delta_{\mathscr{D},M}$ works as before except that if the interpretation of G satisfies the condition of closure then it is revised so that G is true of nothing. It is plain, therefore, that $\delta_{\mathscr{D},M}$ has no n-reflexive hypotheses (n > 0). Hence, for all n > 0,

$$\models_{n}^{\mathscr{D}} \sim AX,$$

and the limit of the systems S_n (n > 0) fails to be weakly conservative.

The above example reveals a property of S_0 that is important to note.

5A.19   Example   (ω-inconsistency in S_0)   Let L, AX, and $\mathscr{D}$ be as in the previous example, and let $\ulcorner n \urcorner$ denote the term formed by n applications of the successor function $'$ to the name 0. It can be verified that, in an arbitrary model M of AX, n + 2 applications of the rule $\delta_{\mathscr{D}, \mathrm{M}}$ to an arbitrary hypothesis h result in an extension for G that contains the denotation of $\ulcorner n \urcorner$. Hence, for all n

$$\models^{\mathscr{D}}_0 AX \to G\ulcorner n \urcorner.$$

But we have also

$$\models^{\mathscr{D}}_0 AX \to {\sim}(\forall x)\, Gx,$$

for after one revision some objects in the domain are bound to fall outside the resulting extensions. Relative to S_0 and $\mathscr{D}$, then, AX implies an ω-inconsistent set of sentences. It follows that if $\mathscr{D}$ is added to Peano Arithmetic and definitions are used in accordance with the system S_0 then an ω-inconsistent set of sentences will be deducible.

Remark   We do not think that this example should be interpreted as showing that S_0 is too strong. First, *the existence of ω-inconsistency ought not be read as ruling out the standard model of the ground language L.* It shows only that in the standard model no possible extension for G will make all the validities true. We can accept this since we have independent reasons for thinking that circular concepts do not always have definite extensions. Second, this aspect of S_0 may actually be useful in explaining certain features of the concept of truth (see section 6C). In any case, we shall later construct not only a system $S^\# > S_0$ but also a system S^* in which definitions never result in the above sort of ω-inconsistency.

5B   Completeness and Conservativeness

The principal goals of this section are to show the completeness of the calculuses C_n with respect to the systems S_n and to construct a semantical system that is weakly, but not strongly, conservative.

The Calculuses C_n

The distinguishing feature of the calculuses C_n is that they weaken the rules of definition, DfI and DfE, through the use of *indices*.[14] Each step in a derivation in these calculuses is assigned an integer as its index. Intuitively, this index can be viewed as giving the relative position of the step in a revision process. Application of DfE or DfI results in a conclusion with an index different from that of the premiss: DfE results in a conclusion with an index one less than that of the premiss, DfI in a conclusion with an index one greater.

We adopt the natural deduction system, as developed by Fitch, for the presentation of the rules of C_n.[15] In this system vertical lines are used to indicate the hypotheses under which a conclusion is drawn. A vertical line may be *flagged* with a variable. This is indicated by putting the variable at the top left of the line; see the rule $\forall$I below. All formulas (and subproofs) to the right of a flagged vertical line are "general" with respect to the flagged variable. Hypotheses are set apart from the rest of the formulas by a horizontal line. Detailed explanations of Fitch's system can be found in many logic books.[16] Note that in the rules and derivations given below we indicate the index of a step by a numeral in superscripted parentheses. Thus, an occurrence of $A^{(i)}$ in a derivation indicates that the index of that occurrence of A is i.

I.   Structural Rules

Hypothesis (Hyp)

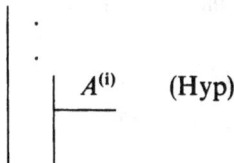

$$\quad\quad A^{(i)} \quad\quad \text{(Hyp)}$$

Restriction on Hyp: i is an integer.

---

[14] Some of this lost power is restored by the rules for shifting indices.
[15] Natural deduction systems were first introduced by Gerhard Gentzen and Stanislaw Jaśkowski.
[16] See, e.g., Fitch 1952, Thomason 1970, Leblanc and Wisdom 1976, Bergmann et al. 1980, and Teller 1989. Be warned that these books present slightly different versions of the system.

Reiteration (Reit)

$$m \quad A^{(i)}$$

$$A^{(i)} \quad \text{(Reit m)}$$

Restriction on Reit: If a subproof is flagged with a variable x then no formula that contains x free can be reiterated into it.

Index Shift (IS)

$$m \quad A^{(i)}$$

$$A^{(j)} \quad \text{(IS m)}$$

Restriction on IS: A must not contain any defined symbols.

II. Logical Rules

Rules for $\sim$

$\sim$ Introduction ($\sim$ I)   *$\sim$ Elimination* ($\sim$ E)

$$m \quad A^{(i)}$$

$$n \quad B^{(i)}$$

$$p \quad \sim B^{(i)}$$
$$\sim A^{(i)} \quad (\sim \text{I } m\text{--}n, p)$$

$$m \quad \sim \sim A^{(i)}$$

$$A^{(i)} \quad (\sim \text{E } m)$$

Rules for &

& Introduction (&I)

m | $A^{(i)}$

n | $B^{(i)}$

  | $(A \,\&\, B)^{(i)}$ (&I m, n)

& Elimination (&E)

m | $(A \,\&\, B)^{(i)}$

  | $A^{(i)}$ (&E m)

m | $(A \,\&\, B)^{(i)}$

  | $B^{(i)}$ (&E m)

Rules for $\perp$

$\perp$ Introduction ($\perp$I)

m | $A^{(i)}$

n | $\sim A^{(i)}$

  | $\perp^{(i)}$ ($\perp$I m, n)

$\perp$ Elimination ($\perp$E)

m | $\perp^{(i)}$

  | $A^{(i)}$ ($\perp$E m)

Rules for $\forall$

$\forall$ Introduction ($\forall$I)

m | x |

n | | $A^{(i)}$
  | $\forall x A^{(i)}$ ($\forall$I m–n)

$\forall$ Elimination ($\forall$E)

m | $\forall x A(x)^{(i)}$

  | $A(t)^{(i)}$ ($\forall$E m)

Restriction on $\forall$E: The term t must be free for x in A.

Rules for $=$

$= Introduction\ (=I)$ $= Elimination\ (=E)$

$$
\begin{array}{c|l}
 & \quad\vdots \\
 & \quad\vdots \\
 & \quad\vdots \\
 & (s = s)^{(i)} \qquad (=I)
\end{array}
$$

$$
\begin{array}{c|l}
 & \quad\vdots \\
m & (s = t)^{(i)} \\
 & \quad\vdots \\
n & A(s)^{(i)} \\
 & \quad\vdots \\
 & A(t)^{(i)} \qquad (=E\ m, n)
\end{array}
$$

Restriction on $=E$: The terms s and t must be free for x in $A(x)$.

Rules for Definitions

Definiendum Introduction (DfI$_r$)   *Definiendum Elimination* (DfE$_r$)

$$
\begin{array}{c|l}
 & \quad\vdots \\
m & A_G(t_1,\ldots,t_n)^{(i)} \\
 & \quad\vdots \\
 & G(t_1,\ldots,t_n)^{(i+1)} \quad (\text{DfI}_r\ m)
\end{array}
$$

$$
\begin{array}{c|l}
 & \quad\vdots \\
m & G(t_1,\ldots,t_n)^{(i+1)} \\
 & \quad\vdots \\
 & A_G(t_1,\ldots,t_n)^{(i)} \quad (\text{DfE}_r\ m)
\end{array}
$$

Condition on DfI$_r$ and DfE$_r$: It is assumed in these rules that

$$G(x_1,\ldots,x_n) =_{\text{Df}} A_G(x_1,\ldots,x_n)$$

belongs to the system of definitions $\mathscr{D}$ and that t_1, ..., t_n are free for x_1, ..., x_n respectively in A_G.

Aside from the rules stated above, the calculus C_n contains one additional rule (IS$_n$) that liberalizes Index Shift. This rule allows us to infer $A^{(i+n)}$ from $A^{(i)}$, and conversely. Note that IS$_n$ places no restrictions on the formula A whose index is shifted. In contrast, the earlier rule IS allows indices to be shifted only when there are no occurrences of the definienda in the formula.

Here are two sample derivations. The first establishes the derivability of the rule $\sim$DfI$_r$:

$$\sim A_G(t_1,\ldots,t_n)^{(i)} \mathrel{\vert\frac{\mathscr{D}}{m}} \sim G(t_1,\ldots,t_n)^{(i+1)}.^{17}$$

[17] Assuming that t_1, ..., t_n are free for x_1, ..., x_n respectively in A_G.

1. | $\sim A_G(t_1,\dots,t_n)^{(i)}$ (Hyp)

2. | $G(t_1,\dots,t_n)^{(i+1)}$ (Hyp)

3. | $A_G(t_1,\dots,t_n)^{(i)}$ (DfE$_r$ 2)

4. | $\sim A_G(t_1,\dots,t_n)^{(i)}$ (Reit 1)

5. | $\perp^{(i)}$ ($\perp$I 3,4)

6. | $\perp^{(i+1)}$ (IS 5)

7. | $\sim G(t_1,\dots,t_n)^{(i+1)}$ ($\perp$E 6)

8. | $\sim G(t_1,\dots,t_n)^{(i+1)}$ ($\sim$I 2–2, 7)

Derivability of $\sim$DfE$_r$,

$$\sim G(t_1,\dots,t_n)^{(i+1)} \mathrel{\vert\!\frac{\mathscr{D}}{\mathsf{m}}} \sim A_G(t_1,\dots,t_n)^{(i)},$$

can be established in a similar manner.

The second example shows that $\perp$ is a theorem of $\mathbf{C}_3$ if the definition

(1) $Gx =_{\mathrm{Df}} \sim Gx$

belongs to $\mathscr{D}$.[18]

1. | | | $\sim Gx^{(0)}$ (Hyp)

2. | | $Gx^{(1)}$ (DfI$_r$ 1)

3. | | | $Gx^{(2)}$ (Hyp)

4. | | $Gx^{(1)}$ (Reit 2)

5. | | $\sim Gx^{(1)}$ (DfE$_r$ 3)

6. | | $\perp^{(1)}$ ($\perp$I 4, 5)

7. | | $\perp^{(2)}$ (IS 6)

8. | | $\sim Gx^{(2)}$ ($\perp$E 7)

9. | | $\sim Gx^{(2)}$ ($\sim$I 3–3, 8)

10. | | $Gx^{(3)}$ (DfI$_r$ 9)

11. | | $Gx^{(0)}$ (IS$_3$ 10)

12. | $\sim\sim Gx^{(0)}$ ($\sim$I 1–1, 11)

13. | $\sim Gx^{(1)}$ ($\sim$DfI$_r$ 12)

---

[18] This should not cast any doubt on the soundness of $\mathbf{C}_3$, since $\perp$ is valid in $\mathbf{S}_{2m+1}$ *if* (1) belongs to $\mathscr{D}$.

14.	$Gx^{(2)}$	(DfI, 13)
15.	$\sim\sim Gx^{(3)}$	(IS$_3$ 12)
16.	$Gx^{(3)}$	($\sim$E 15)
17.	$\sim Gx^{(2)}$	(DfE, 16)
18.	$\perp^{(2)}$	($\perp$I 14, 17)
19.	$\perp^{(0)}$	(IS 18)

The above kind of derivation cannot be constructed in $\mathbf{C_2}$ (and, more generally, $\mathbf{C_{2m}}$). The key problem arises at step (11): IS$_2$ allows us to deduce only the innocuous $Gx^{(1)}$, not the formula $Gx^{(0)}$ needed to complete the reductio.

The Completeness Proof

5B.1   Theorem   (Soundness and Completeness)   For all m $\geq$ 0,

(i) $\mathbf{C_m} \leq \mathbf{S_m}$

and

(ii) $\mathbf{S_m} \leq \mathbf{C_m}$.

Proof   Claim (i), the soundness of $\mathbf{C_m}$, has a straightforward proof, which we omit. Claim (ii), the completeness of $\mathbf{C_m}$, can be established by the Henkin method. We outline this proof below.

For the rest of this section, let us understand by a *theory* Γ a set of indexed *sentences* $A^{(i)}$. Γ is *inconsistent* (in $\mathbf{C_m}$) iff

$$\Gamma \models_{m}^{\mathscr{D}} \perp^{(0)}$$

(see Definition 5A.4); otherwise Γ is *consistent*. Γ is *complete* iff for all sentences A and indices i either $A^{(i)}$ or $\sim A^{(i)}$ belongs to Γ. Finally, Γ is *henkin* iff for all indices i and all formulas $A(x)$ with exactly one free variable there is a closed term t such that

$$((\exists x)A(x) \rightarrow A(t))^{(i)}$$

belongs to Γ. Note that if Γ is complete and consistent in $\mathbf{C_m}$ then Γ is closed under the consequence relation of $\mathbf{C_m}$; i.e., for all sentences A and indices i, if $\Gamma \models_{m}^{\mathscr{D}} A^{(i)}$ then $A^{(i)} \in \Gamma$.

Given a consistent, complete, henkin theory Γ of $\mathbf{C_m}$, we construct a sequence of interpreted languages $\mathscr{L}_j$ ($= \langle L^+, \mathscr{M}_j, \tau \rangle$; $\mathscr{M}_j = \langle D_j, I_j \rangle$) as follows. Define

$t_1 \equiv_j t_2$ iff $(t_1 = t_2)^{(j)} \in \Gamma$.

In virtue of the rules for identity, $\equiv_j$ is an equivalence relation. Let

$Term/\equiv_j$

be the partition of the set of all closed terms of L, and let $[t]$ be the member of this partition that contains t. Set

$D_j = Term/\equiv_j$;

$I_j(a) = [a]$, for all names a;

$I_j(F)([t_1],\ldots,[t_n]) = \mathbf{t}$ iff $F(t_1,\ldots,t_n)^{(j)} \in \Gamma$, for all n-place predicates F;

$I_j(f)([t_1],\ldots,[t_n]) = [f(t_1,\ldots,t_n)]$, for all n-place function symbols f.

(The above definition is satisfactory in virtue of the rules for identity.) The basic fact about the models $\mathscr{L}_j$ is this: For all sentences A,

(2) A is true in $\mathscr{L}_j$ iff $A^{(j)} \in \Gamma$.

Its proof involves nothing essentially new, and we omit it.[19]
     By the rule IS for shifting indices, if a sentence A does not contain any occurrences of the definienda, then for all i and j

$A^{(i)} \in \Gamma$ iff $A^{(j)} \in \Gamma$.

Hence all models $\mathscr{M}_j$ have the same domain and agree on the interpretations of the constants of L. Let M $(= \langle D, I \rangle)$ be the reduct of $\mathscr{M}_j$ to L. We shall call M the *canonical* model generated by Γ. Define hypothesis h_j thus:

$h_j(G,\bar{d}) = I_j(G)(\bar{d})$,

for all n-place definienda G and $\bar{d} \in D^n$. We claim that, for arbitrary integer j and natural number p,

(3) $\delta^p_{\mathscr{D},M}(h_j) = h_{j+p}$.

This can be established by induction on p. The Base Case is trivial. For the Inductive Case, suppose that the claim holds for p and that, for an arbitrary n-place definiendum G and arbitrary $\bar{d} \in D^n$,

---

[19] See, for instance, chapter 2 of Mendelson 1964.

$\delta_{\mathscr{D},M}^{p+1}(h_j)(G,\bar{d}) = t.$[20]

By definition, $\delta_{\mathscr{D},M}^{p+1}(h_j) = \delta_{\mathscr{D},M}(\delta_{\mathscr{D},M}^{p}(h_j))$, and by the inductive hypothesis, $\delta_{\mathscr{D},M}^{p}(h_j) = h_{j+p}$. Hence,

$\delta_{\mathscr{D},M}(h_{j+p})(G,\bar{d}) = t.$

By the definition of $\delta_{\mathscr{D},M}$, the definiens $A_G(x_1,\ldots,x_n)$ of G is true of $\bar{d}$ in $\mathscr{L}_{h_{j+p}}$. Let $\bar{d} = \langle[t_1],\ldots,[t_n]\rangle$. It follows that $A_G(t_1,\ldots,t_n)$ is true in $\mathscr{L}_{h_{j+p}}$ (by a generalized version of Theorem 2A.10). Hence, by (2),

$A_G(t_1,\ldots,t_n)^{(j+p)} \in \Gamma.$

DfI$_r$ yields that

$G(t_1,\ldots,t_n)^{(j+p+1)} \in \Gamma.$

Hence,

$h_{h+p+1}(G,\langle[t_1],\ldots,[t_n]\rangle) = h_{j+p+1}(G,\bar{d})$

$$= t.$$

This establishes (3).

The final part of the argument for the completeness of $\mathbf{C}_m$ can now be given. Suppose A is not a theorem of $\mathbf{C}_m$. Then the theory $\{\langle\sim A,0\rangle\}$ is consistent. This theory can be extended to a complete, consistent, henkin theory of $\mathbf{C}_m$ in the usual way.[21] The above construction yields hypotheses h_j and a canonical model M such that, for all natural numbers p,

(i) $\delta_{\mathscr{D},M}^{p}(h_{-p}) = h_0$

and

(ii) A is false in $\mathscr{L}_{h_0}$.

---

[20] The argument for the other case, $\delta_{\mathscr{D},M}^{p+1}(h_j)(G,\bar{d}) = f$, is parallel.

[21] The proof relies on the following easily verified properties of $\mathbf{C}_m$: (i) If Γ is consistent in $\mathbf{C}_m$, then for all sentences A and indices j either $\Gamma \cup \{\langle A,j\rangle\}$ or $\Gamma \cup \{\langle\sim A,j\rangle\}$ is consistent in $\mathbf{C}_m$. (ii) If $\Gamma \vdash_m^{\mathscr{D}} A(c)^{(i)}$ then $\Gamma \vdash_m^{\mathscr{D}} \forall x A(x)^{(i)}$, provided that Γ and $A(x)$ do not contain any occurrences of the constant c. Note that in order to ensure extendibility to a henkin theory we must have sufficiently many names in the language. The standard procedure for solving this problem works in the present case: One extends the language with sufficiently many new names and constructs the henkin theory in the extended language; one then constructs in the above manner a canonical model for the extended language; finally, one takes the reduct of this model to the initial language. This reduct has the desired properties.

But in virtue of the rule IS_m, h_{-p} is m-reflexive. It follows that A is not valid in S_m.   ■

Skippable remarks

(i) Consider a variant notion of "valid in S_0" by which A counts as valid iff there is a number p such that, for all models M and hypotheses h, A is true in $M + \delta^p_{\mathscr{D},M}(h)$. The only difference between this notion and the one defined in 5A.2 is that the positions of the quantifiers 'there is a number p' and 'all models M' are switched. C_0 is sound for this notion of validity and also, by the above argument, complete.

(ii) Paul Bartha pointed out to us that C_0 is not complete with respect to the notion of validity defined in note 10 of chapter 4. Counterexample: Let $\mathscr{D}$ and AX be as given in 5A.17, but suppose that the language L has an additional constant k. Then the sentence

(4) $AX \rightarrow (Gk \rightarrow Gk')$

is valid in the sense of note 10. However, it is not provable in C_0 since it is not valid in the variant sense defined in the previous remark.

Conservativeness

The above proof enables us to construct a system S_d that is weakly, but not strongly, conservative.

5B.2   Definition   (Descending hypothesis)   A hypothesis h_0 is *descending in M relative to $\mathscr{D}$* iff there are hypotheses h_1, h_2, ... such that, for all $n \geq 0$, $h_n = \delta^p_{\mathscr{D},M}(h_{n+1})$.

Remark   All n-reflexive hypotheses (n > 0) are descending, but there can be descending hypotheses that are not n-reflexive.

5B.3   Definition   (Validity in S_d)   Let A be a sentence of L^+. Then:

(i) A is *valid on $\mathscr{D}$ in M in the system S_d* (notation: $M \models^{\mathscr{D}}_d A$) iff there is a natural number p such that for all descending hypotheses h, A is true in $M + \delta^p_{\mathscr{D},M}(h)$.[22]

(ii) A is *valid on $\mathscr{D}$ in S_d* (notation: $\models^{\mathscr{D}}_d A$) iff, for all classical models M of L, $M \models^{\mathscr{D}}_d A$.

Remark $M \models^{\mathscr{D}}_d A$ iff, for all descending hypotheses h, A is true in $M + h$.

---

[22] This is exactly parallel to Definition 5A.2.

5B.4   Theorem   (A property of S_d) S_d is weakly, but not strongly, conservative.

Proof   That S_d is not strongly conservative can be shown using the language L and definition $\mathscr{D}$ of Example 5A.18. Let M ($= \langle D, I \rangle$) be a model such that $D = \{0, 1, 2, \ldots\}$ and let I assign to the constants of L their usual arithmetical interpretations. It can be verified that, relative to M and $\mathscr{D}$, there are no descending hypotheses. Hence, M $\models_{\mathbf{d}}^{\mathscr{D}} \perp$. But $\perp$ is not a true sentence of $\mathscr{L}$ ($= \langle L, M, \tau \rangle$).

S_d is, however, weakly conservative. The completeness proof sketched above shows that $S_d \leq C_0$. The proof yields, for each sentence A that is not a theorem of C_0, a canonical model M and a descending hypothesis h_0 such that A is not true in M $+ h_0$.   ∎

Remark   Observe that $S_0 \equiv S_d$. S_0 and S_d therefore have the same validities, even though the former is strongly conservative and the latter is not.

5C   Revision Sequences and Their Properties

In this section we define and study the notion of a revision sequence (i.e., a sequence obtained through repeated applications, possibly transfinite, of the revision rule). We shall use this notion in section 5D to build two theories that endow definitions with rich content and are strongly conservative.

It will be useful for later applications to view a rule of revision ρ as an operation on an arbitrary space of functions; that is,

$$\rho: X^D \to X^D,$$

where X and D are nonempty sets. (A good example of ρ to keep in mind is $\delta_{\mathscr{D}, \mathscr{G}}$, described above on p. 146.) We shall call members of X^D *hypotheses*, and use variables 'h', 'h'', ... to range over them. Variables 'α', 'β', 'γ', ... will be used to range over ordinals, and '$\mathscr{S}$', '$\mathscr{S}'$', ... over sequences of hypotheses. We shall be interested in only those sequences $\mathscr{S}$ whose length, $lh(\mathscr{S})$ [$=$ the domain of $\mathscr{S}$], is either a limit ordinal or the class On of all ordinals. Henceforth, we take this restriction as read into the notion of a sequence. If $\beta < lh(\mathscr{S})$ then $\mathscr{S}_\beta$ is the βth member of $\mathscr{S}$, and $\mathscr{S} \restriction \beta$ is the restriction of $\mathscr{S}$ to β.

The following three definitions are fundamental to our theory.

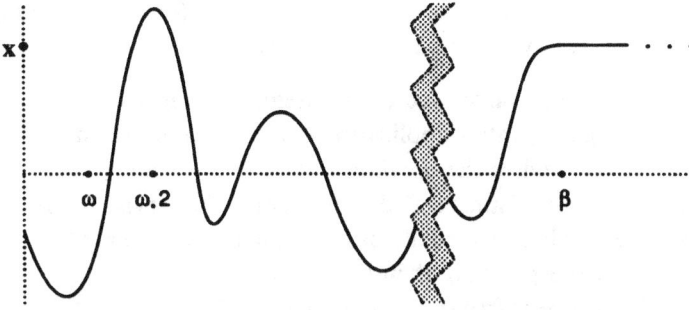

Figure 5.1

5C.1 **Definition** (Stability) Let $x \in X$ and $d \in D$, and let $\mathscr{S}$ be a sequence of hypotheses. Then:

(i) d is *stably* x *in* $\mathscr{S}$ iff there is an ordinal $\beta < \text{lh}(\mathscr{S})$ such that for all ordinals γ if $\beta \leq \gamma < \text{lh}(\mathscr{S})$ then $\mathscr{S}_\gamma(d) = x$;[23] the least such β is *the stabilization point of* d *in* $\mathscr{S}$.

(ii) d is *stable in* $\mathscr{S}$ iff, for some $x \in X$, d is stably x in $\mathscr{S}$; otherwise, d is *unstable in* $\mathscr{S}$.

If d is stably x in $\mathscr{S}$, then it displays a pattern of the kind shown in figure 5.1. The value of d may fluctuate initially—say up to β—but must eventually settle down to x.

5C.2 **Definition** (Coheres) A hypothesis h *coheres with* a sequence $\mathscr{S}$ iff, for all $d \in D$ and all $x \in X$, if d is stably x in $\mathscr{S}$ then $h(d) = x$.

By this definition, if h coheres with $\mathscr{S}$ and an object d is stably x in $\mathscr{S}$, then h must assign x to d; but if d is unstable, then h may assign any member of X to d.

5C.3 **Definition** (Revision sequence) $\mathscr{S}$ is a *revision sequence for* ρ iff for all $\alpha < \text{lh}(\mathscr{S})$

(i) if $\alpha = \beta + 1$ then $\mathscr{S}_\alpha = \rho(\mathscr{S}_\beta)$

and

---

[23] If α is a limit ordinal $< \text{lh}(\mathscr{S})$ and d is stably x in $\mathscr{S} \upharpoonright \alpha$, then we say also that d is *stably* x *at* α *in* $\mathscr{S}$. Similarly for "stable" and "unstable" below.

(ii) if α is a limit ordinal then $\mathcal{S}_\alpha$ coheres with $\mathcal{S}\!\!\upharpoonright\alpha$, i.e., for all d $\in$ D and
all x $\in$ X, if d is stably x in $\mathcal{S}\!\!\upharpoonright\alpha$ then $\mathcal{S}_\alpha(\mathrm{d}) = \mathrm{x}$.

A revision sequence $\mathcal{S}$ can be viewed as an attempt to improve an initial
hypothesis $\mathcal{S}_0$ through repeated applications of the rule ρ. At successor
stages $\alpha\,(=\beta+1)$, one revises the previous outcome $\mathcal{S}_\beta$ by an application
of ρ. At a limit stage α, one "sums up" the effects of earlier revisions: If the
revision process up to α has yielded a definite verdict on an element d (i.e.,
if d has stabilized in the process), then this verdict is reflected in the αth
hypothesis; otherwise, one is free to assign to d any value in X whatsoever.

There are no serious alternatives, as far as we can see, to the treatment
of successor stages in the above definition. The same can also be said of the
treatment of elements stable at a limit stage α, but not of elements unstable
at α. Alternative treatments of these latter elements are possible and may
have useful applications. There are three kinds of alternative treatments
that we would like to note briefly.

(a) One may assign values to the unstable elements according to some
fixed rule—not, as in the above definition, arbitrarily. Hans Herzberger,
when he faced a similar problem in the theory of truth, assigned the value
f to the unstable sentences.[24] In the present context, a *Herzberger Limit
Rule* would assign an antecedently chosen member of X to the unstable
elements. We were initially attracted to the idea that the value of an unstable element should be the same as its value in the initial hypothesis $\mathcal{S}_0$. We
shall call this the *Constant Limit Rule*. There are other rules that one might
follow.[25]

(b) One may impose certain global constraints on the treatment of
unstable elements. For instance, one may require the resulting revision
sequence $\mathcal{S}$ to be *fully varied* in the sense that if a hypothesis h coheres
with $\mathcal{S}$ then h occurs in $\mathcal{S}$.[26]

5C.4 Example   (Fully varied revision sequences)   Suppose that

$$\rho\colon \{\mathbf{t},\mathbf{f}\}^{\{1,2,3\}} \to \{\mathbf{t},\mathbf{f}\}^{\{1,2,3\}}.$$

---

[24] See Herzberger 1982a, 1982b.
[25] In "Truth and paradox," where the Constant Limit Rule is introduced, the revision process
is pictured as generating better and better hypotheses, even at transfinite stages. This picture
is misplaced when, as in Definition 5C.3, arbitrary choices are allowed at limits. ω-long
revision sequences may still be viewed as resulting in progressively better hypotheses. However, choices made at a limit stage may result in a worse hypothesis than those occurring
before it. See, in this connection, Belnap 1982, p. 104.
[26] A stronger constraint is to require that h be cofinal in $\mathcal{S}$ (see Definition 5C.6).

Let h_{12} be the member of $\{t, f\}^{\{1,2,3\}}$ that assigns t to 1 and 2 and f to 3. Let us understand h_{13}, h_3, h_{123}, etc. in a similar way. (So, h assigns f to 1, 2, and 3.) Suppose ρ revises hypotheses as follows:

$$h_{123} \to h \to h_{13} \to h_{23} \to h_{13},$$

and all the remaining hypotheses are revised to h_3. (In the above display, '$h_{13} \to h_{23}$' indicates that $\rho(h_{13}) = h_{23}$.) Let $\mathscr{S}$ be a sequence of length On that assigns to the even ordinals h_{13} and to the odd ordinals h_{23}. $\mathscr{S}$ is a revision sequence that is not fully varied: h_3 coheres with $\mathscr{S}$ but does not occur in $\mathscr{S}$. On the other hand, the revision sequence that assigns h_3 to every ordinal *is* fully varied. (An example of a possible application of fully varied revision sequences is given in section 6C. See 6C.10 and the remark following it.)

(c) One may take the revision process up to a limit ordinal α as giving a definite verdict on *some* of the unstable elements. For instance, this course may be followed on those elements that, though unstable, are *nearly* stable in the following sense.

5C.5 Definition   (Near stability)[27]

(i) The value of d in $\mathscr{S}$ is *nearly stable at* x iff there is a $\beta < lh(\mathscr{S})$ such that, for all γ, if $\beta \leq \gamma < lh(\mathscr{S})$ then there is a natural number m such that, for all $n \geq m$, $\mathscr{S}_{\gamma+n}(d) = x$.

(ii) An element d is *nearly stable* in $\mathscr{S}$ iff for some $x \in X$ the value of d in $\mathscr{S}$ is nearly stable at x.

Stability *simpliciter* requires an element d to settle down to a value x after some initial fluctuations, say up to β (see figure 5.1). In contrast, near stability allows fluctuations after β also, but these fluctuations must be confined to finite regions just after limit ordinals (see figure 5.2). We have chosen to work with the treatment of limit stages given in Definition 5C.3 because it is simple and general, and because it reduces to a minimum reliance on policies not absolutely dictated by the revision rule itself. We do not wish to suggest by making this choice, however, that this is the only coherent treatment. But note that the consequences of opting for a different limit rule, though important, are less radical than they may

---

[27] The notion of near stability will play an important role in the theory S^*, developed in section 5D.

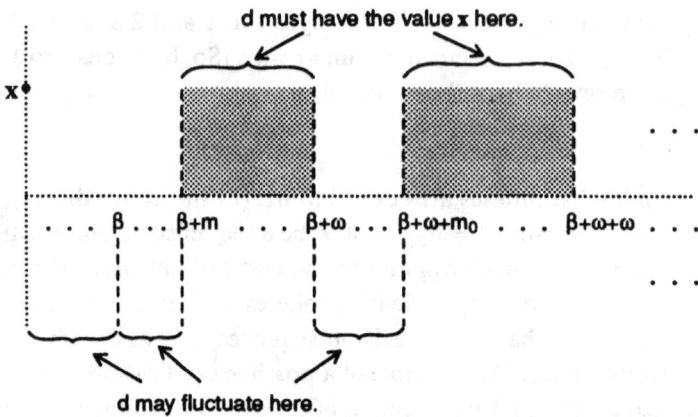

d must have the value x here.

d may fluctuate here.

Figure 5.2

appear at first sight. The alternatives mentioned above yield remarkably similar theories of definitions.

5C.6 Definition (Cofinality) An object h is *cofinal* in a sequence $\mathscr{S}$ iff for all ordinals $\alpha < \mathrm{lh}(\mathscr{S})$ there is a β such that $\alpha \leq \beta < \mathrm{lh}(\mathscr{S})$ and $\mathscr{S}_\beta = h$.

5C.7 Theorem (Cofinal hypotheses) Let $\mathscr{S}$ be a sequence of length On. Then:

(i) There is at least one hypothesis $h \in X^D$ that is cofinal in $\mathscr{S}$.

(ii) There is an ordinal α such that, for all $\beta \geq \alpha$, $\mathscr{S}_\beta$ is cofinal in $\mathscr{S}$; the least such α is *the initial ordinal for $\mathscr{S}$*.

(iii) For all ordinals α there is an ordinal $\beta > \alpha$ satisfying the condition that for all hypotheses h cofinal in $\mathscr{S}$ there is an ordinal γ such that $\alpha \leq \gamma < \beta$ and $\mathscr{S}_\gamma = h$; such an ordinal β is a *completion ordinal for $\mathscr{S}$ above α*.

Proof For each hypothesis h that is *not* cofinal in $\mathscr{S}$, let α_h be the least ordinal after which h does not occur in $\mathscr{S}$, so that, for all $\beta \geq \alpha_h$, $\mathscr{S}_\beta \neq h$. Let α be the supremum of the set of ordinals $\{\alpha_h: h$ is not cofinal in $\mathscr{S}\}$. Clearly, if $\beta \geq \alpha$ then $\mathscr{S}_\beta$ is cofinal in $\mathscr{S}$. Hence (ii) is established. As (ii) implies (i), so is (i) established. (iii) is proved similarly. For each hypothesis h cofinal in $\mathscr{S}$ there is an ordinal δ such that $\alpha \leq \delta$ and $\mathscr{S}_\delta = h$. Let β_h be the successor of the least such δ. The supremum of $\{\beta_h: h$ is cofinal in $\mathscr{S}\}$ is a completion ordinal for $\mathscr{S}$ above α. ∎

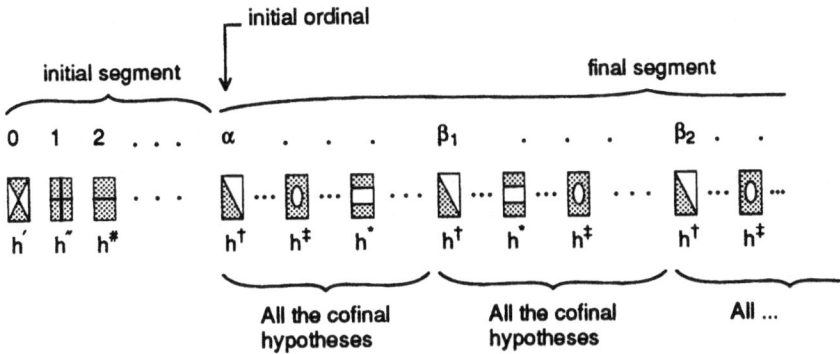

Figure 5.3

A sequence $\mathscr{S}$ of length On consists of two parts: an initial segment that contains hypotheses that are *not* cofinal in $\mathscr{S}$ and a final segment that contains *only* those that are cofinal.[28] The division between the two segments occurs at the initial ordinal, α. Between the initial ordinal and the next completion ordinal β_1 all the cofinal hypotheses can be found. The same happens between β_1 and *its* next completion ordinal, β_2. And so on. The cofinal hypotheses occur over and over again in the final segment.[29] See figure 5.3.

5C.8   Theorem (Cofinal hypotheses and stability)   Let $\mathscr{S}$ be a sequence of hypotheses. Then, for all $d \in D$ and all $x \in X$,

(i) if d is stably x in $\mathscr{S}$ then the value of d is x in all hypotheses cofinal in $\mathscr{S}$;

(ii) the converse of (i) holds if $\mathrm{lh}(\mathscr{S}) = \mathrm{On}$.

Proof
(i) Suppose d is stably x in $\mathscr{S}$ and that its stabilization point is α. For any cofinal hypothesis h there is an ordinal β such that $\alpha \leq \beta < \mathrm{lh}(\mathscr{S})$ and $\mathscr{S}_\beta = h$. Hence, $h(d) = x$.

---

[28] The initial segment may contain some hypotheses that are cofinal in $\mathscr{S}$.
[29] Herzberger (198+) has shown that, in certain kinds of revision sequences, not only do the same hypotheses occur over and over again in the final segment, but they occur in a "periodic" way. (Herzberger's paper remains unpublished. The reader can find proofs of his theorem in Visser 1989 and in McGee 1991.)
    The periodicity phenomenon does not occur in *all* revision sequences. It can be shown that the phenomenon occurs if and only if the treatment of the unstable elements at the limit stages exhibits periodicity.

(ii) If $\mathrm{lh}(\mathscr{S}) = \mathrm{On}$ and the value of d in all cofinal hypotheses is **x**, then $\mathscr{S}_\gamma(\mathrm{d}) = \mathbf{x}$ for all $\gamma \geq$ the initial ordinal for $\mathscr{S}$. So d is stably **x** in $\mathscr{S}$.   ∎

Remarks

(i) Suppose that d is stably **x** in $\mathscr{S}$ and that its stabilization point is α. Then, d is stably **x** at all limit ordinals β such that $\alpha < \beta < \mathrm{lh}(\mathscr{S})$. And if $\mathrm{lh}(\mathscr{S})$ is On then $\alpha \leq$ the initial ordinal for $\mathscr{S}$.

(ii) If two sequences $\mathscr{S}$ and $\mathscr{S}'$ of length On have the same cofinal hypotheses, then stabilities and instabilities in $\mathscr{S}$ and $\mathscr{S}'$ are exactly the same.

5C.9   Definition   (Reflection ordinal)   An ordinal α is a *reflection ordinal for $\mathscr{S}$* iff α is a limit ordinal $< \mathrm{lh}(\mathscr{S})$ such that

(i) $\alpha \geq$ the initial ordinal for $\mathscr{S}$

and

(ii) for all $\mathrm{d} \in \mathrm{D}$ and $\mathbf{x} \in \mathrm{X}$, d is stably **x** in $\mathscr{S}{\upharpoonright}\alpha$ iff d is stably **x** in $\mathscr{S}$.[30]

If α is a reflection ordinal for $\mathscr{S}$, then the segment $\mathscr{S}{\upharpoonright}\alpha$ reflects all the stabilities and instabilities found in $\mathscr{S}$. Our next theorem shows that sequences of length On contain many reflection ordinals. Let us recall some set-theoretic terminology. A class Z of ordinals is *unbounded* iff for all ordinals α there is an ordinal $\beta \geq \alpha$ such that $\beta \in \mathrm{Z}$. Z is *closed* iff Z contains every limit ordinal α satisfying the condition that for all $\beta < \alpha$ there is a γ such that $\beta \leq \gamma < \alpha$ and $\gamma \in \mathrm{Z}$.

5C.10   Theorem   (Reflection Theorem)   Let $\mathscr{S}$ be a sequence of length On. Then the class R of reflection ordinals for $\mathscr{S}$ is closed and unbounded.[31]

Proof

(i) R is closed. Let α be an arbitrary limit ordinal satisfying the condition that

(1)   for all $\beta < \alpha$ there is a γ such that $\beta \leq \gamma < \alpha$ and $\gamma \in \mathrm{R}$.

We need to show that $\alpha \in \mathrm{R}$. Suppose that d is stably **x** in $\mathscr{S}$. Since $\alpha \geq$ the initial ordinal for $\mathscr{S}$, d is stably **x** in $\mathscr{S}{\upharpoonright}\alpha$. Suppose, on the other hand,

---

[30] The notion of reflection ordinal is similar to Herzberger's notion of "alignment point."
[31] This is a generalization of a theorem due to Herzberger.

that d is stably x in $\mathscr{S}\!\upharpoonright \alpha$ and that its stabilization point in $\mathscr{S}\!\upharpoonright \alpha$ is β. By (1) there is a reflection ordinal γ between α and β. Clearly, d is stably x in $\mathscr{S}\!\upharpoonright \gamma$. As γ is a reflection ordinal for $\mathscr{S}$, it follows that d is stably x in $\mathscr{S}$. We conclude that $\alpha \in R$.

(ii) R is unbounded. Let θ > the initial ordinal for $\mathscr{S}$. We show that there is a reflection ordinal > θ.

Define a sequence of ordinals α_n so that $\alpha_0 = \theta$ and α_{n+1} is the least completion ordinal above α_n. By Theorem 5C.7(iii), α_{n+1} exists. Let α be the supremum of $\{\alpha_n : n \in \omega\}$. By an argument very similar to the one given in (i), $\alpha \in R$. Note that if an element d is stably x in $\mathscr{S}\!\upharpoonright \alpha$ then the value of d must be x in all hypotheses cofinal in $\mathscr{S}$. So, d must be stably x in $\mathscr{S}$ (see Theorem 5C.8). ∎

Skippable remark   We can now see that fully varied revision sequences exist. Associate pairwise-disjoint stationary classes of ordinals Z_h with hypotheses $h \in X^D$.[32] Construct an On-long revision sequence $\mathscr{S}$ that assigns to elements d unstable at a limit ordinal $\alpha \in Z_h$ the value h(d). $\mathscr{S}$ is fully varied: Suppose h coheres with $\mathscr{S}$. Let α be a reflection ordinal for $\mathscr{S}$ in Z_h. Since the class of reflection ordinals of $\mathscr{S}$ is closed and unbounded, such an α does exist. We have $\mathscr{S}_\alpha = h$.

The theorems proved so far hold for all sequences of hypotheses. We now turn to some in which the special character of revision sequences comes into play.

5C.11   Theorem   (Miscellaneous properties of revision sequences)   Let $\mathscr{S}$ be a revision sequence for ρ and let $\alpha < \mathrm{lh}(\mathscr{S})$.

(i) For all β such that $\alpha + \beta < \mathrm{lh}(\mathscr{S})$, set $\mathscr{S}'_\beta = \mathscr{S}_{\alpha+\beta}$. Then $\mathscr{S}'$ is a revision sequence for ρ.[33]

(ii) Suppose that there is a $\beta < \alpha$ such that $\mathscr{S}_\beta = \mathscr{S}_\alpha$. Set $H = \{h :$ for some γ, $\mathscr{S}_\gamma = h$ and $\beta \leq \gamma < \alpha\}$. Then there is a revision sequence $\mathscr{S}'$ of length On such that the set of cofinal hypotheses in $\mathscr{S}'$ is H.

(iii) If h is cofinal in $\mathscr{S}$ then so also is $\rho(h)$.

(iv) If $\mathscr{S}_\alpha$ is a fixed point of ρ, then for all β such that $\alpha + \beta < \mathrm{lh}(\mathscr{S})$ we have $\mathscr{S}_{\alpha+\beta} = \mathscr{S}_\alpha$; furthermore, an object $d \in D$ is stably x in $\mathscr{S}$ iff $\mathscr{S}_\alpha(d) = x$.

---

[32] A class is *stationary* iff it intersects every closed and unbounded class.
[33] Note that $\mathscr{S}\!\upharpoonright \alpha$ is also a revision sequence (assuming α is a limit ordinal).

Proof

(i) $\mathscr{S}'$ satisfies the first condition on revision sequences because for all $\gamma < \mathrm{lh}(\mathscr{S}')$

$$\mathscr{S}'_{\gamma+1} = \mathscr{S}_{\alpha+(\gamma+1)} = \mathscr{S}_{(\alpha+\gamma)+1} = \rho(\mathscr{S}_{\alpha+\gamma}) = \rho(\mathscr{S}'_{\gamma}).$$

Further, if d is stably x in $\mathscr{S}'$ at a limit ordinal $\gamma < \mathrm{lh}(\mathscr{S}')$, then, by the definition of $\mathscr{S}'$, d is stably x in $\mathscr{S}$ at $\alpha + \gamma$. Hence, $\mathscr{S}_{\alpha+\gamma}(\mathrm{d}) = \mathrm{x}$. So $\mathscr{S}'_{\gamma}(\mathrm{d}) = \mathrm{x}$, and the second condition on revision sequences is satisfied as well.

(ii) Since $\beta < \alpha$, there is a $\gamma \neq 0$ such that $\beta + \gamma = \alpha$. Construct a sequence $\mathscr{S}'$ of length On in the following manner. For all δ and for all $\mu < \gamma$, set $\mathscr{S}'_{\gamma \cdot \delta + \mu} = \mathscr{S}_{\beta+\mu}$. The set of cofinal hypotheses in $\mathscr{S}'$ is H and, as can be verified, $\mathscr{S}'$ is a revision sequence for ρ.

(iii) If $\mathscr{S}_{\beta} = \mathrm{h}$ then $\mathscr{S}_{\beta+1} = \rho(\mathrm{h})$. So if h is cofinal in $\mathscr{S}$ then $\rho(\mathrm{h})$ is as well.

(iv) By induction on β. The case $\beta = 0$ is trivial. If $\beta = \gamma + 1$ then, by the induction hypothesis, $\mathscr{S}_{\gamma} = \mathscr{S}_{\alpha}$. Hence,

$$\mathscr{S}_{\beta} = \mathscr{S}_{\gamma+1} = \rho(\mathscr{S}_{\gamma}) = \rho(\mathscr{S}_{\alpha}) = \mathscr{S}_{\alpha}.$$

If β is a limit ordinal and, for an arbitrary $\mathrm{d} \in \mathrm{D}$, $\mathscr{S}_{\alpha}(\mathrm{d}) = \mathrm{x}$, then, by the induction hypothesis, the value of d in $\mathscr{S}_{\alpha+\gamma}$ $(\gamma < \beta)$ is x. So d is stably x in $\mathscr{S} \upharpoonright (\alpha + \beta)$, and $\mathscr{S}_{\alpha+\beta}(\mathrm{d}) = \mathrm{x}$. Hence $\mathscr{S}_{\alpha+\beta} = \mathscr{S}_{\alpha}$. The argument for the limit case shows that an object $\mathrm{d} \in \mathrm{D}$ is stably x in $\mathscr{S}$ iff $\mathscr{S}_{\alpha}(\mathrm{d}) = \mathrm{x}$.   ∎

5C.12   Definition   (Recurring and reflexive hypotheses)

(i) A hypothesis h is *recurring for* ρ iff h is cofinal in some revision sequence $\mathscr{S}$ of length On for ρ.

(ii) A hypothesis h is α-*reflexive for* ρ[34] iff there is a revision sequence $\mathscr{S}$ for ρ such that $\alpha < \mathrm{lh}(\mathscr{S})$ and $\mathscr{S}_0 = \mathscr{S}_{\alpha} = \mathrm{h}$; h is *reflexive for* ρ iff h is α-reflexive for some ordinal $\alpha > 0$.

Intuitively, the recurring hypotheses can be thought of as those that survive the revision process. They will be used later to help provide a semantics for definitions.

5C.13   Theorem   (Recurring and reflexive hypotheses)   All and only recurring hypotheses are reflexive.

---

[34] This is a generalization of the notion of m-reflexiveness introduced in section 5A.

Proof   Suppose h is a recurring hypothesis. Then there is a revision sequence $\mathscr{S}$ of length On in which h occurs cofinally. For an α such that $\mathscr{S}_\alpha = $ h, construct a sequence $\mathscr{S}'$ such that for all β

$$\mathscr{S}'_\beta = \mathscr{S}_{\alpha+\beta}.$$

Since h is cofinal in $\mathscr{S}$, there is an ordinal $\gamma > 0$ such that $\mathscr{S}_{\alpha+\gamma} = $ h. So, $\mathscr{S}'_\gamma = $ h. By Theorem 5C.11(i), $\mathscr{S}'$ is a revision sequence for ρ. Hence, h is reflexive for ρ.

Suppose h is a reflexive hypothesis. Then there is a revision sequence $\mathscr{S}$ and an ordinal $\alpha < \mathrm{lh}(\mathscr{S})$ such that $\mathscr{S}_0 = \mathscr{S}_\alpha = $ h $(\alpha > 0)$. By Theorem 5C.11(ii) there is a sequence $\mathscr{S}'$ of length On in which h is cofinal.   ∎

Remark   This theorem shows that the notion of recurring hypothesis, which is defined in 5C.12 using quantification over proper classes, can instead be defined without resorting to such quantification. It can be defined within ZFC.

Skippable Remarks   Let ρ be the revision rule given in Example 5C.4.

(i) If revision sequences are defined using the Herzberger Limit Rule, then the equivalence of recurring and reflexive hypotheses fails. By this rule, all recurring hypotheses are reflexive, but the converse is not true. Counterexample: h_{13} and h_{23} are 2-reflexive for ρ, but there is no Herzberger-style On-sequence in which h_{13} and h_{23} are cofinal (assuming that the unstable elements are assigned the value **f**).

(ii) The equivalence fails also on the Constant Limit Rule. Now all reflexive hypotheses are recurring, but the converse is not true. Counterexample: h recurs in the revision sequence generated by h_{123}, but h is not reflexive by this limit rule.

(iii) Finally, h_{23} is reflexive but is not cofinal in any fully varied revision sequence for ρ.

5C.14   Theorem   (Existence of reflexive hypotheses)   At least one hypothesis is reflexive for ρ.

Proof   On-sequences $\mathscr{S}$ for ρ can always be constructed. By Theorem 5C.7, hypotheses cofinal in $\mathscr{S}$ exist. These hypothesis are, by definition, recurring. By Theorem 5C.13, they are also reflexive.   ∎

5C.15 Theorem (McGee's theorem)   Let h be a reflexive hypothesis for ρ, where $\rho: X^D \to X^D$. Let $m = \max\{|D|, |X|, \aleph_0\}$.[35] Then, for some ordinal α such that $|\alpha| \leq m$, h is α-reflexive.

Proof   The proof relies on the Löwenheim-Skolem-Tarski Theorem (see Chang and Keisler 1977). Suppose $\mathscr{S}$ is a revision sequence for ρ and β an ordinal such that $\mathscr{S}_0 = \mathscr{S}_\beta = h$ and $\beta + \omega \leq \mathrm{lh}(\mathscr{S})$. Consider a classical first-order language $\mathscr{L}$ whose nonlogical constants are the predicates *Ord*, *Obj*, *Val*, *Less*, and *R* and whose interpretation M $(= \langle \mathrm{Dom}, I \rangle)$ satisfies the following conditions:

$\mathrm{Dom} = D \cup X \cup \{\gamma : \gamma < \beta + \omega\}$,

$I(Ord)(d) = t$ iff d is an ordinal $< \beta + \omega$,

$I(Obj)(d) = t$ iff $d \in D$,

$I(Val)(d) = t$ iff $d \in X$,

$I(Less)(d, d') = t$ iff d, d' are ordinals such that $d < d'$,

$I(R)(d, d', d'') = t$ iff $\mathscr{S}_d(d') = d''$.

By the Löwenheim-Skolem-Tarski Theorem, there is an elementary submodel M' $(= \langle \mathrm{Dom}', I' \rangle)$ of M of cardinality m whose domain Dom' includes D, X, and $\{0, \beta\}$. The ordinals in Dom' constitute a well-ordering. Define the isomorphism f between them and an initial segment of ordinals thus: For $\gamma \in \mathrm{Dom}'$,

$f(\gamma) = \bigcup \{f(\delta) + 1 : \delta \in \gamma \cap \mathrm{Dom}'\}$.

Let $\alpha = f(\beta)$. Note that $|\alpha| \leq m$. Define now a sequence $\mathscr{S}'$ of length $\alpha + \omega$: For all $\gamma \leq \alpha + \omega$, and all $d \in D$, and all $x \in X$,

$\mathscr{S}'_\gamma(d) = x$ iff $I'(R)(f^{-1}(\gamma), d, x) = t$.

Note that if an ordinal δ is in Dom' then so also is $\delta + 1$, since "is an immediate successor of" is a first-order condition that is expressible in $\mathscr{L}$.

   We now verify that $\mathscr{S}'$ is a revision sequence for ρ. The requirement on successor stages is met simply because M' is a submodel of M and its domain includes D and X. To verify that the requirement on limit stages is also met, suppose that γ is a limit ordinal $< \mathrm{lh}(\mathscr{S}')$ and that d is stably

---

[35] $|D| =$ the cardinality of D.

x at γ in $\mathscr{S}'$. Let $\delta = f^{-1}(\gamma)$. Since γ is limit, so also is δ. By the definition of $\mathscr{S}'$, we conclude that the formula

$$\exists y[Ord(y) \& Less(y, x_1) \&$$

$$\forall z(Ord(z) \& Less(y, z) \& Less(z, x_1) \rightarrow R(z, x_2, x_3))]$$

is true of δ, d, and x in M', and hence also in M, since M' is an elementary submodel of M. This means that d is stably x at δ in $\mathscr{S}$. So, $\mathscr{S}_\delta(d) = x$. It follows that $\mathscr{S}'_\gamma(d) = x$.

Since $\mathscr{S}'_0 = \mathscr{S}'_\alpha = h$, h is α-reflexive, where $|\alpha| \le m$. ∎

Remark It can be shown similarly that the stabilities and instabilities in a revision sequence $\mathscr{S}$ of length $> m$ can be mirrored in a revision sequence $\mathscr{S}'$ of length $< m^+$. See McGee 1991.

We now study revision sequences in the context of ccpos. Let X be a *finite* set, and $\mathscr{X} = \langle X, \le \rangle$ be a ccpo.[36] We are interested in those revision rules

$$\rho\colon X^D \to X^D$$

that are monotone operations on $\mathscr{X}^D$. Note that by Theorem 2C.4 the structure $\mathscr{X}^D$ is a ccpo.

5C.16 Theorem (Revision sequences in ccpos) Let $\mathscr{S}$ be a revision sequence for a monotone ρ.

(i) If $\mathscr{S}_0$ is sound then, for all $\alpha < \text{lh}(\mathscr{S})$,

(a) $\mathscr{S}_\alpha = \bigvee \{\mathscr{S}_\gamma\colon \gamma < \alpha\}$ if α is a limit ordinal

and

(b) for all $\beta < \text{lh}(\mathscr{S})$, $\mathscr{S}_\beta \le \mathscr{S}_\alpha$ if $\beta < \alpha$.

(ii) If $\mathscr{S}_0$ is replete then, for all $\alpha < \text{lh}(\mathscr{S})$,

(a) $\mathscr{S}_\alpha = \bigwedge \{\mathscr{S}_\gamma\colon \gamma < \alpha\}$ if α is a limit ordinal

and

(b) for all $\beta < \text{lh}(\mathscr{S})$, $\mathscr{S}_\alpha \le \mathscr{S}_\beta$ if $\beta < \alpha$.

(iii) If $\mathscr{S}_0$ is sound and $\text{lh}(\mathscr{S}) = \text{On}$ then there is an ordinal α such that $\mathscr{S}_\alpha$ is the least fixed point of ρ above $\mathscr{S}_0$.

---

[36] The primary example to keep in mind is where $X = \{t, f, n\}$. Note that if X is infinite then the theorems given below hold only for special kinds of revision sequences.

(iv) If $\mathscr{S}_0$ is replete and $\mathrm{lh}(\mathscr{S}) = \mathrm{On}$ then there is an ordinal α such that $\mathscr{S}_\alpha$ is the greatest fixed point of ρ below $\mathscr{S}_0$.

Proof

(i) This is proved by induction on α. Let $\alpha < \mathrm{lh}(\mathscr{S})$ be a limit ordinal. For an arbitrary $d \in D$, consider the sequence of values $\langle x_\gamma \rangle_{\gamma < \alpha}$, where $x_\gamma = \mathscr{S}_\gamma(d)$. Since X is finite and this sequence of values is infinite, some value—say, x_θ—must occur cofinally in it. Consider an ordinal δ such that $\theta \leq \delta < \alpha$. We know there is an ordinal μ such that

$$\delta < \mu < \alpha$$

and

$$x_\mu = x_\theta.$$

By the induction hypothesis,

$$x_\theta \leq x_\delta \leq x_\mu = x_\theta.$$

It follows that $x_\delta = x_\theta$. Hence, d is stably x_θ in $\mathscr{S} \upharpoonright \alpha$. So, $\mathscr{S}_\alpha(d) = x_\theta$. And $\mathscr{S}_\alpha$ is an upper bound of $\{\mathscr{S}_\gamma : \gamma < \alpha\}$. Further, if h is an upper bound of $\{\mathscr{S}_\gamma : \gamma < \alpha\}$ then $h(d) \geq x_\theta$. So, $h(d) \geq \mathscr{S}_\alpha(d)$. $\mathscr{S}_\alpha$ is, therefore, the supremum of $\{\mathscr{S}_\gamma : \gamma < \alpha\}$.

Let us now turn to part (b). If $\alpha = 0$, the claim holds vacuously. If α is limit, the argument already given for part (a) proves the claim. Suppose, then, that $\alpha = \gamma + 1$ and consider cases for β.

Case: $\beta = 0$ Since $\beta < \alpha$, $\beta \leq \gamma$. By the induction hypothesis, $\mathscr{S}_0 \leq \mathscr{S}_\gamma$. By the soundness of $\mathscr{S}_0$ and the monotonicity of ρ, we have

$$\mathscr{S}_0 \leq \rho(\mathscr{S}_0) \leq \rho(\mathscr{S}_\gamma) = \mathscr{S}_\alpha.$$

Case: β *is a successor ordinal*   Say $\beta = \delta + 1$. Then $\delta < \gamma$, and the induction hypothesis implies that $\mathscr{S}_\delta \leq \mathscr{S}_\gamma$. By monotonicity, $\mathscr{S}_{\delta+1} \leq \mathscr{S}_{\gamma+1}$.

Case: β *is a limit ordinal*   Consider a $\delta < \beta$. By the induction hypothesis, $\mathscr{S}_\delta \leq \mathscr{S}_\gamma$. Monotonicity and another application of the induction hypothesis yield

$$\mathscr{S}_\delta \leq \rho(\mathscr{S}_\delta) \leq \rho(\mathscr{S}_\gamma) = \mathscr{S}_\alpha.$$

It follows that $\mathscr{S}_\alpha$ is an upper bound of $\{\mathscr{S}_\delta : \delta < \beta\}$. By part (a) of the induction hypothesis, $\mathscr{S}_\beta$ is the least upper bound of this set. So, $\mathscr{S}_\beta \leq \mathscr{S}_\alpha$.

(ii) This is a dual of the proof of (i).

(iii) By Theorem 5C.7(i), there are hypotheses h that are cofinal in $\mathscr{S}$. Hence, there are ordinals α and β such that $\alpha < \beta$ and $\mathscr{S}_\alpha = \mathscr{S}_\beta = h$. Since $\mathscr{S}_0$ is sound, part (i) implies that

$$h = \mathscr{S}_\alpha \leq \mathscr{S}_{\alpha+1} \leq \mathscr{S}_\beta = h.$$

Hence $\mathscr{S}_{\alpha+1} = h$ and $\mathscr{S}_\alpha$ is a fixed point.

Let $h \geq \mathscr{S}_0$ be an arbitrary fixed point of ρ. One shows by induction that, for all β, $\mathscr{S}_\beta \leq h$. It follows that $\mathscr{S}_\alpha$ is the least fixed point above $\mathscr{S}_0$.

(iv) Similar to the proof of (iii).   ■

Remarks

(i) Revision sequences generated by sound (replete) hypotheses under monotone operations manifest no instability.[37] There are thus no choices to be made at limit stages; the entire sequence is fixed once one is given the initial hypothesis. In these special cases, the revision sequence coincides with that obtained in the process of iteratively building fixed points of monotone operators—a process that is familiar from many branches of mathematics, including lattice theory and the theory of inductive definitions.

(ii) The least element of $\mathscr{S}^D$ is sound. Hence, the revision sequence that starts at this element culminates in the least fixed point of ρ. This sequence is exploited in an illuminating way in Kripke's Theory of Truth (see the first paragraph of section 6A below).

(iii) Visser (1984) has observed that certain kinds of revision sequences invariably culminate in a fixed point; it is immaterial whether the initial hypothesis of revision is sound or not. Suppose $\mathscr{S}$ is a revision sequence of length On for a monotone ρ, and that $\mathscr{S}$ treats elements d unstable at a limit ordinal α thus:

$$(2) \quad \mathscr{S}_\alpha(d) = \bigvee_{0 \leq \beta < \alpha} \left[\bigwedge_{\beta \leq \gamma < \alpha} \mathscr{S}_\gamma(d) \right].^{38}$$

Let θ be a reflection ordinal such that all hypotheses cofinal in $\mathscr{S}$ are cofinal in $\mathscr{S} \restriction \theta$. (By Theorems 5C.7 and 5C.10, such a θ does exist.) Ob-

---

[37] Assuming, as before, that X is finite.
[38] This rule may be followed on stable elements also, for if d is stably x in $\mathscr{S}$ at α then the rule yields that $\mathscr{S}_\alpha(d) = x$.

serve that $\mathscr{S}_{\theta+1}$ is cofinal in $\mathscr{S}$ and, hence, in $\mathscr{S} \upharpoonright \theta$. By condition (2) on $\mathscr{S}$, we have that, for all d unstable in $\mathscr{S}$,

$$\mathscr{S}_\theta(d) \le \mathscr{S}_{\theta+1}(d).$$

Thus,

$$\mathscr{S}_\theta \le \mathscr{S}_{\theta+1}.$$

That is, $\mathscr{S}_\theta$ is sound. Hence, by the above theorem, $\mathscr{S}$ culminates in a fixed point.

5C.17 Definition (Simple ccpo) A ccpo $\mathscr{X}$ $(= \langle X, \le \rangle)$ is *simple* iff every member of X other than the least element is maximal.

Simple ccpos look like this:

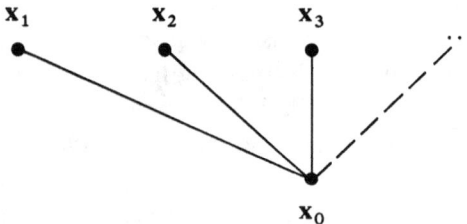

5C.18 Theorem (Comparison of revision sequences I) Let $\mathscr{X}$ $(= \langle X, \le \rangle)$ be a simple ccpo, and let ρ be a monotone operation on $\mathscr{X}^D$. Suppose that $\mathscr{S}$ and $\mathscr{S}'$ are revision sequences for ρ such that $\mathscr{S}_0$ is sound and $\mathscr{S}_0 \le \mathscr{S}_0'$. Then, for all $\alpha < \mathrm{lh}(\mathscr{S})$ and $\mathrm{lh}(\mathscr{S}')$,

$$\mathscr{S}_\alpha \le \mathscr{S}_\alpha'.$$

Proof This is proved by induction on α. For $\alpha = 0$, we are given that $\mathscr{S}_\alpha \le \mathscr{S}_\alpha'$. If α is a successor, say $\beta + 1$, then the induction hypothesis yields that $\mathscr{S}_\beta \le \mathscr{S}_\beta'$. By monotonicity of ρ,

$$\mathscr{S}_{\beta+1} \le \mathscr{S}_{\beta+1}'.$$

If α is a limit, then we have by Theorem 5C.16(i) that

$$\mathscr{S}_\alpha = \bigvee \{\mathscr{S}_\beta : \beta < \alpha\}.$$

We need only show that $\mathscr{S}_\alpha'$ is an upper bound of $\{\mathscr{S}_\beta : \beta < \alpha\}$. Consider an arbitrary $\beta < \alpha$ and an arbitrary $d \in D$. If $\mathscr{S}_\beta(d)$ $(= x$, say) is the least element of $\mathscr{X}$, then

$\mathcal{S}_\beta(d) \le \mathcal{S}'_\beta(d)$.

On the other hand, if x is *not* the least element of $\mathcal{X}$, then x must be maximal since $\mathcal{X}$ is simple. Consider a γ such that $\beta \le \gamma < \alpha$. By Theorem 5C.16(i),

$\mathcal{S}_\beta \le \mathcal{S}_\gamma$.

By the induction hypothesis,

$\mathcal{S}_\gamma \le \mathcal{S}'_\gamma$.

Hence,

$x = \mathcal{S}_\beta(d) \le \mathcal{S}_\gamma(d) \le \mathcal{S}'_\gamma(d)$.

As x is maximal,

$\mathcal{S}'_\gamma(d) = x$.

So d is stably x at α in $\mathcal{S}'$, and

$\mathcal{S}'_\alpha(d) = x$.

We have the desired

$\mathcal{S}_\beta(d) \le \mathcal{S}'_\alpha(d)$.   ∎

The analogue of the above theorem for replete elements fails. It does hold, however, under one special condition:

5C.19 Theorem (Comparison of revision sequences II) Let $\mathcal{X}$ $(= \langle X, \le \rangle)$ be a *two-element* simple ccpo and ρ a monotone operation on $\mathcal{X}^{\mathrm{D}}$. Suppose that $\mathcal{S}$ and $\mathcal{S}'$ are revision sequences for ρ such that $\mathcal{S}_0$ is replete and $\mathcal{S}_0 \ge \mathcal{S}'_0$. Then, for all $\alpha < \mathrm{lh}(\mathcal{S})$ and $\mathrm{lh}(\mathcal{S}')$,

$\mathcal{S}_\alpha \ge \mathcal{S}'_\alpha$.

Proof This is proved by an induction on α.   ∎

Remark Since the two-element ccpo $\mathcal{X}$ is a complete lattice, ρ has a greatest fixed point. In this special case, the reflexive hypotheses of ρ all fall somewhere between the least and the greatest fixed points of ρ.

Historical note The theorems proved in this section give the basic properties of revision sequences. Many of them (or their analogues for the special case of truth) can be found in Belnap 1982, Gupta 1982, and Herzberger 1982a. The notion of reflection ordinal is based on Herzberger's notion of alignment point. The notion of reflexive hypothesis has, curiously, not been articulated before.[39] Theorem 5C.15 is a consequence of a result of McGee (1991). Analogues of Theorem 5C.16 (iii) and (iv) can be found in Visser 1984, Woodruff 1984, and Fitting 1986.

5D   The Semantical Systems $S^\#$ and S^*

Revision sequences provide a way of meeting simultaneously the demands of content and of conservativeness on definitions. The central idea is to interpret definitions in terms of recurring hypotheses. These hypotheses are like the m-reflexive ones (m > 0) in that they embody a degree of closure (see 5C.13); this ensures that definitions have content. They are unlike the m-reflexive hypotheses (m > 0), however, in that they are bound to exist; this ensures that definitions are strongly conservative.

Two systems, $S^\#$ and S^*, both based on recurring hypotheses, will be presented in this section. We begin with the system $S^\#$.

The System $S^\#$

5D.1   Definition   (Validity in $S^\#$)   Let $\mathscr{L} = \langle L, M, \tau \rangle$ and let A be a sentence of the language L^+.[40] Then,

(i) A is *valid on $\mathscr{D}$ in* M *in* the system $S^\#$ (notation: $M \models_{\#}^{\mathscr{D}} A$) iff for all hypotheses h that are recurring for $\delta_{\mathscr{D},M}$ there is a number n such that, for all $p \geq n$, A is true in $M + \delta_{\mathscr{D},M}^p(h)$.[41]

(ii) A is *valid on $\mathscr{D}$ in* $S^\#$ (notation: $\models_{\#}^{\mathscr{D}} A$) iff, for all classical models M of L, $M \models_{\#}^{\mathscr{D}} A$.

See Theorem 5D.14 for some alternative characterizations of $M \models_{\#}^{\mathscr{D}} A$.

---

[39] Perhaps a reason is that this concept appears less natural when it is not equivalent to that of recurring hypothesis. As already remarked, the two are not equivalent if revisions are defined in the manner of Gupta 1982 and Herzberger 1982a.

[40] We use freely the definitions and notational conventions stated in the introduction (see pp. 145–146).

[41] A variant definition of interest is one in which the quantifiers 'for all hypotheses h' and 'there is a number n' are switched. Note that the variant notion of validity is structurally parallel to the one defined in Definition 5A.2 (see also pp. 122–123). By this variant notion, however, there are fewer validities than on the notion defined in the text, and hence lesser content is attributed to definitions.

5D.2 Theorem (Relationships between systems I) Let M and A be as above. Then (i) implies (ii), and (ii) implies (iii).

(i) $M \models_0^{\mathscr{D}} A$

(ii) $M \models_{\#}^{\mathscr{D}} A$

(iii) $M \models_n^{\mathscr{D}} A$ (n > 0).

Proof All recurring hypotheses are 0-reflexive. So (i) implies (ii). All n-reflexive hypotheses h are recurring. So, by (ii), there is a number m such that, for all $p \geq m$, A is true in $M + \delta_{\mathscr{D},M}^p(h)$. Hence, A is true in $M + \delta_{\mathscr{D},M}^{n\cdot m}(h)$. As h is n-reflexive, $\delta_{\mathscr{D},M}^{n\cdot m}(h) = h$. So, A is true in $M + h$ and (iii) holds. ∎

5D.3 Theorem (Relationships between systems II)

$$S_0 < S^{\#} < S_n \quad (n > 0).$$

Proof By the previous theorem,

$$S_0 \leq S^{\#} \leq S_n.$$

Example 5A.17 suffices to establish the first strict inequality. Relative to the system of definitions $\mathscr{D}$ given in this example, the formula

$$AX \to \forall x Gx$$

is valid in $S^{\#}$ but not in S_0. Example 5A.14 can be used to show the second strict inequality. Relative to $\mathscr{D}_n$ constructed in this example, A_n is valid in S_n but not in $S^{\#}$. ∎

Remarks

(i) The system $S^{\#}$ sustains classical reasoning: If A is a classical validity, then $\models_{\#}^{\mathscr{D}} A$.

(ii) The rules of definitions, DfI and DfE, hold in $S^{\#}$ in categorical contexts: For all models M and all closed terms $t_1, \ldots, t_n$, we have

$$M \models_{\#}^{\mathscr{D}} G(t_1, \ldots, t_n) \text{ iff } M \models_{\#}^{\mathscr{D}} A_G(t_1, \ldots, t_n).$$

(Recall the convention, stated in the introduction to this chapter, that the definition

$$G(x_1, \ldots, x_n) =_{Df} A_G(x_1, \ldots, x_n)$$

belongs to the system $\mathscr{D}$.)

(iii) The rules of definitions do not hold, in general, in hypothetical contexts: We do not have

$$\models_{\#}^{\mathscr{D}} (G(t_1,\ldots,t_n) \leftrightarrow A_G(t_1,\ldots,t_n)).$$

But we do have (by Theorem 5A.6(i))

$$C_0 < S^{\#}.$$

Hence, the rules of definitions can be used in hypothetical contexts so long as the restrictions on revision indices are observed.

(iv) Theorem 5D.3 shows that in general $S^{\#}$ attributes a greater content to definitions than S_0. In finite situations, however, $S^{\#}$ and S_0 are equivalent:

5D.4 Theorem (Relationships between systems III) Let the model M and the system of definitions $\mathscr{D}$ be both finite.[42] Then the following are equivalent:

(i) $M \models_{0}^{\mathscr{D}} A.$

(ii) $M \models_{\#}^{\mathscr{D}} A.$

(iii) For all $n > 0$, $M \models_{n}^{\mathscr{D}} A.$

Proof We have seen already in Theorem 5D.2 that (i) implies (ii) and that (ii) implies (iii). We need only show that (iii) implies (i). Since M and $\mathscr{D}$ are finite, there are only finitely many hypotheses. Let the number of hypotheses be p. It is easily verified that, for all $m \geq p$ and all h, $\delta_{\mathscr{D},M}^{m}(h)$ is n-reflexive (for some $n > 0$). Hence, (iii) yields that A is true in $M + \delta_{\mathscr{D},M}^{m}(h)$. So, $M \models_{0}^{\mathscr{D}} A.$ ∎

Remark If M and $\mathscr{D}$ are finite, then $M \models_{\#}^{\mathscr{D}} A$ iff A is true in all $M + h$, where h is an n-reflexive hypothesis ($n > 0$).

The next theorem shows that C_0 is perfectly adequate for reasoning concerning finite models.

5D.5 Definition (Finite sentences) A sentence A of L^{+} is *finite* iff A is true only in finite standard models of L^{+}.

Remark Here is a simple characterization of finite sentences: Let $Exist_{\geq}(n)$ (where $n > 1$) abbreviate the formula

---

[42] That is, the domain of M is finite and $\mathscr{D}$ contains only finitely many definitions.

$$\exists x_1 \ldots \exists x_n \left(\bigwedge_{1 < j \leq n} \left[\bigwedge_{1 \leq i < j} x_i \neq x_j \right] \right).$$

Then A is finite iff for some number $n > 1$, A implies $\sim Exist_{\geq}(n)$.[43]

5D.6 Theorem (Finite sentences and S^{*}) Suppose that the system of definitions $\mathcal{D}$ is finite. Then, for all sentences B and all finite A, if $\models_{\#}^{\mathcal{D}} (A \rightarrow B)$ then $\models_{0}^{\mathcal{D}} (A \rightarrow B)$.

Proof Suppose that $(A \rightarrow B)$ is not provable in C_0. By the argument given in the proof of Theorem 5B.1, there is a model M and hypotheses h_0, $h_1, \ldots$ such that, for all i,

$$h_i = \delta_{\mathcal{D},M}(h_{i+1}),$$

and $(A \rightarrow B)$ is not true in $M + h_0$. So, A is true and B false in $M + h_0$. Since A is finite, M must be finite; consequently, there are only finitely many hypotheses. There must, therefore, be numbers m, $n > 0$ such that $h_m = h_{m+n}$. This entails that h_p is n-reflexive for all $p \leq m + n$. Hence h_0 is n-reflexive. By Theorem 5D.4, $(A \rightarrow B)$ is not valid in M by S^{*}. ■

5D.7 Problem (Calculus for S^{*}) Is a complete calculus for S^{*} possible? If not, what is the complexity of the theorems of S^{*} (relative to that of $\mathcal{D}$)?

Remark C_0 is a complete calculus for a semantical system in the neighborhood of S^{*}. Call a hypothesis *attractive* iff it is either recurring or descending (5B.2). Define validity in the manner of 5A.2, replacing 'n-reflexive' by 'attractive'. The resulting semantic system seems to attribute a rich content to definitions, yet the logic it generates is no stronger than C_0 (see the proof of Theorem 5B.4).

The next three theorems concern ordinary and regular definitions in S^{*}. Note that the notion "regular in S^{*}" is defined as in Definition 5A.8 but with 'm-reflexive' replaced by 'recurring'. Here is an alternative characterization of the notion:

---

[43] Proof: Suppose A is finite. Then the set $\{A, Exist_{\geq}(2), Exist_{\geq}(3), \ldots, Exist_{\geq}(n), \ldots\}$ is inconsistent. Hence some finite subset of this set is inconsistent also. Since $Exist_{\geq}(m)$ implies $Exist_{\geq}(n)$ (for $m \geq n > 1$), $\{A, Exist_{\geq}(n)\}$ is inconsistent for some $n > 1$. The converse is immediate.

5D.8   Theorem   (Regular definitions in $S^\#$)   A system of definitions $\mathscr{D}$ is regular in $S^\#$ iff, for all models M, the rule of revision $\delta_{\mathscr{D},M}$ yielded by $\mathscr{D}$ has a unique recurring hypothesis.

Proof   Let $\mathscr{D}$ be regular in $S^\#$, and let M be an arbitrary model of L. Construct a fixed point h of $\delta_{\mathscr{D},M}$ in the manner given in the proof of Theorem 5A.9(i). Suppose, for *reductio*, that there is a recurring hypothesis h′ (for $\delta_{\mathscr{D},M}$) that is distinct from h. Let $\mathscr{S}$ be a revision sequence of length On in which h′ is cofinal; say $\mathscr{S}_\alpha = $ h′. Since $\mathscr{D}$ is regular, we know that, for any arbitrary n-place definiendum G, there is a number p such that, for all recurring hypotheses h″ and all n-tuples $\bar{d}$ of elements of the domain of M,

$$\delta^p_{\mathscr{D},M}(h'')(G,\bar{d}) = h(G,\bar{d}).$$

Since $\mathscr{S}_\alpha\,(=h')$ is recurring, $\mathscr{S}_{\alpha+m}$ is recurring also (for all m ≥ 0). It follows that, for all q ≥ p,

$$\mathscr{S}_{\alpha+q}(G,\bar{d}) = h(G,\bar{d}).$$

Since $\mathscr{S}$ is a revision sequence,

$$\mathscr{S}_{\alpha+\omega}(G,\bar{d}) = h(G,\bar{d}).$$

As G and $\bar{d}$ are arbitrary, $\mathscr{S}_{\alpha+\omega} = $ h. By Theorem 5C.11(iv), $\mathscr{S}_{\alpha+\beta} = $ h for all $\beta \geq \omega$. This conflicts with the assumption that h′ is cofinal in $\mathscr{S}$.

The converse claim is an immediate consequence of the definitions.   ■

5D.9   Theorem   (Relationships between systems IV)   If $\mathscr{D}$ is regular in S_0 then $\mathscr{D}$ is regular in $S^\#$, and if $\mathscr{D}$ is regular in $S^\#$ then $\mathscr{D}$ is regular in S_n (n > 0). Neither of the converses holds.

Proof   The positive claims are a straightforward consequence of the definitions. The system $\mathscr{D}$ constructed in Example 5A.17 is regular in $S^\#$ but not in S_0, and the one constructed in Example 5A.12 is regular in S_{2n+1} but not in $S^\#$. A modification of this last example (along the lines of 5A.14) suffices to establish the remaining parts of the theorem.   ■

5D.10   Theorem   (Ordinary definitions in $S^\#$)   If $\mathscr{D}$ is ordinary, then $\mathscr{D}$ is regular in $S^\#$.

Proof   We know by Theorem 5A.10 that ordinary definitions are regular in S_0. By the previous theorem, they are regular also in $S^\#$.   ■

We conclude that S^*, like the earlier systems S_n ($n \geq 0$), entails no changes in our ordinary ways of working with noncircular definitions. Unlike S_n ($n > 0$), however, S^* is conservative.

5D.11   Theorem   (Conservativeness of S^*) S^* is strongly conservative.

Proof   Suppose that M is a model and A a sentence of L such that $M \overset{\mathscr{D}}{\underset{\#}{\vDash}} A$. By Theorem 5C.7(i), there is at least one recurring hypothesis h for $\delta_{\mathscr{D},M}$. The definition of validity (5D.1) implies that, for some n, A is true in $M + \delta_{\mathscr{D},M}^n(h)$. Since A contains no occurrences of the definienda, A must also be true in M.   ∎

Fix an $\alpha > 0$. A system that interprets definitions in terms of α-reflexive hypotheses attributes a greater content to definitions than S^*; however, as the following example shows, it violates strong conservativeness.

5D.12   Example   (Failure of strong conservativeness)   Recall the system $\mathscr{D}$ of definitions constructed in Example 5A.18. $\mathscr{D}$ consists of only one definition:

$$Gx =_{Df} [G \text{ is closed } \& \ x \neq x] \vee [\sim(G \text{ is closed}) \& \ \forall y(y < x \rightarrow Gy)],$$

where *G is closed* abbreviates the formula

$$\forall x[\forall y(y < x \rightarrow Gy) \rightarrow Gx].$$

Let $\alpha > 0$ and let M ($= \langle D, I \rangle$) be the model, where $D = \alpha + \alpha$ and $<$ is given its usual interpretation. It can be verified that no hypothesis is α-reflexive for $\delta_{\mathscr{D},M}$. Hence, a system that interprets definitions in terms of α-reflexive hypotheses violates strong conservativeness.

Remark   Strong conservativeness seems to us to be a proper demand on an idealized theory of definitions. This does not mean, however, that it is a proper demand on all definitions in *all* contexts. Sometimes definitions are given and accepted with certain presuppositions in mind. These presuppositions may entitle one to interpret definitions in a stronger way than that given in S^*. One may, for instance, restrict the hypotheses considered to those that satisfy the presuppositions. And one may (justifiably) ignore violations of strong conservativeness so long as they occur in models that fail to satisfy these presuppositions.

Revision processes yield a rich array of semantic distinctions. The following definition is useful in their articulation.

5D.13 Definition   (Evaluation, evaluation sequence)

(i) *The evaluation of $\mathscr{L}^+$ relative to the hypothesis* h *is the member* $E_{\mathscr{L}^+}(h)$ of the set

$$\bigcup_n (\{A: A \text{ a formula with n free variables}\} \times D^n) \to \{t,f\}$$

that satisfies the following condition: For all formulas A containing n free variables and all n-tuples $\bar{d}$ in D^n,

$$E_{\mathscr{L}^+}(h)(\langle A, \bar{d}\rangle) = t \text{ iff } A \text{ is true of } \bar{d} \text{ in } M + h.^{44} \text{ (See Definition 2A.11.)}$$

(ii) Let $\mathscr{S}$ be a revision sequence for $\delta_{\mathscr{D},M}$. *The evaluation sequence of* $\mathscr{L}^+$ *generated by* $\mathscr{S}$ (notation: $E_{\mathscr{L}^+}(\mathscr{S})$) *is the sequence* $\langle E_{\mathscr{L}^+}(\mathscr{S}_\alpha)\rangle_{\alpha < \mathrm{lh}(\mathscr{L})}$. An *evaluation sequence of* $\mathscr{L}^+$ *is one that is generated by some revision sequence for* $\delta_{\mathscr{D},M}$.

Remark   We shall understand the notion of stability (near stability) in an evaluation sequence in the manner of Definition 5C.1 (5C.5).

5D.14 Theorem   (Validity in $S^\#$)   The following are equivalent:

(i) $M \models^{\mathscr{D}}_{\#} A$.

(ii) For all recurring hypotheses h, $\langle A, \langle\rangle\rangle$ is stably t in all evaluation sequences $E_{\mathscr{L}^+}(\langle \delta^n_{\mathscr{D},M}(h)\rangle_{n<\omega})$.

(iii) $\langle A, \langle\rangle\rangle$ is nearly stably t in all On-long evaluation sequences of $\mathscr{L}^+$.

Proof   Straightforward.   ∎

5D.15 Definition   (Pathologicality and other concepts)   The distinctions between the pathological and the nonpathological and between the different kinds of pathologicality can be articulated in $S^\#$ as shown in table 5.1. Note that all concepts are relative to a language $\mathscr{L}^+$ and the system $S^\#$. We let $\mathscr{E}$ range over On-long evaluation sequences of $\mathscr{L}^+$.

A sentence A is *nonpathological* (*paradoxical*,...) iff $\langle A, \langle\rangle\rangle$ is nonpathological (paradoxical,...).

---

[44] Note that $D^0 = \{\langle\rangle\}$.

Table 5.1

Concept	Its definition
Nonpathological	
(i.e. categorical)	either nearly stably **t** in all $\mathscr{E}$ or nearly stably **f** in all $\mathscr{E}$
Pathological	
Paradoxical	not nearly stable in any $\mathscr{E}$.
Truth-Teller-like	nearly stable in every $\mathscr{E}$ and nearly stably **t** in some, but not all, $\mathscr{E}$
Mixed	nearly stable in some, but not all, $\mathscr{E}$

5D.16   Example   (Pathologicality and other concepts)   Suppose that $\mathscr{D}$ consists of just one definition,

$$Gx =_{\text{Df}} [x = a \ \& \ Ga] \lor [x = b \ \& \ \sim Gb] \lor [x = c \ \& \ (Ga \lor \sim Gc)],$$

and that the names a, b, c, and d denote distinct objects in $\mathscr{L}^{+}$. Then Gd is nonpathological but Ga, Gb, and Gc are pathological. Ga is Truth-Teller-like, Gb is paradoxical, and Gc is mixed.

Remark   Definition 5D.15 records only some of the distinctions among the pathological that can be made within the revision theory. Finer distinctions within each of the subcategories defined are possible. Furthermore, distinctions that cut across these subcategories can be made by considering various specific types of revision sequences.

The soundness of the rules of $\mathbf{C_0}$ yields the following theorem concerning paradoxicality in $S^{\#}$.

5D.17   Theorem   (Relationship with $\mathbf{C_0}$)   A sentence A of $\mathscr{L}^{+}$ is paradoxical in $S^{\#}$ in all ground models M, if there are numbers m, n > 0 such that $A^{(0)} \vdash_{0}^{\mathscr{D}} \sim A^{(m)}$ and $\sim A^{(0)} \vdash_{0}^{\mathscr{D}} A^{(n)}$.

5D.18   Definition   (Definability)

(i) A formula A of $\mathscr{L}^{+}$ *weakly defines* a set $X \subseteq D^{n}$ (n > 0) *in* $S^{\#}$ iff A contains exactly n free variables and, for all $\bar{d} \in D^{n}$, $\bar{d} \in X$ iff $\langle A, \bar{d} \rangle$ is nearly stably **t** in all On-long evaluation sequences of $\mathscr{L}^{+}$. If in addition we have $\bar{d} \notin X$ iff $\langle A, \bar{d} \rangle$ is nearly stably **f** in all On-long evaluation sequences of $\mathscr{L}^{+}$, then A *(strongly) defines* X in $\mathscr{L}^{+}$ in $S^{\#}$.

(ii) A set $X \subseteq D^{n}$ (n > 0) is *weakly definable (strongly definable) in* $S^{\#}$ in $\mathscr{L}^{+}$ iff there is a formula A of $\mathscr{L}^{+}$ that weakly defines (defines) X in $S^{\#}$.

5D.19 Example (Definability)   Suppose that the language L has the constants 0 ("zero") and $'$ ("the successor of"), that the domain of the model M is the set of the integers

$$\{\ldots -3, -2, -1, 0, 1, 2, 3, \ldots\},$$

and that M assigns to the constants of L their usual interpretation. Let $\mathscr{D}$ consist of just one definition:

(1) $G(x) =_{\mathrm{Df}} x = 0 \vee \exists y(G(y) \ \& \ x = y').$

(This is a reformulation of the usual inductive definition of natural number.) Finally, let $\delta_{\mathscr{D},\mathrm{M}}$ be the rule of revision yielded by $\mathscr{D}$ in M. The recurring hypotheses here are the two fixed points of $\delta_{\mathscr{D},\mathrm{M}}$—the set of natural numbers and the set of integers[45]—and all sets of the form

$$X \cup \{0, 1, 2, 3, \ldots\},$$

where X and its complement[46] are both infinite subsets of the negative integers. It is easily seen that $\langle G(x), i \rangle$ is nearly stably t in all On-long evaluation sequences iff i is a natural number. Thus, $G(x)$ weakly defines the set of natural numbers. Since $\langle G(x), -n \rangle$ is pathological for all $n > 0$, $G(x)$ does not strongly define the set of natural numbers. A related example: If $\mathscr{D}$ had contained instead the following variant of the above definition

$$G(x) =_{\mathrm{Df}} [(x = 0 \vee \exists y(G(y) \ \& \ x = y')) \ \& \sim A],$$

where A is the formula

$$\exists z(G(z) \ \& \ z' = 0),$$

then the rule $\delta_{\mathscr{D},\mathrm{M}}$ would have a unique recurring hypothesis, namely, the set of natural numbers. In this case, $G(x)$ strongly defines the set of natural numbers.

Remark   The above example shows that definitions, if added in accordance with S^*, can increase the expressive power of the language. In the example given, the set of natural numbers is not first-order definable in terms of 0 and $'$ but is definable once circular definitions are admitted.

---

[45] Here, and below, we identify a hypothesis with the extension that it assigns to G.
[46] With respect to the set of negative integers.

The System S*

Certain circular definitions, if used in accordance with the system $S^\#$, generate "ω-inconsistencies." The definition given in Example 5A.18 generates ω-inconsistencies in S_0 (see 5A.19); since $S_0 < S^\#$, this definition generates ω-inconsistencies in $S^\#$ also. We now sketch a simple alternative S^* to $S^\#$ that does not have this feature.[47]

5D.20   Definition   (Validity in S*)   Let $\mathscr{L} = \langle L, M, \tau \rangle$, and let A be a sentence of the language L^+. Then:

  (i) A is *valid on $\mathscr{D}$ in* M *in* the system S* (notation: $M \overset{\mathscr{D}}{\underset{*}{\models}} A$) iff A is true in all models $M + h$, where h is a recurring hypothesis of $\delta_{\mathscr{D}, M}$.

 (ii) A is *valid on $\mathscr{D}$ in* S* (notation: $\overset{\mathscr{D}}{\underset{*}{\models}} A$) iff, for all classical models M of L, $M \overset{\mathscr{D}}{\underset{*}{\models}} A$.

The key difference between the systems $S^\#$ and S^* can be expressed thus: In S^* the fundamental idea is that of *stability* in an evaluation sequence, whereas in $S^\#$ it is that of *near stability*. Thus, as can easily be verified, A is valid in $\mathscr{L}^+$ in S^* iff $\langle A, \langle \rangle \rangle$ is stably t in all On-long evaluation sequences $\mathscr{E}$ of $\mathscr{L}^+$, whereas (as we know already) A is valid in $\mathscr{L}^+$ in $S^\#$ iff $\langle A, \langle \rangle \rangle$ is nearly stably t in all such $\mathscr{E}$. This difference is reflected also in the definitions of "pathologicality," "paradoxicality," etc. These concepts are defined in S^* as they are in $S^\#$ except that "near stability" is replaced by "stability" (see the chart given in Definition 5D.15).

5D.21   Example   (Validity in S*)   Let $\mathscr{D}$ and $\mathscr{L}^+$ be as in Example 5D.16. Then $\sim Gd$ is valid in S*. And the status of the sentences Ga, Gb, and Gc in S* is the same as that in $S^\#$. The first is Truth-Teller-like, the second paradoxical, and the third mixed. Indeed, in this example $S^\#$ and S^* give the same verdict on all sentences. There are, however, definitions on which the two systems differ radically. An example is the definition constructed in 5A.18. For all n, $G^\ulcorner n \urcorner$ is valid in $S^\#$ in any model of AX (see 5A.17 and 5A.19), but it is paradoxical by S*.

5D.22   Theorem   (Relationships between systems V) $S^* < S^\# < S_n$ $(n > 0)$, but S_0 and S* are incomparable.

---

[47] The order of exposition here does not reflect the historical order. The system S* has an earlier origin—it is essentially a generalization of the theory of truth proposed in Belnap 1982.

Proof It is easily seen that $S^* \leq S^\# < S_n$ (n > 0) (see Theorem 5D.3). Consider the definition of G (and AX) given in Example 5A.17. On this definition, the sentence $(AX \rightarrow \forall x Gx)$ is valid in S^* but not in S_0. Hence, validity in S^* does not imply validity in S_0. On the other hand, if the definition of G is as described in Example 5A.18 then the sentence $(AX \rightarrow {\sim}\forall x Gx)$ is valid in S_0 (and, hence, in $S^\#$), but not in S^*. Hence, neither validity in S_0 nor validity in $S^\#$ implies validity in S^*.   ■

5D.23 Theorem (Relationships between systems VI) If a sentence is paradoxical in $\mathscr{L}^+$ by $S^\#$ then it is paradoxical also by S^*; if it is Truth-Teller-like by S^* then it is so by $S^\#$. Neither of the converses holds.

Proof Straightforward.   ■

Many of the properties of $S^\#$ discussed above hold also of S^*. S^* sustains classical reasoning. It validates the ordinary rules of definitions for categorical contexts. It preserves our normal ways of working with ordinary definitions. It is strongly conservative. Finally, definitions, if used in accordance with S^*, can increase the expressive power of language.

The principal virtue of $S^\#$ over S^* is that it allows one to use, at least to a limited extent, the rules of definitions in hypothetical contexts: We have $C_0 < S^\#$, but this fails for S^*. It is a consequence of this very feature, however, that some definitions generate ω-inconsistencies in $S^\#$. Which of the two systems is more appropriate must depend upon the details of their applications. The differences these systems entail in one such application (the theory of truth) will be examined in section 6C. (Sections 6A and section 6B study the theory of truth within a special context in which the differences between $S^\#$ and S^* are immaterial.)

Comparison with Inductive Definitions

Let us now compare $S^\#$ and S^* with the system of inductive definitions. (On the latter, see Moschovakis 1974, Barwise 1975, and Aczel 1977.)

5D.24 Definition (Positive definitions) The system of definitions $\mathscr{D}$ is *positive* iff all the occurrences of the definienda in the definiens of $\mathscr{D}$ are positive (i.e., if these occurrences are within the scope of an even number of negations).[48]

---

[48] Recall that the primitive connectives of our languages are $\sim$, &, and $\forall$; the remaining connectives are defined in terms of these. If $\rightarrow$ had been a primitive connective, this definition would have required modification.

Suppose that $\mathcal{D}$ is positive. The revision rule $\delta_{\mathcal{D},\mathrm{M}}$ yielded by $\mathcal{D}$ in a model M is an operation on the space $\{\mathbf{t},\mathbf{f}\}^Z$, where Z is some set. Let $\le$ be the pointwise ordering of this space, where the truth-values are ordered thus:

t

●

│

●

f

We shall call this two-element structure **A2**. By Theorem 2C.4, $\mathbf{A2}^Z$ $(=\langle\{\mathbf{t},\mathbf{f}\}^Z, \le\rangle)$ is a complete lattice. It can be verified that $\delta_{\mathcal{D},\mathrm{M}}$ is a monotone operation on this space. Hence, by Tarski's Fixed-Point Theorem (2C.9), the fixed points of $\delta_{\mathcal{D},\mathrm{M}}$ form a complete lattice. In the system of inductive definitions, the interpretation of a definiendum G is that given by the least fixed point of $\delta_{\mathcal{D},\mathrm{M}}$.

5D.25   Definition   (Inductive validity)   Suppose that $\mathcal{D}$ is positive.

(i) A is *inductively valid* (or *valid in* S_i, or *i-valid*) *on* $\mathcal{D}$ *in* M (notation: $\mathrm{M} \models^{\mathcal{D}}_i A$) iff A is a true sentence of the language $\langle L, \mathrm{M} + \mathrm{h}, \tau\rangle$, where h is the least fixed point of $\delta_{\mathcal{D},\mathrm{M}}$.

(ii) A is *inductively valid on* $\mathcal{D}$ (notation: $\models^{\mathcal{D}}_i A$) iff, for all models M, $\mathrm{M} \models^{\mathcal{D}}_i A$.

5D.26   Example   (Inductive validity)   Let L and M be as in Example 5D.19 with the sole exception that we suppose L to have a one-place predicate N whose extension in M is the set of natural numbers. Let $\mathcal{D}$ consist of the definition (1). Since $\mathcal{D}$ is positive, $\delta_{\mathcal{D},\mathrm{M}}$ has a least fixed point, namely the set of natural numbers $\{0, 1, 2, \ldots\}$. Consequently, the following formulas are i-valid in M:

$G(0), G(0'), G(0''), \ldots,$

$\forall x(G(x) \leftrightarrow N(x)).$

However, only the first group of formulas is valid in $\mathbf{S}^\#$ ($\mathbf{S}^*$). $\mathbf{S}^\#$ and $\mathbf{S}^*$ are *not*, therefore, generalizations of the system of inductive definitions.

Remark

(i) Inductive definitions are not strictly circular; the apparent circularity in them is eliminable through higher-order quantification in the following well-known way. Suppose for simplicity that in the definition

(2) $G(x_1,\ldots,x_n) =_{Df} A_G(x_1,\ldots,x_n)$,

G is the only definiendum occurring in A_G. Let A_H be obtained from A_G by replacing all occurrences of G in it by an n-place predicate variable H. Construed inductively, (2) is equivalent to the definition

$$G(x_1,\ldots,x_n) =_{Df} \forall H [\forall x_1 \ldots \forall x_n (H(x_1,\ldots,x_n) \leftrightarrow A_H(x_1,\ldots,x_n))$$

$$\to H(x_1,\ldots,x_n)],$$

which is noncircular. Hence, inductive definitions ascribe definite extensions to their definienda; they do not result in any pathological behavior.

(ii) The system of inductive definitions has two characteristic validities. Suppose $\mathscr{D}$ is positive and contains the definition (2). Then, the universal closure of

(3) $G(x_1,\ldots,x_n) \leftrightarrow A_G(x_1,\ldots,x_n)$

is i-valid because G is interpreted in inductive definitions via a fixed point. The second characteristic validity arises because G is interpreted via the *least* fixed point. Suppose $B(x_1,\ldots,x_n)$ is a formula with n free variables, and $A_B(x_1,\ldots,x_n)$ is obtained from $A_G(x_1,\ldots,x_n)$ by replacing occurrences of $G(t_1,\ldots,t_n)$ by $B(t_1,\ldots,t_n)$, making sure by a change of bound variables that no "new" occurrences of variables become bound. Then the formula

(4) $\forall x_1 \ldots \forall x_n (B(x_1,\ldots,x_n) \leftrightarrow A_B(x_1,\ldots,x_n))$

$$\to \forall x_1 \ldots \forall x_n (G(x_1,\ldots,x_n) \to B(x_1,\ldots,x_n))$$

is i-valid. Both these validities fail in $\mathbf{S}^{\#}$ and $\mathbf{S}^*$; (4) fails even in the strongest system $\mathbf{S}_1$.

5D.27   Theorem   ($\mathbf{S}^{\#}$, $\mathbf{S}^*$, and $\mathbf{S}_i$ compared)   Suppose $\mathscr{D}$ is positive and h is the least fixed point of the revision rule $\delta_{\mathscr{D},M}$ yielded by $\mathscr{D}$ in M ($= \langle D, I \rangle$). Suppose further that G is an n-place definiendum and $\bar{d}$ is an n-tuple of members of D. Then,

(i) $h(G,\bar{d}) = \mathbf{t}$ iff, for all recurring hypotheses h', $h'(G,\bar{d}) = \mathbf{t}$

and

(ii) $M \models_{\bar{\mathbb{1}}}^{\mathscr{D}} G(t_1,\ldots,t_n)$ iff $M \models_{\#}^{\mathscr{D}} G(t_1,\ldots,t_n)$ iff $M \models_{\bullet}^{\mathscr{D}} G(t_1,\ldots,t_n)$, for all closed terms $t_1,\ldots,t_n$.

Proof Suppose that $h(G,\bar{d}) = t$ and that h' is an arbitrary recurring hypothesis of $\delta_{\mathscr{D},M}$. By remark (ii) following Theorem 5C.16, there is a revision sequence $\mathscr{S}$ of length On such that $\mathscr{S}_0$ is the least element of $\mathbf{A2}^D$ and for some α

$$\mathscr{S}_\alpha = h.$$

Since h' is recurring, there is a revision sequence $\mathscr{S}'$ of length On in which h' is cofinal. There is, thus, an ordinal $\beta \geq \alpha$ such that

$$\mathscr{S}'_\beta = h'.$$

The ccpo $\mathbf{A2}$ is simple and $\mathscr{S}_0 \leq \mathscr{S}'_0$. So Theorem 5C.18 applies. We have that

$$\mathscr{S}_\beta \leq \mathscr{S}'_\beta.$$

But $\mathscr{S}_\beta = h$, since h is a fixed point (Theorem 5C.11(iv)). The desired result, $h'(G,\bar{d}) = t$, follows. Since every fixed point is recurring, the converse is immediate, and (i) is proved. (ii) is a consequence of (i). ∎

Remark If $\mathscr{D}$, M, G, and $\bar{d}$ are as in the above theorem and h is the greatest fixed point of $\delta_{\mathscr{D},M}$, then $h(G,\bar{d}) = f$ iff, for all recurring hypotheses h', $h'(G,\bar{d}) = f$. This is a consequence of Theorem 5C.19.

Even for definitions that are not positive, one can establish a relationship between $S^\#$ (S^*) and S_i that is similar to the one given above. The central idea is due to Gilmore (1974) and Feferman (1984). Consider an arbitrary system $\mathscr{D}$. Construct a positive version $\mathscr{D}^+$ of $\mathscr{D}$ as follows: For each definition

$$G(x_1,\ldots,x_n) =_{\mathrm{Df}} A_G(x_1,\ldots,x_n)$$

in $\mathscr{D}$, place two definitions in $\mathscr{D}^+$, one for G^+ and the other for G^-:

$$G^+(x_1,\ldots,x_n) =_{\mathrm{Df}} A_G^+(x_1,\ldots,x_n)$$

$$G^-(x_1,\ldots,x_n) =_{\mathrm{Df}} A_G^-(x_1,\ldots,x_n),$$

where A_G^+ (A_G^-) is obtained by replacing all negative occurrences of all definienda H in A_G ($\sim A_G$) by $\sim H^-$ and all positive occurrences by H^+. Observe that $\mathscr{D}^+$ is positive.

5D.28 Theorem (Relationship between $\mathscr{D}$ and $\mathscr{D}^+$) Let $\mathscr{D}$ and $\mathscr{D}^+$ be as specified above and suppose that they yield, in a model M, the rules $\delta_{\mathscr{D},\mathrm{M}}$ and $\delta_{\mathscr{D}^+,\mathrm{M}}$ respectively. Let h_0 and h_1 be, respectively, the least and the greatest fixed points of $\delta_{\mathscr{D}^+,\mathrm{M}}$. Then, for all n-place definienda G of $\mathscr{D}$ and all n-tuples $\bar{d}$ of the elements of M, we have the following:

(i) If $h_0(G^+,\bar{d}) = \mathbf{t}$ then, for all recurring hypotheses h of $\delta_{\mathscr{D},\mathrm{M}}$, $h(G,\bar{d}) = \mathbf{t}$.

(ii) If $h_1(G^-,\bar{d}) = \mathbf{t}$ then, for all recurring hypotheses h of $\delta_{\mathscr{D},\mathrm{M}}$, $h(G,\bar{d}) = \mathbf{f}$.

(iii) If $G^+(t_1,\ldots,t_n)$ is i-valid in M (relative to $\mathscr{D}^+$), then $G(t_1,\ldots,t_n)$ is valid in M in $S^\#$ and S^* (relative to $\mathscr{D}$). Similarly for G^-.

Proof For a hypothesis h in the domain of $\delta_{\mathscr{D},\mathrm{M}}$ define the hypothesis h^+ in the domain of $\delta_{\mathscr{D}^+,\mathrm{M}}$ as follows: For all definienda G of $\mathscr{D}$ and all $\bar{d}$,

$$h^+(G^+,\bar{d}) = h(G,\bar{d})$$

and

$$h^+(G^-,\bar{d}) = \sim h(G,\bar{d}).$$

Observe that

$$[\delta_{\mathscr{D},\mathrm{M}}(h)]^+ = \delta_{\mathscr{D}^+,\mathrm{M}}(h^+).$$

It follows that if $\mathscr{S}$ is a revision sequence for $\delta_{\mathscr{D},\mathrm{M}}$ then $\langle(\mathscr{S}_\alpha)^+\rangle_{\alpha<\mathrm{lh}(\mathscr{S})}$ is a revision sequence for $\delta_{\mathscr{D}^+,\mathrm{M}}$. Hence, if h is a recurring hypothesis for $\delta_{\mathscr{D},\mathrm{M}}$ then h^+ is a recurring hypothesis for $\delta_{\mathscr{D}^+,\mathrm{M}}$. But every recurring hypothesis h' of $\delta_{\mathscr{D}^+,\mathrm{M}}$ has the property that

$$h_0 \leq h' \leq h_1.$$

(See 5C.18 and 5C.19.) Hence the theorem holds. ∎

Concluding Remarks

The semantical schemes $S^\#$ and S^* can be applied to languages L that contain predicates governed by rules of revision but in which no *definition* is formulable for these predicates. A simple kind of case is this: A predicate

G may be introduced into L through the stipulation that it has the same meaning as the predicate H in another language L', where H is given (in L') a circular definition that is not formulable in L. The semantical theories developed above apply to such cases in the most straightforward way.

An intermediate type of case is this: G is governed by a rule of revision ρ in L; one cannot give a definition of G in L (i.e., no system of definitions formulable in L yields ρ); nonetheless, one can formulate *partial* definitions in L for G. The notion of partial definition can be elucidated as follows. Let $t_1, \ldots, t_n$ be some closed terms of L and suppose that they denote the respective member of the n-tuple $\bar{d}$. Then

$$G(t_1, \ldots, t_n) =_{Df} B(t_1, \ldots, t_n)$$

is a *partial* definition of the predicate G governed by ρ in L iff, for all hypotheses h, $B(t_1, \ldots, t_n)$ is true in L under the hypothesis h iff $\rho(h)(\bar{d}) = t$. Intuitively, partial definitions fix the conditions under which a predicate applies to certain specified objects. If L contains partial definitions for all the objects, then we say that the rule ρ is *weakly expressible* in L. For example, the Tarski biconditionals constitute partial definitions of truth. And, if the language has names for all the objects in its domain, then the rule of revision for truth is weakly expressible in it.

A note on our terminology In this work we have used 'stable' (and its relatives) only for one purpose: to describe the behavior of elements in *particular* revision sequences. In our earlier works (and in those of others), 'stable' served a dual purpose, and the resulting ambiguity has been confusing. Sometimes it was used as in the present work, but sometimes it was used to describe the behavior of an element in all revision sequences. For example, in earlier works, 'stably true' sometimes means that the object behaves a certain way in a certain revision sequence, but sometimes it means that it behaves that way in all revision sequences. To disambiguate, one had to pay attention to whether 'stable truth' was relative to a sequence or to a model. In place of the old terminology 'stably true in M' we now use 'valid in M', and instead of 'stable in M' we use 'categorical in M'.

6 Truth, Categoricalness, and Necessity

In this chapter we apply the theory of definitions to the concepts of truth, categoricalness, and necessity.

6A Truth I: The Main Lemma

Kripke sketches in the following well-known passage an attractive picture of the concept of truth:

We wish to capture an intuition of somewhat the following kind. Suppose we are explaining the word 'true' to someone who does not yet understand it. We may say that we are entitled to assert (or deny) of any sentence that it is true precisely under the circumstances when we can assert (or deny) the sentence itself. Our interlocutor then can understand what it means, say, to attribute truth to (6) ('snow is white') but he will still be puzzled about attributions of truth to sentences containing the word 'true' itself....

Nevertheless, with more thought the notion of truth as applied even to various sentences themselves containing the word 'true' can gradually become clear. Suppose we consider the sentence

(7)   Some sentence printed in the *New York Daily News*, October 7, 1971, is true.

... [I]f (7) is unclear, so still is

(8)   (7) is true.

However, our subject, if he is willing to assert 'snow is white', will according to the rules be willing to assert '(6) is true'. But suppose that among the assertions printed in the *New York Daily News*, October 7, 1971, is (6) itself. Since our subject is willing to assert '(6) is true', and also to assert '(6) is printed in the *New York Daily News*, October 7, 1971', he will deduce (7) by existential generalization. Once he is willing to assert (7), he will also be willing to assert (8). In this manner, the subject will eventually be able to attribute truth to more and more statements involving the notion of truth itself. There is no reason to suppose that *all* statements will become decided in this way, but most will. (Kripke 1975, pp. 65–66)

Kripke goes on to show that the statements so decided can plausibly be identified with those that have a truth value in the least fixed point (the *grounded* statements) of the Strong Kleene scheme.

One part of Kripke's picture can hardly be doubted: that the grounded statements are unproblematic. It is not so plausible to maintain, however, that *only* these statements are unproblematic. The instructions given by Kripke to his imaginary subject leave out something important: *They do not specify how the subject is to work with the concept of truth in hypothetical contexts.* Suppose that the subject does not know that

Gillian owns a lamp that once belonged to Carnap (P),

but that in the course of some reasoning he is led to hypothesize that P. The instructions given by Kripke do not entitle the subject to deduce, under the hypothesis P, that "P" is true. If the subject can *assert* that P, then the instructions entitle him to assert that "P" is true. If the subject can *deny* that P, then again the instructions entitle him to deny that "P" is true. But if the subject merely *supposes* that P, they do not entitle him to conclude that "P" is true.

This points to one important difference between the intuitive picture of truth we wish to put forward and Kripke's. The instructions we would give to the subject consist simply of the Tarski biconditionals (understood definitionally). No restrictions would be placed on their use; in all contexts, categorical or hypothetical, their use would be uniform. What separates the situation under consideration from countless others in which the meaning of a word is explained is that the (partial) definitions we would give our subject are circular. This circularity does not make the definitions illegitimate or wrong or senseless. One does not have to eliminate the circularity of truth (say, via a hierarchy of truth predicates or by invocation of new semantic values) to make sense of the biconditionals. The biconditionals make sense on their own. Indeed, the roots of both the ordinary nonpathological behavior of the concept of truth and its perplexing pathological behavior lie in their circularity.

The picture we wish to put forward retains the legitimacy of Kripke's procedure. It affirms that a sentence is nonpathological if it receives a truth value by this procedure (see Lemma 6B.5). But it denies the converse. Indeed, as we shall see below, there are conditions under which the revision process dictates that truth has a classical signification while Kripke's procedure does not (Examples 6B.6, 6B.7).

Let us apply the theories of definitions we constructed in chapter 5 to the concept of truth. We begin with some notational matters. Let $\mathscr{L}$ ($= \langle L, M, \tau \rangle$; $M = \langle D, I \rangle$) be an interpreted classical language (see pp. 44–45), and let $\mathscr{L}^+$ be obtained by adding a new one-place predicate T to $\mathscr{L}$. We suppose that the set S of the sentences of $\mathscr{L}^+$ is included in the domain D and that $\mathscr{L}$ has a quotation name 'A' for each sentence A of L^+ (so I('A') $= A$). We interpret T as a predicate defined via the partial definitions

$$T(`A') =_{\text{Df}} A.$$

These biconditionals yield the rule of revision τ_M (see Definition 2B.8) as the signification of T.[1] Revision sequences of length On for τ_M will be called τ_M-*sequences* (alternatively, τ-*sequences of* M).

For purposes of comparison, we shall also be interested in the revision sequences for various normal monotonic three- and four-valued schemes. Of particular importance are the schemes μ and κ (introduced in chapter 2) and the supervaluation scheme σ of van Fraassen (1968). Truth and falsity are evaluated in the supervaluation scheme as follows.

6A.1   Definition   (Supervaluation scheme σ)   Let $\mathcal{M}$ be a three-valued model of a language L. A sentence A of $\mathcal{L}$ is *true* (*false*) in $\mathcal{M}$ by the supervaluation scheme σ iff A is true (false) in all classical models $\mathcal{M}' \geq \mathcal{M}$ (see p. 39). σ_M shall be the jump yielded by the supervaluation scheme in a ground model M.

Note that σ is normal and monotonic, but not truth functional. Given a scheme ρ, the revision sequences of length On for ρ_M will be called ρ_M-*sequences* (alternatively, ρ-*sequences of* M). Sentences that have the value **t** (**f**) in the least fixed point of ρ_M will be said to be ρ-*grounded true* (*false*) *in* M; ρ-*grounded* sentences are those that are either ρ-grounded true or ρ-grounded false. We shall understand "ρ-*intrinsic truth*," "ρ_M-*paradoxical*," etc. in a parallel way.[2]

An important feature of the revision theory, and one that prompted our interest in it, is its consequence that truth behaves like an ordinary classical concept under certain conditions—conditions that can roughly be characterized as those in which there is no vicious reference in the language. This can be shown on the basis of the Main Lemma, which we will state after two preliminary definitions.

6A.2   Definition   (Degree)   The *degree of* terms and formulas is defined recursively:

   (i)   The degree of atomic terms (i.e., variables and nonquotational names) and of $\perp$ is 0.

---

[1] We are assuming, as usual, that only sentences are true. If $\mathcal{L}$ has names of all the objects in its domain, then the revision rule is weakly expressible in it.
[2] A sentence A is a ρ_M-intrinsic truth iff it is true in the largest intrinsic fixed point of ρ_M; A is ρ_M-paradoxical iff it is neither true nor false in each fixed point of ρ_M.

(ii) If the degree of a sentence A is n, then the degree of the term 'A' is
n + 1.

(iii) If the degrees of the terms $t_1, \ldots, t_n$ are $i_1, \ldots, i_n$ respectively and f [F]
is an n-place function [predicate] letter, then the degree of $f(t_1, \ldots, t_n)$
[$F(t_1, \ldots, t_n)$] is the maximum of $i_1, \ldots, i_n$.

(iv) If x is a variable and A and B are formulas of degrees m and n,
respectively, then the degree of $\forall x A$ and $\sim A$ is m and the degree of
(A & B) is the maximum of m and n.

6A.3 Definition (X-neutral model) Let X be a subset of the domain of
the model M. We say that M is X-*neutral* iff the interpretations in M of all
the (i) names *other than* the quotational names, (ii) function symbols, and
(iii) predicates are X-neutral (see Definition 2D.2).

The following lemma is the principal tool we shall use to establish properties of τ_M in certain kinds of models M.

6A.4 Lemma (The Main Lemma) Let M ($=\langle D, I \rangle$) be X-neutral
(X $\subseteq$ D), and let S be (as before) the set of sentences of $\mathscr{L}^+$. Further, let
$\mathscr{S}$ and $\mathscr{S}'$ be τ-sequences of M, and let Y be the set of those sentences that
are either stably t in both $\mathscr{S}$ and $\mathscr{S}'$ or stably f in both. If (S $-$ Y) $\subseteq$ X,
then there is an ordinal α such that, for all $\beta \geq \alpha$, $\mathscr{S}_\alpha = \mathscr{S}'_\beta$. (It follows that
$\mathscr{S}_\alpha = \mathscr{S}_\beta = \mathscr{S}'_\beta$.)

Proof Suppose that S $-$ Y $\subseteq$ X. Let θ be an ordinal greater than the
initial ordinals for $\mathscr{S}$ and $\mathscr{S}'$. We claim that for all ordinals α and β,
and all natural numbers n, if α, $\beta > \theta + n + 1$ then for all sentences A of
degree n

$$\mathscr{S}_\alpha(A) = \mathscr{S}'_\beta(A).$$

This claim implies the Main Lemma, since it yields that if $\alpha = \theta + \omega$ and
$\beta \geq \alpha$ then $\mathscr{S}_\alpha = \mathscr{S}'_\beta$. We prove the claim by a double induction.

Induction Hypothesis I For all $\alpha_1 < \alpha$, all β and all n, if α_1, $\beta > \theta +$
n + 1 then for all sentences A of degree n

$$\mathscr{S}_{\alpha_1}(A) = \mathscr{S}'_\beta(A).$$

Induction Hypothesis II For all $\beta_1 < \beta$ and all n, if α, $\beta_1 > \theta + n + 1$
then for all sentences A of degree n

$$\mathscr{S}_\alpha(A) = \mathscr{S}'_{\beta_1}(A).$$

We need to show that for all n, if $\alpha, \beta > \theta + n + 1$ then for all sentences A of degree n

$$\mathscr{S}_\alpha(A) = \mathscr{S}'_\beta(A).$$

Let n be arbitrary and let $\alpha, \beta > \theta + n + 1$.

Case i $\alpha = 0$. Trivial.

Case ii α is a limit ordinal. Let A be an arbitrary sentence of degree n. Suppose that $\mathscr{S}'_\beta(A) = \mathbf{t}$, and consider an arbitrary ordinal μ such that $\theta + n + 1 < \mu < \alpha$. By Induction Hypothesis I,

$$\mathscr{S}_\mu(A) = \mathbf{t}.$$

Hence, A is stably $\mathbf{t}$ at α in $\mathscr{S}$. So,

$$\mathscr{S}_\alpha(A) = \mathbf{t} = \mathscr{S}'_\beta(A).$$

A similar argument works for the other subcase: $\mathscr{S}'_\beta(A) = \mathbf{f}$.

Case iii α is a successor ordinal, say $\alpha = \gamma + 1$. We consider cases for β.

Case iiia $\beta = 0$. Trivial.

Case iiib β is a limit ordinal. Parallel to the argument given for Case ii, but using Induction Hypothesis II.

Case iiic β is a successor ordinal, say $\beta = \delta + 1$. This is the interesting case. To prove the claim we show that the standard models

$$\mathscr{M}_1 = \mathbf{M} + \mathscr{S}_\gamma$$

and

$$\mathscr{M}_2 = \mathbf{M} + \mathscr{S}'_\delta$$

have the same sentences of degree n true, and the same false. We establish this by constructing a restricted isomorphism Ψ between $\mathscr{M}_1$ and $\mathscr{M}_2$ that preserves all constants except possibly quotational names of degree $> n$.

Note that if Y contains all the sentences of degree n then, since $\gamma, \delta >$ the initial ordinals for $\mathscr{S}$ and $\mathscr{S}'$, the same sentences of degree n are true in the models $\mathscr{M}_1$ and $\mathscr{M}_2$, and we have the desired result. So, in the construction of Ψ we may suppose that at least one sentence of degree n does not belong to Y; i.e., there is at least one sentence of degree n that is neither stably $\mathbf{t}$ in both $\mathscr{S}$ and $\mathscr{S}'$ nor stably $\mathbf{f}$ in both $\mathscr{S}$ and $\mathscr{S}'$. It follows that there are denumerably many such sentences,[3] for if B is such a sentence then so also is every sentence of the form $(B \,\&\, B)$. Set

$X_{\gamma,\,\mathbf{t}}$ = the set of sentences $B \in X$ of degree $\geq$ n such that $\mathscr{S}_\gamma(B) = \mathbf{t}$,

$X_{\gamma,\,\mathbf{f}}$ = the set of sentences $B \in X$ of degree $\geq$ n such that $\mathscr{S}_\gamma(B) = \mathbf{f}$,

$X_{\delta,\,\mathbf{t}}$ = the set of sentences $B \in X$ of degree $\geq$ n such that $\mathscr{S}'_\delta(B) = \mathbf{t}$,

and

$X_{\delta,\,\mathbf{f}}$ = the set of sentences $B \in X$ of degree $\geq$ n such that $\mathscr{S}'_\delta(B) = \mathbf{f}$.

Since $(S - Y) \subseteq X$, we know that the set $X_{\gamma,\,\mathbf{t}} \cup X_{\gamma,\,\mathbf{f}}$ is denumerable. We now argue that the sets $X_{\gamma,\,\mathbf{t}}$ and $X_{\gamma,\,\mathbf{f}}$ are individually denumerable. This must be so if γ is a successor ordinal, for then neither $X_{\gamma,\,\mathbf{t}}$ nor $X_{\gamma,\,\mathbf{f}}$ can contain both a sentence and its negation. (Note that $S - Y$ is closed under negation.) If γ is a limit ordinal then $\gamma \geq \theta + \omega$, since $\alpha = \gamma + 1 > \theta + n + 1$. Hence, by Induction Hypothesis I, every sentence is stable at γ in $\mathscr{S}$. So, again, neither $X_{\gamma,\,\mathbf{t}}$ nor $X_{\gamma,\,\mathbf{f}}$ can contain a sentence and also its negation. We conclude that $X_{\gamma,\,\mathbf{t}}$ and $X_{\gamma,\,\mathbf{f}}$ are both denumerable. A parallel argument using Induction Hypothesis II shows that $X_{\delta,\,\mathbf{t}}$ and $X_{\delta,\,\mathbf{f}}$ are denumerable. The four sets $X_{\gamma,\,\mathbf{t}}$, $X_{\gamma,\,\mathbf{f}}$, $X_{\delta,\,\mathbf{t}}$, and $X_{\delta,\,\mathbf{f}}$ have, therefore, the same cardinality, and there are 1-1 mappings f and g that map, respectively, $X_{\gamma,\,\mathbf{t}}$ onto $X_{\delta,\,\mathbf{t}}$ and $X_{\gamma,\,\mathbf{f}}$ onto $X_{\delta,\,\mathbf{f}}$.

We construct Ψ as follows. We let Ψ be identity over $D - (X_{\gamma,\,\mathbf{t}} \cup X_{\gamma,\,\mathbf{t}})$. Over $X_{\gamma,\,\mathbf{t}}$ we let it coincide with f, and over $X_{\gamma,\,\mathbf{f}}$ with g.

Ψ is so constructed that it preserves the interpretation of T in $\mathscr{M}_1$ and $\mathscr{M}_2$: Over sentences not in X, Ψ is identity. But as $(S - Y) \subseteq X$ these sentences are either stably $\mathbf{t}$ in both $\mathscr{S}$ and $\mathscr{S}'$ or stably $\mathbf{f}$ in both. Hence, the values of these sentences in $\mathscr{S}_\gamma$ and $\mathscr{S}'_\delta$ must be the same.[4] The same can also be said, in virtue of Induction Hypothesis I, of the sentences of degree $<$ n. On these Ψ is again identity and, consequently, the interpretation of T is preserved. The remaining sentences are those in $X_{\gamma,\,\mathbf{t}} \cup X_{\gamma,\,\mathbf{f}}$. On these the interpretation of T is preserved in virtue of the definition of Ψ.

Since on sentences of degree $<$ n Ψ is identity, it preserves the interpretation of all quotational names of degree $\leq$ n. It preserves the inter-

---

[3] We are assuming that L is countable. The lemma can be proved, however, without any assumptions concerning the cardinality of L.

[4] Recall that γ and δ are $\geq$ the initial ordinals for $\mathscr{S}$ and $\mathscr{S}'$.

pretation of all the other nonlogical constants because the model M is X-neutral and Ψ is identity over $D - X$. ∎

Here is one simple application of the Main Lemma. Further applications will be given in section 6B.

6A.5   Theorem   (Behavior of τ_M in S-neutral models)   If M is S-neutral then all τ_M-sequences culminate in the same fixed point, h.

Proof   Let h be a hypothesis that recurs in a τ_M-sequence $\mathscr{S}$. Consider an arbitrary τ_M-sequence $\mathscr{S}'$. All conditions for an application of the Main Lemma hold. There is, therefore, an ordinal α such that for all $\beta \geq \alpha$,

$$\mathscr{S}_\alpha = \mathscr{S}_\beta = \mathscr{S}'_\beta.$$

Choose a $\beta \geq \alpha$ such that $\mathscr{S}_\beta = h$. Then

$$\mathscr{S}'_\beta = \mathscr{S}'_{\beta+1} = h. \qquad\qquad ∎$$

In an S-neutral model M, then, the revision rule τ_M has a unique fixed point h and, furthermore, all the revision sequences generated by τ_M converge to h.

Addendum to Section 6A: Proof of the Transfer Theorem

The technique exhibited in the proof of the Main Lemma can be used to prove the Transfer Theorem (2D.4):

The Transfer Theorem   Let R be a reference list for a language N and let M be a quantificational enrichment of R.[5] There is an isomorphism F between the fixed points of ρ_R and those of ρ_M ($\rho = \kappa, \mu, \upsilon, \tau$) such that for all atomic sentences Ga of N and fixed points v of ρ_R

$$v(Ga) = F(v)(Ga)$$

provided that if ρ is not classical then there is a name a in N such that $R(a) = {\sim} Ga$.

Proof   Let ρ be one of the schemes $\kappa, \mu, \upsilon, \tau$, and let v and v′ be arbitrary fixed points of ρ_R. We show that:

(1)   There is a unique fixed point F_v of ρ_M that agrees with v over the atomic sentences of N.

---

[5] See section 2D for an explanation of our notation and terminology.

(2)   If $v \leq v'$ then $F_v \leq F_{v'}$.

Since every fixed point of ρ_M can be "cut down" to a fixed point of ρ_R, these claims suffice to establish the theorem.

Let $\mathscr{S}$ be a ρ-sequence of M such that for all sentences A of N

$\mathscr{S}_0(A)$ = the value of A relative to the interpretation v and the scheme ρ,

and, if $\rho \neq \tau$,

$\mathscr{S}_0(B) = \mathbf{n}$, for all the remaining sentences B of L^+.

Such a sequence $\mathscr{S}$ will be called a *regular ρ-sequence for* v. An inductive argument relying on the local determination property of the schemes shows that, for all ordinals α and all names $a \in N$,

$\mathscr{S}_\alpha(Ga) = v(Ga)$.

Set

S_N = the set of sentences of N.

We know, then, that M is $(S - S_N)$-neutral and that all members of S_N are stable in $\mathscr{S}$. This observation is sufficient to show that $\mathscr{S}$ culminates in a fixed point of ρ_M; i.e., for some ordinal α,

$\mathscr{S}_\alpha = \mathscr{S}_{\alpha+1}.$

If $\rho = \tau$, the claim follows from the Main Lemma.[6] Note that, in fact, the Lemma yields something stronger: All regular τ-sequences for v culminate in the same fixed point, so (1) holds. Since (2) holds vacuously, the theorem is established for case $\rho = \tau$. Henceforth we assume that $\rho \neq \tau$. The observation made earlier tells us, for these cases, that $\mathscr{S}_0$ is sound. By Theorem 5C.16(iii), $\mathscr{S}$ culminates in the least fixed point of ρ_M above $\mathscr{S}_0$. Let F_v be this fixed point.

Let h be an arbitrary fixed point of ρ_M that agrees with v over the atomic sentences of N. We will show that

(3) $F_v = h$.

This will establish (1). And (2) also follows: Suppose that $v \leq v'$. Let $\mathscr{S}'$ be a regular ρ-sequence for v'. We know that $\mathscr{S}$ and $\mathscr{S}'$ culminate in fixed

---

[6] In applying the lemma we let $\mathscr{S}' = \mathscr{S}$.

points (respectively, F_v and $F_{v'}$). One shows by induction that, for all ordinals α, $\mathscr{S}_\alpha \leq \mathscr{S}'_\alpha$. (If $\rho = \mu$ or κ, then Theorem 5C.18 implies this.) It follows that $F_v \leq F_{v'}$.

To establish (3) we prove by induction that

(4)   For all natural numbers n and all sentences A of degree n,
      $F_v(A) = h(A)$.

Suppose that the claim holds for all numbers less than n. Set

$$\mathscr{M}_1 = M + F_v$$

and

$$\mathscr{M}_2 = M + h.$$

We show the claim holds for n by constructing a restricted isomorphism Ψ between $\mathscr{M}_1$ and $\mathscr{M}_2$ that preserves all constants except possibly quotation names of degree $> n$. If $\rho = \mu$ or κ, the construction is similar to the one given in Case iiic in the proof of the Main Lemma—in fact, in the present instance, the construction is easier. Note that the proviso on the Transfer Theorem plays an important role in the proof: It ensures that denumerably many sentences (of any given degree) have the value **n** in F_v and h.

If $\rho = v$, the construction of Ψ is similar except that we have to deal with one complication: What if one of the fixed points, F_v and h, does not assign **b** to any sentences but the other one does?[7] If this possibility is not ruled out, then the desired kind of isomorphism Ψ cannot be constructed.

Suppose without loss of generality that F_v does not assign **b** to any sentence. So, no sentence of N has the value **b** in F_v and, hence, in h. By the proviso on the theorem, there is a Liar-like sentence in the language. It must have the value **n** in F_v and, hence, in h. The remainder of the proof is a reductio of the hypothesis that some sentences have the value **b** in h.

The *reductio* relies on some properties of the scheme v and of the model $\mathscr{M}_2$. Define the *dual* ($[\ ]^\wedge$) of the semantic values in the following standard way:

$[\mathbf{b}]^\wedge = \mathbf{n}$,

$[\mathbf{t}]^\wedge = \mathbf{t}$,

---

[7] There is a parallel complication for **n**; it is treated similarly.

$[\mathbf{f}]\,\hat{} = \mathbf{f},$

$[\mathbf{n}]\,\hat{} = \mathbf{b}.$

For any assignment s, s' of values to the variables, let us say the following:

- s is a *dual of* s' iff s and s' are alike except that, for all variables x and y,

  (i) if $h(s(x))$ or $h(s'(x))$ is $\mathbf{n}$ or $\mathbf{b}$ then $h(s(x)) = [h(s'(x))]\,\hat{}$

  (ii) $s(x) = s(y)$ iff $s'(x) = s'(y)$.

- $s \leq s'$ iff, for all variables x and y, the following three conditions obtain:

  (i) $h(s(x)) \leq h(s'(x))$.

  (ii) $s(x) = s(y)$ iff $s'(x) = s'(y)$.

  (iii) If either $h(s(x))$ or $h(s'(x))$ is $\mathbf{t}$ or $\mathbf{f}$ then $s(x) = s'(x)$.

For notational convenience, set

$\mathrm{Val}_s(A)$ = the semantic value of A according to v in $\mathcal{M}_2$ relative to the
          assignment s.

(See pp. 39–40.) Let A be a formula that contains no occurrences of any names. The following properties can be verified by an inductive argument.

(5)   If s is a dual of s' then $\mathrm{Val}_s(A) = [\mathrm{Val}_{s'}(A)]\,\hat{}$.

(6)   If $s \leq s'$ then $\mathrm{Val}_s(A) \leq \mathrm{Val}_{s'}(A)$.

We can now complete the *reductio*. Let A^* be a sentence of the lowest degree, say m, to which h assigns the value $\mathbf{b}$. Let A be just like A^* except A has new variables in place of the names in A^*. Finally, let s be an assignment of values to the variables such that if a variable x replaces a name t in A^* then $s(x)$ is the denotation of t in $\mathcal{M}_2$; to the remaining variables s assigns the sentence $\perp$. Since h is a fixed point,

$h(A^*) = \mathrm{Val}_s(A) = \mathbf{b}.$

But a dual s' of s exists. By (5),

$\mathrm{Val}_{s'}(A) = [\mathrm{Val}_s(A)]\,\hat{} = \mathbf{n}.$

Since neither sentences of degree lower than m nor sentences of N receive the value $\mathbf{b}$ by h, $s \leq s'$. By (6),

$\text{Val}_s(A) \leq \text{Val}_{s'}(A)$.

That is, $\mathbf{b} \leq \mathbf{n}$. This completes the *reductio*.   ∎

6B   Truth II: Restricted Self-Reference

In this section we study the behavior of the revision rule τ_M in those models M that allow only restricted kinds of self-reference. The principal tool we shall use is the Main Lemma (6A.4).

6B.1   Definition   (Properties of revision rules)   Let $\rho: X^D \to X^D$ be a revision rule.

- (i) ρ is *convergent* iff there is a revision sequence for ρ in which all recurring hypotheses for ρ are cofinal.[8]
- (ii) ρ *settles on fixed points* iff all recurring hypotheses for ρ are fixed points.
- (iii) ρ *converges to a fixed point* iff ρ is convergent and ρ settles on fixed points.

Remarks
   (i) If ρ is convergent, then the outcome of the revision process does not depend on the initial hypothesis. Any recurring hypothesis h can be reached from any initial hypothesis h' by repeatedly applying ρ and by making appropriate choices at limits—in other words, there is a revision sequence $\mathscr{S}$ for ρ such that h is cofinal in $\mathscr{S}$ and $\mathscr{S}_0 = $ h'.
   (ii) ρ converges to a fixed point iff ρ has a unique recurring hypothesis, i.e., iff all revision sequences for ρ culminate in one and *the same* fixed point. Note that "converges to a fixed point" is a stronger condition than "has a unique fixed point"; see Example 6B.3 below.
   Let $\mathscr{L}$ $(= \langle L, M, \tau \rangle; M = \langle D, I \rangle)$, and $\mathscr{L}^+$ be as in section 6A (p. 200).

6B.2   Definition   (Thomason model)   M is a *Thomason model*[9] iff τ_M converges to a fixed point.

If M is Thomason then τ_M has a unique fixed point, but the converse is not true:

---

[8] This notion of convergence is stricter than the one defined in Gupta 1990.
[9] So called because a question raised by Richmond Thomason led us to investigate this notion.

6B.3 Example (A non-Thomason model) Suppose that M ($= \langle D, I \rangle$) is S-neutral except that the interpretations of two names, a and b, are as follows:

I(a) = Ta,

I(b) = $Tb \to Ta$.[10]

By the Transfer Theorem (2D.4), τ_M has a unique fixed point, but M is not Thomason. In fact, τ_M is not convergent, nor does it settle on fixed points.

Let $T^{\#}$ and T^* be the theories of truth based on, respectively, $S^{\#}$ and S^*. Set

$V_M^{\#}$ = {A: A is valid in M by $T^{\#}$}

and

V_M^* = {A: A is valid in M by T^*}.

It is easily verified that

$V_M^{\#}$ = {A: A is *nearly stably* t in all τ-sequences of M}

and

V_M^* = {A: A is *stably* t in all τ-sequences of M}.[11]

It follows that if M is a Thomason model and h is the unique fixed point of τ_M then

$A \in V_M^{\#}$ iff $A \in V_M^*$ iff h(A) = t.

So, both theories $T^{\#}$ and T^* dictate that truth behaves like a classical concept in Thomason models.

6B.4 Theorem (Convergence to a fixed point I) If M is X-neutral, then M is a Thomason model provided that X contains (i) all sentences that have occurrences of T, or (ii) all sentences that are μ-ungrounded in M, or (iii) all that are κ-ungrounded, or (iv) all that are σ-ungrounded.

---

[10] This example was discussed in chapter 3.
[11] See Theorem 5D.14 and the remarks following Definition 5D.20. Note the following equivalence: A sentence B is (nearly) stably t (f) in $\mathscr{S}$ iff $\langle B, \langle \rangle \rangle$ is (nearly) stably t (f) in the evaluation sequence $E_{\mathscr{L}^+}(\mathscr{S})$, where $\mathscr{S}$ is a τ-sequence of M.

Proof Suppose, for *reductio*, that there are two distinct hypotheses—say, h and h'—that are recurring for τ_M. Hence, there are τ-sequences of M—say, $\mathscr{S}$ and $\mathscr{S}'$—in which h and h' are cofinal. Let Y be the set of those sentences that are either stably **t** in both $\mathscr{S}$ and $\mathscr{S}'$ or stably **f** in both. If $S - Y \subseteq X$, then all the conditions for an application of the Main Lemma hold and we have the conclusion that $h = h'$, which contradicts our initial assumption. $S - Y \subseteq X$ holds trivially in case (i). It holds in the remaining cases in virtue of part (i) of the following lemma.   ■

6B.5 Lemma (Stability and fixed points) Let M be an arbitrary ground model, and let ρ be any normal monotonic three-valued scheme.

(i) If A is ρ-grounded true (false) in M, then A is stably **t** (**f**) in all τ-sequences of M. (Hence, if A is ρ-grounded true in M, then $A \in V_M^*$ and, consequently, $A \in V_M^\#$.)

(ii) If A is **t** (**f**) in a fixed point of ρ_M, then A is stably **t** (**f**) in some τ-sequence of M. (Hence, if A is paradoxical in M according to $T^\#$ or T^*, then A is ρ_M-paradoxical.)

Proof

(i) Let $\mathscr{S}'$ be the ρ-sequence that begins with the least element of $\langle \{\mathbf{t}, \mathbf{f}, \mathbf{n}\}^D, \leq \rangle$ and culminates in the least fixed point h' of ρ_M. By remark (ii) after Theorem 5C.16, such a revision sequence does exist. Let $\mathscr{S}$ be an arbitrary τ-sequence of M, and let h be an arbitrary hypothesis cofinal in it. Since ρ is a normal scheme, $\mathscr{S}$ is a ρ-sequence also. Theorem 5C.18 applies and allows us to conclude that $h' \leq h$, which implies the desired conclusion.

(ii) Let h' be an arbitrary fixed point of ρ_M. Consider a τ-sequence $\mathscr{S}$ such that $h' \leq \mathscr{S}_0$. Again, $\mathscr{S}$ is a ρ-sequence of M and Theorem 5C.18 applies. Hence, for all hypotheses h cofinal in $\mathscr{S}$, $h' \leq h$. The desired conclusion follows.   ■

Here are some simple examples that illustrate the usefulness of Theorem 6B.4.

6B.6 Example (Thomason models) Suppose that the ground model $M (= \langle D, I \rangle)$ is S-neutral except for the name a, which denotes the sentence A (so M is $(S - \{A\})$-neutral). Suppose, further, that Hb is true in M. Then Theorem 6B.4 implies that M is a Thomason model if A is any one of the following sentences:

(1)   *Hb*,

(2)   *T*('*Hb*'),

(3)   *Hb* ∨ ~ *Ta*,

(4)   *Ta* ∨ ~ *Ta*.

For (1) we can appeal to clause (i) of the theorem, since in this case the set S − {*A*} contains all sentences that have occurrences of *T*. For (2), clause (i) is insufficient but clause (ii) suffices, since (2) is μ-grounded. Similarly, for (3), clause (iii) suffices but the earlier ones do not; (3) is μ-ungrounded but κ-grounded. Finally, (4) is κ-ungrounded but σ-grounded. In this case we appeal to clause (iv); the earlier clauses are insufficient. (If *A* is the Liar (~ *Ta*) or the Truth Teller (*Ta*), the theorem does not apply, for S − {*A*} does not contain all the σ-ungrounded sentences. In either of these two cases M fails to be a Thomason model.)

Remark   The later clauses of Theorem 6B.4 put weaker conditions on the model M and, consequently, provide more powerful ways of showing that M is Thomason.[12] This is so in virtue of the fact that for all hypotheses h

$$\mu_M(h) \le \kappa_M(h) \le \sigma_M(h).$$

It follows by an inductive argument that if h, h′, and h″ are the least fixed points of, respectively, μ_M, κ_M, and σ_M, then

$$h \le h' \le h''.$$

Hence, all μ-grounded sentences are κ-grounded, and the latter in turn are all σ-grounded. We can conclude also that μ-grounded truth implies κ-grounded truth, which implies σ-grounded truth, which implies membership in V_M^* (see 6B.5), which implies membership in $V_M^{\#}$. None of the converse implications hold.

Theorem 6B.4 is useful, but has its limitations. The next example shows this.

6B.7   Example   (Another Thomason model)   Suppose that M is as in the previous example except that the denotation of *a* is

(5)   *T*('*Ta*') ∨ *T*('~ *Ta*').

---

[12] The earlier clauses are useful nonetheless, because sometimes they are verified more easily.

Because (5) is σ-ungrounded, Theorem 6B.4 cannot be applied. M is, however, a Thomason model, and can be shown to be so by the next theorem. Note that (5) is stably **t** in all τ-sequences of M.

Remark   If the denotation of a is any of (1)–(5) then, for all sentences B, $B \in V_M^*$ or $\sim B \in V_M^*$ (since M is a Thomason model). But not all sentences are κ-grounded in M.[13] It can be shown that in cases (1)–(4) the least fixed point of σ_M is classical; it is not classical, however, in case (5).

6B.8   Theorem   (Convergence to a fixed point II)   Suppose M is an $(S - Y)$-neutral model and that Y contains only sentences that are either stably **t** in all τ-sequences of M or stably **f** in all such sequences—in other words,

$$Y \subseteq \{A: A \in V_M^* \text{ or } \sim A \in V_M^*\}.$$

Then, M is Thomason.

Proof   Similar to the proof of Theorem 6B.4.   ∎

This theorem cannot be strengthened to say that an $(S - Y)$-neutral model is Thomason if $Y \subseteq \{A: A \in V_M^\# \text{ or } \sim A \in V_M^\#\}$.

6B.9   Example   (A counterexample)   Let M be a ground model that, apart from the interpretation of the one-place predicate H, satisfies the condition of S-neutrality. Let the extension of H in M be the set

$\{(\exists x)(Hx \ \& \ \sim Tx),$

$T(`(\exists x)(Hx \ \& \ \sim Tx)'),$

$T(`T(`(\exists x)(Hx \ \& \ \sim Tx)')'),$

$T(`T(`T(`(\exists x)(Hx \ \& \ \sim Tx)')')'),$

$\qquad \vdots$

$\qquad \} \ [= Y].$[14]

It can be verified that for all $A \in Y$

$A \in V_M^\#.$

---

[13] In fact, the least fixed point of κ (also μ) is *never* classical.
[14] This kind of self-referential construction is used by McGee (1985, 1991) in the proof of his ω-inconsistency theorem; see Theorem 6C.8.

In fact, the value of A is $\mathbf{t}$ at almost all stages $\geq \omega$ of a τ-sequence of M; only at stages $\alpha + \mathrm{n}$ (where α is a limit ordinal and n is a fixed positive integer) does A have the value $\mathbf{f}$. So, M is $(S - Y)$-neutral but not Thomason.

Remark   The condition "M is Thomason" is equivalent to

(6)   all sentences are stable in all τ-sequences of M

but not to

(7)   all sentences are nearly stable in all τ-sequences of M.

The model M given in the last example satisfies (7) but is not Thomason.

There is one way in which Theorem 6B.8 can be strengthened. We can allow the language L to contain—and the model M to interpret in the natural way—certain syntactic resources, such as negation (*Neg*) and conjunction (*Conj*). The presence of these resources prevents M from being X-neutral.[15] But M can be shown to be Thomason (assuming it is otherwise X-neutral, for a suitable X). One establishes this by proving an analogue of the Main Lemma. The argument proceeds as before except that the restricted isomorphism Ψ is constructed more carefully so that the interpretations of *Conj* and *Neg* are respected.

6B.10   Problem   (Quantificational instance problem)   Suppose that M is S-neutral except for the interpretation of the three predicates *Neg*, *Conj*, and *Inst*. Suppose, further, that these predicates are interpreted in M in the intended way; in particular, *Inst* is true of pairs of sentences of the form

$$\langle (\forall \mathrm{x}) A(x), A(t) \rangle.$$

Is M Thomason? If not, does τ_M have a fixed point?

Kripke (1975) introduced the following variant of the supervaluation jump operation.

6B.11   Definition   (The jump σ_M^c) σ_M^c is defined only for those three-valued hypotheses h for which $\{A: \mathrm{h}(A) = \mathbf{t}\}$ is consistent. Given such a hypothesis h and a sentence A,

---

[15] For nontrivial $X \subseteq S$; more precisely, for those $X \subseteq S$ whose cardinality is > 1.

$\sigma_M^c(h)(A) = t\,(f)$ iff A is true (false) in all classical models $\mathcal{M}' \geq M + h$ such that the extension of T in $\mathcal{M}'$ is complete and consistent.[16]

Remark   Since the union of a chain of consistent sets is consistent and since σ_M^c is monotone, σ_M^c has a least fixed point.

6B.12 Problem   (Thomason models and the jump σ_M^c)   Does the condition "the least fixed point of σ_M^c is classical" imply "M is Thomason"?

The converse implication is known to fail. There are Thomason models M in which the least fixed point of σ_M^c is not classical:

6B.13   Example   (Thomason models and the jump σ_M^c)   Let M $(=\langle D, I\rangle)$ be a ground model that is S-neutral except for the interpretations of the names b_i $(i \geq 0)$. Let the denotation of b_i in M be the sentence A_i, where

$$A_i = (\sim Tb_0 \And Tb_{i+1}).^{17}$$

It can be verified that A_i $(i \geq 0)$ is stably f in all τ-sequences of M. But M is $(S - \{A_i : i \geq 0\})$-neutral. So Theorem 6B.8 applies and we can conclude that M is Thomason.

We now show that A_i $(i \geq 0)$ has the value n in the least fixed point of σ_M^c. Let $\mathcal{S}$ be the revision sequence that iteratively builds this fixed point from the "null" hypothesis (i.e., $\mathcal{S}_0(d) = n$ for all $d \in D$). Let C_j, for $j > 0$, be the sentence

$$\sim Tb_0 \And \sim Tb_1 \And \cdots \And \sim Tb_{j-1} \And Tb_j.$$

We show by induction that for all ordinals α and all $j > 0$,

$$\mathcal{S}_\alpha(C_j) \neq f.$$

The zero and limit cases are trivial. Suppose then that α is the successor ordinal $\beta + 1$ and that $j > 0$. We know by the induction hypothesis that $\mathcal{S}_\beta(C_{j+1}) \neq f$. Hence, the set

$$\{B : \mathcal{S}_\beta(B) = t\} \cup \{C_{j+1}\}$$

---

[16] Equivalently, iff $\tau_M(h')(A) = t\,(f)$ for all $h' \geq h$ such that $\{A : h'(A) = t\}$ is complete and consistent.

[17] Question: Is there a simpler example of a Thomason M in which the least fixed point of σ_M^c is not classical?

is consistent. So there is a two-valued hypothesis $h' \geq \mathcal{S}_\beta$ such that $h'(C_{j+1}) = t$ and $\{B: h'(B) = t\}$ is complete and consistent. This hypothesis is bound to satisfy the condition that

$h'(A_j) = t$ and $h'(A_k) = f$ $(0 \leq k < j)$.

Consequently,

$\tau_M(h')(Tb_j) = \tau_M(h')(\sim Tb_k) = t$ $(0 \leq k < j)$.

So, $\tau_M(h')(C_j) = t$. By Definition 6B.11, $\mathcal{S}_\alpha(C_j) \neq f$. We conclude that

(8) C_j $(j > 0)$ is not f in the least fixed point of σ_M^c.

To show that A_i $(i \geq 0)$ is n in this fixed point, it suffices to show that all Tb_i are n. Tb_i $(i > 0)$ must be n, since otherwise (8) is violated. Tb_0 cannot be t for the same reason; it cannot be f since Tb_1 is n.

Let us say that a τ-sequence $\mathcal{S}$ of M is *maximally consistent* iff, for all α,

$\{A: \mathcal{S}_\alpha(A) = t\}$ is maximally consistent.

(This condition is satisfied automatically by successor stages; it is significant only for zero and limit stages.) Let T^c be the revision theory of truth based on the system S^* and maximally consistent sequences. More precisely:

6B.14   Definition   (Validity in T^c) A is *valid in* M *according to* T^c (notation: $A \in V_M^c$) iff A is true in all standard models $M + h$, where h is cofinal in a maximally consistent τ-sequence of M.

An immediate consequence is that

$A \in V_M^c$ iff A is stably t in all maximally consistent τ-sequences of M.

6B.15   Problem   (T^c and Thomason models)   Suppose M is $(S - Y)$-neutral and that

$Y \subseteq \{A: A \in V_M^c \text{ or } \sim A \in V_M^c\}$.

Is M Thomason?

Thomason models, we have seen, contain neither the Liar nor the Truth Teller. Let us consider briefly what effects these types of self-reference have on the revision process.

6B.16   Theorem   (Settling on fixed points)   If M is an $(S - Y)$-neutral model and Y contains only sentences that are stable in all τ-sequences of M, then τ_M settles on fixed points.

Proof   This is proved by an application of the Main Lemma.   ∎

6B.17   Theorem   (Convergence)   Let M be a model that is S-neutral except for the interpretation of the names b_i. If each b_i denotes $\sim Tb_i$, then τ_M is convergent.[18]

Proof   This is proved by an argument similar to that given for the Main Lemma.   ∎

Remark   If M is as in the previous theorem except that each b_i denotes the Truth Teller Tb_i, then, by Theorem 6B.16, τ_M settles on fixed points. (Note that Tb_i is stable in all τ-sequences of M.) Thus, the presence of the Truth Tellers destroys the convergence of the revision process but leaves settledness on fixed points intact. The presence of Simple Liars has an opposite effect; it destroys settledness, but leaves convergence intact.

6B.18   Theorem   (Relationship to fixed-point theories)   Let M be a ground model, and let ρ be any one of the three-valued schemes μ, κ, and σ.

(i) If τ_M settles on fixed points, then every fixed point of ρ_M has a cl·ssical fixed point above it.

(ii) If τ_M is convergent, then ρ_M has a largest fixed point.[19]

Proof

(i) Suppose h is a fixed point of ρ_M and $\mathscr{S}$ is a τ-sequence for M such that $h \leq \mathscr{S}_0$. Since τ_M settles on fixed points, $\mathscr{S}$ culminates in a fixed point h'. By Theorem 5C.18, $h \leq h'$.

(ii) Suppose there is not a largest fixed point of ρ_M. Since the fixed points of ρ_M constitute a ccpo (Theorem 2C.8), there must be fixed points h_1 and h_2 that have no common upper bound; otherwise the totality of fixed points would be consistent (see Definition 2C.1(i)) and would have a supremum. Since τ_M is convergent, there are τ-sequences $\mathscr{S}$ and $\mathscr{S}'$ and a hypothesis h such that h is cofinal in both $\mathscr{S}$ and $\mathscr{S}'$ and such that

---

[18] A more general version of this theorem can be proved also.

[19] Claim (i) holds also for σ_M^c; we do not know if claim (ii) holds for σ_M^c.

Table 6.1

	Stage >						
	0	1	2	3	4	5	...
Value of (9)	t	f	t	f	t	f	...
Value of (10)	f	t	f	t	f	t	...

$h_1 \leq \mathscr{S}_0$ and $h_2 \leq \mathscr{S}_0'$ (see remark (i) following 6B.1). By Theorem 5C.18, $h_1, h_2 \leq h$. Thus, $\{h_1, h_2\}$ is consistent (in the ccpo of all hypotheses) and has a supremum, say h'. But as h_1 and h_2 are sound, h' must be sound also. Hence, there is a fixed point of ρ_M above h' (Theorem 2C.6(i)). This makes $\{h_1, h_2\}$ consistent in the ccpo of fixed points.   ∎

Remark   The converses of (i) and (ii) are not true. An example given to us by John Burgess and Saul Kripke shows this. Consider a model M in which a name *b* denotes

(9) $\sim Tb \vee T('Tb')$

and which is otherwise S-neutral. Let $\mathscr{S}$ be a τ-sequence of M such that the value of both (9) and

(10)   *Tb*

in $\mathscr{S}_0$ is **t**. (9) is stably **t** in $\mathscr{S}$. Hence, the Main Lemma applies and yields that $\mathscr{S}$ culminates in a fixed point h. It is easily verified that h is the largest fixed point of ρ_M. Thus, the consequents of (i) and (ii) in 6B.18 hold. But τ_M is not convergent and does not always settle on fixed points, for if one of (9) and (10) is hypothesized as true and the other false they both oscillate. See table 6.1.

Historical remark   The results stated in Lemma 6B.5 can be found in Gupta 1982 and in Herzberger 1982a. The Main Lemma of section 6A is a stronger version of a result proven in section 2 of Gupta 1982. Theorem 6B.8 and subsequent results are, we believe, new.

6C   Truth III: Rich Self-Reference

We have seen that in models that permit only certain restricted kinds of self-reference, the revision process yields a classical extension as the signification of truth. In these models, all our unreflective intuitions are preserved: Classical principles of reasoning hold; so do all the Tarski biconditionals, even when they are construed materially; so also do the semantic principles (e.g., the principle that a conjunction is true iff its conjuncts are true).[20] We now turn to the behavior of the concept of truth in models that allow a rich variety of self-reference. We shall see that in these models the three revision theories considered above—$T^{\#}$, T^{*}, and T^{c}—can yield significantly different results.[21]

Let us first note some properties that all three theories have in *all* models. Recall some terminology and some facts from section 6B:

$V_{M}^{\#} = \{A: A \text{ is valid in M by } T^{\#}\}$

$\quad = \{A: A \text{ is nearly stably } \mathbf{t} \text{ in all } \tau\text{-sequences of M}\}$,

$V_{M}^{*} = \{A: A \text{ is valid in M by } T^{*}\}$

$\quad = \{A: A \text{ is stably } \mathbf{t} \text{ in all } \tau\text{-sequences of M}\}$,

$V_{M}^{c} = \{A: A \text{ is valid in M by } T^{c}\}$

$\quad = \{A: A \text{ is stably } \mathbf{t} \text{ in all maximally consistent } \tau\text{-sequences of M}\}$.

6C.1 Theorem (Some common properties of $T^{\#}$, T^{*}, and T^{c}) Let A be a sentence of $\mathscr{L}^{+}$, and let t be a term that denotes A in M.

(i) $A \in V_{M}^{\#} [V_{M}^{*}; V_{M}^{c}]$ iff $T(t) \in V_{M}^{\#} [V_{M}^{*}; V_{M}^{c}]$.

(ii) $\sim A \in V_{M}^{\#} [V_{M}^{*}; V_{M}^{c}]$ iff $\sim T(t) \in V_{M}^{\#} [V_{M}^{*}; V_{M}^{c}]$.

(iii) If A is a μ-, κ-, or σ-grounded truth, then $A \in V_{M}^{*}$. And, hence, $A \in V_{M}^{\#}$ and $A \in V_{M}^{c}$.[22]

(iv) $V_{M}^{\#}$, V_{M}^{*}, and V_{M}^{c} are closed under classical logical consequence.

(v) $V_{M}^{\#}$, V_{M}^{*}, and V_{M}^{c} are consistent.

Proof We outline a proof of only one part of the theorem: that $V_{M}^{\#}$ is consistent. Suppose not—say A and $\sim A$ both belong to $V_{M}^{\#}$. Let $\mathscr{S}$ be a τ-sequence for M. A and $\sim A$ are then both nearly stably $\mathbf{t}$ in $\mathscr{S}$. Hence, there must be an ordinal α such that $\mathscr{S}_{\alpha+1}(A) = \mathscr{S}_{\alpha+1}(\sim A) = \mathbf{t}$. It follows that both A and $\sim A$ are true in $M + \mathscr{S}_{\alpha}$, which is absurd. ∎

---

[20] Assuming that the notion of conjunction is expressible in the language.
[21] The extent of their agreement, however, exceeds that of their disagreement.
[22] See Lemma 6B.5. If A has the value $\mathbf{t}$ in the least fixed point of σ_{M}^{c}, then A belongs to V_{M}^{c} but may fail to belong to $V_{M}^{\#}$ and V_{M}^{*}.

Remark It is a consequence of (iv) that the sentence $(A \lor \sim A)$ is validated by our theories even when A is the Liar. See chapter 7 for a discussion of some of the philosophical issues this raises.

In the remainder of this section we work with a language, $\mathscr{L}^+$, that contains a rich variety of self-reference. We assume that $\mathscr{L}$ ($= \langle L, M, \tau \rangle$; $M = \langle D, I \rangle$) has the following characteristics:

- It includes the language of arithmetic. In particular, it has a formula $Num(x)$ that is true of all and only the natural numbers; furthermore, it has resources enough to express all the recursive predicates.
- D is countable and $\mathscr{L}$ has one standard name (possibly complex) for each member of D; the standard name of a number is its numeral.
- There is an effective Gödel numbering of the syntax of $\mathscr{L}^+$.
- $\mathscr{L}$ has a formula with two free variables that is true of $\langle d_1, d_2 \rangle$ iff d_1 is the Gödel number of the standard name of d_2.[23]

We let $\ulcorner A \urcorner$ be the numeral for the Gödel number of A and $\ulcorner n \urcorner$ be the numeral for n.

6C.2 Definition (T^n, T-step)

(i) Let A be a sentence of $\mathscr{L}^+$. Set $T^0 A = A$ and $T^{n+1} A = T(\ulcorner T^n A \urcorner)$.

(ii) *T-step* is $T^n A \leftrightarrow T^m A$, where m $\neq$ n.

The conditions on $\mathscr{L}$ ensure that there are formulas $Neg(x, y)$, $UQ(x, y)$, $Conj(x, y, z)$, $In(x, y, z)$, and $D(x, y, z)$ of $\mathscr{L}$ such that

$Neg(x, y)$ expresses "x is a sentence (of $\mathscr{L}^+$) that is a negation of y,"[24]

$UQ(x, y)$ expresses "x is a sentence that is a universal quantification of y,"

$Conj(x, y, z)$ expresses "x is the conjunction of the sentences y and z,"

$In(x, y, z)$ expresses "y is a formula with no more than one free variable and x is obtained from y by replacing the free variables in it by the standard name of z,"

and

---

[23] Below we often identify syntactic items with their Gödel numbers.
[24] Henceforth, we omit the parenthetical qualification.

$D(x, y, z)$ expresses "x and y are the Gödel numbers of some sentences A and B, and $A = T^z B$."

6C.3 Definition (TL) TL is the form

$$(\forall x, y)(In(x, \ulcorner A(z)\urcorner, y)\ \&\ T(x) \to A(y)),$$

where $A(z)$ is a formula of $\mathscr{L}$ with exactly one free variable and y is free for z in $A(z)$.

6C.4 Definition (Semantic principles) Let $T\sim$, $T\&$, and $T\forall$ be the universal closures of the displayed formulas.

(T$\sim$) $Neg(x, y) \to [T(x) \leftrightarrow \sim T(y)]$.

(T&) $Conj(x, y, z) \to [T(x) \leftrightarrow T(y)\ \&\ T(z)]$.

(T$\forall$) $UQ(x, y) \to [T(x) \leftrightarrow (\forall u, v)(In(u, y, v) \to T(u))]$.

6C.5 Theorem (T-step) All instances of TL belong to V_M^* (and, hence, to $V_M^{\#}$ and V_M^c). But, for all m and n (m $\neq$ n), there are instances of the T-step that fail to belong to $V_M^{\#}$ and V_M^c (and, hence, to V_M^*).

Proof Instances of TL are κ-grounded truths; by Theorem 6C.1(iii), they belong to V_M^*.

Let n > m, and let C be a sentence that "says" that the result of prefixing n − (m + 1) occurrences of T to it is not true. That is, C is a sentence such that

$$C \leftrightarrow \exists x(D(x, \ulcorner C\urcorner, \ulcorner n - (m + 1)\urcorner)\ \&\ \sim T(x))$$

is true in all standard models M + h. (Such a C can be constructed using Theorem 2B.6(i).) Hence, if C is true (false) in M + h then so also is $\sim T^{n-m}C$. It follows that $T^m C \equiv T^n C$ is false in M + $\tau_M^m(h)$. As h is arbitrary, this instance of the T-step will belong neither to $V_M^{\#}$ nor to V_M^c. ∎

Remark Theorem 6C.1(i) tells us that $T^m A \in V_M^{\#}$ iff $T^n A \in V_M^{\#}$. By the previous theorem, however, not all instances of the T-step belong to $V_M^{\#}$. $T^m A$ and $T^n A$ are, thus, interchangeable only in categorical contexts; they are not interchangeable when they occur as parts of compound sentences. This is a consequence of *any* theory that maintains the consistency of truth within the context of classical logic, for if B is a Simple Liar then the sentence

(1) $B \leftrightarrow \sim T^1 B$

holds. Consistency requires that $B \leftrightarrow \sim B$ fail. It follows that the sub-formula $T^1 B$ of (1) should not be replaceable by B ($= T^0 B$). (There are cases where one might expect and want the interchangeablility of A and $T^1 A$ to hold but where it is not licensed by any of the three theories. A case of this sort is discussed below in Example 6C.10.)

6C.6 Theorem   (Semantic principles)

(i) $T\sim$, T&, and T∀ all belong to $V_M^\#$.

(ii) $T\sim$ and T&, but not T∀, belong to V_M^c.

(iii) Neither $T\sim$ nor T& nor T∀ belongs to V_M^*.

Proof

(i) Let $\mathscr{S}$ be an arbitrary τ-sequence for M, and let α be an arbitrary limit ordinal. Recall that the sentences assigned the value **t** by $\mathscr{S}_{\alpha+n+1}$ ($n \geq 0$) are those that are true in $M + \mathscr{S}_{\alpha+n}$. Hence, for all sentences A, B, and $\forall x C$,

$$\mathscr{S}_{\alpha+n+1}(A) = \mathbf{t} \text{ iff } \mathscr{S}_{\alpha+n+1}(\sim A) = \mathbf{f},$$

$$\mathscr{S}_{\alpha+n+1}(A \ \& \ B) = \mathbf{t} \text{ iff } \mathscr{S}_{\alpha+n+1}(A) = \mathscr{S}_{\alpha+n+1}(B) = \mathbf{t},$$

and

$$\mathscr{S}_{\alpha+n+1}(\forall x C) = \mathbf{t} \text{ iff, for all sentences } D \text{ that are instances of } \forall x C,$$

$$\mathscr{S}_{\alpha+n+1}(D) = \mathbf{t}.$$

(The right-to-left part of the last equivalence uses the condition that every object in the domain D has a name in $\mathscr{L}$.) It follows that $T\sim$, T&, and T∀ are true in $M + \mathscr{S}_{\alpha+n+1}$. Thus, they are all assigned the value **t** by $\mathscr{S}_{\alpha+n+2}$. Since n is arbitrary, they are nearly stably **t** in $\mathscr{S}$, and hence they belong to $V_M^\#$.

(ii) If $\mathscr{S}$ is maximally consistent, then, by an argument similar to the one given above, $\mathscr{S}_\alpha(T\sim) = \mathscr{S}_\alpha(T\&) = \mathbf{t}$ for all $\alpha > 0$. So, $T\sim$ and T& are stably **t** in $\mathscr{S}$; thus, they belong to V_M^c.

We show that T∀ $\notin V_M^c$ by using the self-referential construction given in Example 6B.9 (see McGee 1985, 1991). Let $A(x)$ be a formula of arithmetic that is true of all and only the sentences in the set

$\{\exists x(A(x) \ \& \ \sim Tx),$

$T(\ulcorner \exists x(A(x) \ \& \ \sim Tx)\urcorner),$

$T(\ulcorner T(\ulcorner \exists x(A(x) \ \& \ \sim Tx)\urcorner)\urcorner),$

$T(\ulcorner T(\ulcorner T(\ulcorner \exists x(A(x) \ \& \ \sim Tx)\urcorner)\urcorner)\urcorner),$

$\vdots$

$\} \ [= \mathrm{Z}].$

Such a formula $A(x)$ can be obtained as follows. Using Gödelian methods (see Theorem 2B.6(i)), construct a sentence B that is equivalent to

$\exists x[\exists y(Num(y) \ \& \ D(x, \ulcorner B \urcorner, y)) \ \& \ \sim T(x)].$

Let $A(x)$ be the formula

$\exists y(Num(y) \ \& \ D(x, \ulcorner B \urcorner, y)).$

Then, $A(x)$ is true of all and only the members of Z.

Let $\mathscr{S}$ be a maximally consistent τ-sequence of M, and let α be greater than the initial ordinal of $\mathscr{S}$. It can be verified that each member of Z is stably **t** in $\mathscr{S}\!\upharpoonright(\alpha + \omega)$. Hence, the formula

$\forall x(A(x) \rightarrow Tx)$

is stably **f**, but all its instances are stably **t**, in $\mathscr{S}\!\upharpoonright(\alpha + \omega)$. Consequently, T∀ is false in M $+ \mathscr{S}_{\alpha+\omega}$. So, T∀ is not stable in $\mathscr{S}$ and, thus, does not belong to V_M^c.

(iii) Since $V_M^* \subseteq V_M^c$, T∀ $\notin V_M^*$. We now show that T$\sim \notin V_M^*$. (The argument for T& is similar.) Let A be a Simple Liar sentence of $\mathscr{L}^+$. The value of A fluctuates in any τ-sequence of M. Consider a τ-sequence $\mathscr{S}$ such that, at all limit ordinals α, both A and $\sim A$ are assigned the value **f** by $\mathscr{S}_\alpha$. T$\sim$, then, is false in the model M $+ \mathscr{S}_\alpha$, so $\mathscr{S}_{\alpha+1}(T\sim) = $ **f**. Consequently, T$\sim$ is not stably **t** in $\mathscr{S}$ and fails to belong to V_M^*.   ∎

Remarks

(i) The theorem implies that the semantic principles

$T^n \sim A \leftrightarrow \sim T^n A,$

$T^n(A \ \& \ B) \leftrightarrow (T^n A \ \& \ T^n B),$

$T^n(A \vee B) \leftrightarrow (T^n A \vee T^n B),$

$T^n(A \to B) \leftrightarrow (T^n A \to T^n B)$

belong to $V_M^\#$ and V_M^c, but not to V_M^*.

(ii) The same holds for the generalized versions of the Principles of Non-Contradiction and Bivalence:

$\sim(T^n A \ \& \ T^n \sim A),$

$(T^n A \vee T^n \sim A).$

We now give an example that illustrates the use of the (generalized) Principle of Non-Contradiction in ordinary reasoning. Similar examples can be constructed to illustrate the use of the other semantic principles.

6C.7 Example (A-B example: variant 1) Let M be a model that represents facts concerning numbers and snow as they are in the actual world and, in addition, represents persons A and B as making these (and only these) statements:

A *says*:

Two plus two is three	$[=A_1]$;
Snow is always black	$[=A_2]$;
Everything B says is true	$[=A_3]$;
Ten is a prime number	$[=A_4]$;
Not everything B says is true	$[=A_5]$.

B *says*:

One plus one is two	$[=B_1]$;
Two is a prime number	$[=B_2]$;
Snow is sometimes white	$[=B_3]$;
At most one thing A says is true	$[=B_4]$.

An intuitive argument shows that A_3 and B_4 are true and A_5 is false:

A contradicts himself by asserting both A_3 and A_5. Hence A_3 and A_5 cannot both be true. Since all the other assertions of A are false, it follows that at most one thing that he says is true. So B's assertion B_4 is true. Hence A_3 is true and A_5 is false.

Curiously, all three theories $T^\#$, T^*, and T^c give the intuitively right verdict on the status of the statements made by A and B; in particular, A_3, B_4, and the negation of A_5 all belong to $V_M^\#$, V_M^*, and V_M^c. However, while $T^\#$ and T^c validate the argument given above, T^* does not.[25] The semantic version of the Principle of Non-Contradiction used in the argument holds only on the former theories, not on the latter.[26]

The theory $T^\#$, we have noted above, preserves all the semantic principles $T\sim$, $T\&$, and $T\forall$; the theories T^* and T^c, however, do not. We have seen also that $T^\#$ is built on a theory of definitions that sometimes results in "ω-inconsistencies"; not so for T^* and T^c. There is an intimate connection between the two phenomena. A theorem of McGee's shows that any theory that validates the semantic principles must countenance ω-inconsistencies.

6C.8 Theorem (McGee's ω-Inconsistency Theorem) Any set Γ of sentences of $\mathscr{L}^+$ that

(i) contains the truths of $\mathscr{L}$,

(ii) is closed under classical first-order consequence,

(iii) contains T^1A if it contains A, and

(iv) contains TL, $T\sim$, $T\&$, and $T\forall$

is ω-inconsistent.[27]

Proof We rely on the self-referential construction given in the proof of Theorem 6C.6(ii), and we use the notational conventions introduced there. Note that the conditions (i) and (ii) on Γ imply that

(2) $B \leftrightarrow \exists x [A(x) \;\& \sim T(x)] \in \Gamma$.

To prove the theorem it suffices to prove that

(3) $\sim B \to T(\ulcorner B \urcorner) \in \Gamma$

and

(4) $T(\ulcorner B \urcorner) \to B \in \Gamma$,

[25] This was pointed out to us by Kripke.
[26] Note that many theories of truth that rely on nonclassical logics not only fail to validate the argument given above but also fail to preserve our intuitive judgments about the status of some of the statements. For instance, A_3, A_5, and B_4 turn out to be neither true nor false in the least fixed point of the Weak and the Strong Kleene schemes.
[27] Some of the clauses given above can be weakened; see McGee 1985, 1991.

for these imply, by (ii), that $B \in \Gamma$ and, hence, by (iii), that, for all natural numbers n, $T^n B \in \Gamma$. The sentence $D(\ulcorner T^n B \urcorner, \ulcorner B \urcorner, \ulcorner n \urcorner)$ is a truth of $\mathscr{L}$ and so belongs to Γ. It follows that for each n

$$\exists x [D(x, \ulcorner B \urcorner, \ulcorner n \urcorner) \ \& \ T(x)] \in \Gamma.$$

Since $B \in \Gamma$, we have by (2) that

(5) $\exists x [\exists y (Num(y) \ \& \ D(x, \ulcorner B \urcorner, y)) \ \& \ \sim T(x)]$

belongs to Γ. The universal closure of

(6) $D(y, \ulcorner B \urcorner, x) \ \& \ D(z, \ulcorner B \urcorner, x) \rightarrow y = z$

belongs to Γ, since it is a truth of $\mathscr{L}$. (5) and (6) logically imply

$$\exists y [Num(y) \ \& \ \sim \exists x [D(x, \ulcorner B \urcorner, y) \ \& \ T(x)]],$$

which, by (ii), must also belong to Γ. This makes Γ ω-inconsistent.

Proof of (3)   The following belong to Γ:

$A(\ulcorner B \urcorner)$ [truth of $\mathscr{L}$]

$\sim B \rightarrow \forall x (A(x) \rightarrow T(x))$ [by (2) and (ii)]

$\forall x (A(x) \rightarrow T(x)) \rightarrow (A(\ulcorner B \urcorner) \rightarrow T(\ulcorner B \urcorner))$ [logical truth]

Hence, by (ii), so does

$\sim B \rightarrow T(\ulcorner B \urcorner)$.

Proof of (4)   In view of (ii) and (iv), it suffices to show that

$\sim B \rightarrow T(\ulcorner \sim B \urcorner) \in \Gamma$.

In virtue of (2) and (iv), we need only show that

$\forall x (A(x) \rightarrow T(x)) \rightarrow T(\ulcorner \forall x (A(x) \rightarrow T(x)) \urcorner) \in \Gamma$.

Since $T \forall \in \Gamma$, we can do this by proving that

(7) $\forall x (A(x) \rightarrow T(x)) \rightarrow (\forall u, v)[In(u, \ulcorner A(x) \rightarrow T(x) \urcorner, v) \rightarrow T(u)]$

belongs to Γ. This is shown by a formalization of the following argument: "Any instance of $(A(x) \rightarrow T(x))$ with respect to a standard name of an object, say v, is a conditional. The antecedent of this conditional is either true or untrue. If the latter, then the conditional is true (by $T\sim$ and T&). If the former, then, by TL, v satisfies the formula $A(x)$. In virtue of the construction of $A(x)$, so must the consequent. Hence, the consequent is true since every A is true. By $T\sim$ and T&, the conditional is true also."

More formally, the conditions on Γ imply that it contains the sentence

(8) $In(u, \ulcorner A(x) \to T(x) \urcorner, v) \to (\exists y, z)[In(y, \ulcorner A(x) \urcorner, v) \,\&\, In(z, \ulcorner T(x) \urcorner, v)$

$$\&\, (T(z) \to T(u)) \,\&\, (\sim T(y) \to T(u))].$$

The following is an instance of TL, and so belongs to Γ:

(9) $(\forall y, v)[(In(y, \ulcorner A(x) \urcorner, v) \,\&\, T(y)) \to A(v)].$

Further, the sentence

(10) $(\forall z, v)[(A(v) \,\&\, In(z, \ulcorner T(x) \urcorner, v)) \to A(z)]$

is a truth of $\mathscr{L}$ and so also belongs to Γ. As (8)–(10) logically imply (7), we have the desired conclusion. ∎

Remarks

(i) The semantic principles, then, can be had only at the price of ω-inconsistency. $T^{\#}$ pays this price; T^{*} and T^{c} do not. The former choice enables one to explain the use of the semantic principles in ordinary reasoning, but results in the counterintuitiveness associated with ω-inconsistency. The latter choice has the opposite effect; we gain ω-consistency but lose some of the semantic principles. McGee's theorem shows that there is no way around this dilemma.

(ii) $T^{\#}$ accords with the Inconsistency View of Tarski and Chihara to a limited degree. By $T^{\#}$, truth is *not* plain inconsistent, but it *is* ω-inconsistent. It should be observed, however, that $T^{\#}$ is not open to the objections leveled against the Inconsistency View in chapter 1.

It will be instructive to consider some variants of Example 6C.7.

6C.9 Example (A-B example: variant 2) Suppose A and B make assertions as in variant 1 except that A says instead of A_5,

Two plus two is four.

Table 6.2

	Stage >						
	0	1	2	3	4	5	...
Value of A_3	t	t	f	f	t	t	...
Value of B_4	t	f	f	t	t	f	...

We now have a Buridanian situation in which A_3 asserts the truth of B_4, and B_4 the falsity of A_3. Calculation shows that if A_3 and B_4 are hypothesized as true, they exhibit the revision pattern shown in table 6.2.[28]

Notice that every hypothesis concerning the truth values of A_3 and B_4 results in an instability. It follows that A_3 and B_4 are judged to be paradoxical by all three theories.

6C.10   Example   (A-B example: variant 3)   Suppose A and B make assertions as in the first variant except that A says, instead of A_5, $T^1 A_5$. The intuitive argument given in variant 1 no longer goes through, since now A's statements A_3 and $T^1 A_5$ do not contradict each other. To show that A_3 and B_4 are true one needs to appeal to an instance of the T-step, e.g.,

$$T^1 A_5 \leftrightarrow A_5,$$

which is not validated by any of the three theories. Neither A_3, A_5, and B_4 nor their negations are valid according to $\mathbf{T}^{\#}$ [nor according to $\mathbf{T}^*$ and $\mathbf{T}^c$].[29] This can be seen by examining table 6.3, which shows the revision pattern for these sentences under the hypothesis that A_3 is true and A_5, $T^1 A_5$, and B_4 false.[30]

Remark   If we work with fully varied revision sequences (see p. 168) then we can preserve the intuition that in this example also A_3 and B_4 are true. If $\mathscr{S}$ is a fully varied sequence then the values of A_3 etc. cannot be unstable in $\mathscr{S}$; if they were, then the hypothesis according to which A_3 and B_4 are true and A_5 and $T^1 A_5$ false would occur in $\mathscr{S}$. But on such a hypothesis the values of these sentences stabilize.

---

[28] Assuming that the true sentences of $\mathscr{L}$ are hypothesized to be true, and the false ones false.
[29] These statements are, of course, ungrounded by the μ, κ, and σ schemes. They also fail to have a truth value in the least fixed point of σ_M^c. A_3 and B_4 are, however, κ- and σ-intrinsic truths.
[30] In the calculation below we assume, as before, that the true sentences of $\mathscr{L}$ are hypothesized to be true, and the false ones false.

Table 6.3

	Stage >					
	0	1	2	3	4	...
Value of A_3	t	f	t	t	f	...
Value of A_5	f	t	f	f	t	...
Value of T^1A_5	f	f	t	f	f	...
Value of B_4	f	t	t	f	t	...

Bibliographical note   The theory of truth **T*** was first proposed in Belnap 1982; **T^c** was introduced (but not discussed) in Gupta 1987; **T^#** is new to this work. The theories studied in Gupta 1981 and 1982 and in Herzberger 1982a and 1982b are based, as was mentioned above, on different limit rules than any of the three theories considered here. The following works contain valuable information about the revision theories of truth: Burgess 1986; McGee 1991; Turner 1987, 1990a, 1990b; Visser 1984, 1989.

6D   The Concept "Categorical in *L*"

The theory developed above shows how a language can contain its own notion of truth. The same kind of account can be given of such other semantic concepts as reference and satisfaction. But what about the semantic concepts that are the products of our theory? Can a language *L* contain, e.g., the notion "categorical in *L*"? (Recall that a sentence is categorical iff it or its negation is valid.) Or must it, and notions like it, be seen as belonging to a distinct metalanguage? We shall argue in this section that the situation with "categorical in *L*" is parallel to that with "true in *L*." Four points of parallelism will be observed: (i) The former, like the latter, is indefinable in certain languages. (ii) The former, like the latter, is a circular concept. Its signification takes the form of a rule of revision. (iii) The behavior of this revision rule is similar to that for truth. In particular, in the absence of vicious reference, it converges to a fixed point. (iv) In the presence of vicious reference, the rule exhibits various forms of pathologicality.

An Indefinability Theorem

6D.1   Theorem   (Indefinability of categoricalness)   Let $\mathscr{L}\,(=\langle L, \mathscr{M}, \tau \rangle)$ be the classical language of arithmetic. Let $\mathscr{L}^+$ be $\mathscr{L}$ extended with a truth predicate T, where T is given a revision semantics. Then the set X of the Gödel numbers of sentences categorical in $\mathscr{L}^+$ (in $\mathbf{T}^\#$)[31] is not definable in $\mathscr{L}^+$.

Proof Suppose, for *reductio*, that $A(x)$ defines X in $\mathscr{L}^+$. Construct by the Gödelian techniques (2B.6(i)) a "fixed point" for the formula

$\sim A(x) \vee \sim T(x);$

i.e., a sentence B such that

(1) $B \leftrightarrow (\sim A(\ulcorner B \urcorner) \vee \sim T(\ulcorner B \urcorner))$

is true in M + g, for all possible classical interpretations g of T. Since $A(x)$ defines X, we know that

(2) B is categorical in $\mathscr{L}^+$ iff $A(\ulcorner B \urcorner)$ is valid in $\mathscr{L}^+$

and that

(3) B is not categorical in $\mathscr{L}^+$ iff $\sim A(\ulcorner B \urcorner)$ is valid in $\mathscr{L}^+$.

(See 5D.14, 5D.18, and 2A.10.) Now, either B is valid or $\sim B$ is valid or B is not categorical. Each of these assumptions can be shown to imply a contradiction. Suppose, for instance, that B is valid. Then $T(\ulcorner B \urcorner)$ must also be valid. Since (1) is valid, and validity is closed under logical consequence, it follows that $\sim A(\ulcorner B \urcorner)$ is valid. This contradicts (2). The arguments for the other two cases are similar.   ∎

Remarks

   (i) The above proof is exactly parallel to the proof of Tarski's Indefinability Theorem. The principal difference between the two is that where the latter uses the Ordinary Liar, the former uses the Strengthened Liar. (See chapter 7 for an informal discussion of the Strengthened Liar.)

   (ii) Similar indefinability theorems can be proved for semantic concepts such as validity and paradoxicality.

Semantics of Categoricalness

Consider a language $\mathscr{L}^+$ obtained by adding to $\mathscr{L}$ ($= \langle L, M, \tau \rangle$; M $= \langle D, I \rangle$) *two* distinguished predicates: T (truth) and K (categoricalness). Assume that D contains all the sentence of $\mathscr{L}^+$. What should the semantics

---

[31] We shall often suppress the parenthetical phrase; our concern throughout will be with the system $\mathbf{T}^\#$. Similar theorems hold also for $\mathbf{T}^*$ and $\mathbf{T}^c$.

of K be? The key thing to observe is that our intuitive understanding of the concept of categoricalness does not give us a method for assigning an extension to it, but it does tell us what the extension should be *once we are given a hypothesis concerning it.* Suppose we are given the hypothesis that the extension of K is $g \in \{t, f\}^D$. Let M_g be just like M except that it assigns the interpretation g to K. Since M_g assigns an interpretation to everything except T, it carries all the information we need to determine the revision process for T. The sentences that are deemed categorical by this process constitute the revised extension for K. The semantics of K is thus exactly parallel to that of T. *The notion K expresses is circular.* Its signification is given by a rule of revision ψ_M, which is defined as follows.

6D.2 Definition (The jump ψ_M) ψ_M is an operation on $\{t, f\}^D$ such that, for all $g \in \{t, f\}^D$ and all $d \in D$,

$$\psi_M(g)(d) = t \text{ iff } d \text{ is a sentence that is categorical (by } T^*) \text{ in the revision process for } \tau_{M_g}.$$

Remarks

(i) If the notion of categoricalness is added to a language L in the above manner, then we can express within L such claims as "The Liar is not categorical," "'The Liar is not categorical' is true," and "some sentences are categorical." We do not have to see these claims as formulated in a metalanguage. Notions such as "valid in L" and "paradoxical in L" can be added to L in a similar way.

(ii) There is a sense in which the semantics given for K is at a higher level than that for T: The definition of ψ_M makes reference to the entire revision process for T. Such a difference in levels would not have occurred if, instead of giving the semantics of a language with its own T and K predicates, we were giving the semantics for a language with, for instance, its own truth and denotation predicates.

6D.3 Example (The Liar and the Truth Teller) Suppose the denotations of the names a and b in M are, respectively, the Truth Teller Ta and the Liar $\sim Tb$. Consider a revision sequence $\mathscr{S}$ for K, a sequence obtained by repeated applications of the revision rule ψ_M to a hypothetical extension. It is easy to see that, irrespective of the interpretation assigned to K, Ta and $\sim Tb$ are bound not to be categorical in the revision process for T. Hence, for all α such that $0 < \alpha < \text{lh}(\mathscr{S})$,

$$\mathscr{S}_\alpha(Ta) = f$$

and

$\mathscr{S}_\alpha(\sim Tb) = \mathbf{f}.$

But note that

$\mathscr{S}_\alpha(Ta \,\&\, \sim Ta) = \mathbf{t}.$

The sentences considered so far stabilize in the revision process for K after one application of ψ_M. Here is an example in which several applications of ψ_M are needed. Set

$A_0 = \sim Tb$

and

$A_{n+1} = K(`A_n\text{'}) \lor A_0.$

Suppose that $\mathscr{S}$ is a revision sequence of length $\geq \omega$ for ψ_M such that

$\mathscr{S}_0(\sim Tb) = \mathbf{t}.$

Then, for all m, n $< \omega$,

$\mathscr{S}_m(A_m) = \mathbf{t}$

and

$\mathscr{S}_{m+n+1}(A_m) = \mathbf{f}.$

Behavior of ψ_M: Absence of Vicious Reference

Let $\mathscr{L}^+$ contain quotational names for all its sentences. We say that a sentence of $\mathscr{L}^+$ is *K-free* iff it contains no occurrences of K, including those within quotational names. Define U to be the set of sentences of $\mathscr{L}^+$ that are *not K*-free.

6D.4 Theorem (Convergence and settledness of ψ_M)   Let M be a U-neutral ground model of L. Suppose that there is a $g \in \{\mathbf{t}, \mathbf{f}\}^D$ such that τ_{M_g} has a fixed point. Then, ψ_M converges to a fixed point.

Proof   The proof is similar to that of Theorem 2 in Gupta 1990.   ∎

The theorem implies that if there is no vicious self-reference for T and the ground model is U-neutral then the revision process for K converges to and settles at a classical extension.

This same phenomenon occurs even if there is every kind of vicious reference for T, provided that the ground model M is U-neutral and there is a Truth Teller in the language:

6D.5   Theorem   (Convergence and settledness of ψ_M)   Let M ($= \langle D, I \rangle$) be a U-neutral ground model. Then, ψ_M converges to a fixed point provided that for some name a in L

$$I(a) = Ta.$$

Proof   The proof is similar to that of Theorem 1 in Gupta 1990.   ∎

Remarks

(i) The proviso in the above theorem—that there be a Truth Teller in the language—can be weakened. We do not know whether it can be completely eliminated.

6D.6   Problem   (The proviso)   Does the theorem hold if the proviso is removed?

The elimination of the proviso is easy in the one special case where we confine ourselves to revision processes in which the extension of truth at limit stages is required to be maximally consistent.

(ii) The condition of U-neutrality can also be considerably weakened. We can allow the language to have certain kinds of self-referential sentences containing K. If, for example, the language has a name c that denotes $\sim Kc$ and is otherwise U-neutral, then the theorems given above continue to hold. The revision process for K converges to, and settles at, a fixed point. If g is this fixed point, then g($\sim Kc$) = t.

Behavior of ψ_M: Presence of Vicious Reference

In the presence of vicious reference, ψ_M displays the familiar kinds of pathologicality.

6D.7   Example   (ψ_M and the Strengthened Truth Teller)   Suppose that the name d denotes in M the Strengthened Truth Teller A, where $A = Kd \vee \sim Td$. It is easily verified that if A is hypothesized as falling in the extension of K, then it stays in the extension of K (since the first disjunct stays true). And if it is hypothesized as falling out of the extension, then it stays out (since the first disjunct is false and, consequently, A behaves like the Liar in the revision process for T). A, thus, behaves like a Truth Teller in the revision process for ψ_M. The analogy goes further. It can be shown that if, apart from the denotation of d, M is U-neutral, then the revision process invariably settles on fixed points (assuming, as in the previous theorem, that an ordinary Truth Teller exists in the language).

6D.8   Example   (ψ_M and the Strengthened Liar)   Suppose that the name e denotes in M the Strengthened Liar B, where $B = \sim Ke \vee \sim Te$. B oscillates in the revision process for K, irrespective of the initial hypothesis. If at one stage it is in the extension of K then at the next stage it falls out of the extension. And at the next, it is back in. Furthermore, if this is the only vicious reference for K, then the revision process for ψ_M is convergent even though it does not culminate in a fixed point (again assuming that there is an ordinary Truth Teller in the language).

In the presence of vicious reference, ψ_M has more than one recurring hypothesis. The notion of validity in $\mathscr{L}^+$ needs to take this fact into account. The following is modeled on the definition of "validity in S*" given in 5D.1.

6D.9   Definition   (Validity)   A sentence A is *valid in $\mathscr{L}^+$* iff for all recurring hypotheses h of ψ_M there is a natural number m such that, for all $n \geq m$,

$$M_{\psi_M^n(h)} \models_{\#} A.$$

6D.10   Example   ("All truths are categorical")   Consider the sentence

(4) $\forall x(Tx \rightarrow Kx)$.

Suppose that there is a Truth Teller Ta in the language. It is easily verified that, for all recurring hypotheses h of ψ_M,

$$h(Ta) = h(\sim Ta) = \mathbf{f}.$$

But if h$'$ is a recurring hypothesis of τ_{M_h}, then either h$'(Ta) = \mathbf{t}$ or h$'(\sim Ta) = \mathbf{t}$. Hence,

$$M_h \models_{\#} \sim\forall x(Tx \rightarrow Kx).$$

Thus, the negation of (4) is valid if there is a Truth Teller in the language. A similar argument shows that the negation is valid if there is any vicious reference for T in the language.

6D.11 Example (Example 6D.7 continued) The argument of Example 6D.7 shows that the Strengthened Truth Teller A has the value t in some recurring hypotheses (say, h) of ψ_M and the value f in others (say, h'). It shows also that, for all $n \geq 0$,

$$\psi_M^n(h)(A) = t$$

and

$$\psi_M^n(h')(A) = f.$$

Hence, for all $n \geq 0$,

$$M_{\psi_M^n(h)} \models_{\#} K(`A').$$

and

$$M_{\psi_M^n(h')} \models_{\#} \sim K(`A').$$

It follows that $\sim K(`A')$ is not valid. Consequently, the pathologicality of the Strengthened Truth Teller cannot be described using K.

Remark The pathological behavior of K requires for its description a higher-order notion of categoricalness. This higher-order notion is also similar in essential respects to truth. It too is circular. It too exhibits pathologicality in the presence of vicious reference. It too points to the existence of a yet higher notion. Observe that the distinction of *orders* in the notions of categoricalness does not imply a distinction in the *languages* to which these notions can belong. See chapter 7 for a discussion of the philosophical issues that arise here.

6E The Logical Grammar of Necessity[32]

Richard Montague wrote, in a well-known passage, that

if necessity is to be treated syntactically, that is, as a predicate of sentences, as Carnap and Quine have urged, then virtually all of modal logic ... must be sacrificed.... if necessity is regarded as a sentential operator, then perfectly natural model-theoretic interpretations may be found. (Montague 1963, p. 294)

---

[32] This section presupposes some familiarity with basic modal logic and with formal systems of arithmetic. For modal logic, the reader may consult Hughes and Cresswell 1968; for formal systems of arithmetic, Boolos and Jeffrey 1980 and Epstein and Carnielli 1989. Boolos 1979 contains valuable information about both.

These remarks occur in a commentary on a group of theorems, the main one of which is the following.

6E.1 Theorem (Montague's theorem)   Let T be an extension of Robinson's arithmetic **Q**, and let $N(x)$ be an arbitrary formula of T that contains only one free variable x. Then T is inconsistent if the theorems of T include, for all sentences A and B of T, the following:

(1) $N(\ulcorner A \urcorner) \to A$,

(2) $N(\ulcorner N(\ulcorner A \urcorner) \to A \urcorner)$,

(3) $N(\ulcorner A \to B \urcorner) \to (N(\ulcorner A \urcorner) \to N(\ulcorner B \urcorner))$,

(4) $N(\ulcorner A \urcorner)$ if A is a logical axiom.

(Here and below, $\ulcorner A \urcorner$ is the numeral for the Gödel number of A.)

Proof See Montague 1963.   ∎

Observe that the theory shown inconsistent by Montague contains, besides **Q**, syntactic analogues of weak modal principles—principles even weaker than those found in the system **T**. (In **T** the consequent of (4) holds for *all* axioms, not just the logical axioms.)

   Two views of the logical grammar of necessity are contrasted in Montague's remarks. The first view—let us call it the *Predicate View*—analyzes sentences such as

(5)   That man is rational is necessary

as built out of a subject term, 'that man is rational', and a predicate, '⸺ is necessary'; furthermore, it takes the denotation of the subject term to be a sentence. The second view—let us call it the *Connective View*—analyzes (5) as built out of a connective (in Montague's terminology, a "sentential operator"), 'that ⸺ is necessary', and a sentence, 'man is rational'. The first view categorizes necessity with such concepts as "red," "sweet," and identity; the second view categorizes it with negation and conjunction.

   Implicit in Montague's remarks is the suggestion that these alternative theories of logical grammar have substantive consequences: They affect the material principles that can consistently be maintained concerning necessity.[33] If one adopts the Connective View, it is being suggested, then one

[33] This is explicitly suggested by some authors (Hintikka 1975, p. 104; Thomason 1980, 1986).

can subscribe to all the principles (1)–(4)[34] in Montague's theorem (and, indeed, even stronger principles); this is not possible, however, if one opts for the Predicate View.

Our aim in this section is to critically examine these suggestions. We shall argue that the acceptability of the substantive principles turns not on the logical form that one attributes to necessity, but on the *contexts* in which these forms occur.

Let us consider, to begin with, two languages, $\mathscr{CL}$ and $\mathscr{PL}$, both extensions of a classical first-order language $\mathscr{L}$ $(= \langle L, \mathcal{M}, \tau \rangle; \mathcal{M} = \langle N, I \rangle)$ whose domain N is the set of natural numbers and whose function I assigns the intended interpretations to the arithmetical constants 0, ′, ·, and +. Both $\mathscr{CL}$ and $\mathscr{PL}$ are like $\mathscr{L}$ except that the former has a connective ($\square$) for necessity and the latter a predicate (*Nec*). $\mathscr{CL}$ is a modal language and, thus, permits quantifiers to bind variables that lie in the scope of necessity—as, for example, in

$\forall x \square Hx.$

This kind of binding is not possible in $\mathscr{PL}$. We can get its effect, however, if we treat *Nec* as a *two*-place predicate that holds between (the Gödel numbers of) formulas and (the codes of) sequences of objects.[35] If the values of x and y are, respectively, the formula A and the sequence $d_1, \ldots, d_n$, then the intuitive meaning of

(6) $Nec(x, y)$

is that the relation expressed by A holds necessarily of $d_1, \ldots, d_n$.[36] The one-place predicate $N(x)$ that holds of necessary truths can then be defined as

(7) $N(x) =_{Df} Nec(x, \ulcorner \langle \rangle \urcorner) \,\&\, S(x),$

where $\langle \rangle$ is the empty sequence and $S(x)$ is a formula that expresses the

There have been dissenting voices too (Skyrms 1978; Perlis 1985, 1988; Savion 1989). The considerations put forward below confirm the dissenting view.

[34] Strictly speaking, their modal analogues. Henceforth we omit this qualification.

[35] We shall sometimes omit the parenthetical qualifiers and speak as if sentences were identical to their Gödel numbers and sequences to their codes. We use $\ulcorner \langle d_1, \ldots, d_n \rangle \urcorner$ for the numeral for the code of the sequence $d_1, \ldots, d_n$. $\ulcorner A \urcorner$ will be, as before, the numeral for the Gödel number of A, and $\ulcorner n \urcorner$ the numeral for the number n.

[36] Assuming that only the first n variables are free in A; otherwise, some special conventions are necessary. See (8) below.

notion "sentence of $\mathscr{PL}$." (Since the set of sentences is recursive and $\mathscr{PL}$ contains arithmetic, such a formula does exist.)

The natural and easiest way of constructing a semantics for *Nec* is to interpret it via a two-place relation on N. This way makes $\mathscr{PL}$ an interpreted classical language (in the sense of pp. 44–45). And Montague's theorem tells us that in the resulting language some of (1)–(4) are bound to be false.

There is, however, as Montague pointed out, a natural model-theoretic semantics for $\mathscr{CL}$ that does make (1)–(4) true. This is the possible-worlds semantics of modal languages due to Kripke and others. The interpretation of $\mathscr{CL}$, on this approach, is given by a *modal model* M, i.e., a quintuple $\langle W, R, @, D, \mathscr{I} \rangle$ satisfying the following conditions:[37]

(i) W is a nonempty set of entities (intuitively thought of as worlds).

(ii) R is a binary accessibility relation on W, i.e., $R \in \{t, f\}^{W^2}$.[38]

(iii) $@ \in W$ (@ is intuitively thought of as the actual world).

(iv) D is a nonempty set of objects (intuitively thought of as the objects existing in the worlds in W).

(v) $\mathscr{I}$ is a function that assigns to each name a member of D, to each n-place function symbol a member of D^{D^n}, and to each n-place predicate a member of $(\{t, f\}^{D^n})^W$.[39]

The notion of "semantic value" (see p. 40),

$$\text{Val}_{M,s}(X, w),$$

is defined in a way parallel to that given in Definition 2A.4. Note that the notion has one additional parameter, namely worlds, and that the definition must contain a clause for necessity:

$$\text{Val}_{M,s}(\Box A, w) = \forall\{\text{Val}_{M,s}(A, w'): wRw'\}.[40]$$

---

[37] We use 'M', 'M'', ... in this section, and only in this section, to range over modal models. 's', 's'', ... will be used, as before, to range over assignments. These are functions from variables into D.

[38] Or, equivalently, $R \subseteq W \times W$.

[39] We have made several simplifying assumptions in this definition. We have assumed that the language contains no nonrigid names, no "nonrigid" function symbols, and no common nouns that supply conflicting principles of identity. We have assumed further that the same objects exist in all the worlds in W (or, equivalently, that quantification is over all possible objects). These assumptions are dispensable at the cost of added complexity.

[40] Here, $\forall: \mathscr{P}\{t, f\} \rightarrow \{t, f\}$; and for all $X \subseteq \{t, f\}$, $\forall X = t$ iff $f \notin X$.

A sentence A is said to be *true in* M (also, *in* $\mathscr{CL}$) iff $\mathrm{Val}_{M,s}(A, @) = \mathbf{t}$ for some assignment s.

Let us say that a modal model M ($= \langle W, R, @, D, \mathscr{I} \rangle$) *is an extension of* a model $\mathscr{M}'$ ($= \langle D', I' \rangle$) iff (i) $D = D'$ and (ii) for all names a, function symbols f, and predicates H,

$$\mathscr{I}(a) = I'(a),$$

$$\mathscr{I}(f) = I'(f),$$

and

$$\mathscr{I}(H)(@) = I'(H).^{41}$$

It is easily verified that an extension of $\mathscr{M}$ whose accessibility relation R is reflexive makes all the axioms of **Q** and all the principles (1)–(4) true.

An important difference exists, then, as Montague observed, between $\mathscr{CL}$ and $\mathscr{PL}$: There are natural interpretations of the former that validate (1)–(4), but there are no such interpretations of the latter. It would be precipitous to conclude from this, however, that the validity of the principles governing necessity turns on logical grammar. It may be that the root cause of the difference between $\mathscr{CL}$ and $\mathscr{PL}$ lies in $\mathscr{L}$. An analogy will make the point clear. Imagine that two kinds of saplings are planted in some soil. One kind flourishes and produces fruit, but the other withers and dies. It would be precipitous to conclude that the first kind is productive and the second not. The difference in behavior may have more to do with the soil than with the saplings. In a different kind of soil both may flourish; in another the second may flourish and the first die.

A key feature of $\mathscr{L}$ is that it has quantifiers that bind variables occurring in name positions but none that bind variables in sentence positions. Consequently, one cannot generalize in $\mathscr{CL}$ over such positions as p in $\Box p$; in contrast, one can generalize in $\mathscr{PL}$ over such positions as x in $N(x)$. This results in a difference in the expressive powers of $\mathscr{CL}$ and $\mathscr{PL}$. In the former, we cannot translate a sentence such as

All the axioms of Peano Arithmetic are necessary truths.[42]

However, in the latter it has an easy translation:

---

[41] If a modal model M of $\mathscr{CL}$ is an extension of $\mathscr{M}'$, then $\mathscr{M}'$ carries all the information needed to evaluate the nonmodal part of $\mathscr{CL}$. The remaining information in M is there because of the presence of necessity.

[42] It follows from Montague's theorem that the set of Gödel numbers of necessary truths is not definable in $\mathscr{CL}$ (assuming that the accessibility relation is reflexive).

$\forall x(PA(x) \rightarrow N(x)),$

where *PA* is a predicate true of all and only the axioms of Peano arithmetic. $\mathscr{L}$ does not provide, therefore, the same kind of environment for $\square$ and *Nec*.

Let us plant the two forms of necessity in different soils. Let us first consider *Nec* in a language weaker than $\mathscr{PL}$. (Later we shall consider $\square$ in a language richer than $\mathscr{CL}$.) Let $\mathscr{PL}^-$ be like $\mathscr{PL}$ except that the first argument of *Nec* may *only* be filled by a numeral $\ulcorner n\urcorner$ and not by any other term. Example: Of the three strings,

$Nec(0''', y),$

$Nec((0''' + 0), y),$

and

$Nec(x, y),$

the first is a formula of $\mathscr{PL}^-$ but the remaining two are not.

Once the occurrences of *Nec* are so restricted, natural back and forth translations between $\mathscr{CL}$ and $\mathscr{PL}^-$ become possible: Let

$Seq(x)$

and

$Val(x, y, z)$

be formulas of $\mathscr{L}$ that express, respectively, the notions "x is (a code of) a finite sequence" and "z is the yth value of the sequence x."[43]

6E.2 Definition (The translation function $[\ ]^N$ from $\mathscr{CL}$ into $\mathscr{PL}^-$)
Let A and B be arbitrary formulas of $\mathscr{CL}$, let F be an n-ary predicate, let x be a variable, and let $t_1, \ldots, t_n$ be terms. Suppose further that the free variables of A are $x_{i_1}, \ldots, x_{i_m}$. Then:

(i) $[F(t_1, \ldots, t_n)]^N = F(t_1, \ldots, t_n).$
(ii) $[\sim A]^N = \sim[A]^N.$
(iii) $[A \ \& \ B]^N = [A]^N \ \& \ [B]^N.$
(iv) $[\forall x A]^N = \forall x[A]^N.$

[43] If y is greater than the length of x, let the yth value of x be 0.

(v) $[\Box A]^N = \exists y(Seq(y) \ \& \ Val(y, \ulcorner i_1 \urcorner, x_{i_1}) \ \& \ \ldots \ \&$

$$Val(y, \ulcorner i_n \urcorner, x_{i_m}) \ \& \ Nec(\ulcorner [A]^N \urcorner, y)).^{44}$$

6E.3   Definition   (The translation function [ ]$^\Box$ from $\mathscr{PL}^-$ into $\mathscr{CL}$)
The clauses for negation, conjunction, quantifiers, and predicates *distinct*
from *Nec* are parallel to those in the previous definition. For example,

$$[\forall x A]^\Box = \forall x [A]^\Box.$$

We need only state the clause for $Nec(\ulcorner p \urcorner, t)$, where p is an arbitrary number and t is an arbitrary term. If p is not a Gödel number of a formula
of $\mathscr{PL}^-$ then

$$[Nec(\ulcorner p \urcorner, t)]^\Box = (0 \neq 0).$$

Otherwise, let p be the Gödel number of a formula A of $\mathscr{PL}^-$ and let the
free variables of A be $y_{j_1}, \ldots, y_{j_m}$. Choose the first m variables $x_{i_1}, \ldots, x_{i_m}$
distinct from those occurring in A and t, and construct a formula B exactly
like A except that it has $x_{i_1}, \ldots, x_{i_m}$ where A has free occurrences of $y_{j_1}, \ldots,$
y_{j_m}. Then,

$$[Nec(\ulcorner p \urcorner, t)^\Box = \exists x_{i_1}, \ldots, x_{i_m}(Seq(t) \ \& \ Val(t, \ulcorner i_1 \urcorner, x_{i_1}) \ \& \ \ldots \ \&$$

$$Val(t, \ulcorner i_m \urcorner, x_{i_m}) \ \& \ \Box[B]^\Box).^{45}$$

Remark   The final clause in the above definition assumes that the Gödel
numbering is of a standard kind. More specifically, it assumes that A is, by
some measure of complexity, less complex than $Nec(\ulcorner p \urcorner, t)$. Nonstandard
Gödel numberings that violate this condition are possible, and back and
forth translations of the above kind may well not exist for them.

In virtue of the above translations, $\mathscr{PL}^-$ and $\mathscr{CL}$ are equivalent. Any
semantics that is given for one can be adapted for the other. Suppose
$\mathscr{PL}^-$ is given a classical two-valued semantics and, so, *Nec* is assigned a
suitable two-place relation X. The same semantics can be adjusted to
apply to $\mathscr{CL}$. The truth conditions for $\Box A$ would be as follows:

$\Box A$ is true relative to an assignment s iff the Gödel number of $[A]^N$ bears the
relation X to a sequence that codes the values s assigns to the free variables of A.

---

[44] Here y is the first variable distinct from those in A. If A has no free variables, then
$[\Box A]^N = \exists y(Seq(y) \ \& \ Nec(\ulcorner [A]^N \urcorner, y))$.
[45] If A has no free variables, then $[Nec(\ulcorner p \urcorner, t)]^\Box = (Seq(t) \ \& \ \Box[A]^\Box)$.

Suppose, on the other hand, that $\mathscr{CL}$ is given a possible-worlds semantics and, so, is interpreted via a modal extension M of $\mathscr{M}$. This same semantics can be applied to $\mathscr{PL}^-$ also. The clause for *Nec* would be this:

(8)   *Nec*(x, y) is true of $\langle m, p \rangle$ in M at a world w iff m is a code of a formula A and p is a code of a sequence $\langle d_1, \ldots, d_n \rangle$ and A is true relative to s in M at all worlds w' accessible from w, where s assigns to the first n variables the values $d_1, \ldots, d_n$ and to the remaining variables some fixed object, say 0.

It can be verified that if A is a sentence of $\mathscr{PL}^-$ then, by this semantics,

A is true at w in M iff $[A]^\square$ is true at w in M

and

$N(\ulcorner A \urcorner)$ is true at w in M iff $\square [A]^\square$ is true at w in M.

It follows that a model in which the principles (1)–(4) are true in $\mathscr{CL}$ is also one in which (1)–(4) are true in $\mathscr{PL}^-$. More generally, *whatever principles can be validated for $\mathscr{CL}$ can also be validated for $\mathscr{PL}^-$*. Despite differences over the logical grammar of necessity, $\mathscr{PL}^-$ and $\mathscr{CL}$ are notational variants.

Why is it that principles such as (1)–(4) can be validated in $\mathscr{PL}^-$ but not in $\mathscr{PL}$? We shall gain illumination on this if we construct a possible-worlds semantics for $\mathscr{PL}$.

From an intuitive standpoint—and as clause (8) shows—a modal model carries sufficient information for an evaluation of all sentences of $\mathscr{PL}$, not just those of $\mathscr{PL}^-$. But notice that with $\mathscr{PL}$ there is no guarantee that such an evaluation does not entangle us in a vicious circle. It may happen, for example, that to determine whether (6) $[= Nec(x, y)]$ is true of a sentence A and the sequence $\langle \rangle$ at the actual world we are required to determine whether A is true at a world w, and to determine this we are required to determine whether (6) is true of A and $\langle \rangle$ at the actual world. This kind of circularity cannot occur in $\mathscr{PL}^-$, because $\mathscr{PL}^-$ is weak in expressive power.[46] But it cannot be excluded from $\mathscr{PL}$ (see Example 6E.6). Because of the threat of vicious circularity, the way

---

[46] And the Gödel numbering used is standard.

to extend the possible-worlds semantics to $\mathscr{PL}$ is to define a rule of revision, v_M.

Given a hypothetical interpretation h of *Nec* in a modal model M $(= \langle W, R, @, D, \mathscr{I} \rangle)$, i.e., a set h such that

$$h \in (\{t, f\}^{D^2})^W,$$

we have enough information to determine the truth values of all sentences of $\mathscr{PL}$ in all worlds. In fact, M and h yield, for each world $w \in W$, a classical interpretation—say, $M_{h,w}$—of $\mathscr{PL}$; thus, the classical truth definition fixes the truth values of all sentences of $\mathscr{PL}$ in all worlds. We can now state what the revised hypothesis $v_M(h)$ is to be. The value of

(9) $v_M(h)(w)(m, p)$

is to be f if m and p are not codes of the appropriate type (i.e., if m is not a Gödel number of a formula or if p is not a code of a sequence). Otherwise, the value of (9) is determined as follows: Suppose that m is the Gödel number of A and that p is the code of $\langle d_1, \ldots, d_n \rangle$. Let s be an assignment that assigns to the first n variables the objects $d_1, \ldots, d_n$ and to the remaining variables 0. Then,

(10) $v_M(h)(w)(m, p) = \forall \{Val_{M_{h,w'},s}(A): wRw'\}$.

Note that the rule v_M revises a hypothesis by using the semantical clause for necessity. Roughly, the revised hypothesis assigns the value t to a sentence A at a world w iff A is true under the original hypothesis at all worlds accessible from w. Let us see how the rule v_M works in some examples.

A relation R is said to be *well capped* iff the converse of R is well founded, i.e., iff there is no infinite sequence of worlds $w_1, w_2, w_3, \ldots$ such that $w_1 R w_2 R w_3 \ldots$. A modal model is *well capped* (*transitive*, etc.) iff its accessibility relation is well capped (transitive, etc.). (Transitive well-capped models are used in giving a semantics for the system G. See Boolos 1979.)

6E.4 Example (The Modal Liar in a well-capped model) Consider the formula $\sim N(x)$ of $\mathscr{PL}$ (see (7)). We construct, by Gödelian techniques, a sentence D such that

(11) $D \leftrightarrow \sim N(\ulcorner D \urcorner)$

is provable from the axioms of $\mathbf{Q}$.[47] D is the *Modal Liar*; it says of itself that it is not a necessary truth. Consider a well-capped model M that is an extension of $\mathcal{M}$. Suppose, to simplify calculations, that M has only two worlds, w_1 and w_2, and that the accessibility relation is as indicated in the diagram below:

w_2
•

↑

•
w_1

Let h be an arbitrary hypothesis concerning the extension of *Nec*. Observe that the axioms of $\mathbf{Q}$ are bound to be true in the classical models $M_{h,w}$ ($w = w_1, w_2$) and, hence, so is (11). Consequently, (10) implies that

$$v_M(h)(w_1)(\ulcorner D\urcorner, \ulcorner \langle \rangle \urcorner) = \sim[h(w_2)(\ulcorner D\urcorner, \ulcorner \langle \rangle \urcorner)]$$

and

$$v_M(h)(w_2)(\ulcorner D\urcorner, \ulcorner \langle \rangle \urcorner) = \mathbf{t}.$$

Thus, after the second stage of revision $\langle \ulcorner D\urcorner, \ulcorner \langle \rangle \urcorner \rangle$ will fall in the extension of *Nec* at w_2 but not at w_1. D thus acquires a stable value in the revision process: After the second stage, D will always be true at w_1 and false at w_2.

The above example is a special case of a more general phenomenon.

6E.5 Theorem (Revisions in well-capped models) If M ($= \langle W, R, @, D, \mathcal{I} \rangle$) is well capped, v_M converges to a fixed point.

Proof Define the *rank*, r(w), of a world w inductively:

$$r(w) = \bigcup \{r(w') + 1 : wRw'\}.$$

Since R is well capped, this is a logically correct inductive definition. Let $\mathcal{S}$ and $\mathcal{S}'$ be revision sequences of length On for v_M. One can show by induction that, for all worlds w of rank α and all $\beta > \alpha$,

[47] Montague 1963, Lemma 1.

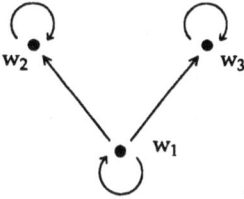

Figure 6.1

$$\mathscr{S}_{\alpha+1}(\mathrm{w}) = \mathscr{S}_{\beta}'(\mathrm{w}).$$

It follows that v_M converges to a fixed point.   ∎

The above proof shows that the truth conditions of *Nec* (see (8)) are not viciously circular if the model is well capped; here the standard semantical clauses extend to $\mathscr{PL}$ without requiring any modification. The next two items show that if the model is reflexive then the circularity *is* vicious.

6E.6 Example (The Modal Liar in a reflexive model) Suppose that a modal model M has only three worlds, w_1, w_2, and w_3, and that the accessibility relation is as indicated in figure 6.1. Let D be, as before, the Modal Liar. Then (10) yields

(i) $v_M(h)(w_1)(\ulcorner D\urcorner,\ulcorner\langle\rangle\urcorner) = (\sim[h(w_1)(\ulcorner D\urcorner,\ulcorner\langle\rangle\urcorner)]$ &
$\qquad\qquad\qquad\qquad\sim[h(w_2)(\ulcorner D\urcorner,\ulcorner\langle\rangle\urcorner)]$ & $\sim[h(w_3)(\ulcorner D\urcorner,\ulcorner\langle\rangle\urcorner)]),$

(ii) $v_M(h)(w_2)(\ulcorner D\urcorner,\ulcorner\langle\rangle\urcorner) = \sim[h(w_2)(\ulcorner D\urcorner,\ulcorner\langle\rangle\urcorner)],$

and

(iii) $v_M(h)(w_3)(\ulcorner D\urcorner,\ulcorner\langle\rangle\urcorner) = \sim[h(w_3)(\ulcorner D\urcorner,\ulcorner\langle\rangle\urcorner)].$

Suppose that the initial hypothesis puts $\langle\ulcorner D\urcorner,\ulcorner\langle\rangle\urcorner\rangle$ in the extension of *Nec* at w_3 but not at w_1 and w_2. D is then true at w_1 and w_2 but not at w_3. By clauses (i)–(iii), the revised hypothesis puts $\langle\ulcorner D\urcorner,\ulcorner\langle\rangle\urcorner\rangle$ in the extension of *Nec* at w_2 but not at w_1 and w_3. Relative to this new hypothesis, D is true at w_1 and w_3 but not at w_2. Further calculations of this sort show that D exhibits the revision pattern displayed in table 6.4.

6E.7 Theorem (The Modal Liar and reflexive models) Let D be the Modal Liar and let M $(=\langle W, R, @, D, \mathscr{I}\rangle)$ be a reflexive extension of $\mathscr{M}$. Then:

Table 6.4

Value of D at	Stage >						
	0	1	2	3	4	5	...
w_1	t	t	t	t	t	t	...
w_2	t	f	t	f	t	f	...
w_3	f	t	f	t	f	t	...

(i) There are at least two recurring hypotheses for v_M.

(ii) The formula

(12) $N(\ulcorner D \urcorner) \rightarrow D$

is not valid at any world in W.

Proof   It suffices to observe that D behaves like the ordinary Liar relative to any hypothesis that treats all worlds uniformly, i.e., one that puts $\langle \ulcorner D \urcorner, p \rangle$ in the extension of *Nec* at all worlds if it puts it in the extension at one world. It is easily verified that in the ω-long revision sequence generated by such a hypothesis if D is true at a world w at a stage n then it is false at w at the next stage n + 1, true at n + 2, and so on. One can, therefore, continue this revision process throughout On by treating all worlds uniformly at all limit stages. Let $\mathscr{S}$ be a revision sequence obtained in this way. Since $\mathscr{S}$ has more than one hypothesis cofinal in it, (i) follows. Further, since (12) is equivalent to D, its truth value at a world w will also oscillate throughout $\mathscr{S}$. Thus, (ii) follows.   ∎

Remarks

(i) It can be shown that if A is a sentence of $\mathscr{PL}^-$ then $N(\ulcorner A \urcorner) \rightarrow A$ is valid. In fact, the following stronger claim can be shown: If a sentence A of $\mathscr{PL}^-$ is true in a modal model M then it is valid by the revision semantics.

(ii) Truth is a special case of necessity; truth and necessary truth are the same if the accessibility relation holds between a world w and w only. Theorem 6E.7(i) is thus a generalization of a result we have already seen for truth: In the context of arithmetic, the revision process for truth does not converge to a fixed point.

(iii) The behavior of the revision process generated by v_M depends, as Nicholas Asher and Hans Kamp (1989) have observed, upon two variables: the kinds of vicious reference present in M and the properties of the accessibility relation. Theorem 6E.5 shows that the revision process converges to a fixed point, irrespective of the vicious reference in M, provided that the accessibility relation is well capped. On the other hand, Asher and Kamp have shown that the revision process behaves the same way, irrespective of the properties of the accessibility relation, provided that M generates no vicious reference for *Nec.*[48]

The foregoing observations suggest that the failure of the modal principles in $\mathscr{PL}$ is due entirely to the vicious reference that its expressive resources make possible. This suggestion is confirmed by the behavior of $\Box$ in richer contexts.

Let $\mathscr{CL}_0^+$ be a language that contains the resources of $\mathscr{CL}$ and (i) a one-place connective ($\bigcirc$), (ii) a propositional quantifier ($\forall$), and (iii) one propositional variable (p). These resources, as we shall see below, suffice for the generation of vicious reference in $\mathscr{CL}_0^+$. They are understood as follows.

Concerning the connective $\bigcirc$ *Syntax*: If A is a sentence of $\mathscr{CL}_0^+$ or the propositional variable p, then $\bigcirc A$ is a formula of $\mathscr{CL}_0^+$. *Semantics*: $\mathscr{CL}_0^+$ provides a set O of natural numbers such that $\bigcirc A$ is true in $\mathscr{CL}_0^+$ iff the Gödel number of A is in O. Further, $\bigcirc$ is rigid: if $\bigcirc A$ is true then so also are $\Box \bigcirc A$, $\Box\Box \bigcirc A$, $\Box\Box\Box \bigcirc A$, ...

Concerning the propositional quantifier $\forall$ It is interpreted substitutionally. A sentence of the form

(13) $\forall p(\text{——} p \text{——})$

is to be true iff all its instances

(14) $\text{——} B \text{——}$

are true. The deduction of (14) from (13) is, therefore, valid in $\mathscr{CL}_0^+$.

Concerning the propositional variable p It may occur in the formulas of $\mathscr{CL}_0^+$ only in the contexts $\forall p$, $\bigcirc p$, and $\Box p$. Thus, the strings p, $\Box\Box p$, and $\bigcirc(p \mathbin{\&} \sim p)$ are not formulas of $\mathscr{CL}_0^+$. But the string

(15) $\forall p(\bigcirc p \to \sim \Box p)$

is a formula.[49]

---

[48] Andrew McCafferty independently proved a similar result.
[49] More precisely, the formulas of $\mathscr{CL}_0^+$ that contain p free are $\bigcirc p$, $\Box p$, and truth-functional compounds of these with other formulas of $\mathscr{CL}_0^+$. There are no restrictions on the contexts in which the *sentences* of $\mathscr{CL}_0^+$ may appear.

The language $\mathscr{CL}_0^+$ treats necessity as a connective, and it is only slightly richer than $\mathscr{CL}$. But, because of the existence of sentences such as (15), it can allow the generation of vicious reference. As a result, a Montague-style theorem can be proved for $\mathscr{CL}_0^+$.

6E.8 Theorem   (Modal principles in $\mathscr{CL}_0^+$)   The theorems of the modal system **T** cannot be true in some languages $\mathscr{CL}_0^+$.

Proof We shall need the following facts concerning the system **T**: that all formulas of the forms

   (i) $\Box(A \to B) \to (\Box A \to \Box B)$

and

   (ii) $\Box A \to A$

are theorems of **T**, and that

   (iii) $\Box A$ is a theorem, if A is a logical truth or a theorem of **T**.

Let C abbreviate (15), and let E abbreviate

$\forall p(\bigcirc p \to (\Box p \leftrightarrow \Box C))$.

Let O be the unit set containing the Gödel number of C. The following, then, are true in $\mathscr{CL}_0^+$:

(16) $\Box \bigcirc C, \Box \Box \bigcirc C,$

(17) $\Box E.$

Suppose, for *reductio*, that the theorems of **T** are also true in $\mathscr{CL}_0^+$. We show that a contradiction is then true in $\mathscr{CL}_0^+$. Observe that the formulas

$C \to (\bigcirc C \to \sim \Box C)$ [$=F$, say]

and

$E \to (\sim \Box C \to C)$

are logical truths (in virtue of the logic of propositional quantification). Hence, their necessitations,

(18) $\Box F, \Box \Box F$

and

(19) $\Box(E \to (\sim \Box C \to C)$,

are theorems of **T** (by (iii)) and, thus, are true in $\mathscr{CL}_0^+$. But the following sentences are deducible in **T** from $\Box \bigcirc C$ and $\Box F$:

(a) $\Box \bigcirc C$ given;

(b) $\Box F$ given;

(c) $\Box C \to (\Box \bigcirc C \to \Box \sim \Box C)$ from (b) using (i);

(d) $\Box C \to \Box \sim \Box C$ from (a) and (c);

(e) $\sim \Box \sim \Box C \to \sim \Box C$ by contraposition of (d);

(f) $\Box \sim \Box C \to \sim \Box C$ by (ii);

(g) $\sim \Box C$ from (e) and (f).

It follows that

$$\Box(\Box \bigcirc C \to (\Box F \to \sim \Box C))$$

is a theorem of **T**. Since we know that $\Box \Box \bigcirc C$ and $\Box \Box F$ are true in $\mathscr{CL}_0^+$, we can deduce that $\Box \sim \Box C$ is also true in $\mathscr{CL}_0^+$. Consequently,

$\sim \Box C$ from (ii)

$\Box C$ from (19) using (i) and (17)

are true in $\mathscr{CL}_0^+$. ∎

Remarks

(i) Sentence (15) is the counterpart of the Modal Liar in $\mathscr{CL}_0^+$. It is the crucial element in the above proof.

(ii) The interpretation of $\bigcirc$ in $\mathscr{CL}_0^+$ is highly *intentional*: Even if sentences A and B are necessarily equivalent, the statement $\bigcirc A \equiv \bigcirc B$ may not be true in $\mathscr{CL}_0^+$. This intentionality is essential to the proof.[50] If $\bigcirc$ is not intentional, it becomes possible to interpret $\forall p$ as ranging over sets of worlds; under this interpretation, the principles of **T** imply no contradictions. Note that any modal system can consistently be enriched with propositional quantification *if* propositions are identified with sets of worlds.

Digression Consider an interpretation that allows propositions to be identified with truth values. Interpret $\Box$ as the vacuous connective "It is true that ..." and $\bigcirc$ as "John says something truth-functionally equivalent to the proposition that...." Thus, $\Box$ and $\bigcirc$ are truth-functional connec-

[50] See Prior 1961 and Thomason 198+.

tives and the theorems of **T** hold vacuously. The above proof shows that under these conditions the sentences

$$\bigcirc \forall p (\bigcirc p \rightarrow \sim \square p) \quad [= \bigcirc C]$$

and

$$\forall p (\bigcirc p \rightarrow (\square p \leftrightarrow \square C)) \quad [= E]$$

cannot be true. But this is intuitively odd: What if John says C and only C? Are not the above two formulas true in such a situation? This difficulty is resolved as follows: There is, in the situation described, a circularity in the meaning of $\bigcirc$. The truth function it expresses depends, in an unstable way, upon a prior hypothesis concerning it. Assume, for example, that it expresses the identity truth function. Then (15) (i.e., $\forall p (\bigcirc p \rightarrow \sim \square p)$) is false. But the meaning of $\bigcirc$ dictates that, if **v** is a truth value,

$$\bigcirc \mathbf{v} = \mathbf{t} =_{\mathrm{Df}} \mathbf{v} = \text{the truth value of (15).}$$

Thus, if (15) is false, it follows that $\bigcirc$ must express the negation truth function. But on *this* hypothesis (15) is true. So the meaning of $\bigcirc$ now dictates that $\bigcirc$ expresses the identity truth function. Similar calculations show that the remaining two hypotheses about the truth function expressed by $\bigcirc$ are revised to either the identity or the negation truth function. Note that the value of C oscillates in the resulting revision process for $\bigcirc$, but the values of $\bigcirc C$ and E stabilize as false. *Moral:* One role of the intentionality of $\bigcirc$ in the above proof is to ensure that $\bigcirc$ is noncircular.

It may appear obvious that if O is arithmetical then there is a function that translates $\mathscr{CL}_{\mathrm{O}}^{+}$ into $\mathscr{PL}$. The construction of such a function is not, however, straightforward.

6E.9 Definition (The translation of $\mathscr{CL}_{\mathrm{O}}^{+}$ into $\mathscr{PL}$) Let O be arithmetical, and let $O(x)$ be a formula of arithmetic that defines O. Suppose A is a formula of $\mathscr{CL}_{\mathrm{O}}^{+}$ with Gödel number j. We define first a translation function $[\ ]^{i,j}$ over the subformulas of A. $[\ ]^{i,j}$ is like $[\ ]^{N}$ defined in 6E.2 with the exceptions that clause (v) in this definition is restricted to those formulas that do not have p free and four new clauses, given below, are added. Let $S^{*}(x)$ be a formula of arithmetic that defines the notion "sentence of $\mathscr{CL}_{\mathrm{O}}^{+}$", and let $B_{\mathrm{i}}(x, y)$ be a formula that expresses ϕ_{i}, the ith of the one-place partial recursive functions in their effective enumeration, and let z be the first variable that does not occur in any of A, O, S^{*}, and B_{i}. Then:

(vi) $[\bigcirc p]^{i,j} = \exists x(O(x)\ \&\ B_i(x,z))$,

(vii) $[\bigcirc C]^{i,j} = O(\ulcorner C\urcorner)$,

(viii) $[\Box p]^{i,j} = N(z)$,

(ix) $[\forall p C]^{i,j} = \forall z(\exists x(S^*(x)\ \&\ B_i(x,z)) \rightarrow [C]^{i,j})$.

Now define a recursive function $f(i,j)$ as follows: If j is not a Gödel number of a formula of $\mathscr{CL}_0^+$, let $f(i,j) = 0$. Otherwise, let $f(i,j) =$ the Gödel number of $[A]^{i,j}$, where A is the formula of $\mathscr{CL}_0^+$ with the Gödel number j. The key here is that $f(i,j)$ is recursive because we can effectively recover B_i from i. By the s-m-n Theorem, there is a recursive function g such that, for all i and j,

$$\phi_{g(i)}(j) = f(i,j).$$

By the Recursion Theorem there is an e such that, for all j,

$$\phi_{g(e)}(j) = \phi_{s^1_1(e)}(j) = f(e,j).$$

ϕ_e is a translation function of the desired sort.

In summary: We have argued for the following conclusions.

- Possible-worlds semantics can be given for necessity even when it is treated as a predicate.
- When necessity is added to a language that is *weak* in expressive power, the principles of the systems T, S5, etc. are consistent. This is so whether necessity is treated as a predicate or as a connective.
- When necessity is added to a language that is *strong* in expressive power, the principles can fail. This failure too is independent of the logical grammar of necessity; it can occur even if necessity is treated as a connective.
- The relevant dimension of expressive power in the previous two points is the capacity to generate vicious reference. The presence of vicious reference makes the truth conditions of some sentences circular and causes the failure of certain principles.

Belnap (1975) observed that syntactic considerations leave one much freedom in logical grammar. It appears that semantic considerations leave this freedom intact.

7 Truth and Other Circular Concepts

The foregoing chapters provide some evidence for our two central claims: that logical and semantical frameworks in which circular concepts make sense are possible and that truth is a circular concept. We cannot claim to have *proved*, once and for all, that these claims are correct. Much more philosophical and technical work must be done before any claim of the sort will be in order. Before we pursue this further work, however, we ought to pause and reflect a little. It is a fact of philosophical life that, although an idea can be given meaning and content only through many long (and sometimes difficult) detailed investigations, in many cases the refutation and the rejection of the idea do not turn on the resulting details. Often the fatal flaw lies at a more elementary and basic level. It would be wise, therefore, to consider whether the same might not be true of the proposal put forward here. We need to reflect a little on the more elementary and basic objections that might be brought against us.

It is a perennial problem with theories of truth that while they apparently resolve one paradox, they allow the generation of another, more vicious one. It may be objected that our account is not exempt from this. For example, a sentence such as (1) presents us with a difficulty.

(1)   Either this sentence is not categorical or it is not true.

If (1) is not categorical then it must be true (because its first disjunct is true) and hence categorical. On the other hand, if it is categorical then it is like the Liar (because its first disjunct is false) and hence noncategorical. In either case we can deduce a contradiction. Our proposal, it may be said, can perhaps account for the *ordinary* versions of the Liar, but it cannot deal with the *strengthened* versions such as (1) above. The central problem raised by the paradoxes, it may appear, is left unresolved in our approach.[1]

It will be best to begin our response to this objection by reviewing the main things we want to say about the Ordinary Liar. We want to hold both of the following theses:

---

[1] See Cargile 1986 and Priest 1987 for arguments along these lines. Hart (1989–90) constructs another kind of Strengthened Liar. He argues that if quantification over indices is allowed then contradictions can be deduced in C_0.

(i) Liar-like paradoxes arise from the very nature of the concept of truth.

(ii) Nonetheless, the principles governing truth are not inconsistent.

We want to hold (ii) because we see little hope of obtaining an adequate description of the concept of truth if the principles governing it (the Tarski biconditionals) are viewed as inconsistent.[2] The reasoning in the Liar argument, we admit, has great force; still, it is not as great as that of the Principle of Noncontradiction. The Liar argument, as we see it, can be read in two ways. We can read the crucial biconditional in it,

The Liar is true if and only if the Liar is not true,

either *materially*,

The Liar is true $\leftrightarrow$ the Liar is not true,

or *definitionally*,

The Liar is true $=_{Df}$ the Liar is not true.

Under the former reading, the Liar argument is valid but the crucial premiss is false. Under the latter reading, all the premisses are true but the argument is invalid. Under no reading is the argument sound.[3]

The claim that the Tarski biconditionals (in their definitional interpretation) are consistent does not imply that everything is in order with the concept of truth, or that truth is like any other ordinary concept, or that there is nothing special about the Liar sentence. On the contrary, a central goal of the theory developed above is to recognize and explain the pathological behavior of the concept of truth while maintaining its consistency. According to our theory, truth exhibits pathologicality because the Tarski biconditionals are definitional of it.[4] These biconditionals make truth a circular concept, and thus generate Liar-like (and other pathological) sentences. The behavior of the pathological sentences, on our view, is rooted in the very meaning of truth.

---

[2] See the discussion of the Inconsistency View in chapter 1.

[3] There is a way of modifying the Liar argument that renders it logically correct. (This may explain some of its great intuitive appeal.) In this modification, one deduces, as usual, 'the Liar is not true' from 'the Liar is true', and then concludes 'the Liar is true', but one associates revision indices with the premisses and the conclusions. Read this way, the Liar reasoning shows, correctly, that if the Liar is true at one revision stage then it is false at the next stage and true again at the very next. No contradiction is implied by the Liar sentence under this reading. See the discussion of the Inconsistency View in chapter 4.

[4] More precisely, the biconditionals fix the signification of truth.

We recognize the Liar to be pathological, but we do not want to say that it is neither true nor false. The sentences 'the Liar is not true' and 'the Liar is not false', whether viewed as belonging to the object language or to some metalanguage, are pathological in exactly the same way as the Liar is pathological.[5] To correctly describe the semantic status of the Liar we need to appeal to notions such as "categoricalness."

Let us turn now to the Strengthened Liar (1). We want to give for it an account parallel to that given for the Ordinary Liar. We believe, in the first place, that the argument in the strengthened paradox is not sound. Not only does it use the Tarski biconditionals in an uncritical manner (a manner that is called into question by our theory); it also relies on a principle, namely

(2)   All truths are categorical,

that is clearly problematic. As we have seen, the Liar sentence is not categorical. This, together with (2), implies, by the rules of Predicate Logic, that the Liar is not true. But this last claim is paradoxical. Hence there is a problem in the argument for the first horn of the Strengthened Liar.[6]

Another problem with the argument is that it assumes that the notion "categorical in L" is in L itself. This assumption can be accepted, but it cannot be assumed that "categorical in L" has an ordinary logic and semantics. On the contrary, we should observe that this notion is just as circular as truth: We can determine the categorical sentences of L *only on the basis of a prior hypothesis concerning the extension of* "categorical in L."[7] Hence, one must exercise more care when working with this notion (especially within the context of hypothetical reasoning) than is shown in the Strengthened Liar argument. It must be borne in mind that the logical

---

[5] Our view here differs from that of Skyrms (1984) and Gaifman (1988), who maintain that the Liar is untrue since it is pathological. It is possible to give a meaning to 'true' by which the pathological sentences would count as 'untrue'—Skyrms's and Gaifman's works show us how. We do not think, however, that this is the ordinary meaning of 'true'. Any assertion that 'the Liar is untrue', even when made with the full consciousness of the Liar's paradoxicality, invites the response that the Liar must then be true, since it asserts its own untruth. The circle of semantical reflection is not naturally broken at any point.

Further, Skyrms' and Gaifman's move can be made for any circular predicate: From the claim that d is pathological with respect to a circular predicate G, we can conclude that d is not G. But here the move seems to us to be very implausible. If so, then it is equally implausible in connection with truth.

[6] By the theory sketched in section 6D, the negation of (2) is valid in the presence of vicious reference (see Example 6D.10).

[7] See section 6D. Note that "categorical in L" is not circular if L does not contain its own notion of categoricalness (or other related notions). In this respect also it is like "true in L."

behavior of definitional equivalences is different from that of material equivalences. The former equivalences force a shift in the index of the conclusion, but the latter equivalences do not.[8] Because of this, the argument for the first horn does not establish that (1) is categorical. It shows only that if (1) falls outside the extension of "categorical" at one stage of the revision process, then it falls in the extension at the next stage. A similar claim holds for the second horn.

We want to say, then, that some of the steps in the Strengthened Liar reasoning are not correct, and, more generally, that the principles governing categoricalness are consistent. Nonetheless, the Strengthened Liar (1) is not to be assimilated to ordinary statements. Its logical behavior is distinctive and is rooted in the very nature (specifically, the circularity) of the concept of categoricalness. The situation is similar in essential respects to that of the Ordinary Liar.

One other point of similarity should be noted. Just as the sentences 'the Liar is true' and 'the Liar is not true' are pathological in the one case, the sentences 'the Strengthened Liar is categorical' and 'the Strengthened Liar is not categorical' are pathological in the other. Hence, the concept of categoricalness that is appropriate for describing the behavior of the Ordinary Liar is not appropriate for the Strengthened Liar. To correctly describe the behavior of the latter we need to appeal to a higher-level notion of categoricalness. This higher-level notion would itself manifest paradoxical behavior in the presence of vicious reference. And we would account for it in the same way. The higher-level paradoxes would demand a still higher-level notion for their description.

But isn't this hierarchy of predicates an embarrassment for us? Doesn't it show that our approach is basically Tarskian? That the essential problem is left unresolved by our theory? More bluntly, can it not be claimed that our investigation is conducted within a framework that makes its results irrelevant to the main problem posed by the paradoxes? The object languages we have investigated are weak in their semantic resources. We have been concerned, for the most part, with languages whose only problematic element is the truth predicate. Even if these languages can be enriched, the strengthened versions of the paradoxes show that an adequate description of any of them requires, within our general framework, a richer metalanguage. But then, it is objected,

---

[8] See the discussion of the calculus C_0 in chapters 4 and 5.

... if we can only give the semantics of our simplified language within an essentially richer metalanguage, the fundamental and difficult problem of how to give the semantics for a language within the language itself will still remain before us. (McGee 1991, p. 147)

Let us call the problem of explaining how a language can be understood from within the "Problem of Semantic Self-Sufficiency." It can be claimed fairly that the very framework we have adopted makes our investigations irrelevant to this problem.[9]

We must confess that we find this kind of criticism perplexing. It requires the theory of truth to explain a phenomenon—"understanding a language from within"—that not only is not known to exist, but even the *possibility* of whose existence can be doubted. Perhaps the response will be that the phenomenon is known to be possible, for natural languages are, in Tarski's terminology, universal ("if we can speak meaningfully about anything at all, we can speak about it in colloquial language" [Tarski 1935/1956, p. 164]). Hence, it may be argued, whatever resources may be necessary for understanding a natural language, they can all be expressed within it. The fundamental problem posed by the paradoxes, on this view, is to show how this universality is possible. And theories of truth and paradox that rely on richer metalanguages contribute little to its solution.

At this point we shall do well to keep firmly in mind Kant's admonition that

[t]o know what questions may reasonably be asked is already a great and necessary proof of sagacity and insight. For if a question is absurd in itself and calls for an answer where none is required, it not only brings shame on the propounder of the question, but may betray an incautious listener into absurd answers, thus presenting, as the ancients said, the ludicrous spectacle of one man milking a he-goat and the other holding a sieve underneath. (1781/1787, A58/B83)

It is being demanded of a theory of truth that it solve the problem of "universality" of natural languages, that it show how a language can be understood from within. But what is this supposed "universality" of natural languages? The claim cannot be that natural languages are universal in the sense that they have the resources to express everything that can be expressed; that is obviously false. Is the claim, then, that natural languages are universal in the weaker sense that anything whatsoever can be expressed in them once suitable resources are added to them? If so, there is

---

[9] Keith Simmons (1990) has put forward similar objections.

nothing very remarkable in this feature. The same is true of any language, natural or artificial. Furthermore, this type of universality does not imply that natural languages, at any stage of their development, can contain their own semantics. Perhaps there is a sense of "universality" in which it applies to natural languages *and* implies that some languages can contain their own semantics. But as far as we know this sense has never been articulated.[10]

There is one sense of "universality" which we can accept and which may be true of natural languages: Universal languages are possible in the sense that for any semantic concept C there is a language L that contains its own C-concept.[11] And it may be a feature of natural languages that they can be extended to include more and more of their own semantic concepts. Note, however, that "universality" in this sense does not imply that there are languages that can be understood from within. Nor does this sense pose a problem for our theory. On the contrary, our theory provides a scheme that can be used to justify this sort of universality: Languages can contain their own semantic concepts because the significations of these concepts take the form of a rule of revision.[12]

Once we abandon the Tarskian claim of universality, few reasons remain for thinking that natural languages can be understood from within. The vast literature on semantics contains, as far as we know, no argument that establishes *a priori* that natural languages *must* be semantically self-sufficient. And as far as *a posteriori* arguments are concerned, it is sufficient to observe that we have at present too poor an understanding of the workings of our language to be able to say, with any clarity and certainty, what resources will be needed for its description.

Whatever the final fate of the Problems of Universality and Semantic Self-Sufficiency may turn out to be, the paradoxes pose a basic challenge that is independent of them. It is plain that we can work coherently with the notion of truth in expressively rich languages, even though it results in paradoxes. The challenge is to find a semantic account of the notion of

[10] Herzberger (1970a), too, gives several arguments for the claim that, as he puts it, "no language is universal in the sense of Tarski."

[11] Note well the order of the quantifiers. It should not be switched, for then not only is the claim false of natural languages but we do not even have an abstract conception of what the requisite L would be like. (The claim *can* be strengthened so that it implies the existence of languages L that contain the concepts "C-in-L" for all C that fall within certain classes of semantic concepts.)

[12] As we argued in chapter 3, this universality cannot be made sense of if languages are viewed in the usual two-, three-, or n-valued way.

truth that will explain this phenomenon. The languages for which this problem arises do not have to be very rich, much less "universal" (in Tarski's sense). The problem arises even for simple extensional first-order languages whose only problematic element is truth. For the sake of simplicity and clarity, we decided to work with such languages. If we can understand the workings of truth in this simplified context, there is hope that we can understand its working within richer ones. We have placed no restrictions on the resources the theory may bring to bear in solving the problem of truth; we have cared only that the problem be solved.[13]

Even if the descriptive problem can be separated from the Problems of Universality and Semantic Self-Sufficiency, and even if the former problem is deemed to be a good one for a theory to tackle, objections that question the very foundations of our theory can nevertheless be put forward. We have insisted that our aim is to arrive at a satisfactory (though, of necessity, idealized) description of our ordinary notion of truth. But, it may be asked, how plausible is it that revision processes, with all their complexity, are relevant to this description? Truth is a notion that most of us, children included, understand. Yet only a very few among us have any idea of the transfinite ordinals used by the revision theory, and fewer still have any conception of revision processes. It is plain, the critic may point out, that we do not ordinarily arrive at our judgments about truth and falsity by revising arbitrary hypotheses concerning the extension of truth. In what sense, then, can the revision theory be taken as providing a *description* of the ordinary notion of truth?[14]

We would like to observe in response, first, that the root conception underlying our theory is not complex at all. We hold that the Tarski biconditionals are definitional of truth. As a consequence, we are led to hold that 'true' is circular and that its meaning is given by a rule with a hypothetical character. There is nothing in this conception that is difficult to attribute to users of 'true', be they adults or children. The Tarski bi-

---

[13] Our criticisms of the Tarskian hierarchy, in chapter 3, were from the perspective of this descriptive problem: We tried to argue that the hierarchy does not provide a promising approach to the problem. We do not want to, nor do we need to, deny the existence of hierarchies of semantic concepts. In fact, we believe that such hierarchies provide an ideal solution for certain kinds of normative problems.

[14] This kind of objection was put to us by several friends, including Geoffrey Hellman, John Macnamara, and Penelope Maddy. They do not necessarily subscribe to it. McGee (1991) also discusses a similar objection and attributes it to Chihara.

conditionals are undeniably an integral part of our concept of truth. We have seen that they do not always fix the truth values of all the sentences; still, we do use them to criticize proposals concerning what is true and what is not true. Let someone assert that the Liar is true (or that it is not true), and we feel entitled to criticize the proposal on the basis of the biconditionals. Let someone propose a complete division of sentences into the true and the false, and we feel entitled to use the biconditionals to determine what would be true and what false *given* the proposed division.

Second, the complexity in our theory appears in the account that it gives of how categorical judgments are founded on the hypothetical rule underlying 'true'. This complexity is due to the fact that the theory considers *arbitrary situations*, including those that contain infinite cross-reference. If we restrict ourselves to situations that do not essentially involve the infinite, even this complexity disappears: There is no need to invoke transfinite revision processes; finite revisions suffice.[15] Our theory is complex, then, only because it is meant to be applicable in all sorts of complex, infinitary situations. Ordinary users of 'true' can bypass this complexity because they do not normally consider—and do not need to consider—such situations.[16]

Third, there is a distinction between "description of a concept" and "description of the psychology (or the sociology) of the users of the concept." To aim to provide the one is not necessarily to aim to provide the other. An account aiming at the latter can afford to ignore uses of the concept that are beyond human ability (e.g., the application of 'true' to exceedingly long sentences), but cannot ignore systematic misuses of the concept. It is just the opposite with an account aiming at a description of the concept. Such an account can afford to ignore systematic misuses but not uses that are beyond human ability. Our aim in this essay has been to give a descriptive account of the concept of truth. We have proposed that revision processes are a useful tool in gaining such a description. This does not imply that users of 'true' arrive at their judgments by revising arbitrary hypotheses, or that the conceptual resources mobilized by the theory are

---

[15] Furthermore, in the context of the theory S^*, the calculus C_0 is perfectly adequate for reasoning concerning finite situations. See Theorems 5D.4 and 5D.6.

[16] Even if infinitary situations are never considered in ordinary practices, it does not follow that they do not fix the application of 'true' in such situations. Ordinary practices point beyond themselves. They guide the application of concepts in new, hitherto unconsidered situations. They may not fix the application of concepts in *all* situations, but they can fix it in *some*.

readily available to them. Users of 'true' arrive at their judgments in a variety of ways—ways that are ill understood at present. A description of the concept of truth does not aim to provide a description of these ways. It aims instead to illuminate the concept of truth by giving a systematic account of the judgments to which these ways lead. The uses of a concept are indeed our primary guide to a philosophical understanding of the concept. However, concepts are reflected only imperfectly in use. No exact rules exist that will separate out uses that provide a clear reflection from those that distort. This is one reason why philosophical analysis of concepts is an art, not a science.

Aside from the methodological objection discussed above, substantive objections may be brought against our theory. It may be argued that the sorting of sentences into such classes as valid, categorical, and paradoxical provided by our theory does not always correspond to ordinary intuition and ordinary usage. For instance, the statement

(3)   The Liar is true or the Liar is not true

turns out, in our theory, to be valid; consequently, it is deemed to be categorically assertible. Neither disjunct of (3), however, is valid; they are both paradoxical. This, it may be said, not only goes against the intuitive classification of (3) but also makes the meaning of 'or' highly mysterious.[17]

It is ironic that this objection should be brought against us. When we first embarked on the project of constructing a theory of truth, a desideratum that was foremost in our minds was the preservation of classical logical laws.[18] Now the very success of our theory in meeting this desideratum is urged as an objection against us. In the theory of truth, more than elsewhere, one man's desideratum is often another man's refuting counterexample!

---

[17] This objection was put to us many years ago by Allen Hazen when we sketched to him (in a conversation) the kind of theory we were attempting to develop. It was urged vigorously by Pierdaniele Giaretta, Paolo Leonardi, Mario Mignucci, and, especially, Enrico Martino in discussions on the theory of truth at the University of Padua. It is also the first of three problem examples raised by Steve Yablo (1985) against the Revision theory. (The remaining two of Yablo's examples reduce to it in the following sense: If we can argue successfully for the Principle of Excluded Middle, then it can be shown, using principles that Yablo would accept, that the Revision theory's classification of his examples is correct.)

[18] Not because we have especial fondness for these laws, but because we felt that the theory of truth should not disturb the logic of the ground language.

An easy way of answering the objection is to challenge the intuition that gives rise to it—the intuition that, because of the Liar's pathologicality, there is something problematic about (3). For, despite the Liar's peculiar behavior, we *do* want to assert that

(4)   If the Liar is true then the Liar is true.

But (4) implies (3) even on the weakest reading of 'if'. Hence, if we are willing to say that (4) is unproblematic and true, we should say the same of (3).[19]

The proponent of the objection may, however, respond thus: One can maintain, and explain, both the intuitions—that there is something right about (4) and that there is something wrong with (3). Many-valued logics provide natural accounts of 'if', 'or', and 'not' that invalidate the argument form

$$(5) \quad \frac{\text{If } p \text{ then } q}{q \text{ or not-}p}$$

used to deduce (3) from (4). Hence, the correctness of (4) cannot be used as an argument for (3).

If what is being suggested in this response is that a many-valued approach better explains the behavior of the English particles 'if', 'or', and 'not', then there is nothing in it with which we need to quarrel (except that it is put forward as a problem for our views). If English is a many-valued language in which the argument form (5) is invalid, then it is possible to maintain and explain that (4) is unproblematic and true and that (3) is pathological. Indeed, the Revision scheme itself can provide such an explanation. Observe that the scheme can be applied to *any* language governed by *any* kind of semantics, be it classical, many-valued, intuitionistic, modal, relevant, or any other. If we apply the scheme to a language in which the Principle of Excluded Middle fails but the principle

If A then A

holds, then (4) will be evaluated as valid but not (3). It is, therefore, not an intrinsic feature of our theory that (3) be ruled unproblematic and true; this is instead a consequence of our *decision* to work with classical ground languages.

---

[19] Kit Fine (1975) has used a similar argument in his defense of the supervaluation account of vagueness.

On the other hand, if what is being suggested is that the addition of a truth predicate to a classical language changes the logic and the semantics of the logical connectives, then we *do* want to quarrel with the response. By shifting the semantics of the connectives we would, it is true, be able to rule (3) pathological, but this seeming gain comes at a high price. First, we would need to explain away the apparent use of the usual logical laws. Second, such a maneuver typically invalidates numerous intuitively correct arguments involving truth (see, for instance, Example 6C.7). We would need to tell some special stories for these also. Third, the maneuver conflicts with two natural ideas: that the Tarski biconditionals are definitional of truth[20] and that definitions do not affect the logic of the ground language. Our understanding of definitions relies on our *prior* understanding of the logical connectives; it does not provide the connectives with new meanings.

One reason why (3) arouses suspicions is that one may easily misread it as saying things that it does not say—e.g., that the Liar or its negation is valid, or that the Liar falls either in the extension or in the antiextenstion of 'true'. But (3) says no such things. It is merely a reflection of a logical feature of the ground language. It is a logical truth, a mere tautology.

II

Which of our ordinary concepts, other than truth, might be circular? This is a large question, and one that is difficult to answer in a definitive way. The following brief discussion of it is divided into three subsections. The first discusses some semantic concepts (reference, satisfaction, etc.), the second is devoted to the set-theoretic and property-theoretic concepts (membership and exemplification), and the third addresses some modal and doxastic concepts (necessity, belief, and knowledge). The question is discussed at a more speculative level in section III.

Reference, satisfaction, etc.

If the above account of the concept of truth is correct, then semantic concepts such as "refers," and "true of," and "satisfies" must also be circular. These concepts exhibit the same kinds of pathological behavior as truth. And, as with truth, their behavior can be traced to a circularity in

---

[20] In the sense that they fix its signification.

their definitions. Consider, for instance, 'refers', which we may view as a two-place predicate that holds between singular terms and their denotations. Berry's paradox shows that certain sentences containing 'refers' behave like the Liar. The term constructed by Berry, 'the least integer not nameable in fewer than nineteen syllables',[21] appears to denote a definite number n,[22] for only a finite number of singular terms can be formulated with a given finite number of syllables. But Berry's term contains only eighteen syllables. Hence, it appears that the statement (6), if true, implies that it is not true; and if not true, that it is true.[23]

(6)   The least integer not nameable in fewer than nineteen syllables is n.

Therefore, (6) behaves like the Liar. The circularity this indicates in "refers" is confirmed by the partial definitions of the concept,

(R)   't' refers to x $=_{Df}$ t is x.

Some of the instances of the form (R) contain "refers" in their definiens and are thus circular. For example:

'The thing referred to by 'Socrates'' refers to x $=_{Df}$ the thing referred to by 'Socrates' is x.

'The least integer not nameable in fewer than nineteen syllables' refers to x $=_{Df}$ the least integer not nameable in fewer than nineteen syllables is x.

One may easily construct a theory of reference by applying the theory of definitions to the partial definitions of the form (R). The resulting theory can be shown to have many of the same nice properties as the theory of truth. Parallel remarks hold for other semantic concepts, such as "satisfaction" and "true of."

A language may contain not just one but several of its semantic concepts. In such a case the partial definitions of one semantic concept will

---

[21] The expression 'x is nameable in fewer than nineteen syllables' is understood here to be synonymous with 'some singular term of fewer than nineteen syllables refers to x'.
[22] Russell (1908) states that it "in fact" denotes 111, 777!
[23] This last implication holds only if we assume, following common practice, that n *is* the least integer not referred to by any singular term distinct from Berry's term that contains fewer than nineteen syllables. The assumption is not unproblematic. There are terms—such as, 'the greatest integer nameable in fewer than nineteen syllables'—that contain fewer than nineteen syllables but which, like Berry's term, are pathological. (This last term behaves like the Truth Teller.) Nonetheless, one can show by a more complex argument that (6) is paradoxical for some values of n. Note that *any* assumption concerning the denotation of Berry's term can be reduced to an absurdity.

make use of the other concepts. Here is an illustrative example. The following partial definitions belong to a language that contains both "reference" and "satisfaction":

'The thing that satisfies A' refers to x =$_{Df}$ x is the thing that satisfies A.

x satisfies "t' refers to y' =$_{Df}$ 't' refers to x.

The first of these is a partial definition of 'refers' and contains 'satisfies' in the definiens; the second is a partial definition of 'satisfies' and contains 'refers' in the definiens. The semantic concepts in such cases constitute a mutually interdependent system. The rule of revision for one concept takes as input not just a hypothesis about that concept's extension but a hypothesis about the extension of all the semantic concepts in the language. The approaches developed in chapter 5 apply to this situation in a straightforward way.

A language may also contain general semantic concepts, such as "true in L" (where L is a variable ranging over languages). An adequate semantic account of these can be given only after a number of difficult questions have been answered:

- What kind of abstract entities are languages? The set-theoretic constructs of section 2A are adequate only for certain kinds of languages and for certain limited kinds of purposes. How is one to give a more adequate account?

- How is one to make sense of the totality of all languages? Such a totality, it appears, can neither be a set nor a proper class, yet it is needed in giving a semantic account of, e.g., "true in L."[24]

- How is one to deal with the paradoxes that these concepts engender?

The theory developed in this essay may contribute to a solution of, at least, the third problem. Suppose we get around the first two through simplification and idealization. Let us restrict ourselves to a *set* X of *extensional first-order* languages. Further, let us suppose that each language in X has only one problematic notion: "true in L," with L ranging over X. The domain of each language contains, therefore, for each L in X, a code

---

[24] Even on the simplest imaginable semantics of "true in L" this is so: Its extension is an abstract object that contains pairs of sentences and languages. (We are assuming that every language has some truths and that something like the Union axiom holds for extensions.)

for L and the sentences of L.[25] The signification of "true in L" would then
be a rule of revision that takes as input a hypothetical extension of "true
in L" and yields as output a new revised extension. Some observations: (a)
To obtain the revised extension of "true in L" in *one* language requires
a semantic evaluation of *all* the languages in X. (b) The revision rule is
the same in all languages: For the same inputs it gives the same outputs
(ignoring nonsentences). (c) The rule may not be expressible[26] in any L in
X. No language in X may be powerful enough to express everything that
is expressible in all others. Hence, no language in X may be able to
express all the Tarski biconditionals for "true in L." This appears to hold
of our ordinary notion of truth. We have the concepts "true in Sanskrit"
and "true in Hebrew," but it may well be that not everything expressible in Sanskrit and Hebrew is expressible in English. (d) Suppose that
'the Liar' is a name in L of a Liar sentence in L*. Then the sentence
of L,

the Liar is true in L*,

is also paradoxical; it oscillates in the revision process. Hence, putting the
concept of truth of L* in another distinct language, even a metalanguage,
does not remove the pathologicality of "true in L*." This too appears to
hold of our ordinary notion of truth: The sentence 'The Liar sentence of
Hebrew is true' is no less perplexing to us than 'the Liar sentence of
English is true'.

Membership and exemplification

The iterative notion of set, which underlies modern set theory, bears
the same relation to Russell's paradox[27] as the Tarskian hierarchy of
truth predicates bears to the Liar paradox. The iterative notion, like the
Tarskian hierarchy, is guaranteed to be free of paradox and circularity; it
is simple and natural; and for many purposes it is perfectly adequate.
However, like the Tarskian hierarchy, it is a descendent of another notion
—one that *is* subject to paradox and circularity. This is the notion of *set*

[25] If we work with non-well-founded sets, we may even identify the code for L with a set-
theoretic construct of section 2A.
[26] I.e., "weakly expressible" in the terminology of section 5D.
[27] This concerns the set or class R that contains all and only those things that are
not members of themselves. R, it appears, is a member of itself iff it is not a member of
itself.

as extension: Given any possible one-place predicate P, there is a totality, the extension of P, or the *class* of things that are P,[28]

$[x: x \text{ is } P]$,[29]

that contains all and only those objects that satisfy P. The iterative conception makes clear that there is no universal set,[30] just as the Tarskian hierarchy makes clear that there is no highest-level truth predicate. There is, however, an extension or class that contains everything, for there are predicates (e.g., x is x) that are true of everything.[31]

Classes and membership ($\in$) are governed by partial definitions of the form

(7) $\quad z \in [x: \text{———} x \text{———}] =_{\text{Df}} \text{———} z \text{———},$

as also are properties and exemplification provided that we read

(8) $\quad [x: \text{———} x \text{———}]$

in (7) as property abstraction and '$\in$' as exemplification. There is a problem in constructing a theory of classes, which we shall discuss shortly. A natural theory of properties, however, can easily be constructed on the basis of (7): We take the terms of the form (8) as noncircular and unproblematic, and we read instances of (7) as partial definitions of "exemplifies." Note that some of these partial definitions are circular, e.g.,

$z \in [x: x \in x] =_{\text{Df}} z \in z$.[32]

Note also that the interpretation of '$\in$' is bound to fluctuate in the revision process generated by any rule that accords with (7).[33] The Russellian property

the property of not exemplifying itself,

---

[28] The use of the term 'class' here is an expository convenience. Classes in this sense are not the classes of the von Neumann-Bernays-Gödel or Morse-Kelly set theories.

[29] We use brackets to distinguish classes from the sets of the iterative conception.

[30] If there were, there would be a stage α of the iterative hierarchy at which the universal set U first appeared. But U, being universal, contains itself as a member. Hence, we have the absurdity that U occurs before α also.

[31] Maddy (1983) develops a theory of classes modeled on Kripke's theory of truth. See Parsons 1974a for a valuable discussion of the set-class distinction.

[32] The sentence, $[x: x \in x] \in [x: x \in x]$, behaves like the Truth Teller.

[33] (7) does not fix completely the rule of revision for "exemplifies," unless we assume that every property has a name of the form (8).

if it exemplifies itself at one stage, will fail to do so at the next stage, and will exemplify itself at the following stage. As with truth, however, many particular instances of exemplification will stabilize in the revision process (see Turner 1987).

The difficulty in extending this kind of theory to classes and membership is as follows: A key feature of classes, and one that distinguishes them from properties, is their extensionality. Classes are determined by their members; classes that have the same members are identical. If, however, we construct a theory of classes in the manner just described for properties, this key feature may not be respected. In such a theory, the denotation of (8) stays the same in the revision process even though the membership relation fluctuates; hence, there is no assurance that extensionality will be preserved. Further, there is no obvious way of reading (7) that will preserve extensionality. We may, for example, try to read (7) as a partial definition of the abstract term (8) and take the membership relation to be noncircular. On this treatment, the interpretation of '$\in$' stays fixed in the revision process; what changes is the denotation of (8). But there are at least two problems with this approach. First, there is no guarantee that we can find a denotation for the abstraction term, since the objects that satisfy the definiens of (7) may not constitute a class *in* the domain. Second, this reading does not capture the pathologicality of classes in the proper way. For instance, the partial definition for the Russell class,

$$z \in [x: x \notin x] =_{\text{Df}} z \notin z,$$

turns out to be noncircular.

The difficulties we are encountering in constructing a theory of classes are indicative of a problem *not* in our general viewpoint but in the conception we are trying to capture. Classes are governed by two principles: abstraction and extensionality. Abstraction shows the membership relation to be circular and prone to pathologicality. Extensionality requires, however, that this relation be as fixed and definite as the identity of classes. It follows that if classes are entities with a definite identity then there is a conflict between the two principles.

This observation suggests a way out of our problem—a way similar to Russell's "No Class" theory. (a) Treat classes as fictions: Analyze "class" talk in terms of "property" talk and the equivalence relation

.... is coextensive with ——— ($\equiv$)

between properties. (b) Read the abstraction principle (7) as giving partial definitions of the exemplification relation. (c) Use the extensionality principle to give partial definitions of $\equiv$: If x and y are properties, then

$$x \equiv y =_{\mathrm{Df}} \text{for all } z, z \in x \text{ iff } z \in y.$$

On this treatment, "coextensiveness" can exhibit pathological behavior since it is defined in terms of a circular concept ($\in$). Thus, from the present viewpoint, extensionality, far from conferring clear objecthood on classes, is responsible for a pathology in their very identity.

Necessity, belief, and knowledge

It is well known that one does not need anything as strong as the Tarski biconditionals to generate a Liar-like phenomenon; much weaker systems of assumptions suffice. An example of such a system follows.

Add to the usual axioms and rules of logic two additional principles,

(AS) $a = \text{`} \sim N(a)\text{'}$

and

(AN)   If $N(\text{`}P\text{'})$ then P,

and one rule of inference,

(RN)   To infer $N(\text{`}P\text{'})$ from P.[34]

Note that AN and RN are logically weaker than the Tarski biconditionals: AN is true and RN is truth-preserving, if N is read as "necessary truth,"[35] but the converse of AN, whose analogue is implied by the Tarski biconditionals, is not true under this reading. A Liar-like argument can be reconstructed in this system as follows:

1. If $N(\text{`} \sim N(a)\text{'})$ then $\sim N(a)$ [AN]
2. If $N(a)$ then $\sim N(a)$ [AS and 1, Logic of $=$]

---

[34] This simple system will suffice for the points we wish to make here. However, systems that are in some respects significantly weaker can also be shown to be subject to paradox (Montague 1963; Thomason 1980; McGee 1985; Koons 1987). Montague, for instance, proves the inconsistency of a system in which RN holds only for those P that are valid formulas of first-order logic (and in which 'if … then …' is read materially). See section 6E.
[35] We are assuming that a and the quotational names are rigid designators. Note that RN may fail to be truth-preserving if additional axioms are added to the system. Even in the present system, RN holds only in categorical reasoning, not in hypothetical. Thus, the Deduction theorem fails in the system.

3. $\sim N(a)$ [2, Propositional Logic]

4. $N(`\sim N(a)`)$ [3, RN]

5. $N(a)$ [AS and 4, Logic of $=$].

The argument shows that all concepts for which the principles AS and AN and the rule RN hold are subject to pathological behavior. Two prime candidates are necessity and knowledge.

Of these two concepts, necessity is more readily seen to be circular. First, the *Modal Liar*, 'this very sentence is not necessarily true', is intuitively paradoxical. Second, even though we do not have exact definitions of necessity, all existing explanations of the concept point to a circularity in it. Consider the explanation given of it in the possible-worlds semantics:

(9) P is a necessary truth (at a world) iff P is true in all possible worlds.[36]

But P may itself assert of some sentences that they are necessary truths. Thus, the necessary truth of some proposition P is explained here in terms of the necessary truth of some other propositions. In certain cases these other propositions may include P. For example, to determine if the Modal Liar is true at any given world, we need first to determine whether it is true at all the worlds.

Consider another explanation of necessity:

(10) P is a necessary truth iff P is a consequence of a collection X of laws and propositions.

There is a circularity here too, though it is a little hidden. P is said to be a necessary truth if P is a consequence of X. Thus, to determine if 'P is a necessary truth' is a necessary truth we need to see if 'P is a necessary truth' is a consequence of X. This shows that the rule (10) is itself a part of the notion of consequence. But (10) uses the notion of consequence. We have thus a circle here: The notion of consequence involves a rule that itself uses the notion of consequence.

Whether the concept of knowledge is circular is not so clear.[37] Of course, knowledge inherits the circularity of truth.[38] The question is

---

[36] We ignore the accessibility relation for simplicity; see section 6E.

[37] We shall treat knowledge and belief as two-place relations holding between knowers and sentences. This assumption is not essential to our argument, however. See section 6E for our views on logical grammar.

[38] This is reflected in the fact that the sentence 'the knower k knows L', where L is a contin-

whether it has some circularity over and above that of truth—i.e., whether any of its other constituents (e.g., belief) are circular also.[39] On the side of circularity are these considerations. First, knowledge and belief do generate self-referential sentences that appear to be pathological. Consider, for instance, the *Believer* sentence (11).

(11)   This very sentence is not believed by k.[40]

There is something very peculiar about this sentence. Suppose k begins reflecting on it without any preconceived ideas about it. At the start of reflection, then, k does not believe (11), and hence (11) is true. Reflection reveals this to k. So at the first stage of reflection, k comes to believe (11). But now (11) is false. So further reflection leads k to disbelieve (11). And this cyclical process can be continued indefinitely.[41] Similar difficulties arise with the *Knower* sentence (12).

(12)   This very sentence is not known by k.

Second, the most prominent philosophical theory of belief, Functionalism, makes it a circular concept. According to Functionalism, beliefs are explained in terms of their functional roles. Very roughly, a state fulfills the functional role of "believing that P" iff it satisfies numerous conditions of the form "causes a disposition to exhibit X kinds of behavior in the presence of such and such desires and beliefs." Since these conditions refer to the beliefs and desires of the agent, the definition of the functional role associated with a belief makes reference to various beliefs and desires.

There are also strong arguments on the side of noncircularity of knowledge and belief. First, the rule RN is not truth preserving if N is interpreted as "is known by k" or as "is believed by k"; hence, the argument of the Liar

gent Liar, is sometimes paradoxical. Suppose k believes L and is justified in believing L. (L may be the sentence 'everything John says is true', and k may have good reasons for trusting John.) Then 'k knows L' is equivalent to L and, hence, paradoxical.

[39] We shall not consider here whether the remaining component of knowledge, justification, is circular.

[40] A more natural, but also more complex, example occurs in Buridan's thirteenth sophism, "Socrates knows the proposition written on the wall to be doubtful to him," where it is posited "that this proposition and no other is written on a wall, that Socrates looks at it, considers it, is in a state of doubt about whether it is true or false, and knows perfectly well that he is in such a state of doubt" (Hughes 1982, p. 93). Further examples can be found in the Surprise Examination Paradox and the closely related Hangman Paradox. See Kaplan and Montague 1960, Anderson 1983, Burge 1984, Grim 1988, and Sainsbury 1988 for discussions of these and related paradoxes.

[41] Asher and Kamp (1986, 1989) use the Revision theory to represent the cyclicity here.

cannot be reconstructed for knowledge and belief. This is further confirmed by the fact that the Knower and Believer sentences can, unlike the Liar, be imagined to be true. We need only imagine a situation in which k has never thought about (11) and (12) and, consequently, has no views concerning them. In such a situation, k believes neither (11) nor (12) and, therefore, (11) and (12) are true. Second, the functionalist account does not bring out the logical difference between "believing 'snow is white'" and "believing (11)"; the functional roles of both seem to be equally enmeshed in vicious circularity. Furthermore, Functionalists themselves view the circularity in their theory as an embarrassment and attempt to remove it. Their attempts to do so do not seem to us to result in a differential treatment of the two belief states. Finally, Functionalists typically are physicalists. They hold that states that exemplify the functional roles of beliefs, desires, etc. are physical.[42] This makes it seem that there is a physical fact of the matter whether k believes (11) or not, and thus that (11) is nonpathological.

It is tempting to resolve the dilemma as follows:

Beliefs (and, hence, also knowledge) have two aspects. They are, on the one hand, *states* of a thinking organism. On the other, they are a product of reasoning and reflection. Beliefs-as-states are not circular; there is a fact of the matter whether an organism has certain beliefs—self-referential or not. The notion of *rational* belief, however, is circular. Whether a certain belief is rational can depend upon the rationality of other beliefs, which may include the original belief. Further, the Believer sentence (11) is perplexing only when we consider k's reflections on it; by itself there is nothing paradoxical in it.

Such a resolution is tempting, but it is unlikely to be the last word. The notions of belief state and rationality are too intimately linked for all circularity to be pinned on the one notion.

III

The framework of circular definitions may be applicable to problems that appear at first sight to have little in common with those due to self-reference. It may be that some of the conceptual problems and perplexities that afflict philosophy have their roots in the circularity or the mutual

---

[42] They do not generally subscribe to a type-by-type identity between the mental and the physical; only to a token-by-token identity.

dependency of some of our concepts. These problems and perplexities, like the Liar, may not be solvable in the usual sense. They may be merely symptoms of the logical peculiarities of the underlying concepts. This possibility becomes a little more credible if one bears in mind the fact that sentences need not be self-referential to exhibit pathological and even paradoxical behavior.[43] Artificial examples of such sentences are easy to construct. Consider the definition

(13) x is G $=_{Df} x$ is not G.

This definition is admittedly strange and doubtless defines a notion that is completely useless. Still, the general theory of definitions recognizes it to be legitimate. According to this definition, sentence (14) is paradoxical.

(14) Socrates is G.

But (14) is not self-referential. It is not about itself, even indirectly; it is about Socrates.[44]

Less artificial definitions that yield non-self-referential but pathological sentences can be given. Constructing one such definition will illustrate the possibility envisioned above. Consider the Continuity analysis of the persistence of physical objects, in which the persistence of physical objects is explained in terms of relations obtaining between temporal *stages* or *slices* of objects. (The notion of stage or slice is generally assumed to be unproblematic and given. Let us go along with this assumption.) Two temporal stages are said, on this analysis, to belong to the *same body* if and only

[43] We mean 'self-reference' in a general sense: A sentence A is self-referential if it is about itself or is about a sentence B that is about A or .... We shall not try to make the notion of "aboutness" precise.
[44] The fact that certain self-referential sentences involving truth are paradoxical is to be explained in terms of the particular features of the definition of truth. The Tarski biconditionals attribute viciously circular truth conditions to these sentences.

Note that definitions can be constructed by which a concept is nonpathological only over the self-referential sentences! A simple example: Let a denote 'a is G', and let the definition of G be

x is G $=_{Df}$ either $x = $ 'a is G' or ($x \neq$ 'a is G' and x is not G).

By this definition G is unproblematic over only one object, namely the self-referential sentence 'a is G'. The root cause of the Liar paradox, therefore, is not self-reference but the circularity of concepts. This explains why 'this very sentence has six words' is completely unproblematic whereas 'this very sentence is true', which has the same form, is pathological. The difference lies in the logic of the concepts "has six words" and "true"—one is circular and the other is not.

if the stages can be so connected by intermediate stages that the whole displays "continuity of displacement, continuity of deformation, continuity of chemical change" (Quine 1976, p. 125). Continuity of displacement can be explained (roughly) as requiring that stages that are near each other in time are near each other in space.[45] Nearness in space of stages x and y means, in turn, that the place of x is near the place of y. As x and y may belong to different temporal moments, the notion "nearness of place" presupposes identification or persistence of places through time. In short, the Continuity analysis appeals to the notion of persistence of places in its explanation of the persistence of physical objects.

How is the persistence of places to be analyzed? One prominent idea explains it in terms of the persistence of physical objects. The resulting circularity is noted, and even embraced, by some. P. F. Strawson (1959, p. 37) wrote:

... places are defined only by the relations of things; and ... one of the requirements for the identity of a material thing is that its existence, as well as being continuous in time, should be continuous in space.... So the identification and distinction of places turn on the identification and distinction of things; and the identification and distinction of things turn, in part, on the identification and distinction of places. There is no mystery about this mutual dependence.[46]

Let us examine the resulting mutual dependence. First we need to be clear on how the persistence of places is to be defined. Since our primary goal is not to provide an analysis of the concepts "physical object" and "places" but only to construct an illustration, let us make our task easier and accept some simplifying assumptions. Let us assume that we are given the notion of "place-time" (i.e., "place-at-a-time"). Our goal is to define how these place-times can be "stacked" together to form places *simpliciter*; in other words, given place-times p_1 and p_2, we need to state conditions under which they bear the relation "is the same place as." In stating these conditions, let us assume that we have available relations such as "distance" between place-times that are simultaneous, and, more significantly, that we have some "reference bodies" (such as the Earth or the fixed stars) that can be assumed to be eternal and motionless. Then we can say that p_1 is the *same place* as p_2 if and only if the distance between p_1 and (the place

[45] A more rigorous definition is possible. Fortunately, our purposes do not require it.
[46] We, like Strawson, find no mystery in the claimed mutual dependence; but we, unlike Strawson, have the framework of circular definitions to remove any lingering mystery.

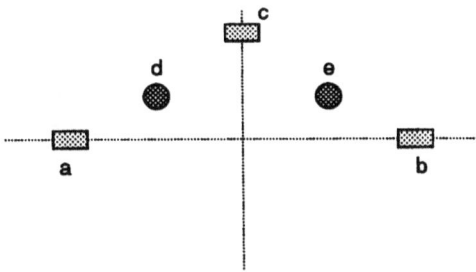

Figure 7.1

occupied by) an arbitrary reference body is the same as the distance between p_2 and the *same* reference body. This definition uses the notion of
persistence of physical objects to explain the persistence of places.

Even though the resulting definitions are circular, the two notions need
not exhibit any pathologicality. Suppose, for example, that the reference
bodies are chemically very different from each other and are spatially
separated in a suitable way. Then there would be at most one way of
stacking their stages together to form physical objects. (Any nonstandard
stacking would violate the requirement of continuity of chemical change.)
Once we have fixed the identities of the reference bodies, we shall have a
unique stacking of place-times into places. Thus, the notion "same place"
would be nonpathological, and, consequently, so would the notion "same
body."[47]

There are conditions, however, under which the definitions do exhibit
pathologicality. Suppose that reference bodies happen to be qualitatively
similar to each other in all respects, and that at a certain time t they are
symmetrically located—say, as in figure 7.1.[48] Here a, b, and c are the
stages of the reference bodies, and d and e are the stages of two qualitatively identical physical objects that are symmetrically located with respect to the reference bodies.

Suppose that the situation portrayed in figure 7.1 continues unchanged
for some time but that at t' it changes to the situation shown in figure 7.2.

[47] We are taking the simplifying assumptions of the example as restricting the initial hypotheses of revision to those that validate these assumptions. Without this there is no reason
to believe that the notions "same place" and "same body" will be ruled by the revision
process to be completely nonpathological.
[48] For simplicity we ignore the third dimension.

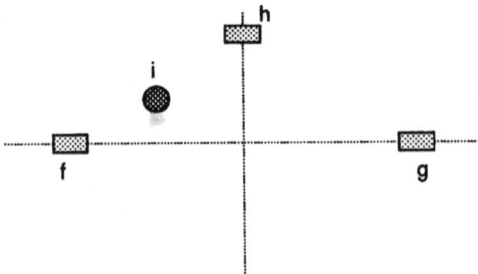

Figure 7.2

Here f, g, and h are the stages of the reference bodies and i is a stage of a physical object. We assume that f, g, and h are qualitatively exactly like a, b, and c, and that i is exactly like d and e. In this example, one admissible hypothesis concerning the identification of the reference bodies is that a, b, and c are the same as, respectively, f, g, and h. This hypothesis in conjunction with the definition of "same place" yields the natural identification of places. Definition of "same body" now confirms our initial identification of the reference bodies and implies that d and i are the stages of the same body.

There is another, equally admissible hypothesis concerning the identification of the reference bodies. According to it, a, b, and c are the same bodies as, respectively, g, f, and h. This latter hypothesis yields, in virtue of the definition of "same place," that the place-times occupied by a, b, c, and e are the same places as, respectively, the place-times occupied by g, f, h, and i. This confirms, in virtue of the definition of "same body", our original hypothesis, and it leads us to say that e and i are stages of the same body. Let X be the physical object whose "time-slice" at t is d. Then the above considerations show that the statement "X exists at t'" behaves like the Truth Teller (see note 47).

Our aim in the above is *not* to establish the logical character of "identity" or "persistence," but only to illustrate our earlier claim that pathological behavior does not require self-reference. The example shows, we hope, that circularity and mutual dependency *may* exist even among ordinary nonsemantic (and nonepistemic) concepts, and that some of the perplexing behavior of these concepts may have its roots in this circularity and mutual dependency. It is not easy to *prove* that this possibility is realized among our concepts, for outside of logic and semantics definitional links between concepts are hard to establish. Nonetheless, we find encouragement in the fact that for many concepts there are persistent puzzles, and in the fact that philosophers in their analyses often go around in circles.[49]

IV

We have been taught to judge philosophical analyses in terms of two criteria. These are, in Tarski's terminology, the criterion of *formal correctness* and that of *material adequacy*. The first requires us to judge an analysis from a formal, logical point of view; it is the one cited in the rejection of circularity. The second requires us to judge the faithfulness of the analysis to the ordinary notion being analyzed. As we have seen above, sometimes the two criteria come into conflict. The analysis that is materially adequate sometimes violates the demand of formal correctness. This conflict, we have argued, should be resolved in favor of the second requirement (material adequacy).[50] We would like to go further in this direction and propose that in philosophical theorizing we should abandon the primacy of formal correctness: A definition should be evaluated only by how well it captures the material aspects of a notion.

Under this liberalization, trivial definitions such as

(15) x is a person $=_{Df} x$ is a person

are admitted as logically proper, but they are usually materially inadequate. Thus, (15) fails to be a materially adequate definition of "person"; it implies that "x is a person" is like the Truth Teller for all objects x, whereas an adequate definition should yield (for example) that Socrates is a person and that Chicago is not. The burden that has traditionally been

---

[49] Friends and colleagues have suggested to us several possible applications of the framework of circular definitions. Charles Chastain and Walter Edelberg have pointed out that it may be applicable to the analysis of meaning and may provide an answer to the circularity objection of Quine (1951). Mark Wilson has suggested that certain episodes in the history of mathematics (e.g., the definition of the imaginary number i) may provide useful illustrations and applications.

[50] Jerrold Levinson (1987, p. 145) has written that "a circular definition, however segmented, no more clarifies anything than it informs or instructs—one simply cannot *elucidate* the content of a concept by *using* and *presupposing* it in the course of the elucidation." We are in complete disagreement with this claim. Sometimes a circular definition provides the most informative and instructive elucidation of a concept.

André Chapuis has recently drawn our attention to a paper in which C. Mason Myers (1978) defends certain kinds of circularity.

borne by certain requirements of formal correctness is better carried, on our view, by the requirement of material adequacy.

The philosophical moral most often drawn from the paradoxes is that the domain of the meaningful is *less* extensive than it appears to be, that certain seemingly meaningful concepts are in fact meaningless. Russell's Vicious Circle Principle is the classic attempt to demarcate the meaningful from the meaningless. In contrast, the moral we draw from the paradoxes is that the domain of the meaningful is *more* extensive than it appears to be, that certain seemingly meaningless concepts are in fact meaningful. The universe of concepts is rich indeed.

Bibliography

Ackrill, J. L. 1963. *Aristotle's "Categories" and "De interpretatione": Translated with Notes.* Oxford University Press.

Aczel, Peter. 1977. "An introduction to inductive definitions." In Barwise 1977.

Aczel, Peter. 1980. "Frege structures and the notions of proposition, truth and set." In Barwise et al. 1980.

Aczel, Peter. 1988. *Non-Well-Founded Sets.* Lecture notes 14, Center for the Study of Language and Information, Stanford University.

Aczel, Peter, and Solomon Feferman. 1980. "Consistency of the unrestricted abstraction principle using an intensional equivalence operator." In Seldin and Hindley 1980.

Anderson, Alan Ross, and Nuel D. Belnap, Jr. 1975. *Entailment: The Logic of Relevance and Necessity*, volume 1. Princeton University Press.

Anderson, Alan Ross, Ruth Barcan Marcus, and Richard M. Martin, eds. 1975. *The Logical Enterprise.* Yale University Press.

Anderson, C. Anthony. 1983. "The paradox of the knower." *Journal of Philosophy* 80: 338–355.

Asher, Nicholas, and Hans Kamp. 1986. "The knower's paradox and representational theories of attitudes." In Halpern 1986.

Asher, Nicholas, and Hans Kamp. 1989. "Self-reference, attitudes, and paradox." In Chierchia et al. 1989.

Bar-Hillel, Yehoshua. 1966. "Do natural languages contain paradoxes?" *Studium Generale* 19: 391–397. (Reprinted in Bar-Hillel 1970; page references are given for that volume.)

Bar-Hillel, Yehoshua. 1970. *Aspects of Language.* Magnes.

Bartlett, Steven J., and Peter Suber, eds. 1987. *Self-Reference: Reflections on Reflexivity.* Martinus Nijhoff.

Barwise, Jon. 1975. *Admissible Sets and Structures: An Approach to Definability Theory.* Springer-Verlag.

Barwise, Jon, ed. 1977. *Handbook of Mathematical Logic.* North-Holland.

Barwise, Jon, and John Etchemendy. 1987. *The Liar: An Essay on Truth and Circularity.* Oxford University Press.

Barwise, Jon, H. Jerome Keisler, and Kenneth Kunen, eds. 1980. *The Kleene Symposium.* North-Holland.

Belnap, Nuel D. 1975. "Grammatical propaedeutic." In Anderson et al. 1975. (Reprinted in Anderson and Belnap 1975.)

Belnap, Nuel D. 1976. "How a computer should think." In Ryle 1976.

Belnap, Nuel D. 1977. "A useful four-valued logic." In Dunn and Epstein 1977.

Belnap, Nuel D. 1982. "Gupta's rule of revision theory of truth." *Journal of Philosophical Logic* 11: 103–116.

Belnap, Nuel D., and Dorothy L. Grover. 1973. "Quantifying in and out of quotes." In Leblanc 1973.

Bergmann, Merrie, James Moor, and Jack Nelson. 1980. *The Logic Book.* Random House.

Bocheński, I. M. 1961. *A History of Formal Logic.* Chelsea.

Bochvar, D. A. 1937/1981. "On a three-valued logical calculus and its application to the analysis of the paradoxes of the classical extended functional calculus." *History and Philosophy of Logic* 2 (1981): 87–112. (Originally published in Russian in *Mathematicheskii Sbornik* 46 [1937].)

Böhm, C., ed. 1975. *λ-Calculus and Computer Science Theory.* Springer-Verlag.

Boolos, George. 1979. *The Unprovability of Consistency: An Essay in Modal Logic*. Cambridge University Press.

Boolos, George, and Richard C. Jeffrey. 1980. *Computability and Logic*, second edition. Cambridge University Press.

Brady, Ross T. 1971. "The consistency of the axioms of abstraction and extensionality in three-valued logic." *Notre Dame Journal of Formal Logic* 12: 447–453.

Burge, Tyler. 1979. "Semantical paradox." *Journal of Philosophy* 76: 169–198. (Reprinted, with a postscript, in Martin 1984.)

Burge, Tyler. 1984. "Epistemic paradox." *Journal of Philosophy* 81: 5–29.

Burgess, John P. 1986. "The truth is never simple." *Journal of Symbolic Logic* 51: 663–681.

Cargile, James. 1986. Critical notice of Martin 1984. *Mind* 95: 116–126.

Chang, C. C., and H. Jerome Keisler. 1977. *Model Theory*, second edition. North-Holland.

Chierchia, Gennaro, Barbara H. Partee, and Raymond Turner, eds. 1989. *Properties, Types and Meaning*, volume 1. Kluwer.

Chihara, Charles S. 1979. "The semantic paradoxes: A diagnostic investigation." *Philosophical Review* 88: 590–618.

Chihara, Charles S. 1984. "The semantic paradoxes: Some second thoughts." *Philosophical Studies* 45: 223–229.

Davidson, Donald. 1973. "In defence of Convention T." In Leblanc 1973. (Also reprinted in Davidson 1984; page references are given for that reprinting.)

Davidson, Donald. 1984. *Inquiries into Truth and Interpretation*. Oxford University Press.

Davidson, Donald, and Gilbert Harman, eds. 1972. *Semantics of Natural Language*. Reidel.

Devitt, Michael. 1984. *Realism and Truth*. Princeton University Press.

Dickie, George. 1984. *The Art Circle*. Haven.

Dowden, Bradley H. 1984. "Accepting inconsistencies from the paradoxes." *Journal of Philosophical Logic* 13: 125–130.

Dunn, J. Michael. 1976. "Intuitive semantics for first-degree entailments and 'coupled trees'." *Philosophical Studies* 29: 149–168.

Dunn, J. Michael, and George Epstein, eds. 1977. *Modern Uses of Multiple-Valued Logic*. Reidel.

Dunn, J. Michael, and Anil Gupta, eds. 1990. *Truth or Consequences: Essays in Honor of Nuel Belnap*. Kluwer.

Emig, J. A., J. T. Fleming, and H. M. Popps, eds. 1966. *Language and Learning*. Harcourt, Brace and World.

Epstein, Richard L., and Walter A. Carnielli. 1989. *Computability: Computable functions, Logic, and the Foundations of Mathematics*. Wadsworth and Brooks/Cole.

Etchemendy, John. 1988. "Tarski on truth and logical consequence." *Journal of Symbolic Logic* 53: 51–79.

Feferman, Solomon. 1984. "Toward useful type-free theories I." *Journal of Symbolic Logic* 49: 75–111. (Reprinted in Martin 1984.)

Field, Hartry. 1972. "Tarski's theory of truth." *Journal of Philosophy* 69: 347–375. (Reprinted in Platts 1980.)

Fine, Kit. 1975. "Vagueness, truth and logic." *Synthese* 30: 265–300.

Fitch, Fredric B. 1946. "Self-reference in philosophy." *Mind* 55: 64–73. (A revised version appears in Fitch 1952.)

Fitch, Fredric B. 1948. "An extension of basic logic." *Journal of Symbolic Logic* 13: 95–106.

Fitch, Fredric B. 1952. *Symbolic Logic: An Introduction*. Ronald.

Fitch, Fredric B. 1964. "Universal metalanguages for philosophy." *Review of Metaphysics* 17: 396–402.

Fitting, Melvin. 1986. "Notes on the mathematical aspects of Kripke's theory of truth." *Notre Dame Journal of Formal Logic* 27: 75–88.

Frege, Gottlob. 1918/1956. "Der Gedanke: Eine logische Untersuchung." *Beiträge zur Philosphie des Deutschen Idealismus* 1: 58–77. (An English translation appeared in *Mind* 65 (1956): 289–311, and is reprinted in Strawson 1967; page references are given for the reprint.)

Friedman, Harvey, and Michael Sheard. 1987. "An axiomatic approach to self-referential truth." *Annals of Pure and Applied Logic* 33: 1–21.

Gabbay, Dov, and Franz Guenthner, eds. 1983–1989. *Handbook of Philosophical Logic*, four volumes. Reidel.

Gaifman, Haim. 1988. "Operational pointer semantics: Solution to self-referential puzzles I." In Vardi 1988.

Gilmore, Paul C. 1974. "The consistency of partial set theory without extensionality." In Jech 1974.

Grim, Patrick. 1988. "Truth, omniscience, and the Knower." *Philosophical Studies* 54: 9–41.

Grover, Dorothy L. 1977. "Inheritors and paradox." *Journal of Philosophy* 74: 590–604.

Grover, Dorothy L., Joseph L. Camp, and Nuel D. Belnap. 1975. "A prosentential theory of truth." *Philosophical Studies* 27: 73–125.

Guenthner, Franz, and S. J. Schmidt, eds. 1978. *Formal Semantics and Pragmatics of Natural Languages*. Reidel.

Gupta, Anil. 1978. "Modal logic and truth." *Journal of Philosophical Logic* 7: 441–472. (A revised version of this paper, with a new section 4, appears as chapter 5 of Gupta 1980.)

Gupta, Anil. 1980. *The Logic of Common Nouns: An Investigation in Quantified Modal Logic*. Yale University Press.

Gupta, Anil. 1981. "Truth and paradox" (abstract). *Journal of Philosophy* 78: 735–736.

Gupta, Anil. 1982. "Truth and paradox." *Journal of Philosophical Logic* 11: 1–60. (A revised version, with a brief postscript, is reprinted in Martin 1984.)

Gupta, Anil. 1987. "The meaning of truth." In LePore 1987.

Gupta, Anil. 1988–89. "Remarks on definitions and the concept of truth." *Proceedings of the Aristotelian Society* 89: 227–246.

Gupta, Anil. 1990. "Two theorems concerning stability." In Dunn and Gupta 1990.

Gupta, Anil, and Nuel D. Belnap. 1987. "A note on extension, intension, and truth." *Journal of Philosophy* 84: 168–174.

Gupta, Anil, and Robert L. Martin. 1984. "A fixed point theorem for the weak Kleene valuation scheme." *Journal of Philosophical Logic* 13: 131–135. (A correction appears on p. 229 of volume 14 [1985].)

Halpern, Joseph Y. 1986. *Theoretical Aspects of Reasoning about Knowledge: Proceedings of the 1986 Conference*. Morgan Kaufmann.

Hart, W. 1989–90. "For Anil Gupta." *Proceedings of the Aristotelian Society* 90: 161–165.

Hawthorn, John. 1983. The Liar and Theories of Truth. Doctoral dissertation, McGill University.

Hazen, Allen. 1983. "Predicative Logics." In volume 1 of Gabbay and Guenthner 1983–1989.

Hazen, Allen. 1987. "Contra Buridanum." *Canadian Journal of Philosophy* 17: 875–880.

Hellman, Geoffrey. 1985. Review of Martin and Woodruff 1975, Kripke 1975, Gupta 1982, and Herzberger 1982. *Journal of Symbolic Logic* 50: 1068–1071.

Herzberger, Hans G. 1966. "The logical consistency of language." In Emig et al. 1966.

Herzberger, Hans G. 1967. "The truth-conditional consistency of natural languages." *Journal of Philosophy* 64: 29–35.

Herzberger, Hans G. 1970a. "Paradoxes of grounding in semantics." *Journal of Philosophy* 67: 145–167.

Herzberger, Hans G. 1970b. "Truth and modality in semantically closed languages." In Martin 1970a.

Herzberger, Hans G. 1982a. "Notes on naive semantics." *Journal of Philosophical Logic* 11: 61–102. (Reprinted in Martin 1984.)

Herzberger, Hans G. 1982b. "Naive semantics and the Liar paradox." *Journal of Philosophy* 79: 479–497.

Herzberger, Hans G. 198+. Notes on periodicity. Typescript, University of Toronto.

Hintikka, Jaakko. 1975. *The Intentions of Intentionality and Other New Models for Modalities.* Reidel.

Horwich, Paul. 1990. *Truth.* Blackwell.

Hughes, G. E. 1982. *John Buridan on Self-Reference: Chapter Eight of Buridan's "Sophismata."* Cambridge University Press.

Hughes, G. E., and M. J. Cresswell. 1968. *An Introduction to Modal Logic.* Methuen.

Jech, T., ed. 1974. *Axiomatic Set Theory.* Proceedings of Symposia in Pure Mathematics 13, part II. American Mathematical Society.

Kant, Immanuel. 1781/1787. *Critique of Pure Reason*, tr. Norman Kemp Smith. Macmillan, 1964. (Kemp Smith's translation first appeared in 1929.)

Kaplan, David, and Richard Montague. 1960. "A paradox regained." *Notre Dame Journal of Formal Logic* 1: 79–90. (Reprinted in Thomason 1974.)

Kapus, Jerry. 1992. Truth and Explanation. Doctoral dissertation, University of Illinois, Chicago.

Kindt, Walther. 1978. "The introduction of truth predicates into first-order languages." In Guenthner and Schmidt 1978.

Kleene, Stephen Cole. 1938. "On notations for ordinal numbers." *Journal of Symbolic Logic* 3: 150–155.

Kleene, Stephen Cole. 1952. *Introduction to Metamathematics.* Van Nostrand.

Kneale, William. 1971. "Russell's paradox and some others." *British Journal for the Philosophy of Science* 22: 321–338.

Kneale, William. 1972. "Propositions and truth in natural languages." *Mind* 81: 225–243.

Koons, Robert C. 1987. Analogues of the Liar Paradox in Systems of Epistemic Logic. Doctoral dissertation, University of California, Los Angeles.

Kremer, Michael. 1986. Logic and Truth. Doctoral dissertation, University of Pittsburgh.

Kremer, Michael. 1988. "Kripke and the logic of truth." *Journal of Philosophical Logic* 17: 225–78.

Kripke, Saul A. 1975. "Outline of a theory of truth." *Journal of Philosophy* 72: 690–716. (Reprinted in Martin 1984; page references are given for that reprinting.)

Kripke, Saul A. 1976. "A theory of truth I & II" (abstracts). *Journal of Symbolic Logic* 41: 556–557.

Lawvere, F. W., ed. 1972. *Toposes, Algebraic Geometry and Logic.* Lecture Notes in Mathematics 274. Springer-Verlag.

Leblanc, Hugues, ed. 1973. *Truth, Syntax and Modality.* North-Holland.

Leblanc, Hugues, and Wiliam A. Wisdom. 1976. *Deductive Logic,* second edition. Allyn and Bacon.

LePore, Ernest, ed. 1987. *New Directions in Semantics.* Academic Press.

Levinson, Jerrold. 1987. Review of Dickie 1984. *Philosophical Review* 96: 141–146.

Linsky, Leonard, ed. 1952. *Semantics and the Philosophy of Language: A Collection of Readings.* University of Illinois Press.

Maddy, Penelope. 1983. "Proper classes." *Journal of Symbolic Logic* 48: 113–139.

Manna, Z., and A. Shamir. 1976. "The theoretical aspects of the optimal fixedpoint." *SIAM Journal of Computing* 5: 414–426.

Martin, Robert L. 1967. "Toward a solution to the Liar paradox." *Philosophical Review* 76: 279–311.

Martin, Robert L. 1968. "On Grelling's paradox." *Philosophical Review* 77: 321–331.

Martin, Robert L., ed. 1970a. *The Paradox of the Liar.* Yale University Press. (The second edition was published in 1978 by Ridgeview.)

Martin, Robert L. 1970b. "A category solution to the Liar." In Martin 1970a.

Martin, Robert L., ed. 1984. *Recent Essays on Truth and the Liar Paradox.* Oxford University Press.

Martin, Robert L., and Peter W. Woodruff. 1975. "On representing 'true-in-L' in L." *Philosophia* 5: 217–221. (Reprinted in Martin 1984; page references are given for that reprinting.)

Mates, Benson. 1981. *Skeptical Essays.* University of Chicago Press.

McCarthy, Timothy. 1985. "Abstraction and definability in semantically closed structures." *Journal of Philosophical Logic* 14: 255–266.

McGee, Vann. 1985. "How truthlike can a predicate be? A negative result." *Journal of Philosophical Logic* 14: 399–410.

McGee, Vann. 1991. *Truth, Vagueness, and Paradox: An Essay on the Logic of Truth.* Hackett.

Mendelson, Elliott. 1964. *Introduction to Mathematical Logic.* Van Nostrand.

Montague, Richard. 1963. "Syntactical treatments of modality, with corollaries on reflexion principles and finite axiomatizability." *Acta Philosophica Fennica* 16: 153–167. (Reprinted in Thomason 1974; page numbers are given for the reprint.)

Moschovakis, Yiannis N. 1974. *Elementary Induction on Abstract Structures.* North-Holland.

Myers, C. Mason. 1978. "Circular explication." *Metaphilosophy* 9: 1–13.

Myhill, John R. 1950. "A complete theory of natural, rational, and real numbers." *Journal of Symbolic Logic* 15: 185–196.

Nepeivoda, N. N. 1973. "A new concept of predicative truth and definability." *Mathematical Notes* 13: 439–445. (Originally published in Russian in *Matematicheskie Zametki* 13 [1973].)

Parsons, Charles. 1974a. "Sets and classes." *Noûs* 8: 1–12. (Reprinted in Parsons 1983a.)

Parsons, Charles. 1974b. "The Liar paradox." *Journal of Philosophical Logic* 3: 381–412. (Reprinted in Parsons 1983a and Martin 1984. The Martin volume includes a condensed version of the Postscript [Parsons 1983b].)

Parsons, Charles. 1983a. *Mathematics in Philosophy: Selected Essays.* Cornell University Press.

Parsons, Charles. 1983b. "Postscript." In Parsons 1983a (pp. 251–267).

Perlis, Donald. 1985. "Languages with self-reference I: Foundations." *Artificial Intelligence* 25: 301–322.

Perlis, Donald. 1988. "Languages with self-reference II: Knowledge, belief, and modality." *Artificial Intelligence* 34: 179–212.

Platts, Mark. 1980. *Reference, Truth, and Reality: Essays on the Philosophy of Language.* Routledge & Kegan Paul.

Priest, Graham. 1979. "The logic of paradox." *Journal of Philosophical Logic* 8: 219–241.

Priest, Graham. 1984. "Logic of paradox revisited." *Journal of Philosophical Logic* 13: 153–179.

Priest, Graham. 1985–86. "Contradiction, belief, and rationality." *Proceedings of the Aristotelian Society* 86: 99–116.

Priest, Graham. 1987. "Unstable solutions to the Liar paradox." In Bartlett and Suber 1987.

Prior, Arthur N. 1961. "On a family of paradoxes." *Notre Dame Journal of Formal Logic* 2: 16–32.

Quine, Willard Van Orman. 1951. "Two dogmas of empiricism." *Philosophical Review* 60: 20–43. (Reprinted in Quine 1953a.)

Quine, Willard Van Orman. 1953a. *From a Logical Point of View.* Harvard University Press.

Quine, Willard Van Orman. 1953b. "Notes on the theory of reference." In Quine 1953a.

Quine, Willard Van Orman. 1970. *Philosophy of Logic.* Prentice-Hall.

Quine, Willard Van Orman. 1976. "Worlds away." *Journal of Philosophy* 73: 359–364. (Reprinted in Quine 1981; page references are given for the reprint.)

Quine, Willard Van Orman. 1981. *Theories and Things.* Harvard University Press.

Ramsey, Frank P. 1927. "Facts and propositions." *Proceedings of the Aristotelian Society,* supplementary volume 7: 153–170. (Reprinted in Ramsey 1978; page references are given for the reprint.)

Ramsey, Frank P. 1978. *Foundations: Essays in Philosophy, Logic, Mathematics and Economics,* ed. D. H. Mellor. Humanities Press.

Russell, Bertrand. 1908. "Mathematical logic as based on the theory of types." *American Journal of Mathematics* 30: 222–262. (Reprinted in Russell 1956.)

Russell, Bertrand. 1956. *Logic and Knowledge,* ed. Robert C. Marsh. Macmillan.

Ryle, Gilbert. 1976. *Contemporary Aspects of Philosophy.* Oriel.

Sainsbury, R. M. 1988. *Paradoxes.* Cambridge University Press.

Savion, Leah. 1989. Semantics for Belief Attribution. Doctoral dissertation, City University of New York.

Scott, Dana. 1972. "Continuous lattices." In Lawvere 1972.

Scott, Dana. 1973. "Models for various type-free calculi." In Suppes 1973.

Scott, Dana. 1975. "Combinators and classes." In Böhm 1975.

Scott, Dana. 1980. "Lambda calculus: some models, some philosophy." In Barwise et al. 1980.

Seldin, J. P., and J. R. Hindley, eds. 1980. *To H. B. Curry: Essays on Combinatory Logic, Lambda Calculus and Formalism.* Academic Press.

Simmons, Keith. 1990. "The diagonal argument and the Liar." *Journal of Philosophical Logic* 19: 277–303.

Skolem, Thoralf A. 1960. "A set theory based on a certain three-valued logic." *Mathematica Scandinavica* 8: 127–136.

Skolem, Thoralf A. 1963. "Studies on the axiom of comprehension." *Notre Dame Journal of Formal Logic* 4: 162–170.

Skyrms, Brian. 1970a. "Return of the Liar: Three-valued logic and the concept of truth." *American Philosophical Quarterly* 7: 153–161.

Skyrms, Brian. 1970b. "Notes on quantification and reference." In Martin 1970a.

Skyrms, Brian. 1978. "An immaculate conception of modality." *Journal of Philosophy* 75: 368–387.

Skyrms, Brian. 1984. "Intensional aspects of semantical self-reference." In Martin 1984.

Smullyan, Raymond M. 1984. "Chameleonic languages." *Synthese* 60: 201–224.

Soames, Scott. 1984. "What is a theory of truth?" *Journal of Philosophy* 81: 411–429.

Sobel, Jordan Howard. 1992. "Lies, lies, and more lies: A plea for propositions." *Philosophical Studies* 67: 51–69.

Spade, Paul Vincent. 1973. "The origins of the mediaeval *insolubilia* literature." *Franciscan Studies* 33: 292–309.

Spade, Paul Vincent. 1975. "On a conservative attitude toward some naive semantic principles." *Notre Dame Journal of Formal Logic* 16: 597–602.

Spade, Paul Vincent. 1979. *William Heytesbury's "On 'insoluble' sentences," Chapter One of his "Rules for Solving Sophisms."* Pontifical Institute of Mediaeval Studies.

Spade, Paul Vincent. 1987. "Five early theories in the mediaeval *insolubilia*-literature." *Vivarium* 25: 24–46.

Strawson, P. F. 1959. *Individuals: An Essay in Descriptive Metaphysics*. Methuen.

Strawson, P. F., ed. 1967. *Philosophical Logic*. Oxford University Press.

Suppes, Patrick, ed. 1973. *Proceedings of the Fourth International Conference for Logic, Methodology and the Philosophy of Science*. North-Holland.

Szaniawski, Klemens, ed. 1989. *The Vienna Circle and the Lvov-Warsaw School*. Kluwer.

Tarski, Alfred. 1935/1956. "Der Wahrheitsbegriff in den formalisierten Sprachen." *Studia Philosophica* 1: 261–405. (An English translation by J. H. Woodger appears in Tarski 1956 under the title "The concept of truth in formalized languages"; page references are given for that translation. For full bibliographical information see the note on p. 152 of Tarski 1956.)

Tarski, Alfred. 1936/1956. "Grundlegung der wissenschaftlichen Semantik." *Actes du Congrès International de Philosophie Scientifique* 3. (An English translation by J. H. Woodger appears in Tarski 1956 under the title "The establishment of scientific semantics"; page references are given for that translation. For full bibliographical information see the note on p. 401 of Tarski 1956.)

Tarski, Alfred. 1944. "The semantic conception of truth." *Philosophy and Phenomenological Research* 4: 341–376. (Reprinted in Linsky 1952.)

Tarski, Alfred. 1956. *Logic, Semantics, Metamathematics: Papers from 1923 to 1938*. Clarendon. (A second edition, edited and introduced by John Corcoran, was published by Hackett in 1983.)

Tarski, Alfred. 1969. "Truth and proof." *Scientific American* 220 (6): 63–77.

Teller, Paul. 1983. "A poor man's guide to supervenience and determination." *Southern Journal of Philosophy* 22 (supplement): 137–162.

Teller, Paul. 1989. *A Modern Formal Logic Primer*. Two volumes. Prentice-Hall.

Thomason, Richmond H. 1970. *Symbolic Logic: An Introduction*. Macmillan.

Thomason, Richmond H., ed. 1974. *Formal Philosophy: Selected Papers of Richard Montague*. Yale University Press.

Thomason, Richmond H. 1980. "A note on syntactical treatments of modality." *Synthese* 44: 391–395.

Thomason, Richmond H. 198+. "Paradoxes of Intentionality?" Typescript, University of Pittsburgh.

Turner, Raymond. 1987. "A theory of properties." *Journal of Symbolic Logic* 52: 445–472.

Turner, Raymond. 1990a. "Logics of truth." *Notre Dame Journal of Formal Logic* 31: 308–329.

Turner, Raymond. 1990b. *Truth and Modality for Knowledge Representation*. Pitman.

van Fraassen, Bas. 1968. "Presupposition, implication, and self-reference." *Journal of Philosophy* 65: 136–152.

van Fraassen, Bas. 1970a. "Truth and paradoxical consequences." In Martin 1970a.

van Fraassen, Bas. 1970b. "Inference and self-reference." *Synthese* 22: 425–438. (Reprinted in Davidson and Harman 1972.)

Vardi, Moshe Y. 1988. *Proceedings of the Second Conference on Theoretical Aspects of Reasoning about Knowledge*. Morgan Kaufmann.

Visser, Albert. 1984. "Four valued semantics and the Liar." *Journal of Philosophical Logic* 13: 181–212.

Visser, Albert. 1989. "Semantics and the Liar paradox." In volume 4 of Gabbay and Guenthner 1983–1989.

Wang, Hao. 1961. "The calculus of partial predicates and its extension to set theory I." *Zeitschrift für mathematische Logik und Grundlagen der Mathematik* 7: 283–288.

Whitehead, Alfred North, and Bertrand Russell. 1910. *Principia Mathematica*, volume 1. Cambridge University Press. (Second edition, 1925.)

Woleński, Jan, and Peter Simons. 1989. "De veritate: Austro-Polish contributions to the theory of truth from Brentano to Tarski." In Szaniawski 1989.

Woodruff, Peter W. 1984. "Paradox, truth and logic I." *Journal of Philosophical Logic* 13: 213–232.

Yablo, Steve. 1985. "Truth and reflection." *Journal of Philosophical Logic* 14: 297–349.

Index

We list symbols at the beginning of the index, and Greek letters at the end. We omit cross-references to "Examples" and "Theorems"; their subentries should be scanned for key words.

'A' (quotation name), 75
@ (actual world), 238
↓ (connective in extended μ), 80–81
↔ (material equivalence), 33
⊥ (falsity), 33
  ⊥I and ⊥E rules, 159
∧ (infimum), 36
∨ (supremum), 36
& (conjunction), 33
  &I and &E rules, 159
  tables for, 40–44
⊨ (semantic implication and validity)
  $\models_{\mathscr{F}}$ (implication in fixed-point theory $\mathscr{F}$), 98
  $\models_{\overline{d}}$ (valid in S*), 182
  $\models_{d}$ (valid in S_d), 165
  $\models_{i}$ (valid in S_i), 193
  $\models_{n}$ (valid in S_n), 147
  $\models_{*}$ (valid in S*), 191
  $\models_{\rho}$ (implication in scheme ρ), 49
  $\models_{c}$ (classical implication), 48
∈ (class membership, exemplification), 267
∃ (existential quantifier), 33
≡
  coextensiveness, 268
  Łukasiewicz biconditional, 93
  relationship between systems, 148
= (identity), 33
  =I and =E rules, 160
⟨ ⟩ (empty sequence), 237
⌜A⌝ (Gödel numeral of A), 220, 237n35
⌜n⌝ (numeral for n), 156, 220, 237n35
< (relationship between systems), 148
≤
  partial order, 34, 38, 45
  relationship between systems, 148
□ (necessity connective), 237–238
~ (negation, choice negation), 33
  ~I and ~E rules, 158
  tables for, 40–44
$\overline{A}$ (exclusion negation), 94
○ (special modal connective), 247
  intentionality of, 249
↾ (restriction), 38n
$\mathscr{S} \restriction \beta$ (sequence restricted to first β values), 166
→ (material conditional), 33
$\vdash_{n}$ (deducibility, theoremhood in C_n), 148
∀
  generalized truth function, 40–44, 238n40
  propositional quantifier, 247

universal quantifier, 33
  ∀I and ∀E rules, 159
∨ (disjunction), 33
[x: __x__] (class or property abstraction), 267
[ ]$^{\square}$ (translation from $\mathscr{PL}^-$ into $\mathscr{CL}$), 241
[ ]^N (translation from $\mathscr{CL}$ into $\mathscr{PL}^-$), 240–241

A_G (definiens for G), 145
a (name), 33
A, B (formulas), 33
A2, 193
A3, 34–35, 63
A4, 34–35
Absolute truth, 22–25
Abstraction ([x: __x__]), 267
Ackrill, J. L., 1
Aczel, Peter, 9n18, 57n22, 132n, 192
Anderson, Alan Ross, 43n, 49
Anderson, C. Anthony, 271n40
Antiextension, 38, 47
Antisymmetry, 35
Aristotle, 1
Aristotle's Rule, 1
Arithmetic, 55–56, 155–156, 220
Asher, Nicholas, 246–247, 271n41
Assignment (of values to variables), 39, 238n37
Attractive hypothesis, 185

b (The Both-True-And-False), 34
Bar-Hillel, Yehoshua, 7, 11
Bartha, Paul, 165
Barwise, Jon, 9n18, 11n22, 54n, 192
Basic intuition. *See* Truth, fundamental intuition for
Belief, 270–272
Belief sentences, 8–9
Believer (self-referential sentence), 271
Belnap, Nuel, 12n22, 24, 34, 43n, 49, 168n25, 182, 191n, 229, 251
Bergmann, Merrie, 157n16
Berman, Joel, 79
Berry's paradox, 264
Beth's Definability Theorem, 151–152
Biconditional, material vs. definitional, 138–139, 254–256
Bivalence, Principle of, 224
Blok, Wim, 79
Bocheński, I. M., 7n14, 10n21, 57n21

Bochvar, D. A., 41n, 42, 57
Boolos, George, 235n, 243
Brady, Ross T., 58n23
Burge, Tyler, 11, 102, 103, 104n45, 271n40
Burgess, John P., 218, 229
Buridan, John, 1, 7n13, 10n20, 271n40

$\mathscr{C}$ (a community), 85
C_0 (calculus for definitions), 126–128, 157–165
    adequacy of, 260n15
    creativity in, 127, 253n
    strong semantical system for, 185
C_n (calculuses for definitions), 148–149, 157–165
Calculus for definitions. See C_0; C_n
Camp, Joseph L., 12n22
Canonical model, 163
Cargile, James, 253n
Carnielli, Walter A., 235n
Categorical, 121, 122, 146, 188–189, 191, 197
    circularity of, 231, 255
    higher order, 235, 256
    K and its revision theory, 230–231. See also Ψ_M
    parallels with truth, 229–235, 255–256
    pathology of, 235, 253. See also Liar, Strengthened
ccpo (coherent complete partial order), 36, 63–71
    simple, 180
Chameleonic Languages, 54
Chang, C. C., 176
Chapuis, André, 277n50
Chastain, Charles, 277n49
Chihara, Charles S., 12–19, 138, 259n14
Choice negation, 94
Chrysippus, 7n14
Circularity, 113, 117–118n5, 129. See also Categorical; Reference; Truth
    in C_0, 127
    can increase expressive power, 190
    of consequence, 270
    extensional adequacy of, 131
    of Functionalism, 272
    inductive definitions do not exhibit, 194
    legitimacy of, 129
    of necessity, 270
    of rationality, 272
    vicious. See Pathologicality
    without self-reference, 273–277
$\mathscr{CL}$ (language with necessity as connective), 237

$\mathscr{CL}_0^+$ (extension of $\mathscr{CL}$), 247
Class (extension of predicate), 267, 268
Classical
    implication, 48
    jump (τ_M), 133
    language or scheme (τ), 41, 45
Closed (set of ordinals), 172
Coding, 50, 51n. See also Gödel numbering
Cofinal, 170
Cognitive synonymy, 130
Coherence theory, 26–27
Coherent complete partial order, 36, 63–71
Coheres with, 167
Complete
    lattice, 36
    poset, 67
    theory, 162
Completeness
    of C_0, 127, 165
    of C_n, 149, 165
Completion ordinal, 170
Conj (syntactic predicate), 220
Connective View (of necessity), 236
Consequence, circularity of, 270
Conservativeness requirement (on theory of definitions), 146
    and logical connectives, 263
    propriety of, 187
    strong vs. weak, 152. See also Logic, conservation of
Consistent (in $\mathscr{X}$), 36, 63
Consistent theory, 162
Constant Limit Rule, 168, 175
Content requirement (on theory of definitions), 146
Contingent Liar, 6, 9
Convention T, 1–5, 132
    and absolute vs. relativized truth, 23–24
    domain of applicability of, 20–24
    as essence of Tarski, 5
    and logical notion of truth, 21–22
    and logical structure, 24
    for natural languages, 2
    and philosophical theories, 27
    and weak notion of truth, 22
Convergence, 135
Convergent revision rule, 209
Converges to a fixed point, 209
Correspondence theory, 25–26
Creative definition, 113. See also Noncreativity requirement
    in C_0, 127
Cresswell, M. J., 235n
Curry's Paradox for truth, 14–16

D (domain), 37
  containing sentences of L, 59
$\bar{d}$ (n-tuples from domain), 38n6
D (syntactic predicate for T^n), 220
$\mathscr{D}$ (set of definitions), 145
$\mathscr{D}^+$ (positive version of $\mathscr{D}$), 195–196
D3, 38
D3, 38
D4, 38
D4, 38
Davidson, Donald, 2, 23–24n41
Davidsonian semantics, 2, 23–24
Deducible (on basis of definitions), 127, 148
Definability
  theorems, 49–50, 57–63, 96, 97, 151–152
  of truth, 51, 97
  weak vs. strong, 189
Defines, 46–47
  weakly vs. strongly, 189
Definiendum, 113, 145
Definiens, 113
Definition
  calculus for. *See* C_0; C_n
  categorical judgments based on, 121
  circular, 116–117. *See also* Circularity
  explicit, 152
  extension ascribed by, 118, 129, 151, 194
  finite, 184n
  as fixing meaning, 118–119
  formal correctness of, 132, 277
  hypothetical character of, 119–120
  inductive, 192–196
  material adequacy of, 132, 277
  natural deduction systems for, 157–162
  ordinary, 149
  partial, 131–132, 197
  positive, 192
  problem of, 121
  and problem of truth and paradox, 113–117
  regular, 149
  revision theory of. *See* Revision rule;
  Revision theory of definition
  rules for, 126–127
  semantical systems for, 146. *See also*
  various S's
  simultaneous, 145
  standards of adequacy for descriptive, 130–131, 260–261
  validity relative to, 147
Definition of truth. *See also* Convention T;
  Implication Thesis
  circularity of, 132–134
  formal correctness of, 132, 277

material adequacy of, 5, 277
  and T-biconditionals, 1–5
Deflationist view, 27–28
Degree (of term or formula), 201–202
Dependency range, 110
Depends on (between definitions), 149
Descending hypothesis, 165
Descriptive problem of truth and paradox, 10–11, 97, 260–261
  and expressive power, 101–102
  and theory of levels, 103–104
Devitt, Michael, 28n48
DfE, DfE$_r$ (Definiendum Elimination), 114, 126, 160
DfI, DfI$_r$ (Definiendum Introduction), 114, 126, 160
Directed set, 67
Disquotational view, 27–28
Dowden, Bradley H., 61n30
Dunn, J. Michael, 43n

$\mathscr{E}$ (evaluation sequence), 188
$\mathscr{E}_{\mathscr{L}+}(\mathscr{S})$ (evaluation sequence), 188
Edelberg, Walter, 277n49
Eliminability requirement, 128–129, 151–152
Epimenides, 6, 114–116
Epstein, Richard L., 235n
Equivalence, material vs. definitional, 138–139, 254–256
Etchemendy, John, 9n18, 11n22, 21n38, 54n
Eubulides of Miletus, 6
Evaluation (sequence), 188
Examples
  $\perp$ a theorem of C_3, 161
  A-B discourses, 224–225, 227–229
  "All truths are categorical," 234
  C_0 derivation, 127
  for ccpos, 63
  circular definition, 119, 123–125
  circularity of $\bigcirc$, 249–250
  classicality of least fixed point of σ_M, 213
  classical unique fixed point that is not truth, 109–112
  conservativeness, 152–153
  convergence to a fixed point, neutrality, and $V_M^\#$, 213
  definability, 190
  derivations in C_n, 160–162
  extensional equivalence, 130
  failure of strong conservativeness and α-reflexiveness, 187
  $\mathscr{F}$(**D3**, h), fixed points, 68–69
  fixed points of κ_M, 70–71, 78–79

Examples (cont.)
  fixed points of $\kappa_{R'}$, 73–74
  fixed points of υ_M, 79–80
  fully varied revision sequence, 168–169
  inductive validity, 193
  intrinsic elements, 70
  largest fixed point without convergence or
    settling on fixed points, 218
  Liar, Truth Teller, Ψ_M, and K, 231–232
  Liar in C_0, 138–139
  Modal Liar in reflexive modal model, 245
  nonconservativeness of limit of S_n, 155–
    156
  nonordinary regular definition, 151
  non-Thomason model, 210
  p + 1 fixed points, 77
  pathological, paradoxical,
    Truth-Teller-like, mixed, 189
  proviso on Transfer Theorem, 77
  revision sequence, 122–123
  settledness and convergence, 135–136
  Strengthened Truth Teller, 235
  Tarski jump, 133–134
  Thomason models, 211–213
  Thomason models and σ_M^c, 215–216
  T-predicate for arithmetic, 76
  truth of "I am not categorical," 233
  validity in S^*, 191
  validity in S_n, 147–148
  weakness of S_0, 154–155
  κ-ungroundedness, 213
  Ψ_M and Strengthened Liar, 234
  Ψ_M and Strengthened Truth Teller, 233–
    234
  ω-inconsistency in S_0, 156
Excluded middle, in revision theory, 220,
    261–262
Exclusion Liar, 141
Exclusion negation, 94, 102
Exemplification, 267
Expressible, weakly, 197
Expression, 39
Expressive power
  and fixed points, 94–96, 108, 214
  and fixed-point theories, 103–104, 108
  increased by circular definitions, 190
  limitation of, as solution to normative
    problem, 10–11
  limited through hierarchies, 102–104
  limited through meaninglessness, 102
  logical, 94, 107–108
  of pre-necessity languages, 239
  of quantification into sentential positions,
    239

semantic, 95
  and semantic ascent, 27
  syntactic, 96
  and vicious circularity, 242, 251
Extension, 30–31, 38, 47
  as ascribed by definitions, 118, 129, 151, 194
  relation between model and modal model,
    239
  set as, 266–267
  of truth, 140, 263
Extensional adequacy, 130–131
Extensional equivalence, 29n50, 130
Extensionality, 268–269

$F(X, f)$ (set of fixed points), 67
F, G (predicates), 33
f, g (function symbols), 33
$\mathbf{f}$ (The False), 34
$\mathscr{F}$ (fixed-point theory), 97
$\mathscr{F}_M$ (interpretation of truth in $\mathscr{F}$), 97
$\mathscr{F}(\mathscr{X}, f)$ (structure of fixed points), 67
False (of), 47
Feferman, Solomon, 58n23, 103n, 132n, 195
Field, Hartry, 4n8, 26
Fine, Kit, 262n
Finite
  definition, 184n
  sentence, 184–185
Fitch, Frederic, 57n23, 94n, 157
Fitting, Melvin, 58, 63, 182
Fixed-point property (of schemes), 61
Fixed points, 59, 66, 67. See also
    T-predicate
  existence of, 109, 215
  and expressive incompleteness, 92–94
  general framework of, 91
  and inductive definitions, 194
  intuitive meaning of, 91
  least, 70–71, 199
  and logical incompleteness, 94–96
  may not be extension of truth, 85, 90–91,
    106
  and (non)monotonicity, 62, 80–83
  (non)uniqueness of, 107, 109
  number of, 78
  of positive fragment, 94
  and reflexive hypotheses, 147n4
  of revision rule for truth, 134
  and revision rules, 209
  in revision sequences, 173, 177–179
  and semantic concepts, 95
  as solution to normative problem, 10
  structure of, 79–80
  unique classical, and truth, 134

Fixed-point theories, 97, 101n, 117n4
  and hierarchies, 102–104
  and hypothetical contexts, 199–200
  implication in, 97–99
  Kripke motivation of, 199–200
  lack of fit, 98–100
  pathological sentences in, 99–100
  relevance of other fixed points, 100
  and Signification Thesis, 104–109
  and "universality" of languages, 258n12
Flag (in a subproof), 157–162
Formal correctness, 132
  to be abandoned, 277
Formula, 33
Four-valued language or scheme (v), 34, 42–
  43, 45
Free in, 33
Frege, Gottlob, 1, 5n10
Friedman, Harvey, 97n
Fully varied revision sequence, 168, 175
Function space, 65
Fundamental intuition. *See* Truth,
  fundamental intuition for

G (candidate T-predicate), 59
G (n-place definiendum of L^+), 145
g (possible interpretation of G), 59
Gaifman, Haim, 255n5
Gap, truth-value, 56, 92
Gentzen, Gerhard, 157n15
Giaretta, Pierdaniele, 261n
Gilmore, Paul C., 57n23, 94n, 103n, 195
Glut, truth-value, 92
Gödel, Kurt, 53
Gödel numbering, 55, 220
  indefinability of, 76
Grammar
  of necessity languages, 235–237, 242, 251
  of truth, 11–12
Greatest lower bound, 36
Grelling's paradox, 108n54
Grim, Patrick, 271n40
Grounded sentences, 137, 140, 199
  ρ-, 201
Ground model, 59
Ground predicate, 59n28
Grover, Dorothy L., 12n22, 24
Gupta, Anil, 19n34, 24, 81n, 87n8, 92n23,
  104nn, 168n25, 182, 218, 229, 232, 233

h (hypothesis), 146, 166
Hangman Paradox, 12n23
Hart, W., 253n
Hawthorn, John, 92nn, 95n28

Hazen, Allen, 10n20, 102n41, 261n
Hellman, Geoffrey, 92nn, 259n14
Henkin theory, 162
Herzberger, Hans G., 14n, 41n, 71n, 168,
  171n29, 172nn, 182, 218, 229, 258n10
Herzberger Limit Rule, 168, 175
Heytesbury, William, 137n
Hierarchy of truth predicates, 117n4
  and of categoricalness, 231, 235, 256
  as solution to descriptive problem, 11,
    102–104, 259n13
  as solution to normative problem, 10
Hintikka, Jaakko, 236n
Horwich, Paul, 28n48
Hughes, G. E., 1n1, 7n13, 235n, 271n40
Hypothesis (argument for revision rule),
  145, 166
  descending, 165
  n-reflexive, 147
Hypothesis (in a subproof), 157–162
Hypothetical contexts, 199–200, 221–222
Hyp (rule), 157

I (interpretation), 37
  except for G, 59
I($\mathfrak{X}$) (set of intrinsic elements), 69
$\mathscr{I}$($\mathfrak{X}$) (structure of intrinsic elements), 69
Identity, 33
iff (if and only if), 35n, 92–93, 108
Implication. *See also* deducible
  classical, 48
  in fixed-point theories, 97–99
  in four schemes, 49
Implication Thesis, 4n8, 25, 28–29
In (syntactic predicate), 220
Inconsistency View, 12–19, 117n4, 138, 227
Inconsistent theory, 162
Indefinability Theorems, 49–50, 52–56, 61,
  95–97, 229–230. *See also* Chameleonic
  Languages
  extensional vs. intensional, 106
Indexed formula, 148
Indexed sentence, 162
Index Shift, 126–127, 159
Inductive definitions, 192–196
Infimum, 36
Initial ordinal, 170
Intension, 25n44, 31
  of truth, 3
Intensional equivalence, 130
Intension Thesis, 25, 28–29, 31. *See also*
  Convention T; T-biconditionals
Interpretation, 34
  for N, 72
  of a predicate, 37

Interpreted language, 44–45
Intrinsic
  element, 69
  fixed point, 71
  truth, ρ-, 201
IS (Index Shift), 159
IS_n (Index Shift by n), 148, 160

$\mathcal{J}$ (modal interpretation), 238
Jaśkowski, Stanislaw, 157n15
Jeffrey, Richard C., 235n
jump, 59. See also κ_M; μ_M; ν_M; ρ_M; τ_M; υ_M

K (categorical), 230
K-free, 232
Kamp, Hans, 246–247, 271n41
Kant, Immanuel, 257
Kaplan, David, 271n40
Kapus, Jerry, 28n48
Keisler, H. Jerome, 176
Kindt, Walther, 57n22
Kleene, Stephen Cole, 41
Kneale, William, 6n12, 7n14
Knower (self-referential sentence), 271
Knowledge, 270–272
Koons, Robert C., 104n44, 269n34
Kremer, Michael, 49, 88n9, 89n14, 98n30,
  99n33
Kripke, Saul A., 6n12, 8n13, 10, 11n22, 50,
  57, 58, 61n30, 69nn, 70, 71n, 87n8, 91–
  92, 96, 98–99n32, 100, 102n42, 140n,
  179, 199–200, 214, 218, 225n25, 238,
  267n31

L (language syntactically construed), 33,
  86n4, 146
  with G, 59
L^+ (L + definienda), 145
$\mathcal{L}$ (interpreted language), 45, 86n4
  as ground language, 145, 200
  including arithmetic, 229
  as pre-modal for $\mathcal{CL}$ and $\mathcal{PL}$, 237
$\mathcal{L}_g$ (interpreted language including G), 59,
  86n5
$\mathcal{L}_h$ (interpreted language including
  definienda), 146
$\mathcal{L}^+$
  $\mathcal{L}$ + definienda, 145
  $\mathcal{L}$ + truth predicate T, 200
  $\mathcal{L}$ + truth T + categoricalness K, 229
$\mathcal{L}_n$ (language in hierarchy), 102
L (language intentionally construed), 86n4
L3, 44
L4, 43

Language. See also Scheme
  extensional first-order, 33
  intentional aspects, 86n4
  interpreted, 44–45
  totality of, 265–266
  "universal," 101, 257–259
Lattice (complete), 36
Least upper bound, 36
Leblanc, Hughes, 157n16
Leonardi, Paolo, 261n
Levels, theory of, 103–104
Levinson, Jerrold, 277n50
lh (length), 166
Liar, 5, 117n4, 137n, 138–139, 266
  Contingent, 6
  and convergence, 136–137
  Exclusion, 141
  and expressive power, 96
  in fixed-point theories, 99–100, 106–107
  Modal, 243–244, 249, 270
  as neither true nor false, 58, 255
  paradox, 5, 6, 253–254
  presupposition failure of, 58
  Simple, 6, 221–222
  sortal incorrectness of, 58
  Strengthened, 58n25, 230, 234, 253–256.
    See also Categorical
  and T-biconditionals, 254
"Limit" of S_n, 155
Limit rules for revision sequences, 168–169
Local determinability, 110–112
Local determination, 46, 99n35
Logic, conservation of, 141–142, 151,
  261–263
Logical constants, 33, 40–44
Logical notion of truth, 20–21
Logical richness vs. incompleteness, 94–96,
  107–108
  and fixed points, 95–96
Lower bound, 36
Löb's Theorem, 15n28
Łukasiewicz, Jan, 41n
Łukasiewicz biconditional, 93, 102, 108

M (ground model = $\langle D, I \rangle$), 59, 146
M (modal model), 238
M + g (ground model + intepetation of
  G), 59
$\mathcal{M}$ (standard n-valued model), 38n6, 201
  including interpretation of G), 59
McCafferty, Andrew, 247n48
McCarthy, Timothy, 95n28
McGee, Vann, 97n, 171n29, 176–177, 182,
  213n14, 222, 225–227, 229, 257, 259n14,
  269n34

Macnamara, John, 259n14
Maddy, Penelope, 259n14, 267n31
Main Lemma, 202
Manna, Z., 70n
Martin, Robert L., 10, 11n22, 50, 57, 58, 61n30, 66n36, 81n, 90n20, 91, 92n22, 96, 140n
Martino, Enrico, 261n
Material adequacy, 132
  as sole criterion, 277
Mates, Benson, 10n20
Maximal consistent τ-sequence, 216
Meaning, 45n
Membership, 267
Mendelson, Elliott, 163n
Metalanguage, 2
Mignucci, Mario, 261n
Mill, John Stuart, 89n16
Mixed (semantic status), 188–189, 191
Model, 37, 48, 238
Monotone, monotonic, 41, 66
  leading to fixed points, 62
  not needed for fixed points, 80–83
Montague, Richard, 96–97n, 235–239, 269n34, 271n40
Moschovakis, Yiannis N., 192
Myers, C. Mason, 277n50
Myhill, John R., 58n23, 94n

N (natural numbers), 237
n-reflexive, 147
N (necessity predicate, one-place), 237
N (set of names; language so based), 71
n (The Neither-True-Nor-False), 34, 42
Natural deduction system, 157–162
Natural language. See Truth, in natural languages
Nearly stable, 169
  and S*, 191
Nec (necessity predicate, two-place), 237
Necessity languages. See also 𝒞ℒ; 𝒫ℒ; Revision theory, for necessity languages
  circularity in, 269–270
  grammar of, 235–237, 242, 251
  intertranslatability among, 240–242, 250–251
  Predicate and Connective Views of, 236
  quantification differences among, 239
  revision semantics for, 243
Negation, 33, 94
Neg (syntactic predicate), 220
Neither true nor false, 95. See also n
Nepeivoda, N. N., 58n23
Neutral, X-, 74, 202

"No Class" theory, Russell's, 268–269
Non-contradiction, Principle of, 224–225
Noncreativity requirement, 128–129
Nonlogical notion of truth, 20–21
Nonpathological (=categorical), 188–189, 191
Nonsemantical facts, 18
Normal (scheme), 41
Normative problem of paradoxes, 10–11
Normore, Calvin, 137n
Num (natural number predicate), 220

O (interpretation of ○), 247
Object language, 2
Open problem, 63, 99n34, 123n10, 185, 214, 215, 215n17, 216, 233
Ordinary definition, 149

p (propositional variable), 247
Paradoxes. See also Problem of truth and paradox
  and belief sentences, 8–9
  of Believer, 271
  Berry's, 264
  blocked in three-valued languages, 56–57
  and ex falso quodlibet, 14
  as not expressing propositions, 8–10, 117n4
  and expressive power of language, 10–11
  Grelling's, 108n54
  Hangman, 12n23
  insolubility of, 7, 12
  of Knower, 271
  Liar. See Liar
  and modality, 9
  moral of, 278
  naturalness of, 142
  and nondenoting singular terms, 7–8
  normative vs. descriptive problems of, 10, 260–261
  and ordinary uses, 17
  on the revision theory, 140–143
  Russell's, 266
  simple solutions to, 7–12
  and sortal incorrectness, 13n26
  for "true in L," 265–266
  in truth-functional compounds, 9
  and truth of contradictions, 12n24
  vs. theorems, 56
Paradoxical, 100, 122, 188–189, 191
  indefinability of, 230
  -ρ_M, 201
Parsons, Charles, 8n13, 10n19, 11, 103, 104n45, 267n31

Partial definitions, 131–132, 197, 264
Partial order, 35
Pathologicality, 123, 188–189, 191
  behavior of K, 235
  due to extensionality, 269
  explanation of, 140, 254, 269
  kinds of, 140
  of knowledge or belief, 270–272
  and vicious reference, 135n, 201, 242, 246–247, 251
  vs. ungroundedness, 199–200
  without vicious reference, 273–277
Paul of Venice, 10, 57n21
Paul, Saint, 6
Perlis, Donald, 237n33
Persistence (of physical objects), 273–277
Physicalism, 4n8, 26, 272
$\mathscr{PL}$ (language with necessity as predicate), 237
  revision semantics for, 243
$\mathscr{PL}^-$ (restricted $\mathscr{PL}$), 240
Positive definition, 192
Positive logic, 94
Possible situation, 31–32, 37, 48
Predicate, 50n18
Predicate View of necessity, 236
Presupposition failure of Liar, 58
Priest, Graham, 12n24, 253n
Prior, Arthur N., 8n13, 249n
Problem. See Open problem
Problem of Semantic Self-Sufficiency, 257–259
Problem of truth and paradox, 6, 19, 29, 31–32, 88n9. See also Paradoxes
  and definitions, 113–117, 137
  idealization of, 30
  normative vs. descriptive, 10–11, 260–261
  vs. problem of "universality," 258–259
Properties, 267–269
Propositional function, 45
Propositional quantification, 247–249
Propositions, as objects of truth, 8. See also Paradoxes, as not expressing propositions
Prosentential theory of truth, 12n22

Q (Robinson arithmetic), 236
Quantificational enrichment, 75
Quine, Willard Van Orman, 4n8, 27, 274, 277n49

R (accessibility relation), 238
Ramified type theory, 10, 102
Ramsey, Frank P., 1, 87

Range of applicability, 38, 47
Rank
  of a definition, 149
  of a world, 244
Recurring hypothesis, 174–175
Redundancy Theory of Truth, 87
Reference, 229, 263–264. See also Vicious reference
Reference list, 72
Reflection ordinal, 172
Reflexive, 174, 182
  n-, 147
  α-, 174
Reflexivity, 35
Regular definition, 149, 151–152, 185
Regular ρ-sequence, 206
Reit (rule), 158
Relationships among S_n, 153–154
Relativized truth, 22–25
Replete, 66
Revision rule, 121, 145. See also δ
  properties of, 209
  as signification of truth, 134–135
Revision sequence, 121, 167–168
  alternate treatment of limits in, 168–169
  basic picture of, 171
  fixed points in, 173, 177–179
  as improving, 121, 168
Revision theory
  applicable beyond definitions, 196–197
  applicable to nonclassical languages, 262
  of categoricalness, 230–231
  of classes and membership, 268–269
  conservation of ground logic by, 141–142, 261–262
  of knowledge or belief, 270–272
  for many-valued languages, 262
  for necessity languages, 243, 269–270
  for persistence of physical objects (for example), 272–277
  of properties and exemplification, 266–267
  of reference, satisfaction, etc., 263–266
  and "universality" of languages, 258
Revision theory of definition, 125
  conservativeness requirement on, 146
  content requirement on, 146
  and meaning of connectives, 263
Revision theory of truth, 137. See also Logic, conservation of
  applicability to any (fixed) language, 141
  bibliographic note, 229
  excluded middle in, 220, 261–262
  in hypothetical contexts, 200, 221–222
  and Inconsistency View, 138–139

objections from complexity of theory,
259–262
objections from conservation of ground
logic, 261–263
objections from no "Semantic
Self-Sufficiency," 256–259
objections from Strengthened Liar, 253–
256
semantic principles in, 221–224
simplicity of, 259–260
and three-valued approaches, 139–142,
200
ω-inconsistency in, 225–227
Russell's "No Class" theory, 268–269
Russell's paradox, 266
Russell, Bertrand, 8, 10, 102, 103, 264n22,
278

S (set of all sentences), 75, 200
s (assignment of values), 39
s[d/x] (shifted assignment), 39
S (sentence-of-$\mathscr{PL}$ predicate), 237–238
s, t (terms), 33
S_0 (semantical system for definitions), 121,
125, 129
categorical in, 123
paradoxical in, 122
strongly conservative, 153–154
valid in, 123
variant validity in, 165
weakness of, 154
ω-inconsistency in, 156
S_n (semantical systems for definitions), 147–
156
eliminability in, 151–152
"limit" of, 155
$S^\#$ (semantical system for definitions), 182–
190
applicable beyond definitions, 196–197
compared with S*, 191, 192
and inductive definitions, 194–196
nearby semantical system, 185
ω-inconsistency in, 191
S* (semantical system for definitions), 191–
192
applicable beyond definitions, 196–197
compared with $S^\#$, 192
and inductive definitions, 194–196
S_d (semantical system of descending
hypotheses), 165–166
S_i (semantical system of inductive
definitions), 193–194
$\mathscr{S}$ (sequence of hypotheses), 166
$\mathscr{S} \upharpoonright \beta$ (sequence restricted to first β values),
166

$\mathscr{S}_\beta$ (βth member of $\mathscr{S}$), 166
Sainsbury, R. M., 271n40
Satisfaction, 107–108, 229, 263–265
Savion, Leah, 237n33
Scheme (for interpreting logical constants),
40–44
Scott, Dana, 49, 58n23, 67
Self-reference, 56–57, 209–218, 273
Semantical systems for definitions, 146. See
also various S's
Semantic ascent, 27
Semantic closure, 76n44
Semantic principles, 221, 227
Semantics
Davidsonian. See Davidsonian semantics
traditional, 97, 108–109
Semantic Self-Sufficiency, Problem of, 257–
259
Semantic value, 39
Sentence, 33
Seq (finite-sequence predicate), 240
Sequence, ρ-, 201
Set, iterative notion vs. as extension, 266–
267
Settledness, 135
Settles on fixed points, 209
Shamir, A., 70n
Sheard, Michael, 97n
Signification, 30, 31n54, 45n, 47
of a predicate, 37
traditional accounts, 33–34, 97, 108–109
of truth, 87, 134–135, 140. See also
Supervenience of signification of truth
Signification Thesis, 31, 104–109, 111,
112n62. See also Convention T;
T-biconditionals
Simmons, Keith, 257n
Simons, Peter, 4n9
Simple ccpo, 180
Simple Liar, 6
and Inconsistency View, 13
and simple solutions to paradoxes, 9
Skolem, Thoralf A., 58n23
Skyrms, Brian, 58nn, 237n33, 255n5
Smiley, T. J., 43n
Smullyan, Raymond, 54
Soames, Scott, 4n8
Sobel, Jordan Howard, 7n14
Sortal incorrectness and paradox, 13n26,
58, 140
Sound (element of poset), 66
Soundness
of C_0, 127, 165
of C_n, 149, 161, 165

Spade, Paul Vincent, 6n11, 7n14, 112n61, 137n
Stabilization point, 167
Stable in, 167, 197
  and S*, 191
Stably x, 167
Standard name, 220
Standard (n-valued) model, 37
Stationary (class of ordinals), 173n32
Strawson, P. F., 274
Strong Kleene scheme or language (κ), 42, 45, 142
Strongly conservative, 152
Strong truth and falsity, 22, 95
Supervaluation language or scheme (σ), 201
  variant, 214
Supervenience of signification of truth, 18, 87–88, 97, 105, 111
Supremum, 36

T$\sim$ (semantic principle), 221
T& (semantic principle), 221
TV (semantic principle), 221
T-step, 220
T (modal system), 236, 248
T* (theory of truth based on near stability), 210
T^c (theory of truth based on stability and maximal consistency), 216
T* (theory of truth based on stability), 210
t (The True), 34
T^n (truth-predicate self-applied), 220
T (truth predicate), 30, 200
Tarski, Alfred, 1–5, 10, 12, 15n28, 20, 23–24n41, 24, 25, 27n, 76n44, 103, 132, 138, 257–258, 277
Tarski biconditionals. See T-biconditionals
Tarski jump, 133
T-biconditionals, 2. See also Intension Thesis; Signification Thesis
  and absolute truth, 23–24
  as analytic of truth, 3, 6
  circularity of, 132–133
  consistency of, 254
  definitional vs. material, 138–139
  and definition of truth, 1–5, 259–260
  expressibility of, 93
  inadequacy of on traditional account, 112
  and Inconsistency View, 14–16, 254
  for Liar, 221–222, 254
  and logical notion of truth, 21
  meaning of 'iff' in, 92–93, 108, 112, 138
  as partial definitions, 132–134, 142, 197
  and philosophical theories, 25–26

on revision theory, 138–139, 200, 254
and Signification Thesis, 31
triviality of, 3
truth value of, 92–93
and uses of 'true', 19–20
variants for necessity, 269–270
and weak notion of truth, 22
Teller, Paul, 88n10, 157n16
Term, 33
TE (Truth Elimination), 114
Theorems
  C_0 and paradoxicality in S*, 189
  $C_0 < S^*$, 184–185
  C_0 on variant notions of validity, 165
  ccpo properties, 64
  $\mathscr{CL}_0^+$ and $\mathscr{PL}$ are notational variants, 250–251
  cofinal hypotheses, 170
  cofinal hypotheses and stability, 171–172
  comparison of revision sequences, 180–181
  condition for $A(x)$ not classical T-predicate, 51
  connectives in τ, κ, and υ, 48
  convergence, neutrality, and Simple Liars, 217
  convergence and settledness of Ψ_M, 232–233
  convergence to a fixed point, neutrality, and groundedness in μ, κ, σ, 210
  convergence to a fixed point, neutrality, and V$_M^*$, 213
  convergence to a fixed point with stronger syntactic resources, 214
  $\mathscr{D}$ and its positive version $\mathscr{D}^+$, 196
  existence of completion ordinal, 170
  existence of fully varied sequences, 173
  existence of initial ordinal, 170
  existence of reflexive hypotheses, 175
  finite definitions in S$_0$, S$_n$, S*, 184
  finite sentences in S$_0$, S$_n$, S*, 185
  fixed-point, 61
  Fixed-Point, Knaster-Tarski, 68n
  Fixed-Point, Tarski's, 68
  Fixed-Point, Visser's, 67
  fixed-point relationships, 60
  fixed points in ccpos, 66
  fixed points in nonmonotonically extended μ, 81
  function-space ccpos, 65
  indefinability, blocked, 57
  Indefinability, Tarski's, 56
  Indefinability I-V, 52–53, 53–54, 54–55, 56, 61

indefinability of categoricalness in
arithmetic + revision theory of truth, 229
intrinsic elements, 69–70
local determination property, 46
Łukasiewicz biconditional implies absence
of fixed points, 93
Main Lemma, 202
Modal Liar and reflexive modal models,
245–246
modal principles in $\mathscr{CL}_0^+$, 248
monotonicity of jumps, 61–62
monotony, 46
Montague's, 236
ordinary definitions, 150
paradoxical and Truth-Teller-like in S^*
and $S^\#$, 192
paradoxicality in $T^\#$, T^*, and ρ_M, 211
$\mathscr{PL}^-$ and $\mathscr{CL}$ are notational variants,
241–242
positive fragment, fixed points of, 94
properties of revision sequences, 173
recurring and reflexive hypotheses, 174
reflection, McGee's, 176
reflection ordinal, 172
regular and ordinary definitions in $S^\#$,
186
regular definitions, 149–150
regularity in S_0, S_n, $S^\#$, 186
relationships among S^*, $S^\#$, S_n, S_0, 191–
192
relationships between S_0, S_n, $S^\#$, 182–184
revision sequences, ccpos and fixed points,
177–182
revisions in well-capped modal models,
244
$S^\#$, S^*, S_i compared on positive
definitions, 194–195
$S^\#$ admits indexed definition rules
hypothetically, 184
$S^\#$ conserves logic, 183
$S^\#$ strongly conservative, 187
$S^\#$ sustains definition rules categorically,
183
S_0 strongly conservative, 153
S_d weakly but not strongly conservative,
166
S_n not weakly conservative, 153
S^* and strong conservativeness, ordinary
definitions, and expressive power, 192
schemes compared, 46
semantic principles and ω-inconsistency,
225
semantic principles in $T^\#$, T^*, T^c, 222
semantics of substitution, 47

settling on fixed points, convergence, and
μ, κ, σ, 217
settling on fixed points, neutrality, and
Truth Tellers, 217
shared properies of $T^\#$, T^*, T^c, 219
soundness and completeness of C_n, 162–
165
stability, fixed points, and groundedness in
three-valued schemes, 211
TL and T-step in revision theories, 221
T-predicate characterized, 51
Transfer, 75, 205
truth and falsity in τ, μ, and κ, 47–48
truths of $\mathscr{PL}^-$ valid on revision
semantics, 246
$V_M^\#$ and $V_M^{\#*}$ and μ-, κ-, σ-groundedness, 212
vicious reference, modal accessibility, and
convergence to fixed point, 247
vs. paradox, 56
τ_M in S-neutral models, 205
ω-Inconsistency, McGee's, 225
Theorems (relative to definitions), 148
Theory, 162
Thomason, Richmond, 8n13, 10n19, 97n,
157n16, 209n9, 236n, 249n, 269n34
Thomason model, 135n, 209–216
Three-valued, 45. See also Paradoxes,
blocked in three-valued languages
interpretation, 34
Three-valued approaches. See also Logic,
conservation of
and Exclusion Liar, 141
and revision theory, 139–142
TI (Truth Introduction), 114
TL (semantic instantiation principle), 221
"Told" interpretation, 34, 42
T-predicate, 50, 86
and fixed points, 60
and truth, 88n11, 90–91
Transitivity, 35
Translation, 28–29
True (of), 47
Truth. See also Definition of truth; Problem
of truth and paradox
absolute vs. relativized, 22–25
beauty of, 90
circularity of, 129, 137, 142–143, 253, 254
definability of, 51
determination by nonsemantical facts, 18–
19, 87–88
extension of, 140, 263
and fixed points, 91, 109
fundamental intuition for, 1, 6, 19, 25, 109
global uses of, 103

Truth (cont.)
  grammar of, 11–12
  in hypothetical contexts, 199–200, 221–222
  importance of, 28
  in, 39, 48, 122. *See also* Truth, absolute vs. relativized
  in **L**, for variable **L**, 265–266
  in modal models, 239
  in natural languages, 2, 12, 257–258
  Inconsistency View of. *See* Inconsistency View
  intension of, 3
  introduction/elimination rules, 114
  is unique classical fixed point iff no vicious reference, 112, 134, 201
  -like predicates, 96, 103
  logical vs. nonlogical, 20–21
  logic of, and circular definitions, 116–117, 255
  objects of, 2, 8, 12
  ordinary uses of, 16–19, 117
  partial definitions for, 132–134
  physicalism and, 4n8, 26
  predicate, 86
  as predicate of sentences, 12
  prosentential theory of, 12n22
  revision theory of. *See* T^*; $T^\#$; T^c
  signification of, 87, 134–135, 137, 139–140
  simpliciter. *See* Truth, absolute vs. relativized
  simplicity of, 90
  stipulating extensions for, 90n17
  strong, 95, 102
  and T-biconditionals. *See* T-biconditionals, as analytic of truth
  and T-predicates, 86n4
  and translation, 28–29
  utility of, 27
  weak vs. strong, 22
Truth conditions, 21
Truth-functional (scheme), 41
Truth Teller, 87, 100nn, 106, 116
  -like, 188–189, 264n22, 267n32
  and settledness, 136
  stipulating a value for, 89–90, 90n17
  Strengthened, 233–234
Truth values, information-ordering on, 34
Turner, Raymond, 229, 268
Two-valued interpretation, 34

Unbounded (set of ordinals), 172
Universality of language, 257–259
Unstable in, 167

Upper bound, 35
UQ (syntactic predicate), 220

v (interpretation for N), 72
$V_M^\#$ (validities of $T^\#$), 210, 219
V_M^c (validities of T^c), 216, 219
V_M^* (validities of T^*), 210, 219
Valid
  i-, 193
  indefinability of, 230
  inductively, 193
  in $\mathscr{L}^+$ (with T and K), 234
  in S^*, 191
  in $S^\#$, 182
  in S_d, 165
  in S_i, 193
  in S_n, 147
  in T^*, 210
  in $T^\#$, 210
  in T^c, 216
  variant for S_0, 165
  variant near $S^\#$, 182n41, 185
Val (semantic value), 39–40
  $Val_{\mathscr{L},s}(X)$, 45
  $Val_{\mathscr{L}}(X)$, 46
  $Val_{\mathscr{L}}(X, \bar{d})$, 46
  $Val_{\mathscr{M},s}(X)$, 39–40, 45
  $Val_{M,s}(X, w)$, 238
Val (value-of predicate), 240
van Fraassen, Bas, 54n, 58, 140n, 201
Variable, 33
Vicious reference, 85
  and pathology, 135n, 201, 246–247, 251
Visser, Albert, 58, 61n30, 63, 70n, 72n, 79, 80n48, 92n22, 99n33, 100n39, 171n29, 179, 182, 229

W (set of worlds), 238
w (world), 85
Wang, Hao, 49
Weak and strong notions of truth, 22, 107
Weak Kleene language or scheme (μ), 41–42, 45, 142
  nonmonotonically extended, 80–83
Weakly conservative, 152. *See also* Logic, conservation of
Weakly expressible rule, 197
Well capped, 243
Whitehead, Alfred North, 102n41
Wilson, Mark, 28n49, 277n49
Wisdom, William A., 157n16
Woleński, Jan, 4n9
Woodruff, Peter W., 10, 11n22, 50, 57, 58, 61n30, 66nn, 80n48, 89n13, 90n20, 91, 92n22, 96, 182

X (subset of domain), 74
X (expression), 33
x (variable), 33
$\mathscr{X}$ (ccpo), 177
$\mathscr{X}^{\mathbf{D}}$ (function space), 65

Yablo, Steve, 22, 261n

$\alpha, \beta, \gamma, \ldots$ (ordinals), 166
α-reflexive, 174
Γ (set of [indexed] sentences), 48, 162
δ
  $\delta_{\mathscr{D},\mathscr{S}}$ (revision rule), 145
  $\delta_{\mathrm{D,M}}$ (revision rule), 120–121
  $\delta_{\mathscr{D},\mathrm{M}}$ (revision rule), 146
  $\delta_{\mathscr{D},\mathrm{M}}^{n}$ (stage in revision sequence), 147
κ (Strong Kleene language or scheme), 42
  κ_{M} (jump for κ), 59
μ (Weak Kleene language or scheme), 41–42
  μ_{M} (jump for κ), 59
  μ_{M}^{+} (jump for extended μ), 81
  $\mu_{\mathrm{M,N}}^{+}$ (deviant jump for extended μ), 82
ν_{M} (jump for necessity language), 243
ρ (scheme $\tau, \mu, \kappa, \upsilon$, or σ), 44
  -grounded (true, false), 201
  -sequence, 201
ρ (revision rule), 166
ρ_{M} (jump), 59
  -sequence, 201
ρ_{R} (jump for reference list), 72
σ (supervaluation language or scheme), 201
  σ_{M} (jump for σ), 201
  σ_{M}^{c} (jump for supervaluation variant), 214
τ (classical language or scheme), 41
  τ_{M} (Tarski or classical jump), 59, 133
  τ_{M} as signification of truth, 134, 137, 201
  τ_{M}-sequence, 201
  τ-sequence, 201
  τ_{M}^{+} (jump for positive τ), 94
υ (four-valued language or scheme), 43
  υ_{M} (jump for υ), 59
ϕ_{e} (translation from $\mathscr{CL}_{0}^{+}$ into $\mathscr{PL}$), 251
Ψ_{M} (jump for categoricalness), 231
ω-inconsistency, 156, 191, 227

www.ingramcontent.com/pod-product-compliance
Lightning Source LLC
Chambersburg PA
CBHW070601270326
41926CB00013B/2383